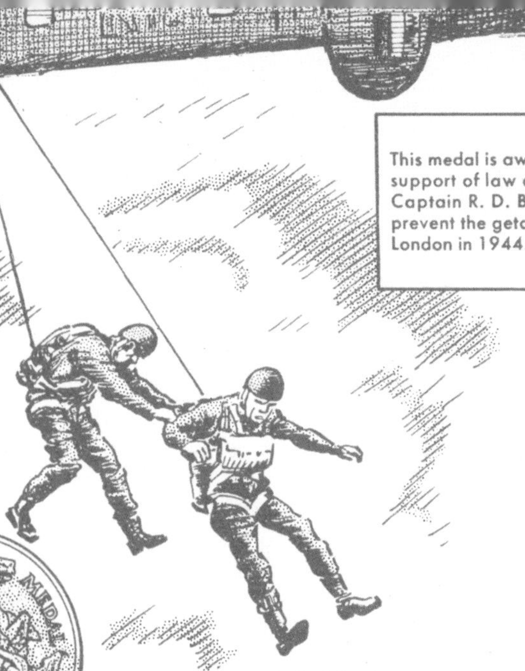

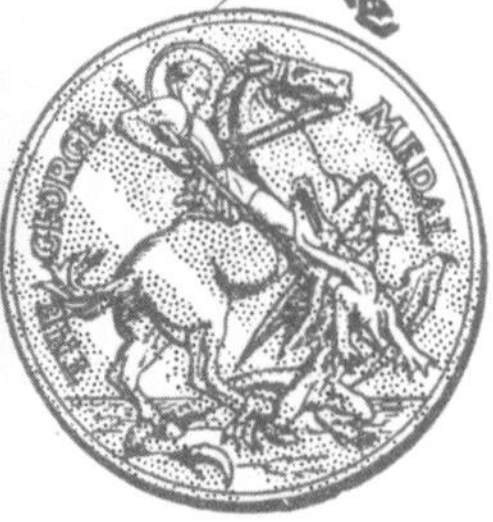
GEORGE
MEDAL

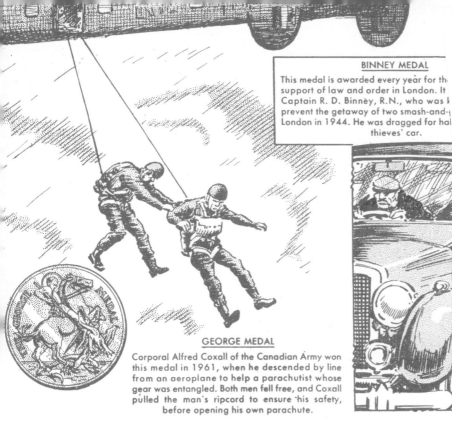

BINNEY MEDAL

This medal is awarded every year for th
support of law and order in London. It
Captain R. D. Binney, R.N., who was k
prevent the getaway of two smash-and-g
London in 1944. He was dragged for hal
thieves' car.

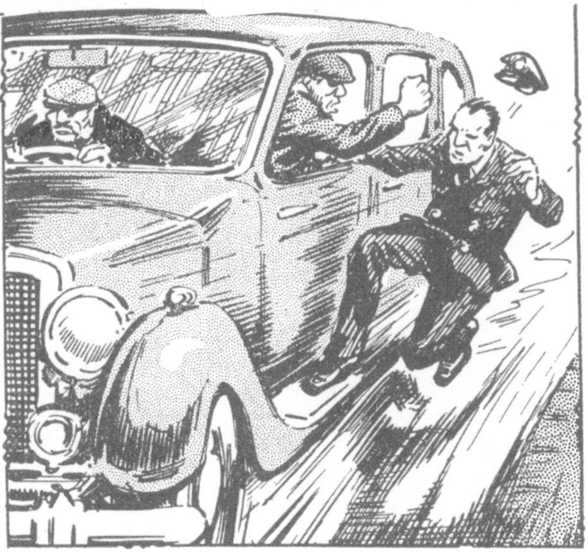

GEORGE MEDAL

Corporal Alfred Coxall of the Canadian Army won this medal in 1961, when he descended by line from an aeroplane to help a parachutist whose gear was entangled. Both men fell free, and Coxall pulled the man's ripcord to ensure his safety, before opening his own parachute.

HEROES OF LAND SEA AND AIR

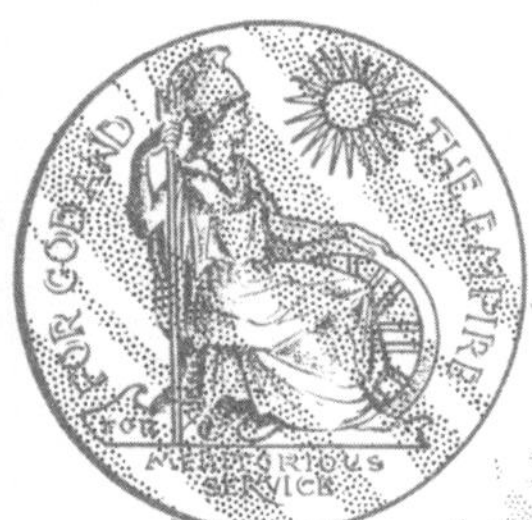
FOR GOD AND THE EMPIRE
FOR MERITORIOUS SERVICE

BRITISH EMPIRE MEDAL

Sixteen-year-old Ronald Heys, of Bootle, won this medal in 1941, during a big German air-raid. A messenger in the Auxiliary Fire Service, he continued to carry important messages although five bicycles which he used were damaged by bomb blast. He was blown off one machine and knocked unconscious.

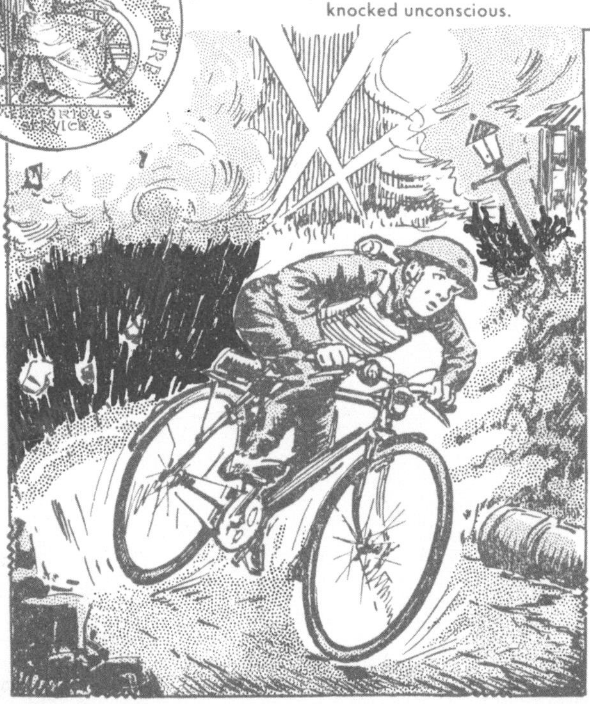

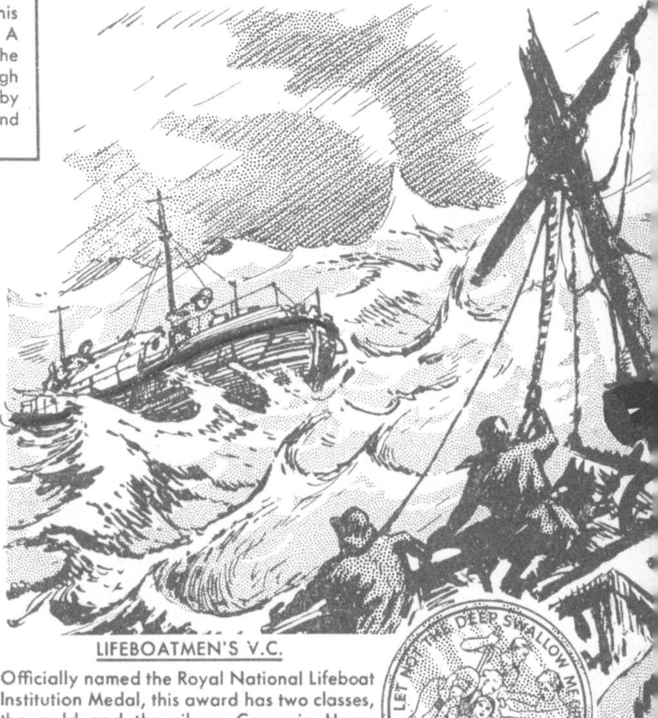

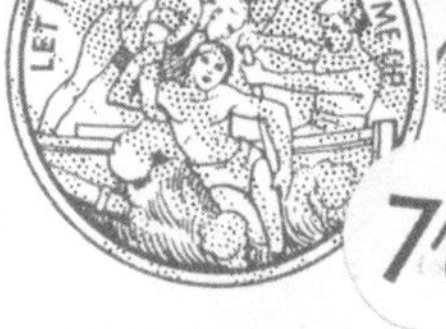
LET NOT THE DEEP SWALLOW ME

LIFEBOATMEN'S V.C.

Officially named the Royal National Lifeboat Institution Medal, this award has two classes, the gold and the silver. Coxwain Henry Blogg, who served in the Cromer lifeboat for 53 years, won the gold medal three times and the silver medal on four occasions. He helped to save the lives of nearly 900 men.

The BEST of The VICTOR
BOOK FOR BOYS

Edited by
Morris Heggie

Foreword by
Andy McNab

PRION

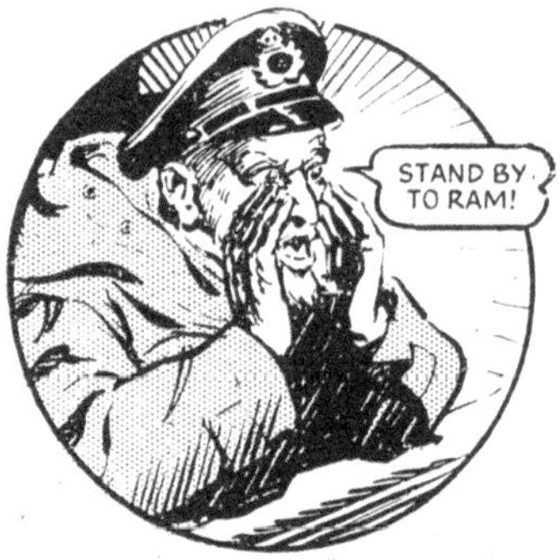
STAND BY
TO RAM!

This edition first published in 2011 by Prion
an imprint of the Carlton Publishing Group
20 Mortimer Street
London W1T 3JW

A catalogue record for this book is available in the British Library.

ISBN 978-1-85375-818-8

Printed and bound in Dubai

1 3 5 7 9 10 8 6 4 2

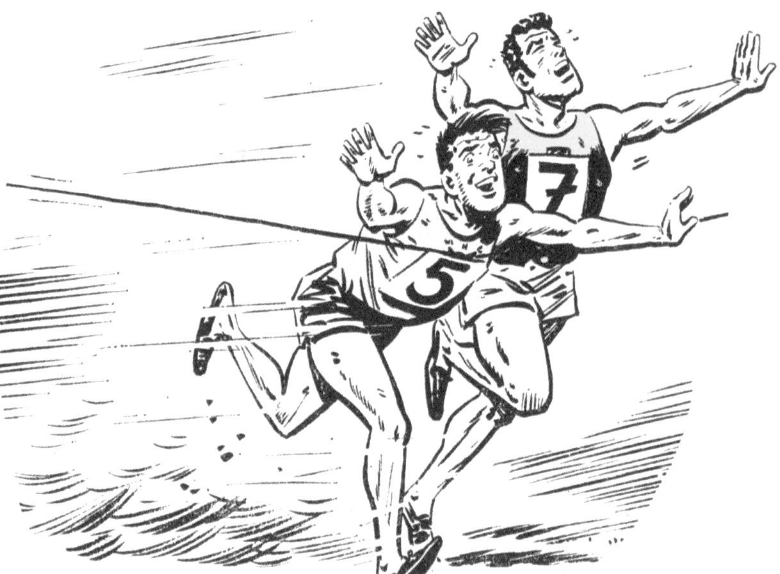

CONTENTS

Foreword by Andy McNab 4

Introduction by Morris Heggie, DC Thomson. 5

Weird Weapons of War 6

The Raid on St Nazaire. 7

Gorgeous Gus 19

The Battalion. 27

Morgyn the Mighty 35

Here Come the Paras. 44

I Flew with Braddock 45

The Lancer Laughed Last! 61

Sniper Dennison 69

Build a Battle Gun 78

Games They Used to Play 80

The Town Tamers. 81

No Cricket for Charlesworth 89

The Flying Cowboy 97

Odd Cars 102

The Mysterious Mister Navaran 103

Come Away The United. 111

The Fight of Forgotten Punches 128

The Tough of the Track 135

FOREWORD

This second helping from *The Victor* archives is even bigger and better than the first, and I'm sure you're going to get as much out of it as I have. OK, there may be the odd jingoistic phrase like "Take that, you ugly square head", but when you compare these stories to most of today's mindlessly violent films and graphic novels, *The Victor Book for Boys* still leaves them in the dust. Because it's always had something which so many of today's stories lack: a moral framework. And *The Victor Book for Boys* has that in spades.

The core values that run through these pages reflect those that lie at the heart of the modern British Army, and pretty much always have done: *Selfless Commitment, Courage, Discipline, Loyalty, Integrity* and *Respect for Others*. They may all sound as if they belong in the Victorian era, but these six principles still hold the Army together. These core values bind every serving soldier from the Day-One recruit to the highest-ranking General. No matter who you are in the Army, every soldier is expected to live by them.

It is these core values that make young men and women, like the ones in *The Victor Book for Boys*, prepared to risk their own lives to save those who stand alongside them. I've been with our troops in Iraq and Afghanistan during the current conflicts and seen these values put into practice time after time. It's what makes a nineteen-year-old squaddie take off his body armour and helmet so he can run faster through enemy fire to rescue another solider he doesn't even know. It's what makes a wounded soldier refuse medical aid so that he can stay on and fight alongside his mates. These core values are what turn ordinary, everyday soldiers into heroes, just as they do in *The Victor Book for Boys*.

So immerse yourself in Victor's world and you might end up becoming a better version of yourself. Who knows?!

Andy McNab

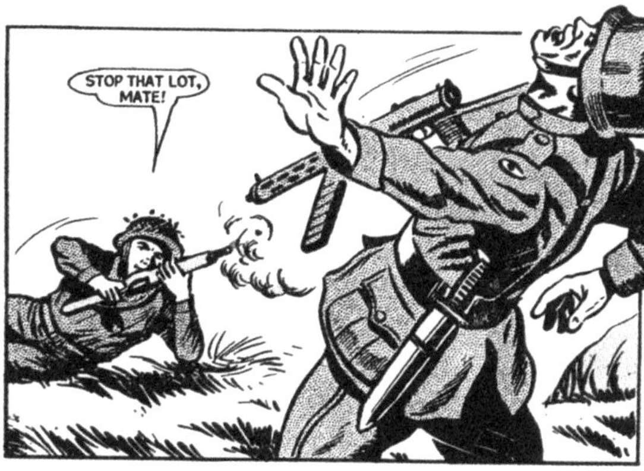
STOP THAT LOT, MATE!

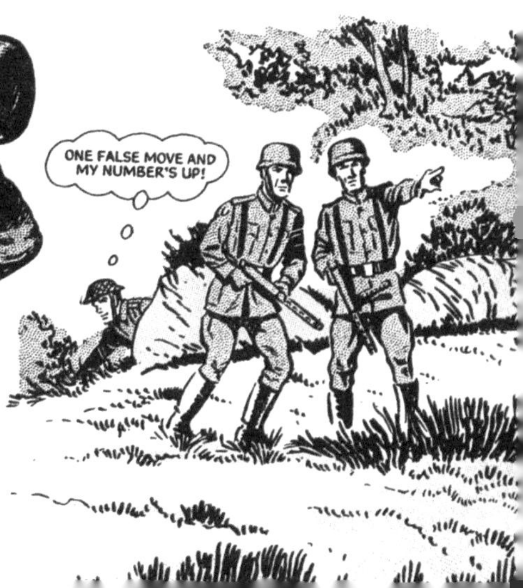
ONE FALSE MOVE AND MY NUMBER'S UP!

INTRODUCTION

For a *Victor* weekly comic reader like myself, a Christmas gift of *The Victor Book for Boys* was the memorable and exciting. I remember clearly the first one I ever received on Christmas day 1963. (I can even recall the unique inky smell you got when you first opened these DC Thomson printed books). Its full colour cover showed Commandos going into action at St. Nazaire, two pages later, the complete story – 'The Raid on St Nazaire', twelve pages in length and with spot-red colouring, especially effective on the explosions and gunfire. It was the best war strip I had ever seen.

On choosing a lead story to kick off this collection it was the top candidate. Reading it again reminded me just how good it was – it stands out strongly even after all these years.

The *Victor* book series started with that 1964 dated book and ran for thirty years. The book was like a super-weekly comic, the same mix of terrific *Victor* characters but they were given much longer stories and very clever single colour highlighting. It would be into the nineties before this simplified colouring style changed to more graphic full colour. I loved the longer stories because they were completes – with the weekly *Victor* the stories were in two- or three-page instalments. Waiting for a whole seven days for a lad like me was near impossible. The book also included features on action topics, my personal favourites being the in-depth looks at armaments and weaponry and the real-life heroes who operated them.

I always thought *The Victor Books for Boys* had a special quality and the only way I can describe it is that for me, they had a "holiday feeling". Something to relax with and to enjoy reading. After I started work on DC Thomson's boys' adventure titles I realised that some of this feeling came over from the authors, artists and editorial staff who all especially enjoyed producing the book. The authors found the compact complete stories a break from the twenty plus instalments they usually produced *Victor* work in. The artists got freedom to express themselves better with having less panels to a page and the magazine editorial team loved the challenge of producing a quality book.

I feel confident you will find this marvellous collection a very worthwhile read. The material was chosen from twelve different years of *Victor Book for Boys* and includes all the most famous *Victor* strips like 'Gorgeous Gus', 'Tough of the Track', 'I Flew With Braddock' and 'Morgyn the Mighty'. It is the best of what was a very high quality series.

Morris Heggie

Morris Heggie.

Editor. DC Thomson & Co Ltd.

Six weird and wonderful weapons of World War Two.

WEIRD WEAPONS OF WAR

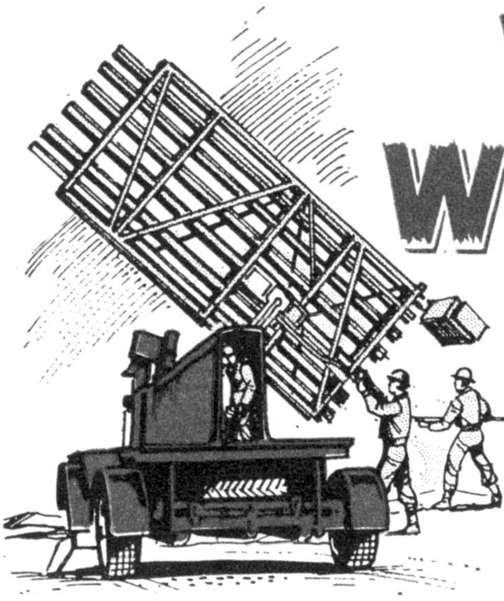

This completely mobile weapon was called the "Z" gun. It was dreaded by enemy bomber pilots because it could fire a salvo of powerful rockets to a great height. The first kill made by a battery of "Z" guns was early in 1941.

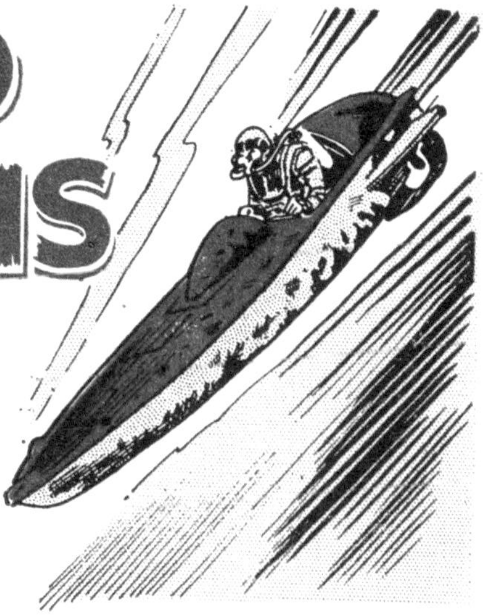

Submersible canoes were used to carry British frogmen on their strikes against enemy shipping. The 12½ foot long canoes were motor-driven, had a range of over 40 miles and a speed of 4 knots. They travelled underwater when they neared the target.

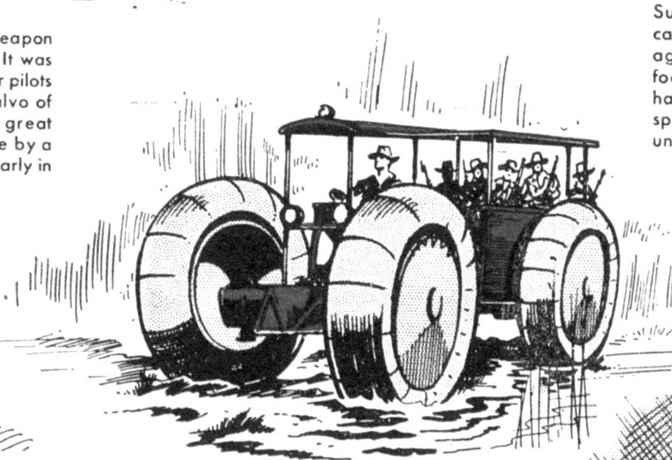

This strange-looking machine was called the Marsh Buggy and it was fitted with huge tyres. They were 10 feet high and weighed 315 lbs. These tyres and the light, hollow aluminium wheels enabled the Buggy to cross otherwise impassable swamps. They were used in the war against the Japanese.

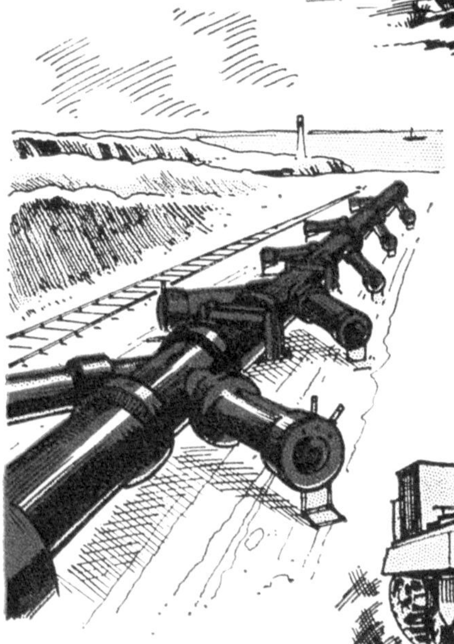

The weapon shown here was a German long-range gun. The barrel was a tube 400 feet long, designed to fire six-inch shells on London. Booster chambers at intervals were ignited in succession to give additional thrust to the shells. The gun was captured before it could be used.

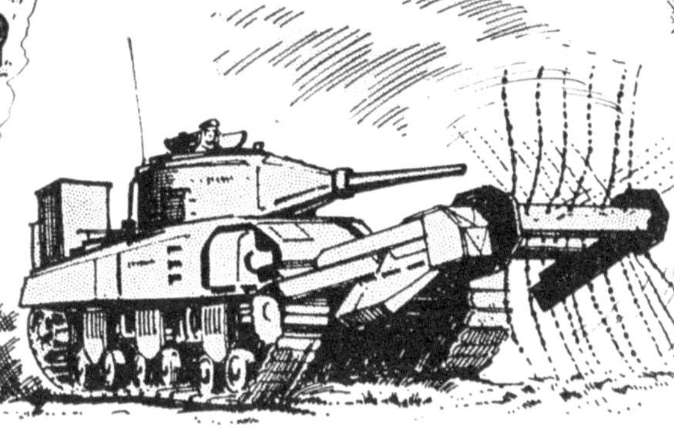

When a path through a minefield had to be quickly cleared, a tank fitted with heavy, whirling chains was brought up. These chains beat the ground and detonated any mines in the way of the tank. The tanks fitted with these flails were called Scorpions.

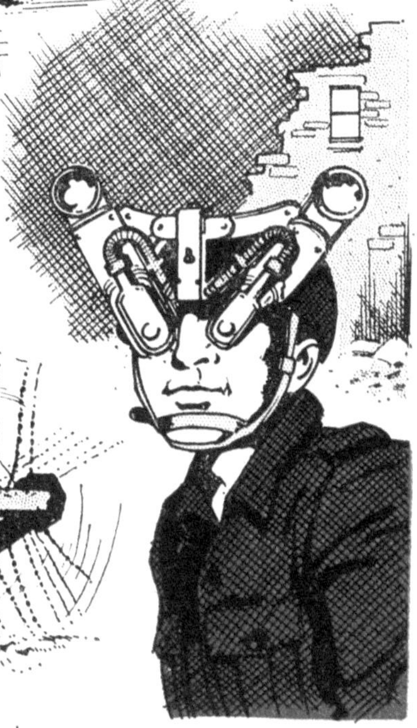

This device used by the Allies was called the Snooperscope. It worked on the infra-red principle and enabled a sentry to see clearly even on the darkest night. It was used extensively by snipers.

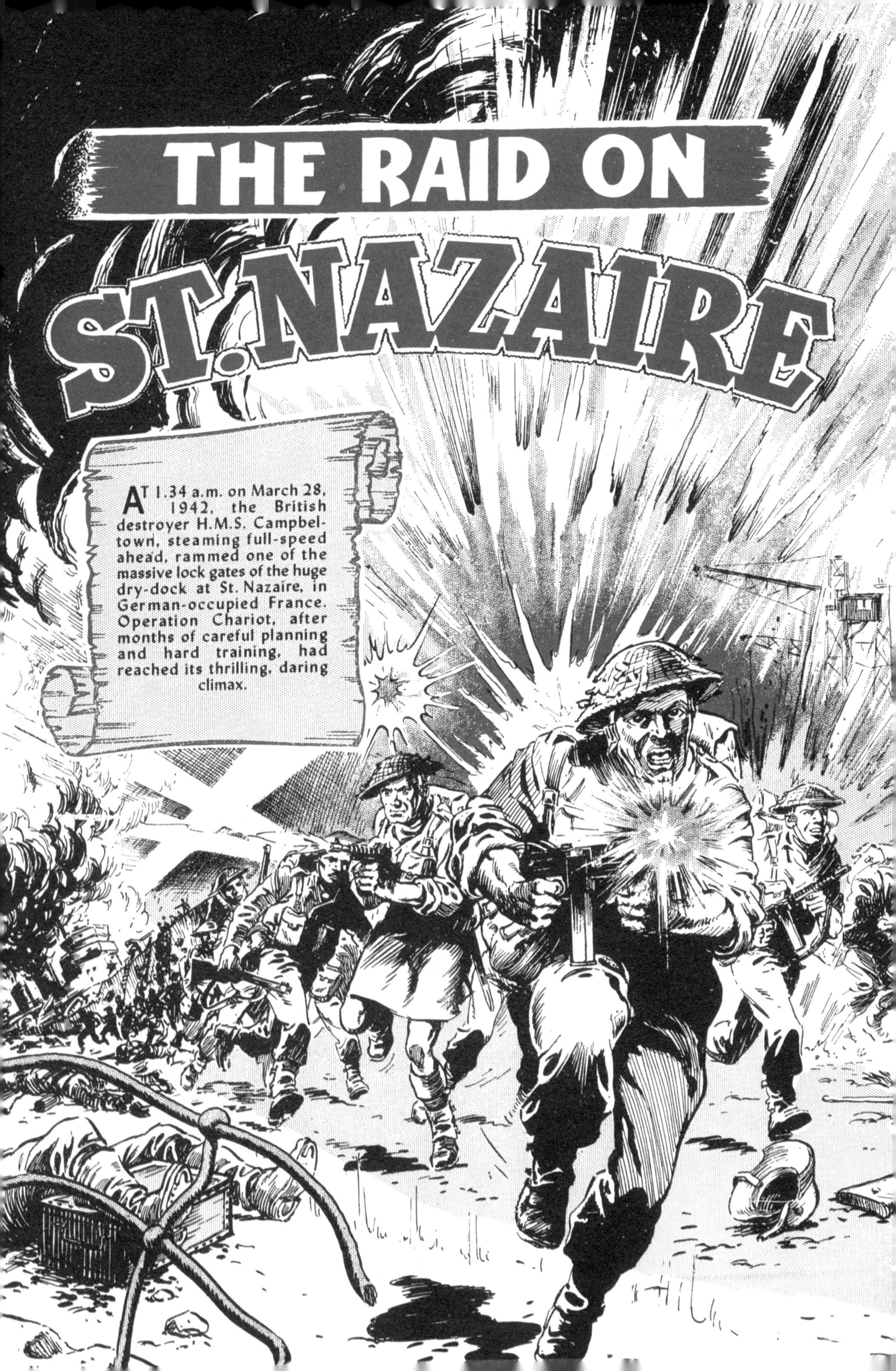
THE RAID ON
ST. NAZAIRE
AT 1.34 a.m. on March 28, 1942, the British destroyer H.M.S. Campbeltown, steaming full-speed ahead, rammed one of the massive lock gates of the huge dry-dock at St. Nazaire, in German-occupied France. Operation Chariot, after months of careful planning and hard training, had reached its thrilling, daring climax.

8

The toughest task Commandos ever tackled!

Nine days previously, Colonel Newman, Army Commander of the operation, had addressed his men.

WELL THAT'S ABOUT ALL, GENTLEMEN. I'VE TOLD YOU ALL ABOUT THE TARGET—SAINT NAZAIRE, THE MOST DANGEROUS JOB THE COMMANDOS HAVE EVER TACKLED. SO DANGEROUS THAT THE COMMANDER-IN-CHIEF HAS ASKED ME TO POINT OUT THAT ANY MAN MAY STAND DOWN. SO, IF ANYONE DOESN'T WANT TO GO—LET HIM STEP FORWARD!

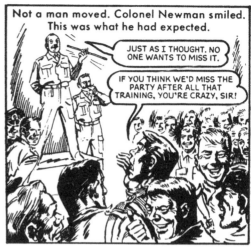

Not a man moved. Colonel Newman smiled. This was what he had expected.

JUST AS I THOUGHT. NO ONE WANTS TO MISS IT.

IF YOU THINK WE'D MISS THE PARTY AFTER ALL THAT TRAINING, YOU'RE CRAZY, SIR!

On March 25, 1942, the Commandos embarked on board the destroyer Campbeltown and set out on one of the most audacious raids in the history of war.

Even at sea, secrecy was of the utmost importance!

SIGNALLER, TELL MY COMMANDOS THEY MUST KEEP OUT OF SIGHT. THERE ARE TOO MANY OF THEM ON DECK.

AY, AY, SIR.

At 7 a.m. on March 27, nearing the French coast, a look-out's warning rang out.

U-BOAT ON THE PORT BOW!

DEPTH CHARGES AWAY!

The Campbeltown's escorting destroyers attacked, and the U-boat disappeared in a welter of foam—presumed sunk! That night, the Campbeltown, and the launches that carried the rest of the Commando assault parties, took up their attack formation—and said goodbye to the escort ships.

" Get that blooming rag down and put up a decent flag."

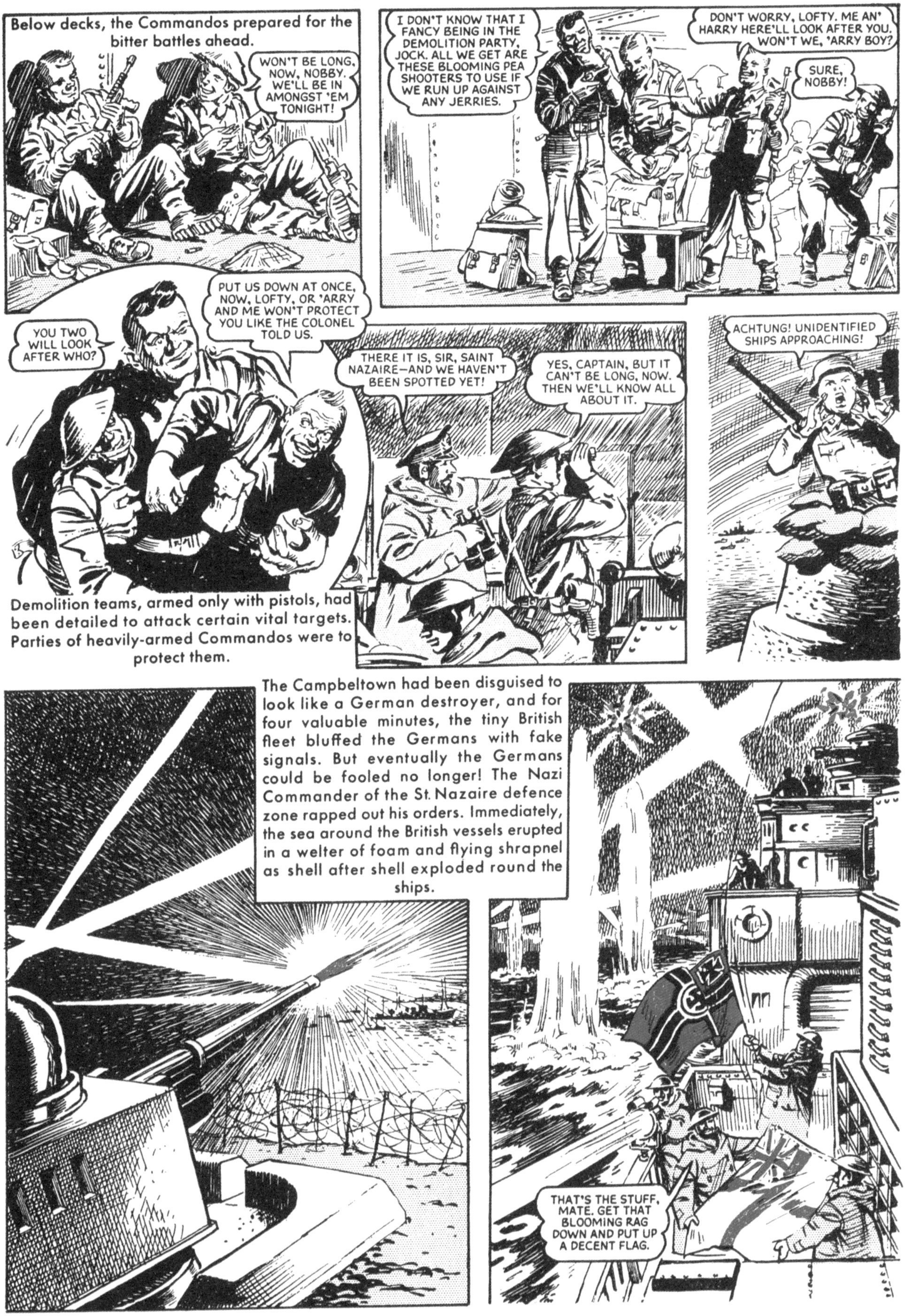

Below decks, the Commandos prepared for the bitter battles ahead.
WON'T BE LONG, NOW, NOBBY. WE'LL BE IN AMONGST 'EM TONIGHT!
I DON'T KNOW THAT I FANCY BEING IN THE DEMOLITION PARTY, JOCK. ALL WE GET ARE THESE BLOOMING PEA SHOOTERS TO USE IF WE RUN UP AGAINST ANY JERRIES.
DON'T WORRY, LOFTY. ME AN' HARRY HERE'LL LOOK AFTER YOU. WON'T WE, 'ARRY BOY?
SURE, NOBBY!
YOU TWO WILL LOOK AFTER WHO?
PUT US DOWN AT ONCE, NOW, LOFTY, OR 'ARRY AND ME WON'T PROTECT YOU LIKE THE COLONEL TOLD US.
Demolition teams, armed only with pistols, had been detailed to attack certain vital targets. Parties of heavily-armed Commandos were to protect them.
THERE IT IS, SIR, SAINT NAZAIRE—AND WE HAVEN'T BEEN SPOTTED YET!
YES, CAPTAIN, BUT IT CAN'T BE LONG, NOW. THEN WE'LL KNOW ALL ABOUT IT.
ACHTUNG! UNIDENTIFIED SHIPS APPROACHING!
The Campbeltown had been disguised to look like a German destroyer, and for four valuable minutes, the tiny British fleet bluffed the Germans with fake signals. But eventually the Germans could be fooled no longer! The Nazi Commander of the St. Nazaire defence zone rapped out his orders. Immediately, the sea around the British vessels erupted in a welter of foam and flying shrapnel as shell after shell exploded round the ships.
THAT'S THE STUFF, MATE. GET THAT BLOOMING RAG DOWN AND PUT UP A DECENT FLAG.

10

"Stand by to ram!"

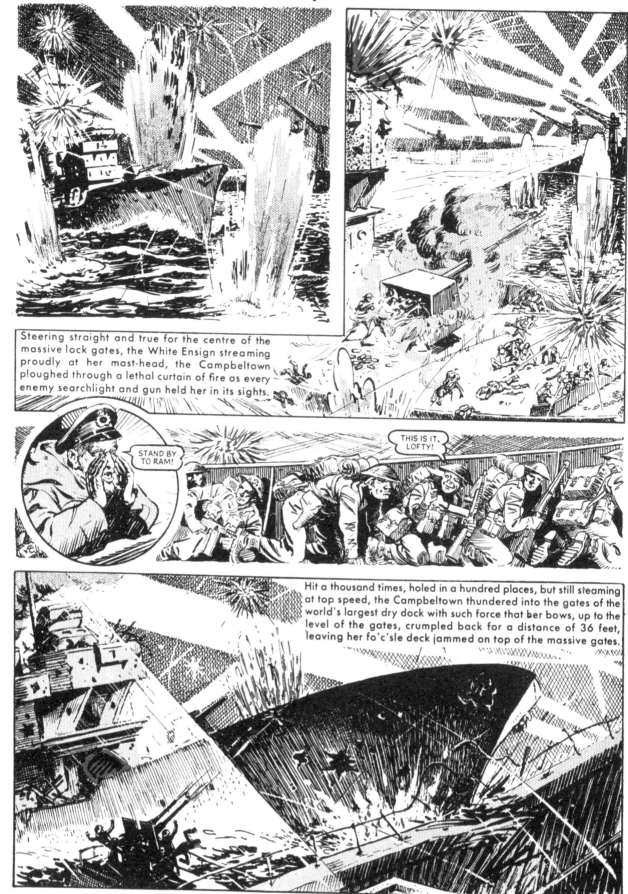

Steering straight and true for the centre of the massive lock gates, the White Ensign streaming proudly at her mast-head, the Campbeltown ploughed through a lethal curtain of fire as every enemy searchlight and gun held her in its sights.

STAND BY TO RAM!

THIS IS IT, LOFTY!

Hit a thousand times, holed in a hundred places, but still steaming at top speed, the Campbeltown thundered into the gates of the world's largest dry dock with such force that her bows, up to the level of the gates, crumpled back for a distance of 36 feet, leaving her fo'c'sle deck jammed on top of the massive gates.

" Commandos away ! "

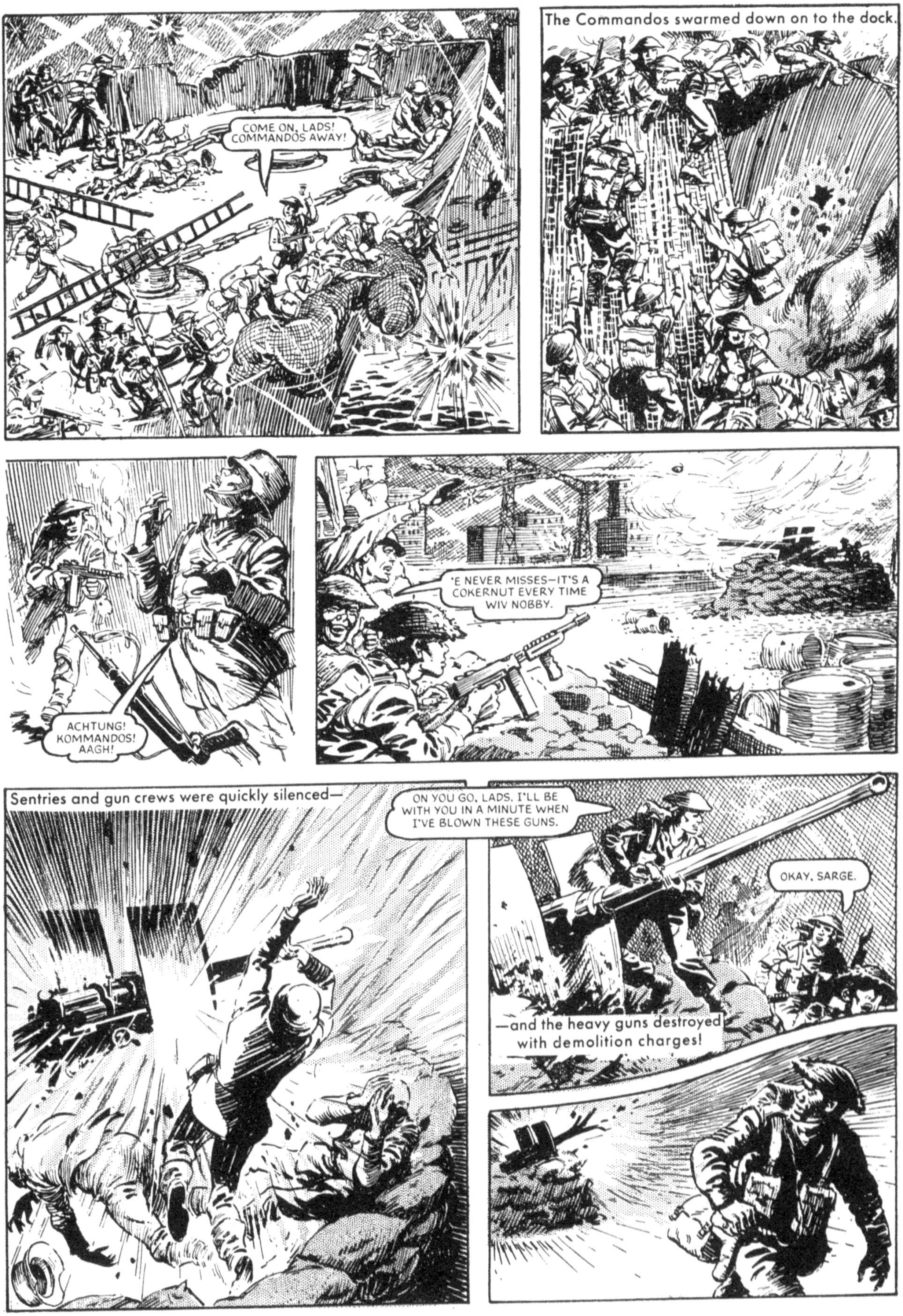
COME ON, LADS! COMMANDOS AWAY!
The Commandos swarmed down on to the dock.
ACHTUNG! KOMMANDOS! AAGH!
'E NEVER MISSES—IT'S A COKERNUT EVERY TIME WIV NOBBY.
Sentries and gun crews were quickly silenced—
ON YOU GO, LADS. I'LL BE WITH YOU IN A MINUTE WHEN I'VE BLOWN THESE GUNS.
OKAY, SARGE.
—and the heavy guns destroyed with demolition charges!

The key to any door!

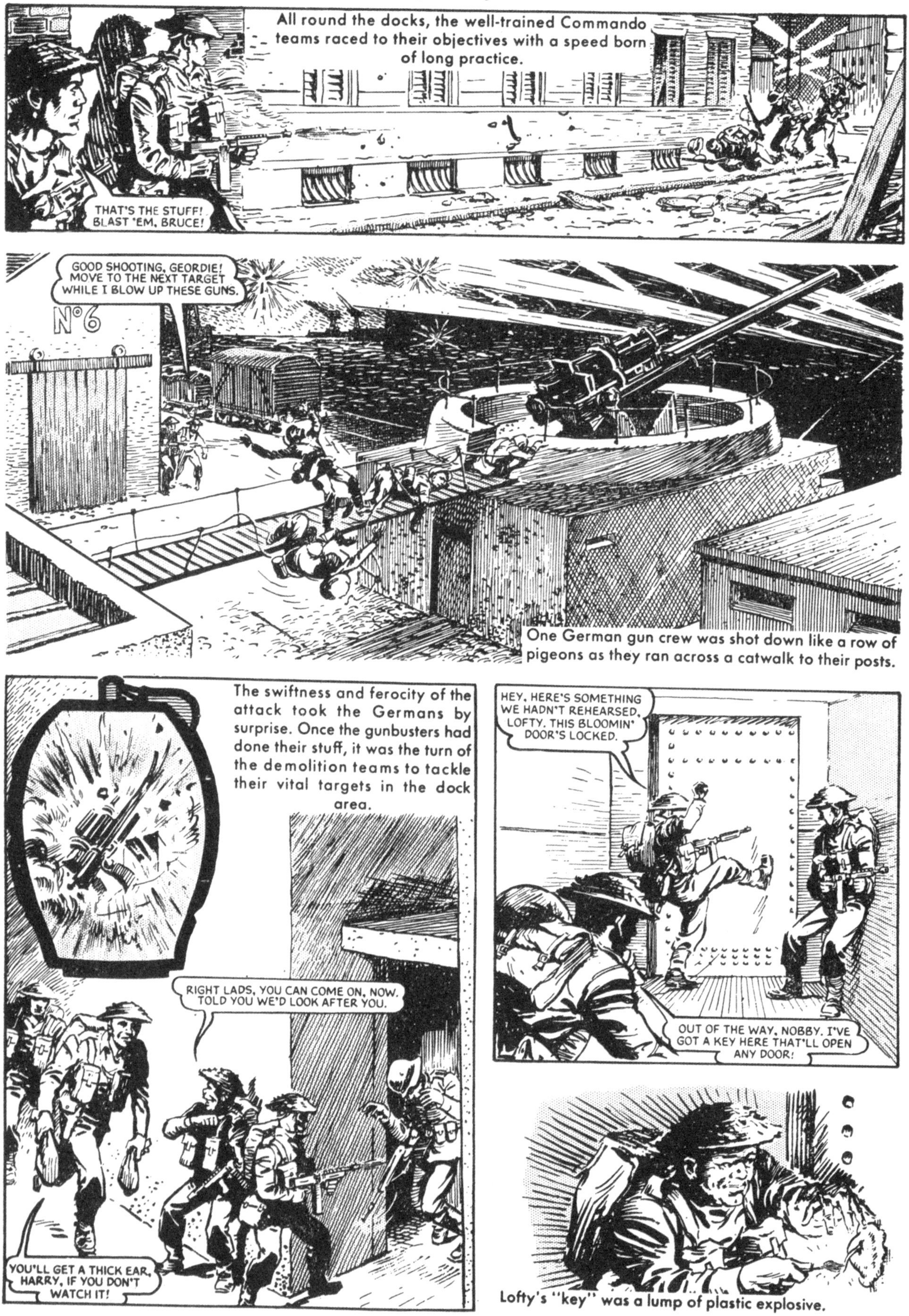
All round the docks, the well-trained Commando teams raced to their objectives with a speed born of long practice.
THAT'S THE STUFF! BLAST 'EM, BRUCE!
GOOD SHOOTING, GEORDIE! MOVE TO THE NEXT TARGET WHILE I BLOW UP THESE GUNS.
Nº6
One German gun crew was shot down like a row of pigeons as they ran across a catwalk to their posts.
The swiftness and ferocity of the attack took the Germans by surprise. Once the gunbusters had done their stuff, it was the turn of the demolition teams to tackle their vital targets in the dock area.
RIGHT LADS, YOU CAN COME ON, NOW. TOLD YOU WE'D LOOK AFTER YOU.
YOU'LL GET A THICK EAR, HARRY, IF YOU DON'T WATCH IT!
HEY, HERE'S SOMETHING WE HADN'T REHEARSED, LOFTY. THIS BLOOMIN' DOOR'S LOCKED.
OUT OF THE WAY, NOBBY. I'VE GOT A KEY HERE THAT'LL OPEN ANY DOOR!

Lofty's "key" was a lump of plastic explosive.

Looking after Lofty.

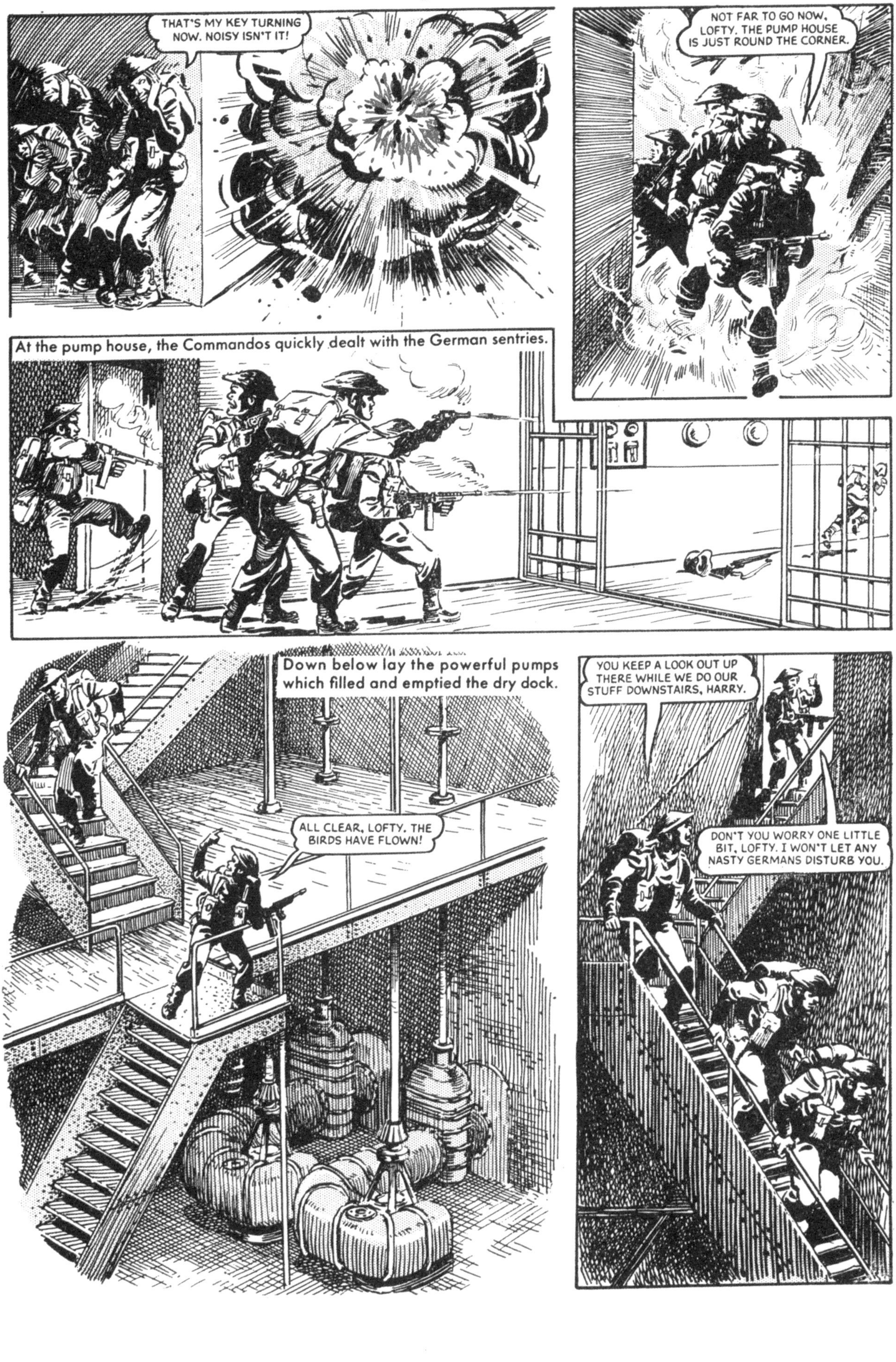
THAT'S MY KEY TURNING NOW. NOISY ISN'T IT!
NOT FAR TO GO NOW, LOFTY. THE PUMP HOUSE IS JUST ROUND THE CORNER.
At the pump house, the Commandos quickly dealt with the German sentries.
Down below lay the powerful pumps which filled and emptied the dry dock.
ALL CLEAR, LOFTY, THE BIRDS HAVE FLOWN!
YOU KEEP A LOOK OUT UP THERE WHILE WE DO OUR STUFF DOWNSTAIRS, HARRY.
DON'T YOU WORRY ONE LITTLE BIT, LOFTY. I WON'T LET ANY NASTY GERMANS DISTURB YOU.

" The Nazis are getting nasty ! "

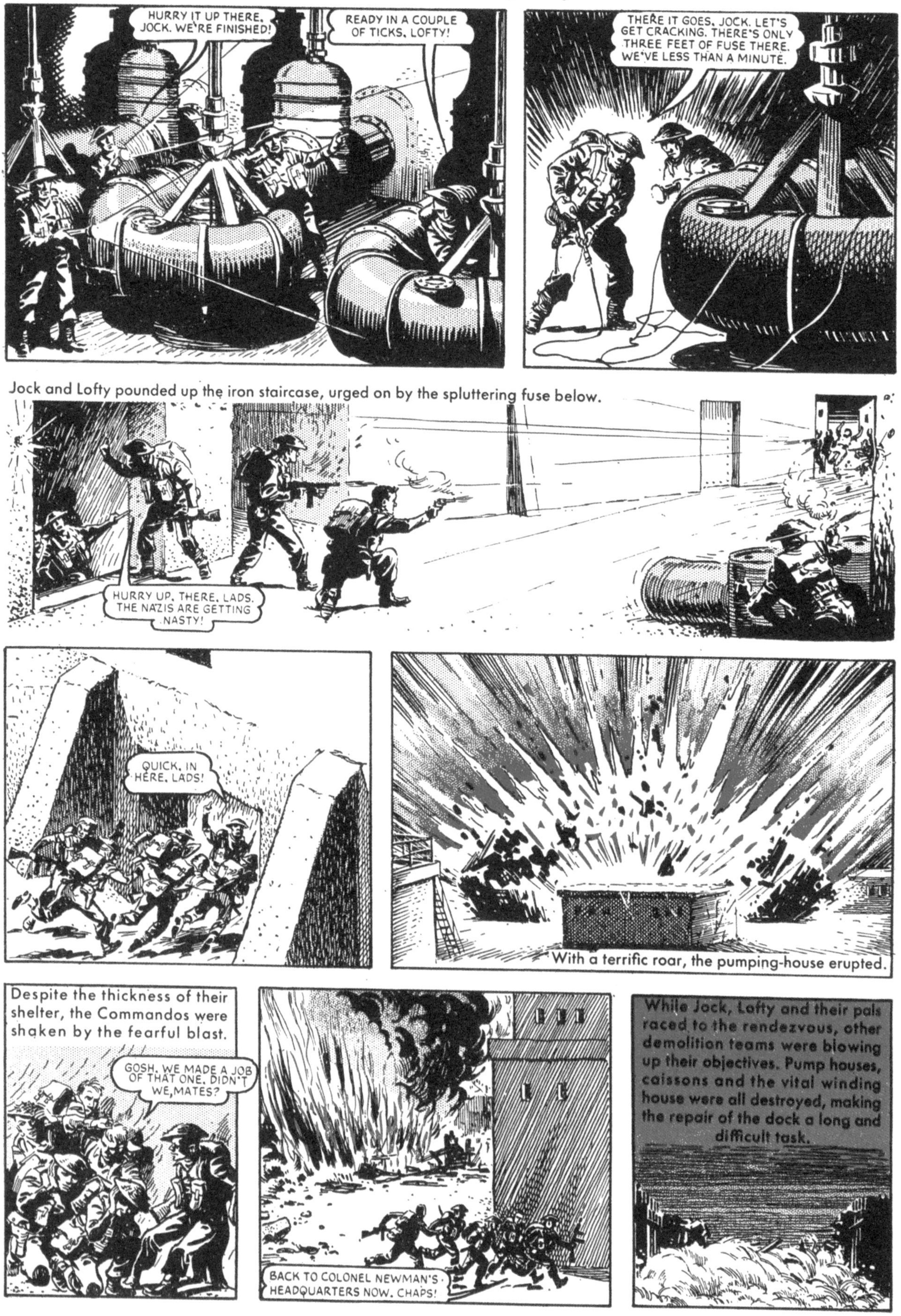
HURRY IT UP THERE, JOCK. WE'RE FINISHED!
READY IN A COUPLE OF TICKS, LOFTY!
THERE IT GOES, JOCK. LET'S GET CRACKING. THERE'S ONLY THREE FEET OF FUSE THERE. WE'VE LESS THAN A MINUTE.
Jock and Lofty pounded up the iron staircase, urged on by the spluttering fuse below.
HURRY UP, THERE, LADS. THE NAZIS ARE GETTING NASTY!
QUICK, IN HERE, LADS!
With a terrific roar, the pumping-house erupted.
Despite the thickness of their shelter, the Commandos were shaken by the fearful blast.
GOSH, WE MADE A JOB OF THAT ONE, DIDN'T WE, MATES?
BACK TO COLONEL NEWMAN'S HEADQUARTERS NOW, CHAPS!
While Jock, Lofty and their pals raced to the rendezvous, other demolition teams were blowing up their objectives. Pump houses, caissons and the vital winding house were all destroyed, making the repair of the dock a long and difficult task.

The death of the little ships!

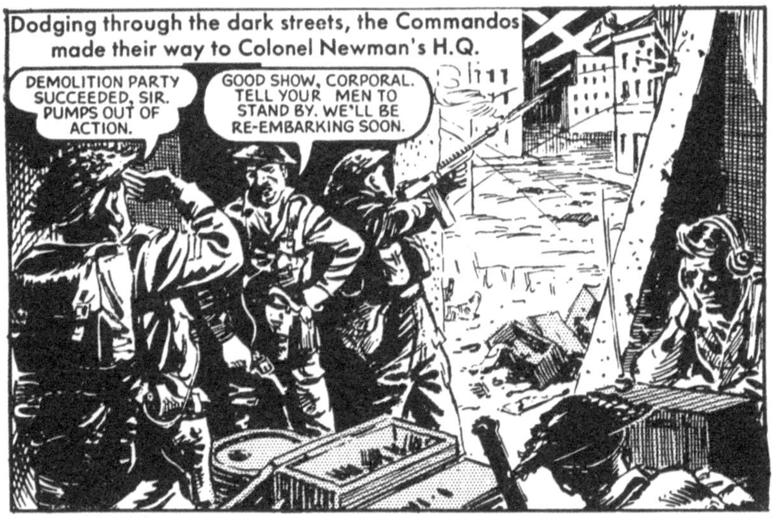
Dodging through the dark streets, the Commandos made their way to Colonel Newman's H.Q.
DEMOLITION PARTY SUCCEEDED, SIR. PUMPS OUT OF ACTION.
GOOD SHOW, CORPORAL. TELL YOUR MEN TO STAND BY. WE'LL BE RE-EMBARKING SOON.

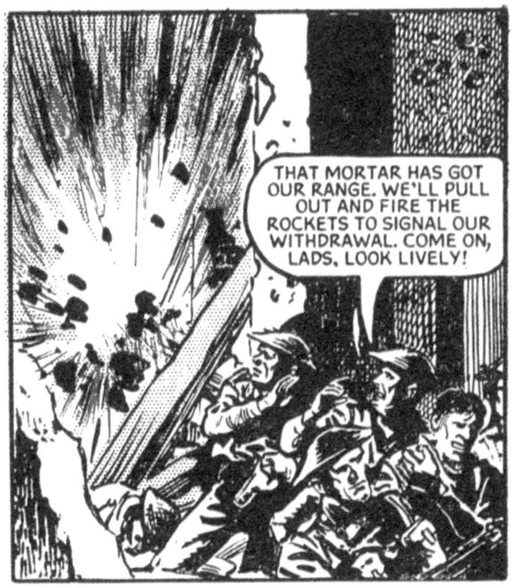
THAT MORTAR HAS GOT OUR RANGE. WE'LL PULL OUT AND FIRE THE ROCKETS TO SIGNAL OUR WITHDRAWAL. COME ON, LADS, LOOK LIVELY!

But when the Commando units retired to their re-embarkation rendezvous, they saw that escape was impossible. Once the Campbeltown had rammed herself on the dock gates, the Germans had turned every gun on the frail launches. Now, despite the bravery of the crews, who manned their guns to the bitter end, every launch was either sunk, ablaze or badly damaged.

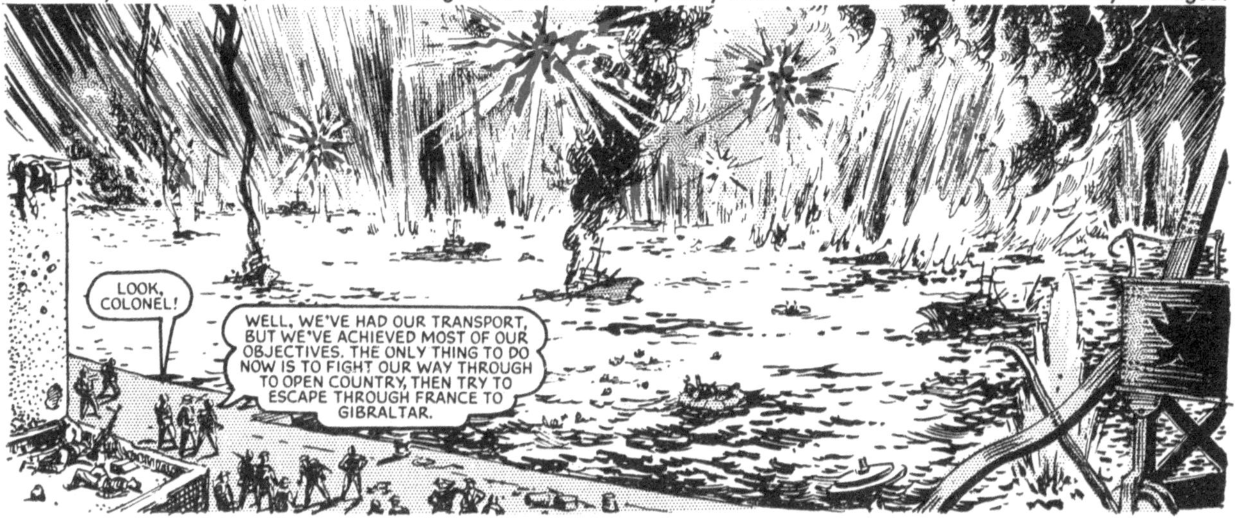
LOOK, COLONEL!
WELL, WE'VE HAD OUR TRANSPORT, BUT WE'VE ACHIEVED MOST OF OUR OBJECTIVES. THE ONLY THING TO DO NOW IS TO FIGHT OUR WAY THROUGH TO OPEN COUNTRY, THEN TRY TO ESCAPE THROUGH FRANCE TO GIBRALTAR.

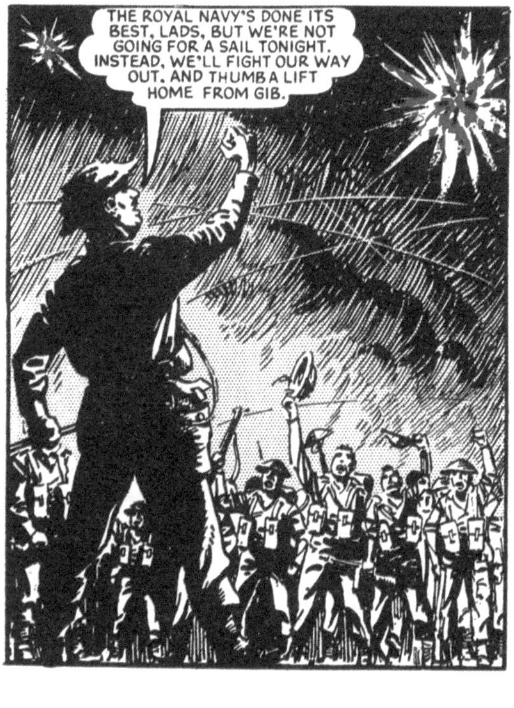
THE ROYAL NAVY'S DONE ITS BEST, LADS, BUT WE'RE NOT GOING FOR A SAIL TONIGHT. INSTEAD, WE'LL FIGHT OUR WAY OUT, AND THUMB A LIFT HOME FROM GIB.

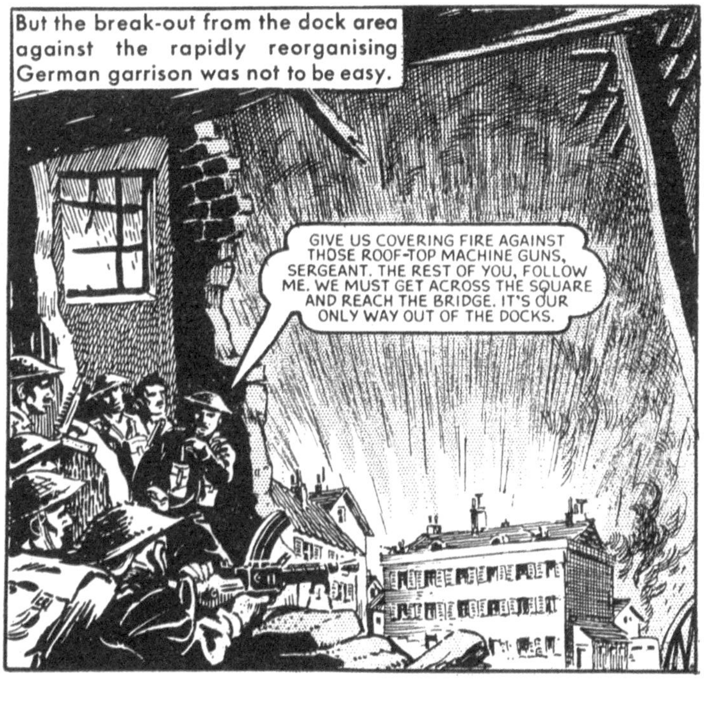
But the break-out from the dock area against the rapidly reorganising German garrison was not to be easy.
GIVE US COVERING FIRE AGAINST THOSE ROOF-TOP MACHINE GUNS, SERGEANT. THE REST OF YOU, FOLLOW ME. WE MUST GET ACROSS THE SQUARE AND REACH THE BRIDGE. IT'S OUR ONLY WAY OUT OF THE DOCKS.

The charge of the lost Commandos!

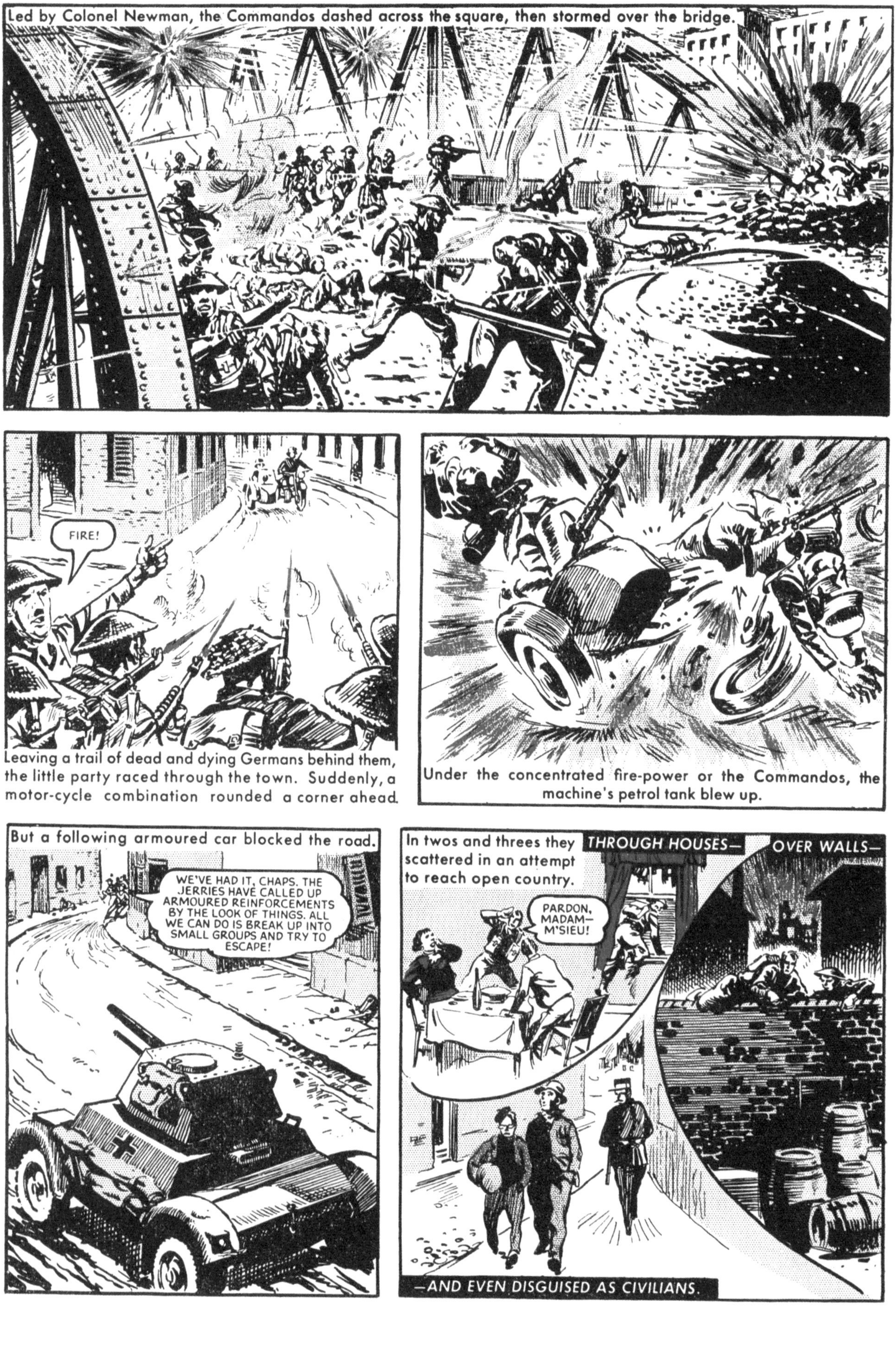
Led by Colonel Newman, the Commandos dashed across the square, then stormed over the bridge.
FIRE!
Leaving a trail of dead and dying Germans behind them, the little party raced through the town. Suddenly, a motor-cycle combination rounded a corner ahead.
Under the concentrated fire-power or the Commandos, the machine's petrol tank blew up.
But a following armoured car blocked the road.
WE'VE HAD IT, CHAPS. THE JERRIES HAVE CALLED UP ARMOURED REINFORCEMENTS BY THE LOOK OF THINGS. ALL WE CAN DO IS BREAK UP INTO SMALL GROUPS AND TRY TO ESCAPE!
In twos and threes they scattered in an attempt to reach open country.
THROUGH HOUSES—
PARDON, MADAM—M'SIEU!
OVER WALLS—
—AND EVEN DISGUISED AS CIVILIANS.

Surrender or die!

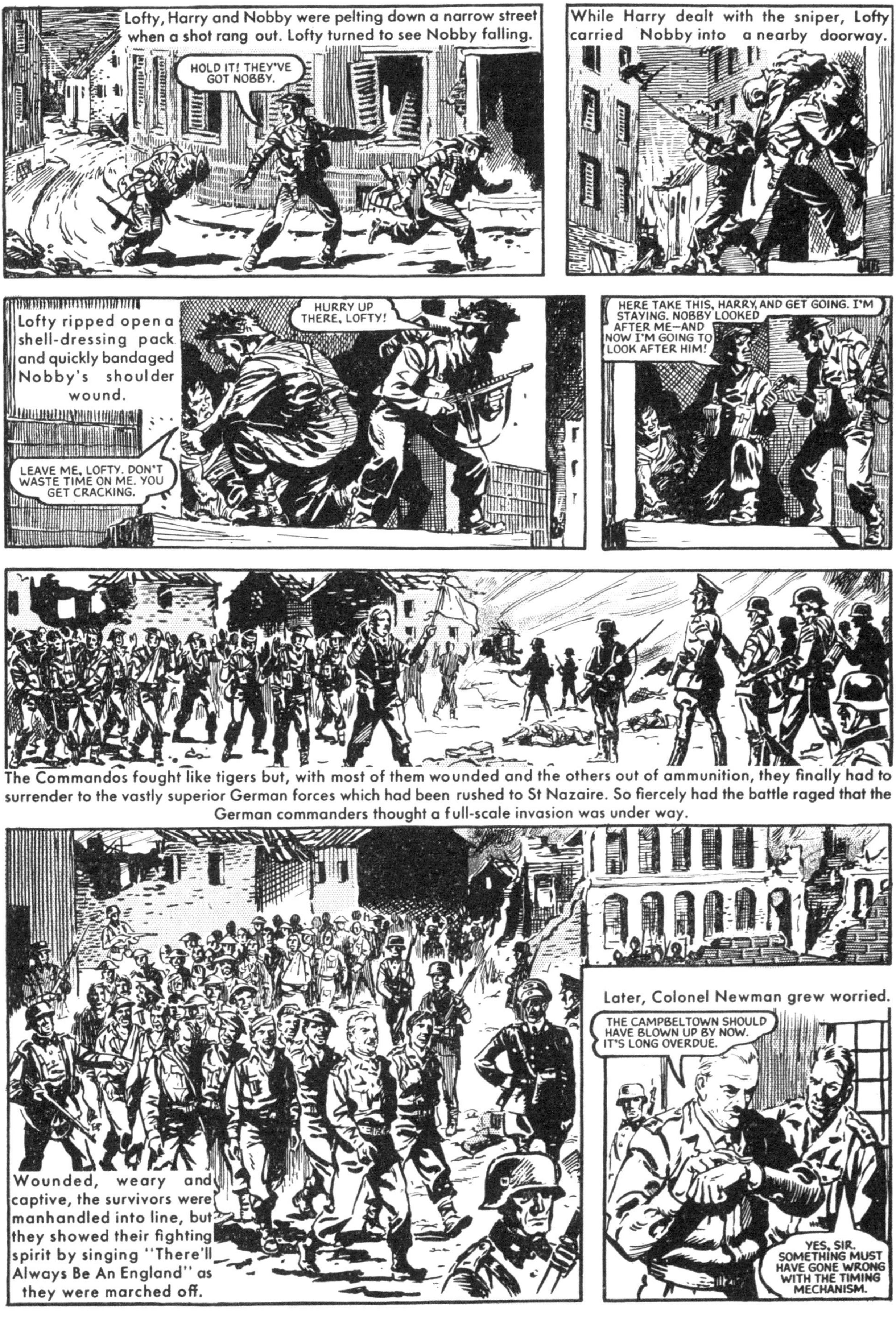

Lofty, Harry and Nobby were pelting down a narrow street when a shot rang out. Lofty turned to see Nobby falling.
HOLD IT! THEY'VE GOT NOBBY.
While Harry dealt with the sniper, Lofty carried Nobby into a nearby doorway.
Lofty ripped open a shell-dressing pack and quickly bandaged Nobby's shoulder wound.
HURRY UP THERE, LOFTY!
LEAVE ME, LOFTY. DON'T WASTE TIME ON ME. YOU GET CRACKING.
HERE TAKE THIS, HARRY, AND GET GOING. I'M STAYING. NOBBY LOOKED AFTER ME—AND NOW I'M GOING TO LOOK AFTER HIM!
The Commandos fought like tigers but, with most of them wounded and the others out of ammunition, they finally had to surrender to the vastly superior German forces which had been rushed to St Nazaire. So fiercely had the battle raged that the German commanders thought a full-scale invasion was under way.
Wounded, weary and captive, the survivors were manhandled into line, but they showed their fighting spirit by singing "There'll Always Be An England" as they were marched off.
Later, Colonel Newman grew worried.
THE CAMPBELTOWN SHOULD HAVE BLOWN UP BY NOW. IT'S LONG OVERDUE.
YES, SIR. SOMETHING MUST HAVE GONE WRONG WITH THE TIMING MECHANISM.

Five Victoria Crosses for the gallant six hundred!

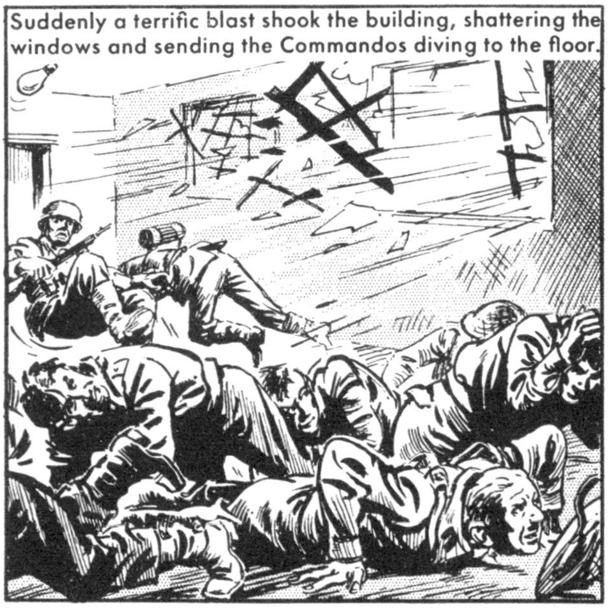
Suddenly a terrific blast shook the building, shattering the windows and sending the Commandos diving to the floor.

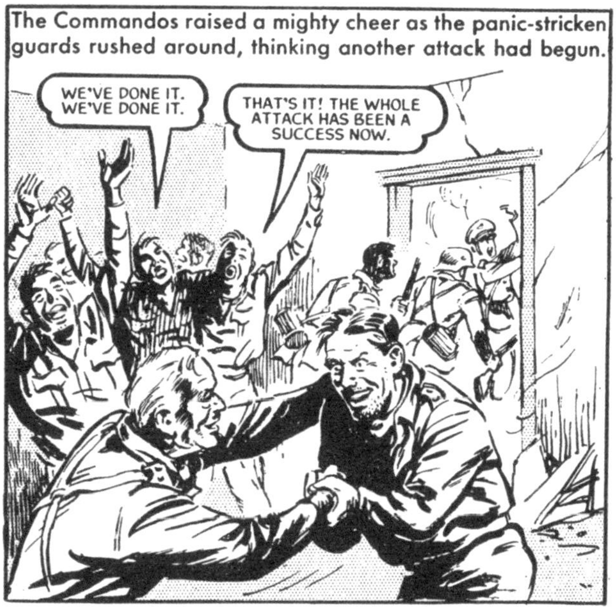
The Commandos raised a mighty cheer as the panic-stricken guards rushed around, thinking another attack had begun.
WE'VE DONE IT. WE'VE DONE IT.
THAT'S IT! THE WHOLE ATTACK HAS BEEN A SUCCESS NOW.

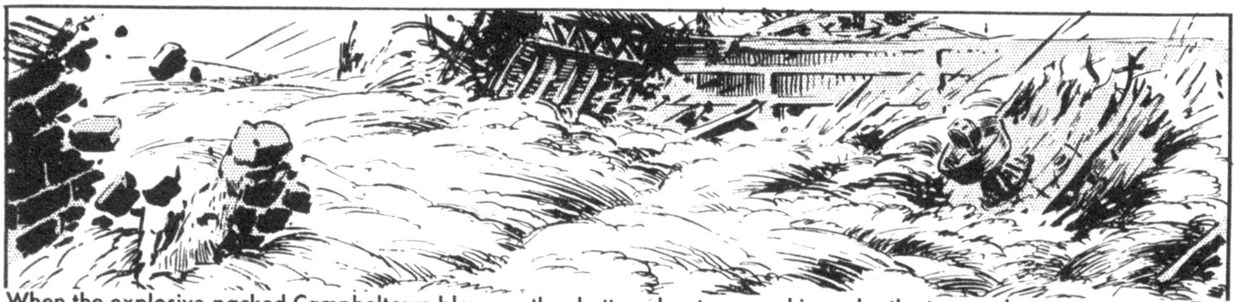

When the explosive-packed Campbeltown blew up, the shattered gates caved in under the tremendous sea pressure. Two tankers and the stern of the Campbeltown were swept far inside—and hundreds of German troops, were killed.

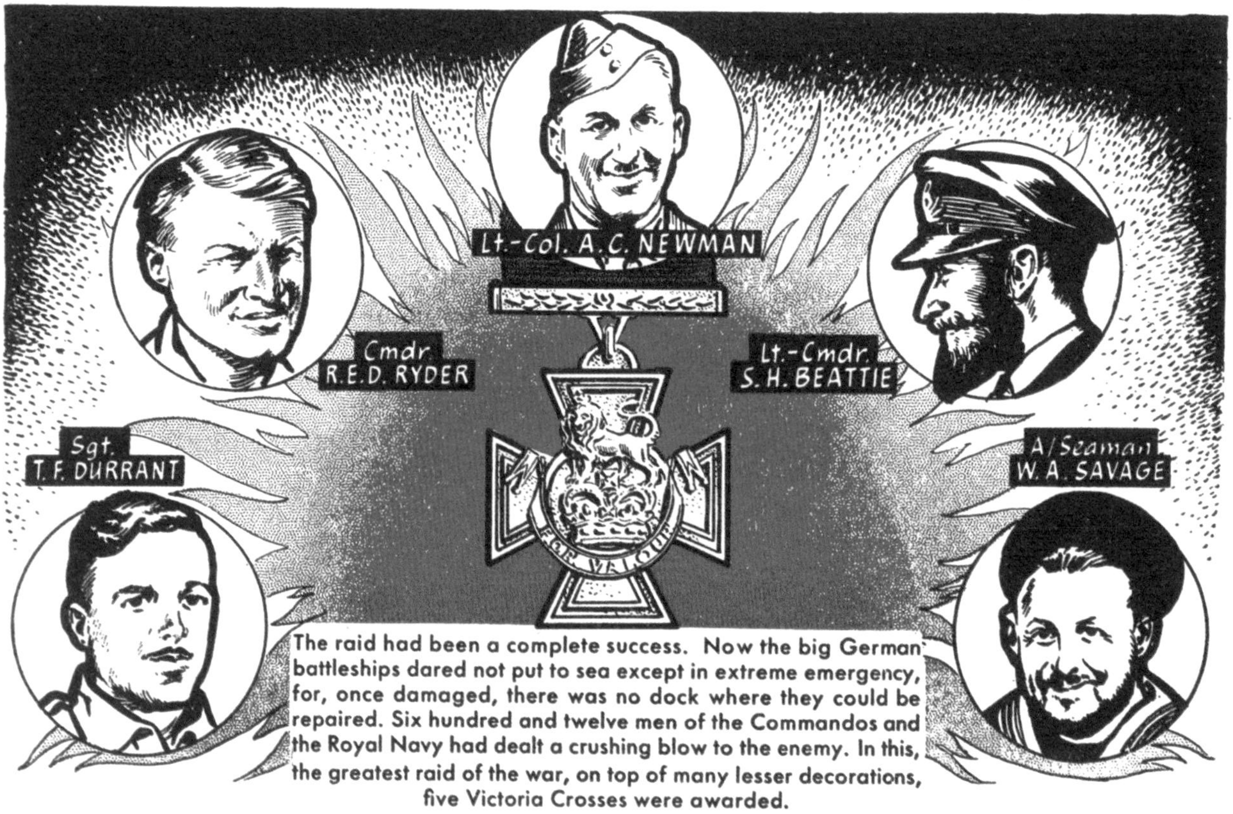
Lt.-Col. A.C. NEWMAN
Cmdr. R.E.D. RYDER
Lt.-Cmdr. S.H. BEATTIE
Sgt. T.F. DURRANT
A/Seaman W.A. SAVAGE
The raid had been a complete success. Now the big German battleships dared not put to sea except in extreme emergency, for, once damaged, there was no dock where they could be repaired. Six hundred and twelve men of the Commandos and the Royal Navy had dealt a crushing blow to the enemy. In this, the greatest raid of the war, on top of many lesser decorations, five Victoria Crosses were awarded.

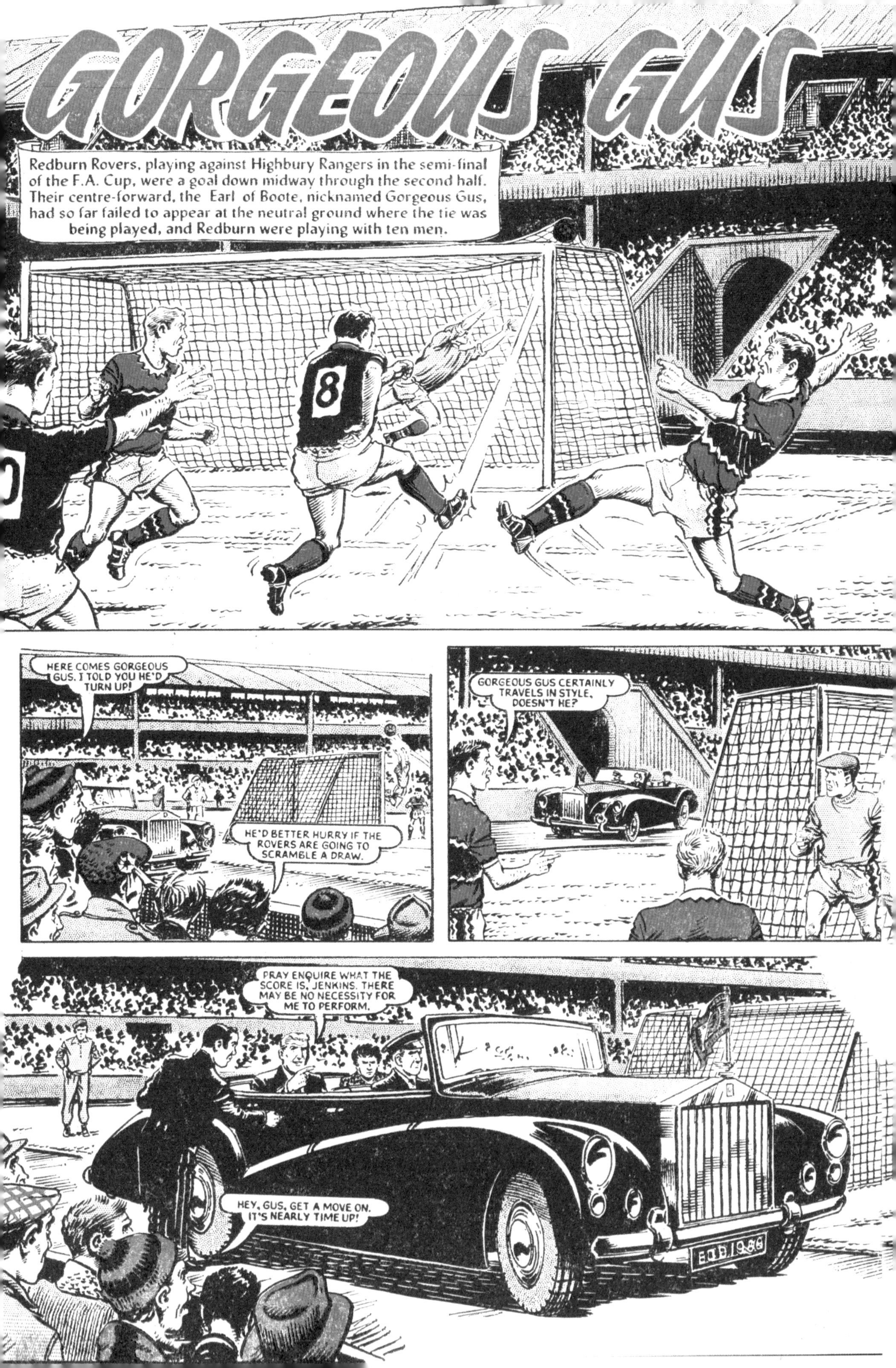
GORGEOUS GUS
Redburn Rovers, playing against Highbury Rangers in the semi-final of the F.A. Cup, were a goal down midway through the second half. Their centre-forward, the Earl of Boote, nicknamed Gorgeous Gus, had so far failed to appear at the neutral ground where the tie was being played, and Redburn were playing with ten men.
HERE COMES GORGEOUS GUS. I TOLD YOU HE'D TURN UP!
HE'D BETTER HURRY IF THE ROVERS ARE GOING TO SCRAMBLE A DRAW.
GORGEOUS GUS CERTAINLY TRAVELS IN STYLE, DOESN'T HE?
PRAY ENQUIRE WHAT THE SCORE IS, JENKINS. THERE MAY BE NO NECESSITY FOR ME TO PERFORM.
HEY, GUS, GET A MOVE ON. IT'S NEARLY TIME UP!

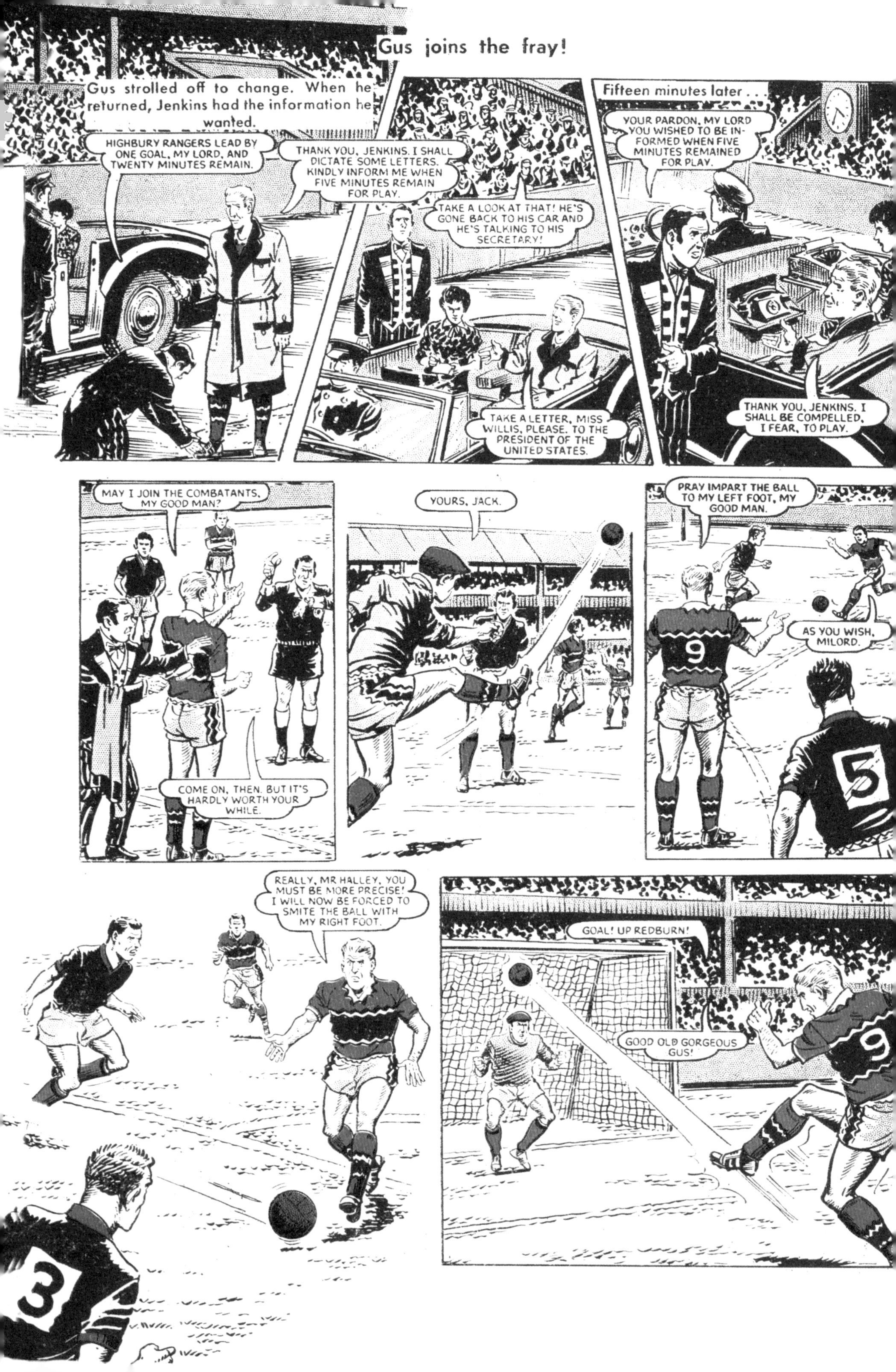
Gus joins the fray!
Gus strolled off to change. When he returned, Jenkins had the information he wanted.
HIGHBURY RANGERS LEAD BY ONE GOAL, MY LORD, AND TWENTY MINUTES REMAIN.
THANK YOU, JENKINS. I SHALL DICTATE SOME LETTERS. KINDLY INFORM ME WHEN FIVE MINUTES REMAIN FOR PLAY.
TAKE A LOOK AT THAT! HE'S GONE BACK TO HIS CAR AND HE'S TALKING TO HIS SECRETARY!
TAKE A LETTER, MISS WILLIS, PLEASE. TO THE PRESIDENT OF THE UNITED STATES.
Fifteen minutes later . . .
YOUR PARDON, MY LORD YOU WISHED TO BE INFORMED WHEN FIVE MINUTES REMAINED FOR PLAY.
THANK YOU, JENKINS. I SHALL BE COMPELLED, I FEAR, TO PLAY.
MAY I JOIN THE COMBATANTS, MY GOOD MAN?
COME ON, THEN. BUT IT'S HARDLY WORTH YOUR WHILE.
YOURS, JACK.
PRAY IMPART THE BALL TO MY LEFT FOOT, MY GOOD MAN.
AS YOU WISH, MILORD.
REALLY, MR HALLEY, YOU MUST BE MORE PRECISE! I WILL NOW BE FORCED TO SMITE THE BALL WITH MY RIGHT FOOT.
GOAL! UP REDBURN!
GOOD OLD GORGEOUS GUS!

The winning goal!

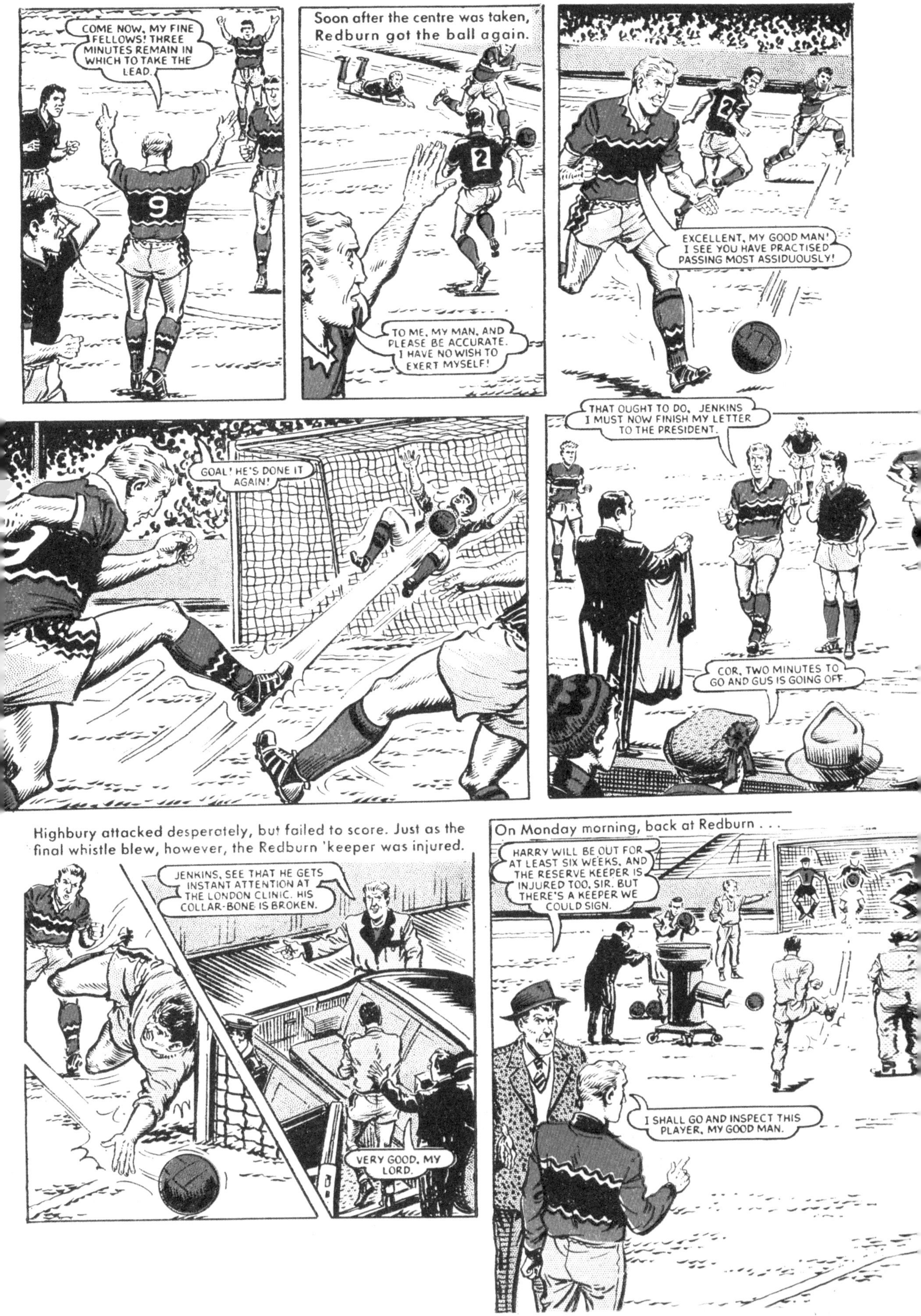
COME NOW, MY FINE FELLOWS! THREE MINUTES REMAIN IN WHICH TO TAKE THE LEAD.
Soon after the centre was taken, Redburn got the ball again.
TO ME, MY MAN, AND PLEASE BE ACCURATE. I HAVE NO WISH TO EXERT MYSELF!
EXCELLENT, MY GOOD MAN! I SEE YOU HAVE PRACTISED PASSING MOST ASSIDUOUSLY!
GOAL! HE'S DONE IT AGAIN!
THAT OUGHT TO DO, JENKINS. I MUST NOW FINISH MY LETTER TO THE PRESIDENT.
COR, TWO MINUTES TO GO AND GUS IS GOING OFF.
Highbury attacked desperately, but failed to score. Just as the final whistle blew, however, the Redburn 'keeper was injured.
JENKINS, SEE THAT HE GETS INSTANT ATTENTION AT THE LONDON CLINIC. HIS COLLAR-BONE IS BROKEN.
VERY GOOD, MY LORD.
On Monday morning, back at Redburn . . .
HARRY WILL BE OUT FOR AT LEAST SIX WEEKS, AND THE RESERVE KEEPER IS INJURED TOO, SIR. BUT THERE'S A KEEPER WE COULD SIGN.
I SHALL GO AND INSPECT THIS PLAYER, MY GOOD MAN.

Twenty thousand pounds for a fullback!

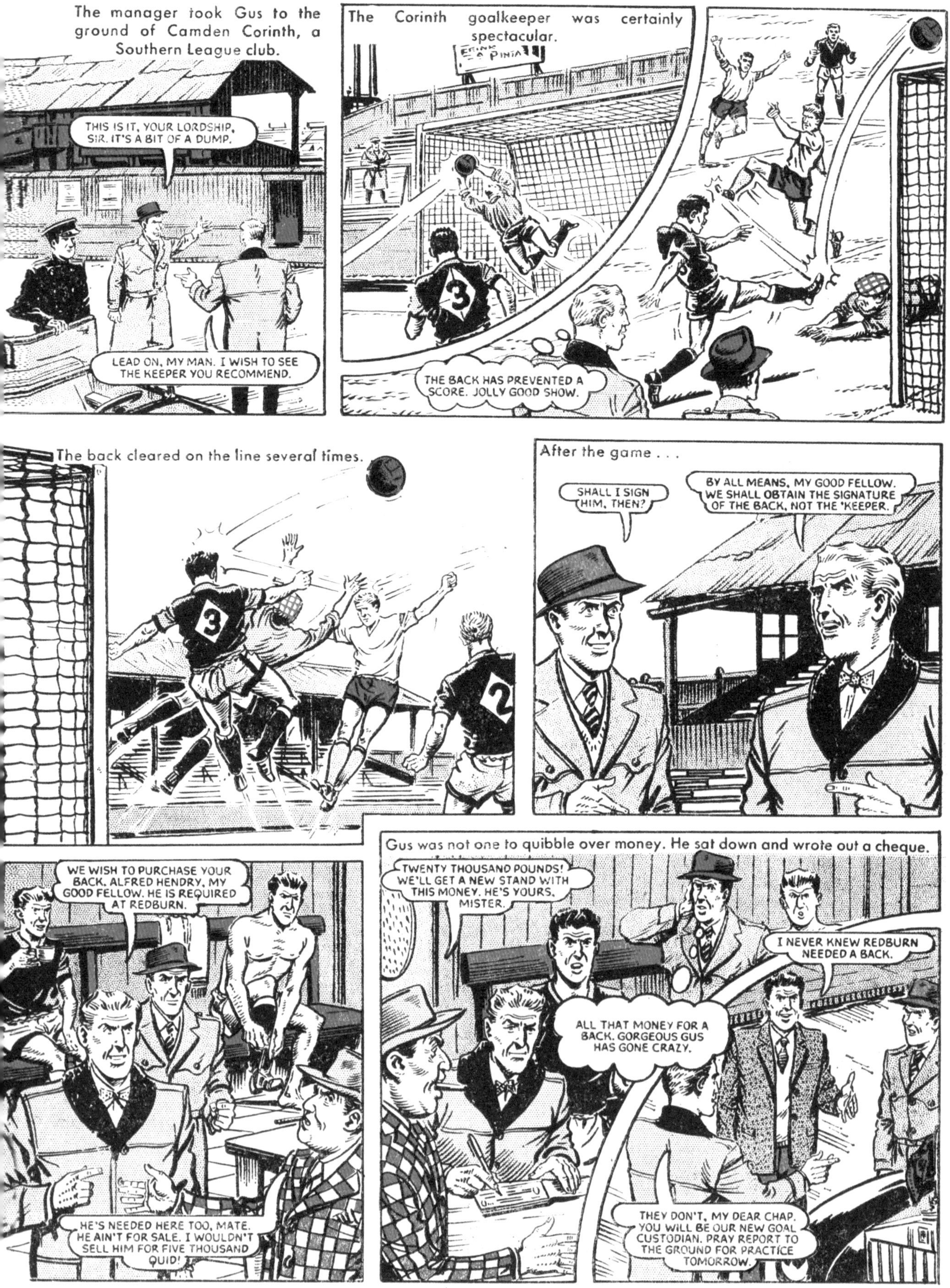
The manager took Gus to the ground of Camden Corinth, a Southern League club.
THIS IS IT, YOUR LORDSHIP, SIR. IT'S A BIT OF A DUMP.
LEAD ON, MY MAN. I WISH TO SEE THE KEEPER YOU RECOMMEND.
The Corinth goalkeeper was certainly spectacular.
THE BACK HAS PREVENTED A SCORE. JOLLY GOOD SHOW.
The back cleared on the line several times.
After the game . . .
SHALL I SIGN HIM, THEN?
BY ALL MEANS, MY GOOD FELLOW. WE SHALL OBTAIN THE SIGNATURE OF THE BACK, NOT THE 'KEEPER.
WE WISH TO PURCHASE YOUR BACK. ALFRED HENDRY, MY GOOD FELLOW. HE IS REQUIRED AT REDBURN.
HE'S NEEDED HERE TOO, MATE. HE AIN'T FOR SALE. I WOULDN'T SELL HIM FOR FIVE THOUSAND QUID!
Gus was not one to quibble over money. He sat down and wrote out a cheque.
TWENTY THOUSAND POUNDS! WE'LL GET A NEW STAND WITH THIS MONEY. HE'S YOURS, MISTER.
I NEVER KNEW REDBURN NEEDED A BACK.
ALL THAT MONEY FOR A BACK. GORGEOUS GUS HAS GONE CRAZY.
THEY DON'T, MY DEAR CHAP. YOU WILL BE OUR NEW GOAL CUSTODIAN. PRAY REPORT TO THE GROUND FOR PRACTICE TOMORROW.

"Gus must be crazy!"

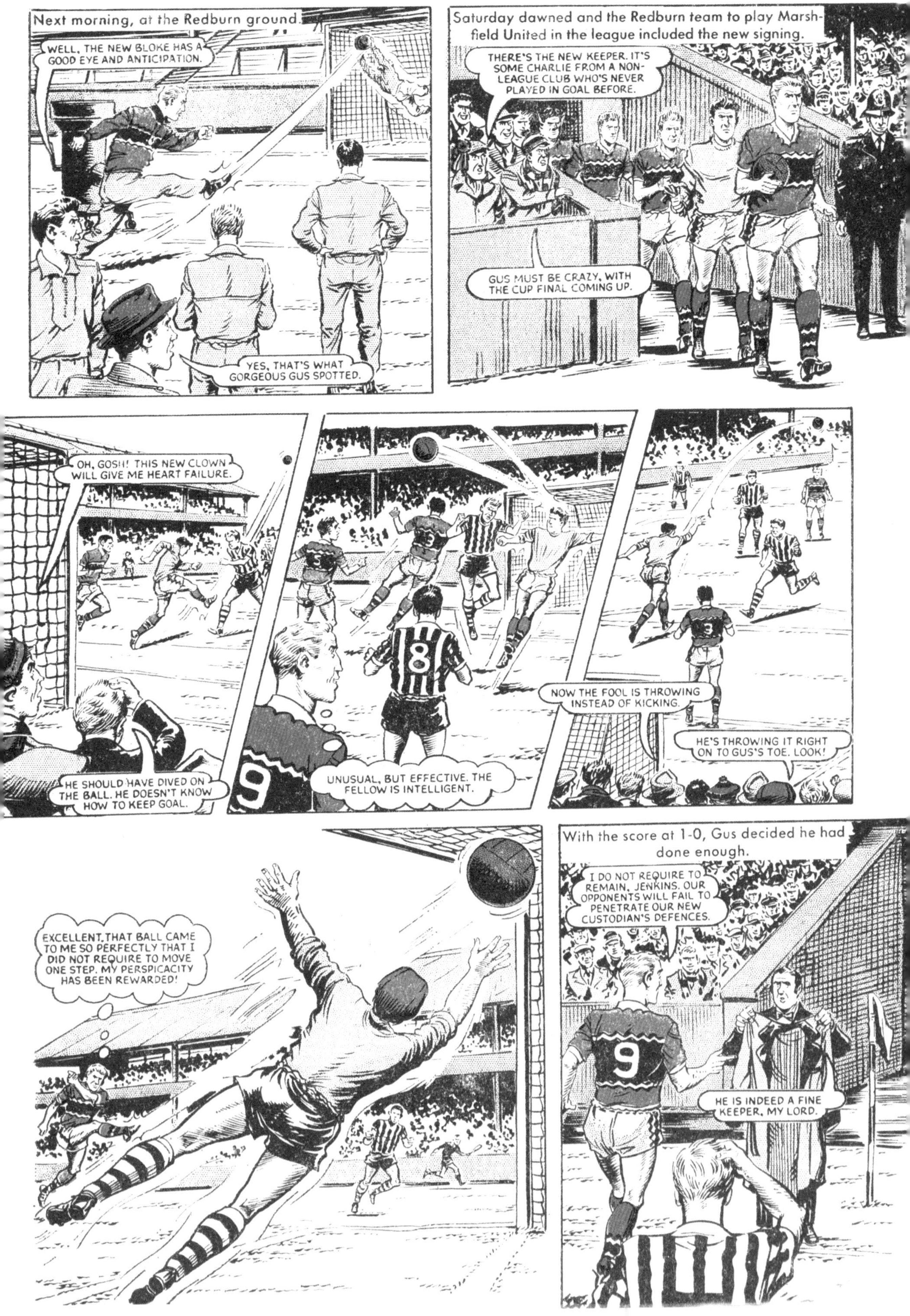
Next morning, at the Redburn ground.
WELL, THE NEW BLOKE HAS A GOOD EYE AND ANTICIPATION.
YES, THAT'S WHAT GORGEOUS GUS SPOTTED.
Saturday dawned and the Redburn team to play Marshfield United in the league included the new signing.
THERE'S THE NEW KEEPER. IT'S SOME CHARLIE FROM A NON-LEAGUE CLUB WHO'S NEVER PLAYED IN GOAL BEFORE.
GUS MUST BE CRAZY, WITH THE CUP FINAL COMING UP.
OH, GOSH! THIS NEW CLOWN WILL GIVE ME HEART FAILURE.
HE SHOULD HAVE DIVED ON THE BALL. HE DOESN'T KNOW HOW TO KEEP GOAL.
UNUSUAL, BUT EFFECTIVE. THE FELLOW IS INTELLIGENT.
NOW THE FOOL IS THROWING INSTEAD OF KICKING.
HE'S THROWING IT RIGHT ON TO GUS'S TOE. LOOK!
EXCELLENT. THAT BALL CAME TO ME SO PERFECTLY THAT I DID NOT REQUIRE TO MOVE ONE STEP. MY PERSPICACITY HAS BEEN REWARDED!
With the score at 1-0, Gus decided he had done enough.
I DO NOT REQUIRE TO REMAIN, JENKINS. OUR OPPONENTS WILL FAIL TO PENETRATE OUR NEW CUSTODIAN'S DEFENCES.
HE IS INDEED A FINE KEEPER, MY LORD.

Only ten men in the Cup-tie team!

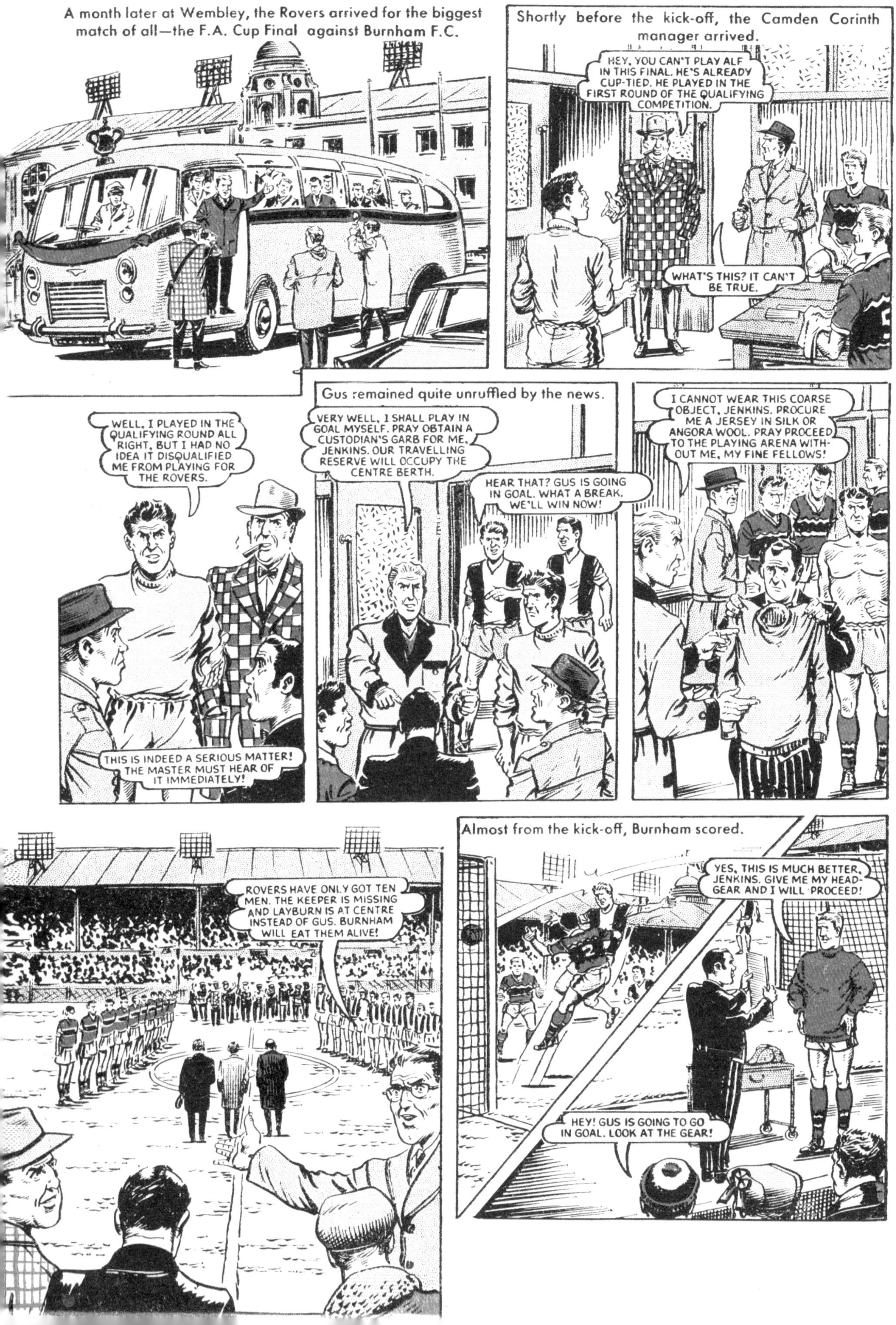
A month later at Wembley, the Rovers arrived for the biggest match of all—the F.A. Cup Final against Burnham F.C.
Shortly before the kick-off, the Camden Corinth manager arrived.
HEY, YOU CAN'T PLAY ALF IN THIS FINAL. HE'S ALREADY CUP-TIED. HE PLAYED IN THE FIRST ROUND OF THE QUALIFYING COMPETITION.
WHAT'S THIS? IT CAN'T BE TRUE.
WELL, I PLAYED IN THE QUALIFYING ROUND ALL RIGHT, BUT I HAD NO IDEA IT DISQUALIFIED ME FROM PLAYING FOR THE ROVERS.
THIS IS INDEED A SERIOUS MATTER! THE MASTER MUST HEAR OF IT IMMEDIATELY!
Gus remained quite unruffled by the news.
VERY WELL, I SHALL PLAY IN GOAL MYSELF. PRAY OBTAIN A CUSTODIAN'S GARB FOR ME, JENKINS. OUR TRAVELLING RESERVE WILL OCCUPY THE CENTRE BERTH.
HEAR THAT? GUS IS GOING IN GOAL. WHAT A BREAK. WE'LL WIN NOW!
I CANNOT WEAR THIS COARSE OBJECT, JENKINS. PROCURE ME A JERSEY IN SILK OR ANGORA WOOL. PRAY PROCEED TO THE PLAYING ARENA WITHOUT ME, MY FINE FELLOWS!
ROVERS HAVE ONLY GOT TEN MEN. THE KEEPER IS MISSING AND LAYBURN IS AT CENTRE INSTEAD OF GUS. BURNHAM WILL EAT THEM ALIVE!
Almost from the kick-off, Burnham scored.
YES, THIS IS MUCH BETTER, JENKINS. GIVE ME MY HEADGEAR AND I WILL PROCEED!
HEY! GUS IS GOING TO GO IN GOAL. LOOK AT THE GEAR!

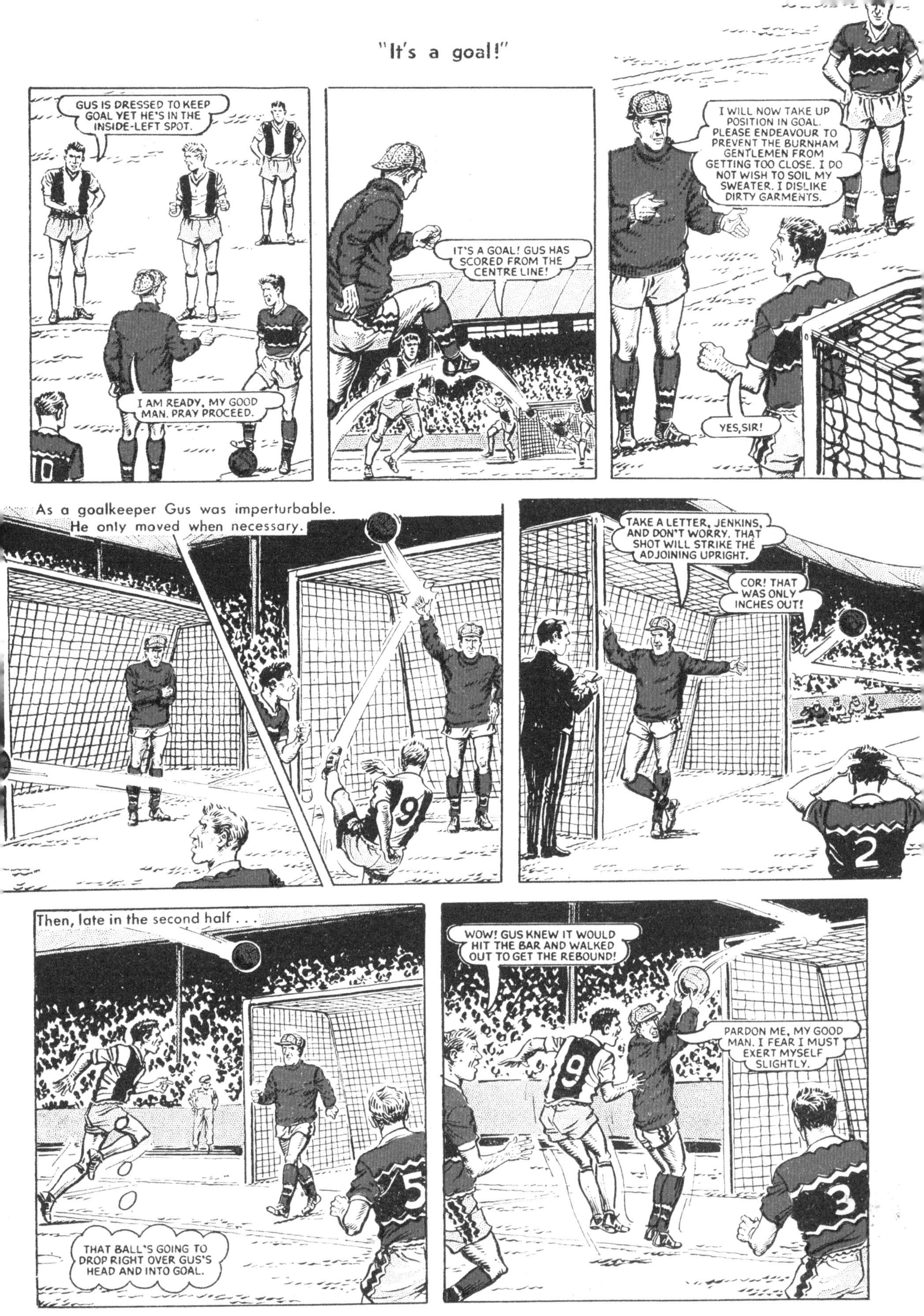
"It's a goal!"
GUS IS DRESSED TO KEEP GOAL YET HE'S IN THE INSIDE-LEFT SPOT.
I AM READY, MY GOOD MAN. PRAY PROCEED.
IT'S A GOAL! GUS HAS SCORED FROM THE CENTRE LINE!
I WILL NOW TAKE UP POSITION IN GOAL. PLEASE ENDEAVOUR TO PREVENT THE BURNHAM GENTLEMEN FROM GETTING TOO CLOSE. I DO NOT WISH TO SOIL MY SWEATER. I DISLIKE DIRTY GARMENTS.
YES, SIR!
As a goalkeeper Gus was imperturbable. He only moved when necessary.
TAKE A LETTER, JENKINS, AND DON'T WORRY. THAT SHOT WILL STRIKE THE ADJOINING UPRIGHT.
COR! THAT WAS ONLY INCHES OUT!
Then, late in the second half . . .
THAT BALL'S GOING TO DROP RIGHT OVER GUS'S HEAD AND INTO GOAL.
WOW! GUS KNEW IT WOULD HIT THE BAR AND WALKED OUT TO GET THE REBOUND!
PARDON ME, MY GOOD MAN. I FEAR I MUST EXERT MYSELF SLIGHTLY.

Goal-scoring goal-keeper!

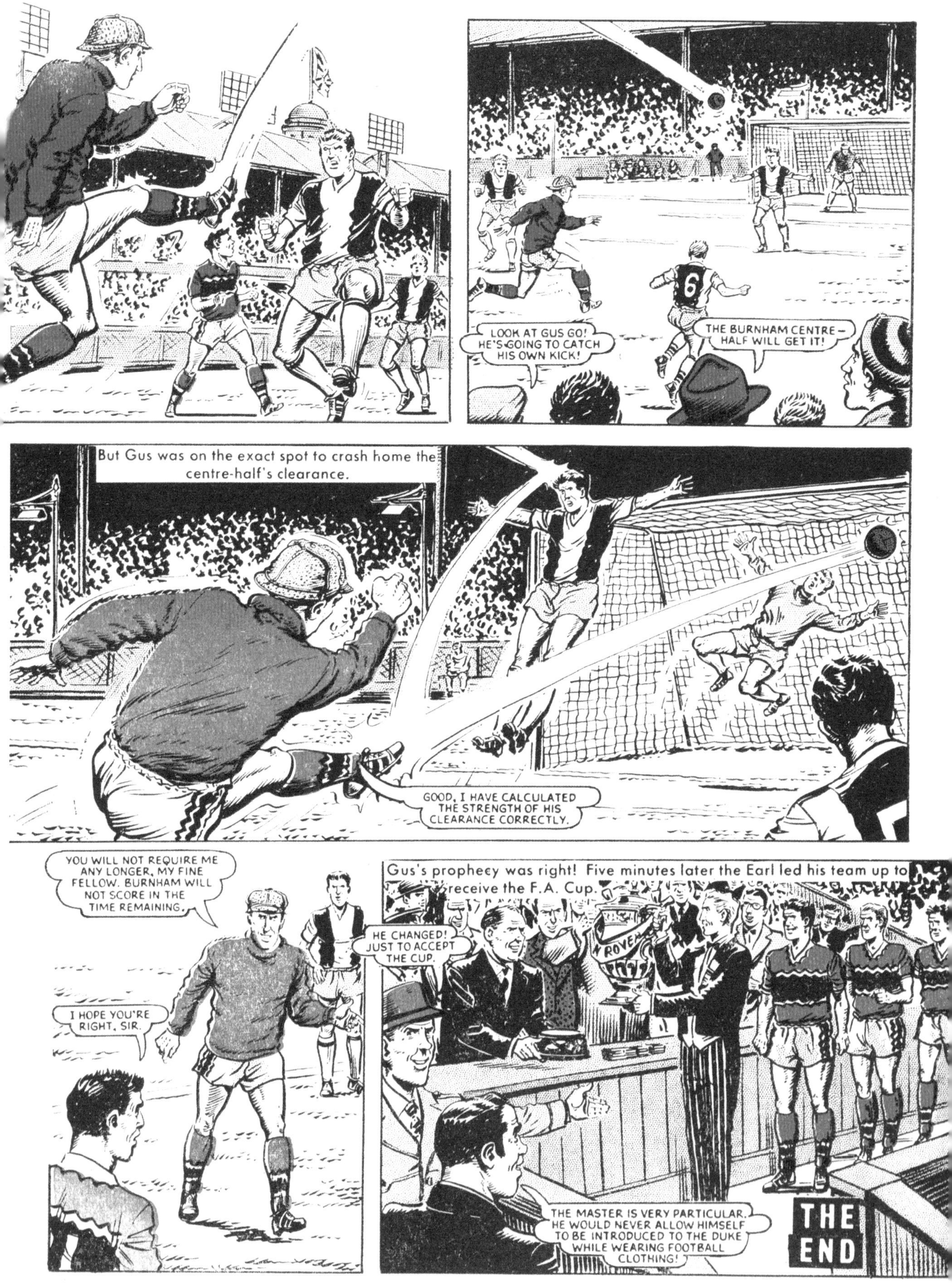

LOOK AT GUS GO! HE'S GOING TO CATCH HIS OWN KICK!
THE BURNHAM CENTRE-HALF WILL GET IT!
But Gus was on the exact spot to crash home the centre-half's clearance.
GOOD, I HAVE CALCULATED THE STRENGTH OF HIS CLEARANCE CORRECTLY.
YOU WILL NOT REQUIRE ME ANY LONGER, MY FINE FELLOW. BURNHAM WILL NOT SCORE IN THE TIME REMAINING.
I HOPE YOU'RE RIGHT, SIR.
Gus's prophecy was right! Five minutes later the Earl led his team up to receive the F.A. Cup.
HE CHANGED! JUST TO ACCEPT THE CUP.
THE MASTER IS VERY PARTICULAR. HE WOULD NEVER ALLOW HIMSELF TO BE INTRODUCED TO THE DUKE WHILE WEARING FOOTBALL CLOTHING!
THE END

THE BATTALION

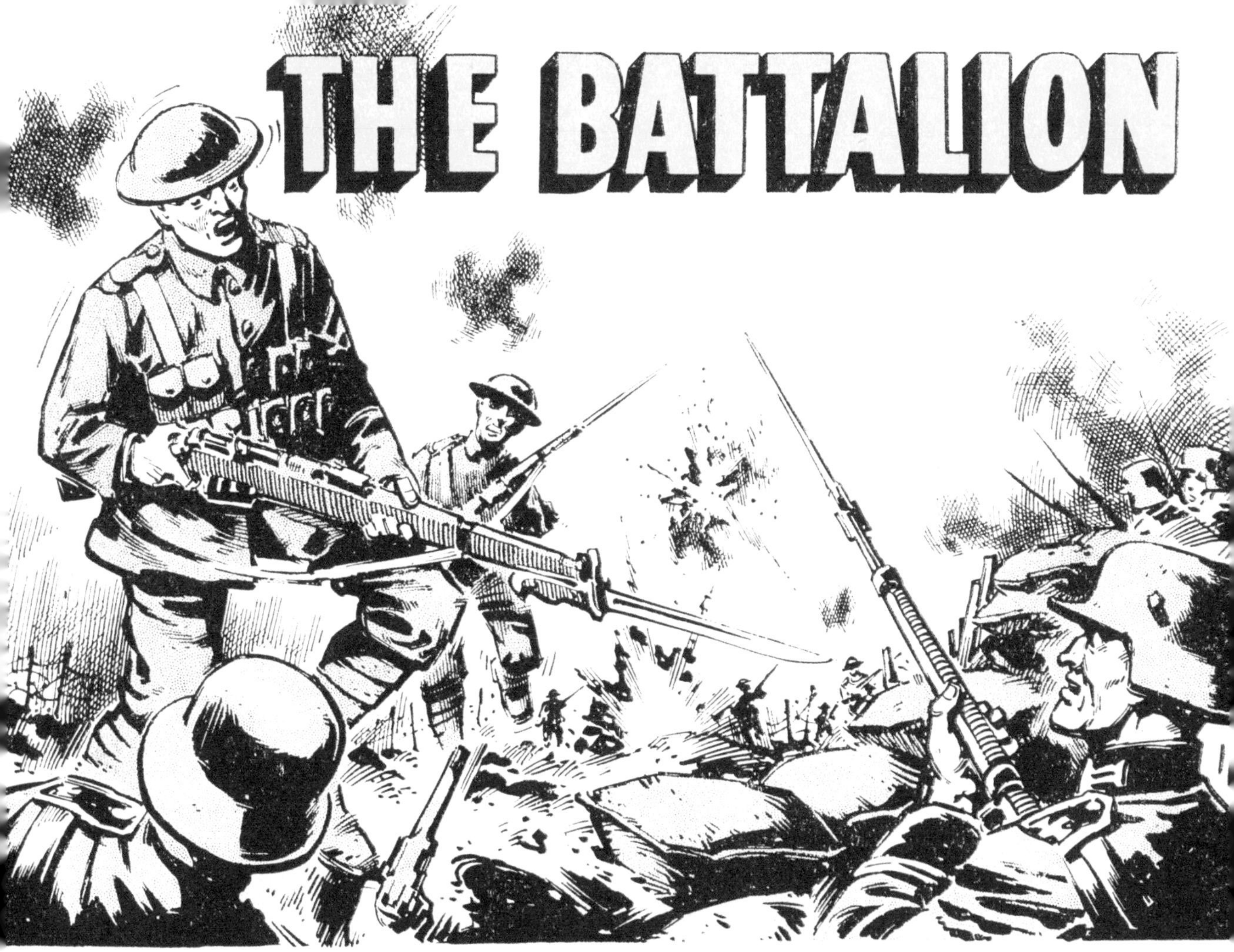

THE battalion sang as it swung along the muddy Belgian road. The song was a popular one—one that would be echoed by marching British troops in two world wars.

"Pack up your troubles in your old kitbag,
And smile, smile, smile . . ."

In the distance, the muffled rumble of the guns added their grim accompaniment. The rain dripped from the tall poplars lining the road, running down the steel helmets of the troops and trickling into gaps between waterproof cape and tunic.

It was the autumn of 1917, and the First World War had been dragging on for three bloodstained years. The regular British Army, the "Old Contemptibles," had long since been ground out of existence in the early battles at Mons and the Ypres Salient.

The Kitchener volunteers, the flower of British manhood, were gone, too, sacrificed by indifferent generalship on the Somme in 1916.

And now, with the Russians capitulating, the French cracking and the Americans barely into the war, it was the turn of the British conscripts. The darkest days of the war were upon them.

Jim Barford, a stocky young private, turned to his pal, Reg Waterforth, who was marching at his side. The song had ended and each man was busy with his own thoughts.

"Won't be long now," grinned Jim.

The conscripts went into the line as rookies—but they came out veterans!

"Aye," said Reg. "We'll be at the front by nightfall."

The front in question was a winding system of muddy trenches and dank dug-outs, hacked out of the French and Belgian clay and stretching, in an unbroken line, from the borders of Switzerland to the Belgian coast.

It was a war in which the machine-gun, the trench mortar, the barbed wire, and the high-explosive shell reigned supreme. It was a war in which men were pawns to be uselessly expended in the mud. And these young, hastily-trained conscripts of the Third Kingsford Light Infantry were about to be caught up in it.

Fred Plant, a thin-faced, undersized soldier in a uniform that looked several sizes too large, spoke up.

"Wonder what it's like in the line," he said anxiously. "Hope I don't get the wind up when I see my first Jerry"

Spud Rogers, a large, beefy-faced youth, chipped in.

"I shouldn't worry," he sneered. "It'll take the Jerries all their time to see you!"

"Leave him alone," rapped Jim, who had fallen foul of the bully several times during training. "We'll see how you behave when the Huns get their sights on you!"

Rogers scowled. "They'll get plenty of chance," he snarled. "I ain't scared of any sausage-eating Jerries!"

The booming tones of Sergeant Major Matlock ended the con-

28

versation. He was a burly, red-faced n.c.o. with a huge, waxed moustache that had earned him the nickname of "Kitchener" in the ranks.

"Keep your mouths shut, you lot, and save your breath for when we get into the line!" he bellowed. "As for you, Rogers, I don't suppose the Huns are scared of you, either!"

The others grinned. The sergeant major had fought at Mons and on the Somme, and was returning to the front after a spell with a training battalion. He was a just man, whose bark was

sprawled stiffly by the roadside, still harnessed to the wreckage of an ammunition limber.

A column of men came marching by—muddy, hollow-eyed and gaunt of cheek. There were walking wounded amongst them, some assisted by more fortunate comrades, and others limping along with the aid of roughly-hewn sticks.

They were dead tired, moving like men in their sleep, but they were veterans every one, from the cloth-bound muzzles of their rifles to the purposeful set of the mud-caked steel helmets on their

artillery drew nearer, and the ominous tac-tac-tac of machine-guns could be heard.

Piccadilly

THE communication trench was narrow and badly shored-up. Mud fell from the crumbling sides and caked on the greatcoats of the long file of men. The trench had left the poplar-lined road as a sunken path, but had deepened until the parapet was more than head high.

As the new battalion marched towards the front, they passed the survivors of another battalion —and realised for the first time just how tough it was going to be!

considerably worse than his bite.

Battered Battalion

THE scenery had changed. There were heavy artillery emplacements in the fields at the side of the road. Huge 9.2-inch howitzers poked menacing blunt snouts from camouflaged, sand-bagged pits. A heavy shell rumbled overhead with a noise like an express train, as distant German gunners searched out vital British targets in back areas.

Shattered cottages could be seen through the trees, and shell-holes formed muddy ponds in abandoned fields. A team of dead horses

heads. They were men who had tasted the bitterness of war.

"What mob are you, mate?" Spud Rogers hailed a tall, thin soldier as the two columns passed.

The man grinned mirthlessly. "Second Battalion of the Westfordshire Regiment!" he shouted. "What's left of us, that is! We ain't got an officer to our name, and only two hundred of us came out of the line!"

"That's right," shouted another private with a grimy bandage round his head. "And over eight hundred of us went in!"

The survivors seemed to have a macabre pride in their appalling losses.

As the two columns marched in their opposite ways, a gloomy silence fell upon the battalion moving up. The rumble of the

Star-shells and parachute flares penetrated the darkness with an intermittent brilliance. They soared up into the sky and drifted slowly to earth, casting harsh black and white shadows over the shell-spattered landscape.

From the direction of the German lines came the harsh chatter of a machine-gun. A rifle cracked and a bullet sang overhead. Jim Barford ducked instinctively. He felt as though the Germans were watching his every move.

Immediately in front of him, he saw Reg Waterforth flinch, too. Suddenly he felt better. By the light of a flare he was able to read the words on a crudely-painted board fastened to the side of the trench. It said: "Regent Street."

"You're in for a tough time!"

Jim grunted as he stumbled over a loose duckboard. Farther down the line a rifle glanced off the wooden trench wall with a clatter. He heard Sergeant Major Matlock mutter a bloodthirsty warning to the offender.

All at once they emerged into a wider, better-maintained trench, which ran at right-angles to the communication trench. The junction was signposted as " Piccadilly Circus." A board pointing to the left said " Piccadilly," and another pointing in the opposite direction indicated that the right-hand turn was " Coventry Street."

Jim caught his breath. They were in the front line. A few hundred yards away, the Germans would be watching and waiting in a line of similar entrenchments.

They turned left into " Piccadilly." The trench was about eight feet in depth from the duckboards lining the bottom to the top row of sandbags protecting the parapet. At intervals, sentries stood on the raised fire-step gazing out across no-man's land.

The trench had many twists and turns, each traverse designed to prevent the enemy permeating the line should any section of the trench be taken. They passed a small sap which ran out from the front line towards the German positions. There would be a listening post at the end of the sap, its occupants waiting tensely for signs of enemy activity.

They squeezed past the last of the troops they were relieving. As another flare burst over the battlefield, Jim could see the strained expressions on their grimy faces. One of the men muttered to Jim as he brushed by :

" Looks like you're in for a tough time, mate ! The Jerries are planning an attack !"

A series of short, sharp explosions burst just in front of the parapet. The line of men froze and Jim heard little Fred Plant give a strangled gasp as a shower of mud spattered into the trench.

Jim and Reg exchanged apprehensive glances. Was this the signal for a German bombardment of their section of the line ? There would be heavy casualties in the crowded trench as the relief took place.

Lieutenant Powers, the subaltern in charge of Jim's platoon, came

Jim and Reg gasped in dismay as they saw their quarters —there wasn't room to swing a cat !

hurrying by. He was followed by Sergeant Frost, the senior platoon n.c.o.

" Keep moving," growled the subaltern. " They're only rifle-grenades !"

" *Only* !" muttered Reg with an old-fashioned glance at Jim. Plant tittered nervously as the file trudged on. The air in the trench was thick with the acrid stench of explosives.

Farther down the line, Jim and Reg found themselves berthed in a six-man dug-out under the orders of weasel-faced Corporal Ferris. Ferris was one of the most unpopular n.c.o.'s in the battalion, and bore down particularly hard on the two pals.

The others in the damp, earthy-smelling shelter were Fred Plant, Spud Rogers and a rather quiet soldier called Simpson.

Simpson was a good deal older than the other privates in the platoon and a bit of a mystery man. He had seen service in Gallipoli and Mesopotamia, but never had much to say about his experiences. He hated Corporal Ferris like poison.

Six bunks had been squeezed along the walls of the dug-out, which had a corrugated iron roof covered with sandbags and several feet of clay. Illumination was provided by a solitary candle, flickering from a bottle standing upon an empty biscuit box.

Fred Plant's pale eyes darted round the shelter. " Crikey," he gasped. " It ain't exactly the Ritz ! Good job I don't suffer from claustrophobia !"

" I'm having one of the bottom bunks," announced Spud Rogers.

" You'll sleep where you're told," snarled Ferris. " I'm in charge here !"

He turned to Jim and Reg, who were unstrapping their heavy packs.

" Needn't think you're turning in !" he barked. " The pair of you can take the first watch in the listening post ! Lieutenant Powers will issue you with a Verey pistol !"

" And don't fall asleep out there," jeered Rogers. " We don't want murdered in our beds !"

Trench Battle

THE two soldiers crouched in the narrow sap and gazed across the shell-pocked landscape. Their nerves were jumpy and their feet were balls of sodden clay. A drifting flare threw shadows that seemed to leap on them from out of the gloom.

Jim's hand gripped the stocky butt of the Verey pistol which was loaded with the red signal cartridge that would announce an enemy attack or raid.

Sentries under attack!

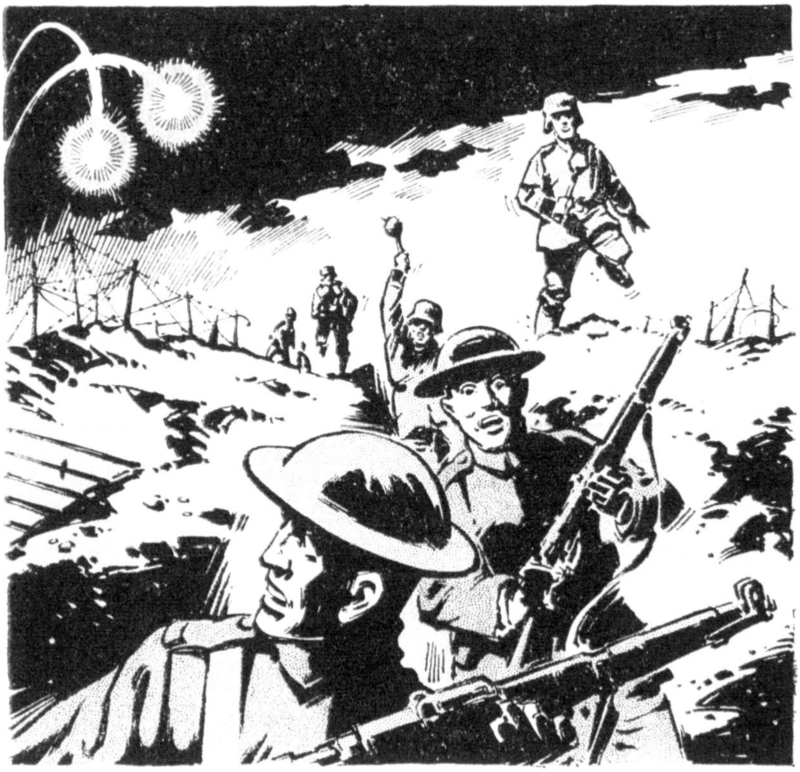

The flare Jim had fired had warned the British lines about the Germans — but it had also shown the Germans where the two sentries were!

Their rifles were nearby, propped against the sides of the sap, with the muzzles well away from the mud. They were armed with trench clubs, too, short stubby weapons that could disable a man quietly in a hand-to-hand combat.

"Look!" Reg grabbed Jim's arm and pointed towards an abandoned tank that had been rusting in the mud since a previous offensive. "There's something moving out there!"

Jim's finger tightened on the trigger of the pistol as he peered in the direction of the tank. At that moment, the flare that had been lighting the scene fell to the ground and extinguished itself in a muddy crater.

Suddenly there was a muffled chink of equipment and a guttural exclamation from a shadowy form stumbling over tangled strands of barbed wire. Other forms flitted from behind the derelict tank.

"It's a Jerry patrol!" hissed Jim, crouching low in the sap to screen the flash from the muzzle as he squeezed the trigger of the signal pistol. A ball of red fire soared high into the sky. Almost at once, whistles began to shrill from the direction of the British lines.

"Quick," grunted Reg, making a dive for his rifle. "Let's get out of here!"

They squelched hurriedly up the sap, hoping to reach the first traverse before the enemy patrol spotted them. Flares were shooting up, and rifles began to crack.

In a last desperate attempt to secure prisoners, the German soldiers leapt into the sap and plunged through the mud after the two Englishmen.

At the traverse, Jim and Reg turned and faced the oncoming Huns. Steadying hands that were trembling with shock and exertion, Jim snapped off a shot at one of the Germans.

The man uttered a cry of pain and slumped to the ground. At the same time, Reg triggered off several rounds and stopped another German in his tracks.

Baffled, the enemy soldiers paused. The bright light of the flares outlined their coal-scuttle helmets. They were about to retreat when a magnesium flare drifted into the sap near the two Britishers, dazzling them with its harsh light.

A voice yelled a harsh order, and four burly German privates plunged forward to seize the two pals. They were armed with daggers and clubs, and their pockets bulged with bombs.

Plunging over the spluttering flare, they grappled with the blinded Tommies, who fought back desperately with their rifle butts.

Jim felt one huge German go down as he jabbed wildly with his Lee Enfield. Reg had his rifle knocked from his grasp, but defended himself stoutly with his trench club.

Weight of numbers began to tell. Reg reeled as a large fist exploded on his chin. A heavy, clubbing blow numbed Jim's shoulder. And then a cheer came from the sap behind them as Sergeant Major Matlock led a party of the Third Kingsford into action.

In a few moments the fight was over, and the surviving Germans were scrambling from the sap under cover of their smoke bombs. Six of their dead were left behind them.

The Kingsfords' First Casualties

AND so began the battalion's six desperate days in the Flanders mud. The casualties were to come later . . .

At dawn, the battalion stood-to, manning the fire-steps and machine-gun emplacements as a precaution against a surprise attack. Only the cooks were exempted, and from the fires and stoves in "Piccadilly" and "Regent Street" drifted the fragrant smell of frying bacon.

Corporal Ferris was in a foul mood. He had missed the excitement of the previous night, and resented the fact that Jim and Reg had been the first of the platoon to see action.

"If you think you're perishing heroes, forget it," he snarled, as they sat on their bunks eating their breakfasts. "If it hadn't have been for the sergeant major and his rescue party, you'd have been eating German sausage for breakfast!"

"There's a big attack coming!"

Reg, who was tucking into a thick slice of fried bread, flushed angrily. He had a hot temper, and the corporal's unfair remarks stung him.

But a sharp kick from Simpson, who was seated at his side, silenced him. It was the veteran who answered Ferris.

"Pity that mortar shell, bursting about fifty yards away made you dive head first into the dug-out, Corp," he grinned. "You missed all the fun!"

Fred Plant gave a high-pitched laugh. He had been terrified himself, but had been one of the first to reach the parapet after the alarm had been raised.

Ferris rounded on the little private angrily.

"Shut your face, Plant," he hooted. "You won't be so cheerful when you know what's in store for us! Those Jerries last night were from the Prussian Guard!"

Even Simpson stopped smiling. The Prussian Guards were crack storm troops and ferocious fighters. Their presence in this sector of the front was ominous.

"Sausage-eaters are the same whatever you call 'em!" blustered Spud Rogers. "You won't find me running from 'em!"

For once his remarks went unanswered. Jim Barford was remembering the gaunt veteran who had passed him in the trench.

"Looks like you're in for a tough time," he had said.

How tough, this battalion of raw conscripts was soon to find out . . .

The first losses were both heavy and unexpected. Shortly after noon, the German guns roared and flamed and poured a concentrated barrage on the section of the line held by "A" Company in "Coventry Street."

The British artillery bellowed back in reply, the lyddite-filled shells raising billowing columns of yellow smoke on the German parapets.

But when the guns had ceased, three officers and twenty men were lying dead in the churned-up mud of the British trenches. Among them was the company commander, Captain Forrester, who had been one of the few experienced officers in the battalion.

At the dusk stand-to, the Germans opened fire again and caught the men on the fire-steps with vicious "whizz-bangs"—high-velocity shrapnel shells which burst on their targets almost simultaneously with the sound of their approach.

As the enemy fire swept along the line, Jim had a narrow escape when the blast from a "whizz-bang" flung him from the fire-step and into the bottom of the trench. The same shell killed Sergeant Frost, who had been inspecting the forward positions. Altogether, they lost six men from their platoon, which formed one of the sections of "C" Company.

Shortly after midnight, wiring parties were sent out to strengthen the defences in front of the British line. Once again, Jim and Reg found themselves in the grim desolation of no-man's land.

This time they were part of a detail under Corporal Ferris, laden with rolls of barbed wire, sledge-hammers, wire-cutters, pliers and the hedgehog-like supports which carried the wire.

Straight away, it was obvious that Ferris had the jitters. As a result, much of the responsibility fell on the shoulders of the veteran, Simpson, who gave his orders in a quiet voice.

They froze, as a trench-flare went up near the "Coventry Street" sector of the front.

"Get a move on," snarled Ferris. "The sooner we're out of here the better!"

"Put a sock in it," growled Simpson, with no respect for the n.c.o.'s rank. "The job has to be done properly before the Germans attack! We might not get another chance!"

There was no answer from the corporal and the men worked on with a will, snagging their mud-stained uniforms and tearing their hands on the wicked barbs. At Simpson's direction, a deliberately-weak section was left in the wire. A machine-gun would be trained on this gap in case the Germans came bunching through.

The task was completed shortly before dawn. By now, Ferris was almost a nervous wreck as he led them back into the trenches. Jim gave Reg a nudge as they trudged through the mud.

"Don't reckon much for our chances under him when the attack comes," he muttered.

"Nor I," answered Reg glumly, floundering across the edge of a shallow crater.

Behind them, they could hear the rumble of iron-shod wheels on the paved roads in the rear of the German lines. The puff-puffing of shunting locomotives was carried on the night air.

"There's a big attack coming, all right," said Simpson. "The Jerries are bringing up stuff by the minute!"

"Let 'em come," grunted Spud Rogers. "I'll be ready for 'em!"

"Quiet there," squeaked Ferris. "You'll have the Huns down on us!"

Wire-laying in no man's land was a nerve-wracking job—any noise above a whisper could mean death for the entire party!

The British troops cheered as the German plane plunged earthwards — one more threat to their safety had been removed!

Simpson regarded the n.c.o.'s back contemplatively. "He's windy," he stated. "And so am I! And I reckon the old Prussian Guards are feeling windy right now! Wouldn't fancy their job trying to get through this little lot"! Suddenly Jim and Reg felt a lot better.

Artillery Barrage

THE next day and the next night saw little activity along the line. The battalion improved its entrenchments and listened to the rumble of the traffic coming from the rear of the German positions. During the afternoon a cheer came from the men, when a black-crossed plane was shot down over the German lines during a dog-fight with a British fighter.

Another quiet day followed, with a hectic skirmish on the "Coventry Street" front during the night when a patrol from "A" Company slipped into the German trenches and spirited away a dumbfounded Prussian.

The prisoner was whisked away to battalion headquarters. He seemed glad to be out of the war, and told them more than his name, rank, and number.

He told them that at dawn, ten divisions including three crack guards units would be flung against the five, under-strength British divisions holding the area. The attack would follow a short but devastating artillery bombardment, which would blow holes in the British wire and shatter the front line.

There was little sleep in the dug-out that night. Jim and Reg were writing letters, while Simpson checked his equipment methodically. Fred Plant lay on his bunk and stared up at the corrugated iron roof. Even Spud Rogers was quiet.

Ferris glanced at his watch nervously. His thin features were pale and drawn in the flickering light of the candle. A muscle in his right cheek twitched.

"It's almost half-past," he announced edgily. "Perhaps the attack's been postponed!"

"Some hope," grunted Simpson. And almost at once the barrage started with an ear-splitting roar. Shell after shell screamed through the air and pounded the British line. Weeks of patient registering had gone into the artillery preparation, and the German gunners did their work well.

The dug-out rocked. Jim and Reg gritted their teeth and clung to their Lee Enfields grimly. Their letters were forgotten. Ferris gripped the edge of his bunk, and Fred Plant uttered a harsh gasp.

One of the occupants whimpered as a "whizz-bang" burst in the trench outside and poured a cloud of acrid fumes into the dug-out. Spud Rogers' nerve was going. He sobbed with fear, his beefy face distorted.

And then the heavens themselves seemed to fall in as a tremendous curtain of steel descended on the British positions. The shelling rose to a crescendo as the moment of attack drew near.

A terrific blast brought pieces of earth and shrapnel spattering on to the floor near the entrance to the dug-out. The candle went out and the glare of flames was reflected from outside.

Rogers moaned. "Let me out of here!" he screamed, as he staggered to his feet and dashed for the entrance. Simpson stuck out a putteed leg and tripped him. Jim and Reg piled in and tried to hold him down.

But fear had given Rogers more than double his strength. In the end, Ferris had to join in and quieten him with a light tap of his trench club.

"Always knew Spud would crack," said Fred Plant with a thin smile. "He was as windy as the rest of us!"

Jim stared at Ferris. The n.c.o.'s face was stern and set. His nerves seemed to have vanished. Fred Plant was standing up well, too. It was as if the sight of Spud Rogers cracking had pulled them together.

Field Promotion

THE barrage began to lift as the German gunners lengthened their range and saturated the British artillery which was roaring back defiantly. Shells began to fall on the support trenches in the rear, causing heavy casualties among the pitifully few British reserves.

Outside the dug-out, whistles shrilled. The raucous, barrack-square tones of Sergeant Major Matlock blended with the roar of the barrage.

"Come on," grunted Ferris, grabbing his Lee Enfield. "Let's get up there and welcome the Jerries! Rogers can stay where he is!"

Jim and Reg followed the corporal up on to the remains of the fire-step. To the left, Lieutenant Powers was shouting instructions to a Lewis gun team as field-grey figures appeared out of the early morning mist, the light glinting palely on their polished bayonets.

Lee-Enfields began to crack as the Germans plunged forward relentlessly. Rifle grenades and mortar shells blew gaps in the oncoming ranks. As the Germans bunched at the gap in the wire, the Lewis gun stuttered into action and scythed them into the mud.

Jim worked his rifle until the

barrel and breech almost burnt to the touch. Already the first wave of attackers had melted away, but almost at once a second wave was rising out of the ground and surging forward.

On the left of Jim a soldier grunted with pain and slid off the fire-step. It was Corporal Ferris. The n.c.o. staggered to his feet again and triggered off several shots at the approaching Germans. Another bullet hit him and he slumped back into the bottom of the trench.

Simpson took over the section in matter-of-fact fashion. Grabbing a small sack of Mills bombs from a recess in the side of the trench, he began heaving them at the oncoming Prussians.

Dropping his smoking rifle, Jim followed the veteran's example. The range was short. He pulled out the pin and counted to three. A quick throw, and the grenade exploded in mid-air amongst a group of Prussians.

A burly German rose up out of a shallow crater and hurled a stick grenade in retaliation. Fred Plant shot him down almost as he threw. Reg Waterforth dived for the enemy bomb and heaved it back. Several more Germans fell back into the mud.

And then the enemy were upon them. A squad of enormous Prussian Guards loomed over the parapet, teeth bared and bayonets jabbing.

Jim missed his footing on the slippery fire-step and fell into the trench. He rolled to one side as a Prussian tried to pin him to the duckboards. The German grunted and folded up as Fred Plant shot him.

"They're breaking, lads," yelled Simpson encouragingly. The words choked in his throat as he went down from a thrust in the chest. With his last breath, the veteran grabbed the enemy rifle and heaved backwards. Reg finished the enemy soldier off with a clubbing blow to the temple.

All at once, the Germans were either dead or retreating. But the British losses had been heavy all along the line. "C" Company had had a particularly tough time. Jim's section was now without an n.c.o.

Jim glanced at his watch. It was barely eight o'clock. They seemed to have been fighting for hours. The trench was a shambles.

"Come on," he said to the others. "Let's get the place cleaned up a bit before the Jerries come back again!"

They were working with a will when Lieutenant Powers came up. With the subaltern was the tall figure of Captain Lee, the company commander.

The officers came over to Jim. They returned his salute.

"Where's Corporal Ferris?" rapped Lieutenant Powers.

"He's dead, sir," said Jim.

"Private Simpson?"

"Dead, sir!"

Reg Waterforth made a desperate attempt to save his mates' lives — by throwing himself at a German grenade!

Captain Lee gave Jim a penetrating glance. He liked the look of the young soldier's determined chin and the unflinching grey eyes staring back at him from the smoke-blackened face.

"Take over the section, corporal," he said. "Chalk on the stripes if you have to, but put them up! We're going to need n.c.o.'s today!"

Attack and Counter-Attack

AT nine o'clock the Germans came again. They followed hard on the heels of a short but vicious mortar bombardment. This time they were supported by the dreaded "Flammenwerfen" — flamethrowers which sent their searing fingers of flame roaring along the sparsely-manned British parapets.

The Kingsfords held firm. The ground in front of their parapets was covered with the enemy dead. But the battalion on their left was overrun, and the Germans were into the British front line.

Soon, the Prussians were bombing their way along the trench, clearing out isolated pockets of resistance. Then, at "Piccadilly," they came up against determined opposition from the survivors of "C" Company.

In the fighting with bomb and bayonet, Lieutenant Powers was killed and Reg Waterforth wounded in the arm. Jim's section was in the thick of the battle. Even Spud Rogers had pulled himself together and was fighting with all the desperation of a cornered animal.

German dead littered the trench as the company retreated foot by foot, past "Piccadilly Circus" and into "Coventry Street" where "A" and "B" Companies were holding firm.

And then the Germans launched another powerful frontal attack and the battalion found itself assailed on two sides. For a while it looked as though the Kingsfords were to be annihilated, until the order came for a withdrawal into the support line.

As they mustered in the support trench, the full extent of the battalion's casualties were seen for the first time. Colonel Evans, the C.O., was dead. So, too, was Major Stafford, the second-in-command. Only Captain Lee of the company commanders remained, and he found himself at the head of the shattered battalion.

Of the senior n.c.o.s, only two platoon sergeants and the indestructible Sergeant Major Matlock remained. Jim received his second promotion on the field and chalked up his third stripe. Reg Waterforth, whose wound was only a slight one, became a corporal.

At noon, the British were ordered to counter-attack and retake the lost trenches. A short bombardment from their depleted artillery, and they went over the top against their own machine guns, which the Germans were turning upon them.

Captain Lee and Sergeant Major Matlock led the remnants of the Kingsfords in that last desperate charge. Almost at once, the captain was hit and flung into the mud. He raised himself up on his elbow and urged the battalion on. Then he fell forward on to his face.

Jim caught up to the sergeant major. The older man was breathing hard as he pounded through the clinging mud. His magnificent moustaches bristled and his eyes shone with the pure joy of battle.

There was no stopping the Kingsfords now. Their blood was up, and suddenly they were leaping into the trench, amongst upturned faces in coal-scuttle helmets. The air was filled with the shouts, curses and screams of men in mortal combat.

Jim bayonetted a bull-necked Prussian. Reg clubbed down on another. Spud Rogers, finding at last that fear was an adequate substitute for courage, flailed around him desperately.

Fred Plant went down with a bullet through the thigh. The sergeant major was taking on the crew of the captured machine-gun single-handed. Other British troops were jumping into the trench.

" Come on !" Jim led his section down the trench, past the dugout where they had cowered long hours ago. The entrance had fallen in. A shot came from behind a sand-bagged traverse. Jim drew the pin from a hand grenade and lobbed it over the top.

The British swept along " Piccadilly." Bombs were rolled down dug-outs. Germans were throwing up their hands. The sergeant major was bellowing in triumph—an' awe-inspiring sound.

And then the battalion was digging in again and strengthening shattered emplacements. The wounded were tended, the dead removed, and the machine-guns turned round again. Soon, there would be another German attack —and another.

The line must be held at all costs until reserves could be despatched from other, less hard-pressed sectors of the front.

Smile, Smile, Smile!

THREE days later, a battalion of fresh-faced young conscripts marched along a muddy Belgian road on their way up to the front line. They sang as they marched.

" Pack up your troubles in your old kitbag,
And smile, smile, smile——"

Suddenly the singing stopped as a column of soldiers approached. There were no commissioned officers at the head of this column— only a huge sergeant major with a bristling Kitchener-style moustache. The column moved slowly to keep pace with the many walking wounded amongst them.

The faces of the men in the slowly-moving column were haggard and drawn, and the red-rimmed eyes were those of men who had seen their comrades die. And yet, there was an air of grim jauntiness about this column of mud-stained soldiers marching from the front.

The conscripts stared. One, greatly daring, shouted out to a young sergeant who was helping a corporal with a bandaged arm to support a thin, under-sized soldier with a severe leg wound.

" What mob are you, mate ?" shouted the conscript.

The young sergeant didn't answer. The reply came from a burly, red-faced soldier who marched with a trace of a swagger.

" First battalion of the Third Kingsford Light Infantry !" he called back proudly. " And we stopped the sausage-eaters back there !"

One of the conscripts had been counting the column as it trudged by. He turned to a comrade in the ranks.

" Blimey," he gasped. " There's only a hundred and fifty of the poor perishers !"

And then the new battalion swung up the poplar-lined Menin Road towards the line, while the veterans of the Third Kingsford marched slowly but proudly away from the rumble of the guns.

THE END

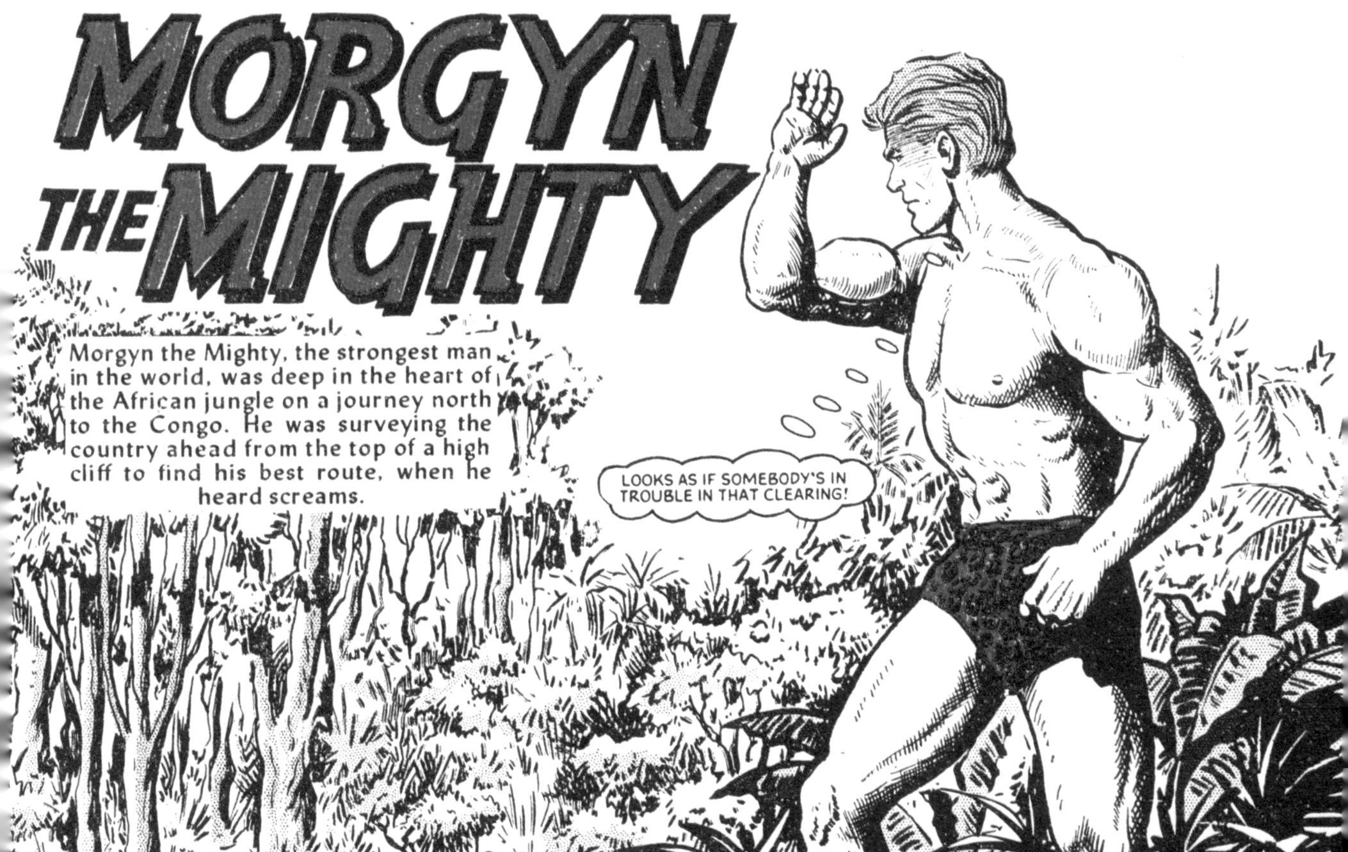
MORGYN THE MIGHTY
Morgyn the Mighty, the strongest man in the world, was deep in the heart of the African jungle on a journey north to the Congo. He was surveying the country ahead from the top of a high cliff to find his best route, when he heard screams.
LOOKS AS IF SOMEBODY'S IN TROUBLE IN THAT CLEARING!

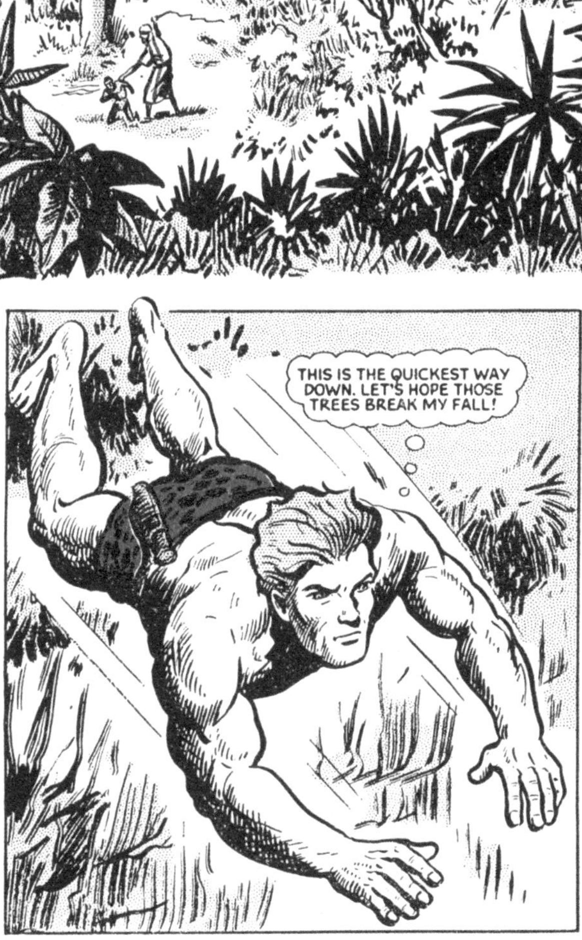
THIS IS THE QUICKEST WAY DOWN. LET'S HOPE THOSE TREES BREAK MY FALL!

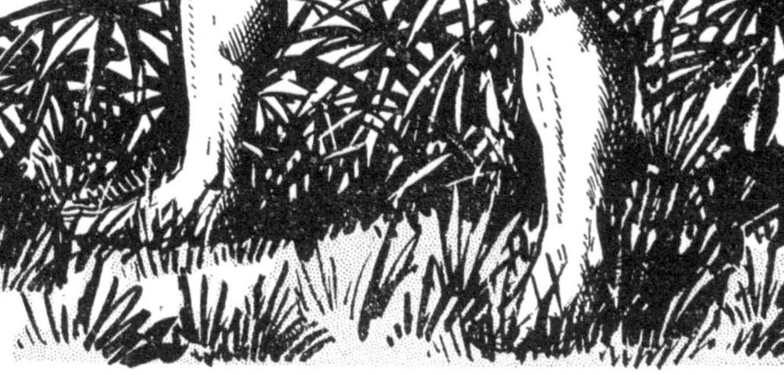
PHEW! MADE IT! NOW TO PUT A STOP TO THIS!

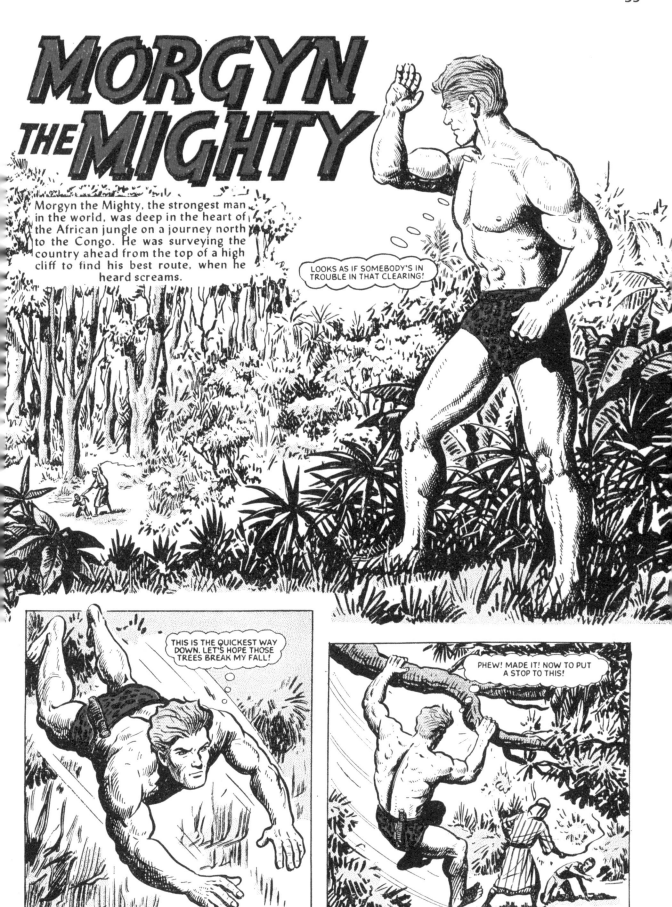

"You will strangle me!"

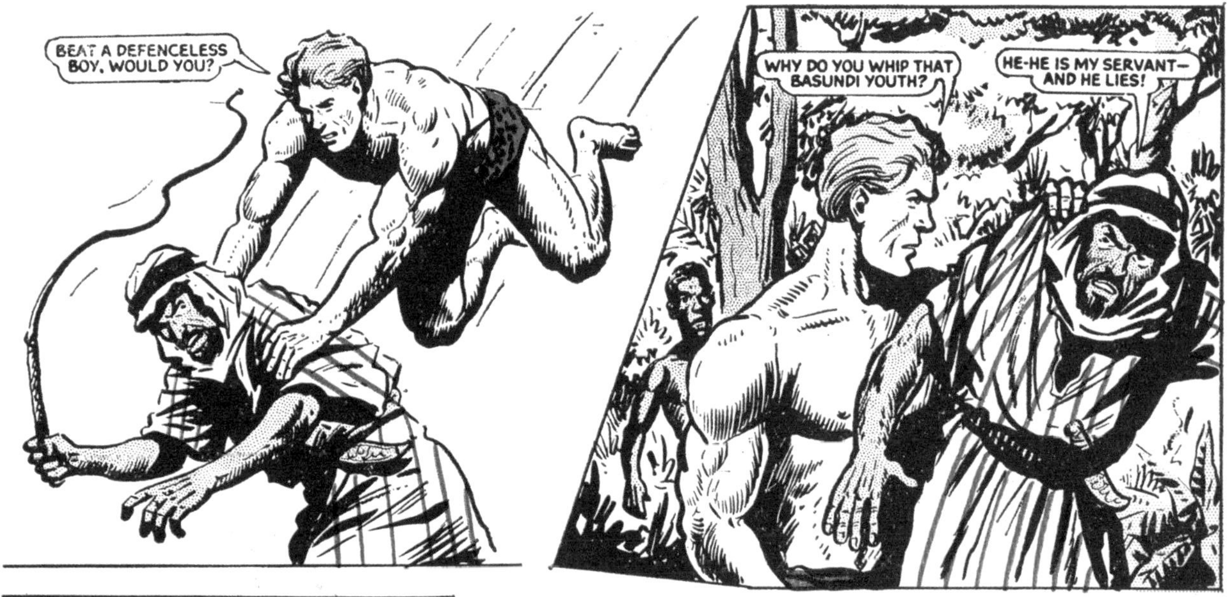
BEAT A DEFENCELESS BOY, WOULD YOU?
WHY DO YOU WHIP THAT BASUNDI YOUTH?
HE-HE IS MY SERVANT— AND HE LIES!

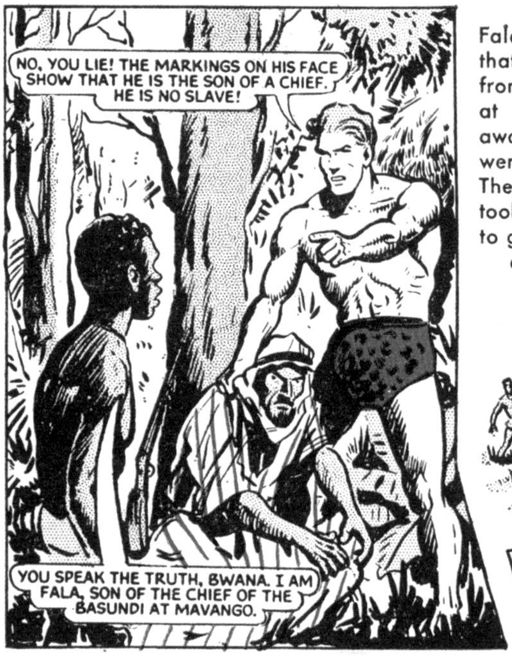
NO, YOU LIE! THE MARKINGS ON HIS FACE SHOW THAT HE IS THE SON OF A CHIEF. HE IS NO SLAVE!
YOU SPEAK THE TRUTH, BWANA. I AM FALA, SON OF THE CHIEF OF THE BASUNDI AT MAVANGO.

Fala went on to tell Morgyn that he had been on his way from his village to the school at the mission, 50 miles away, when he and his guide were ambushed by the Arab. The Arab shot the guide and took Fala prisoner, intending to get a good price for him at the slave market.

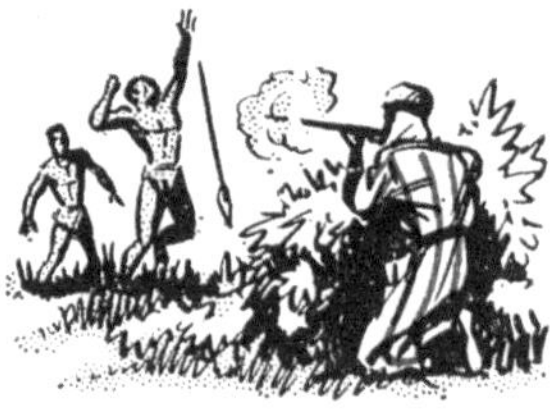

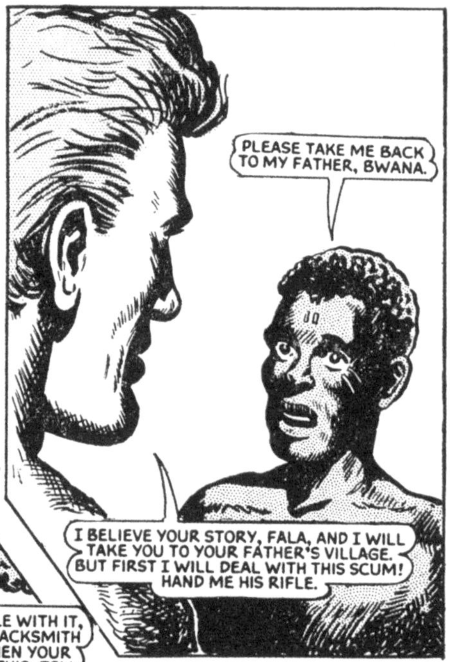
PLEASE TAKE ME BACK TO MY FATHER, BWANA.
I BELIEVE YOUR STORY, FALA, AND I WILL TAKE YOU TO YOUR FATHER'S VILLAGE. BUT FIRST I WILL DEAL WITH THIS SCUM! HAND ME HIS RIFLE.

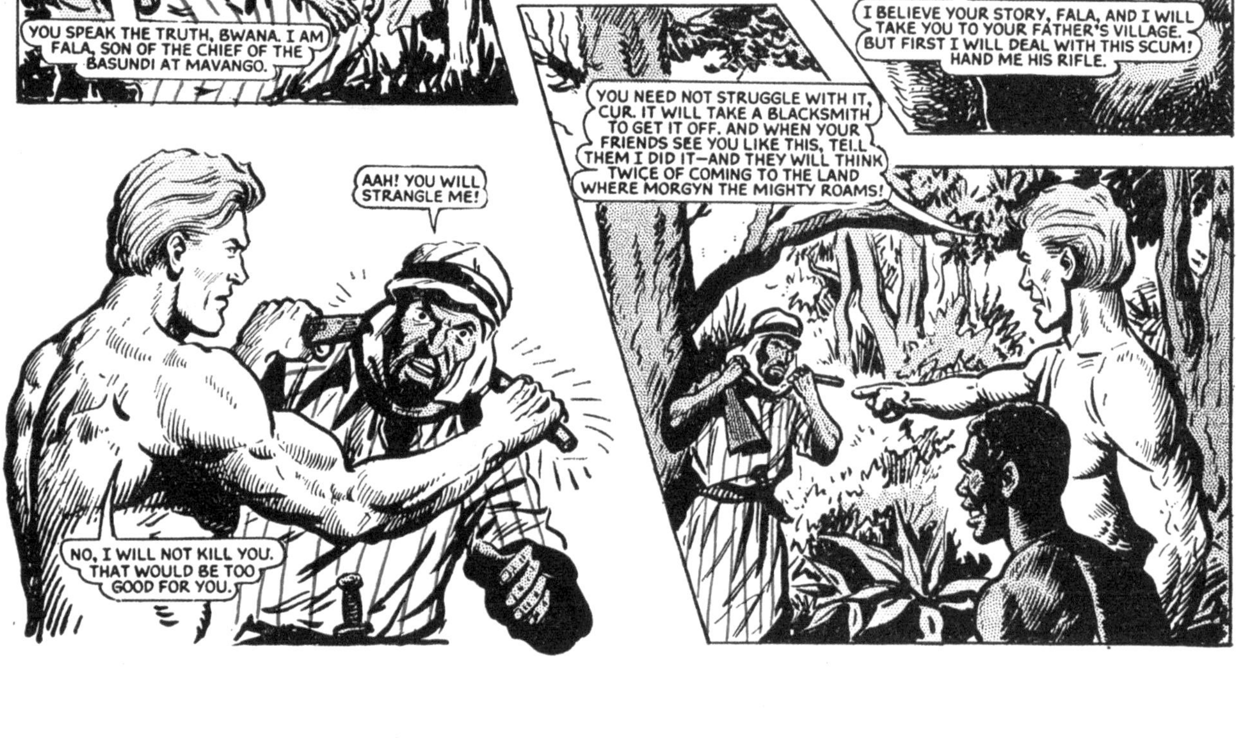
AAH! YOU WILL STRANGLE ME!
NO, I WILL NOT KILL YOU. THAT WOULD BE TOO GOOD FOR YOU.
YOU NEED NOT STRUGGLE WITH IT, CUR. IT WILL TAKE A BLACKSMITH TO GET IT OFF. AND WHEN YOUR FRIENDS SEE YOU LIKE THIS, TELL THEM I DID IT—AND THEY WILL THINK TWICE OF COMING TO THE LAND WHERE MORGYN THE MIGHTY ROAMS!

Ordeal in the rapids.

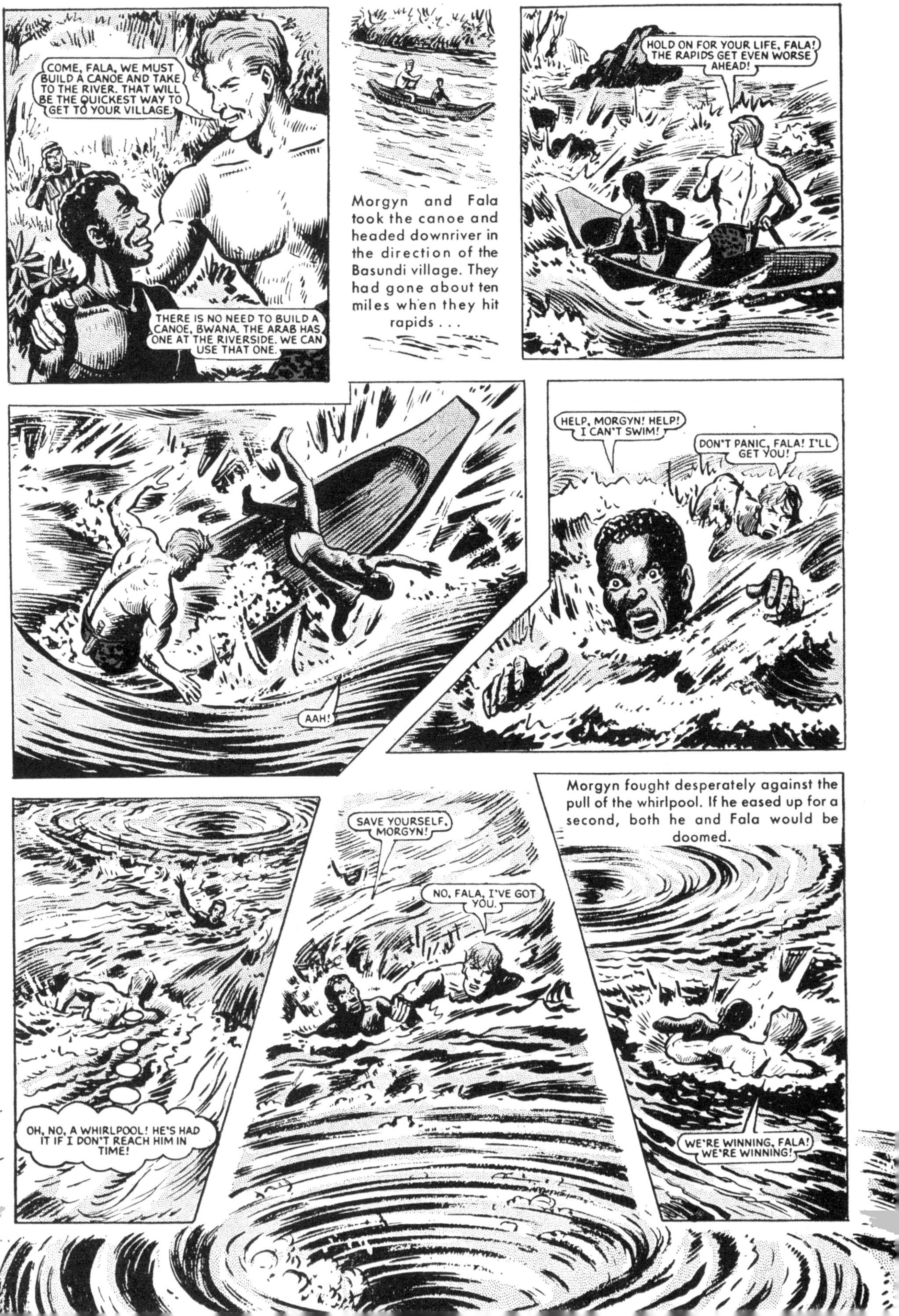
COME, FALA, WE MUST BUILD A CANOE AND TAKE TO THE RIVER. THAT WILL BE THE QUICKEST WAY TO GET TO YOUR VILLAGE.
THERE IS NO NEED TO BUILD A CANOE, BWANA. THE ARAB HAS ONE AT THE RIVERSIDE. WE CAN USE THAT ONE.
Morgyn and Fala took the canoe and headed downriver in the direction of the Basundi village. They had gone about ten miles when they hit rapids . . .
HOLD ON FOR YOUR LIFE, FALA! THE RAPIDS GET EVEN WORSE AHEAD!
AAH!
HELP, MORGYN! HELP! I CAN'T SWIM!
DON'T PANIC, FALA! I'LL GET YOU!
OH, NO, A WHIRLPOOL! HE'S HAD IT IF I DON'T REACH HIM IN TIME!
SAVE YOURSELF, MORGYN!
NO, FALA, I'VE GOT YOU.
Morgyn fought desperately against the pull of the whirlpool. If he eased up for a second, both he and Fala would be doomed.
WE'RE WINNING, FALA! WE'RE WINNING!

"The battle with the river is won!"

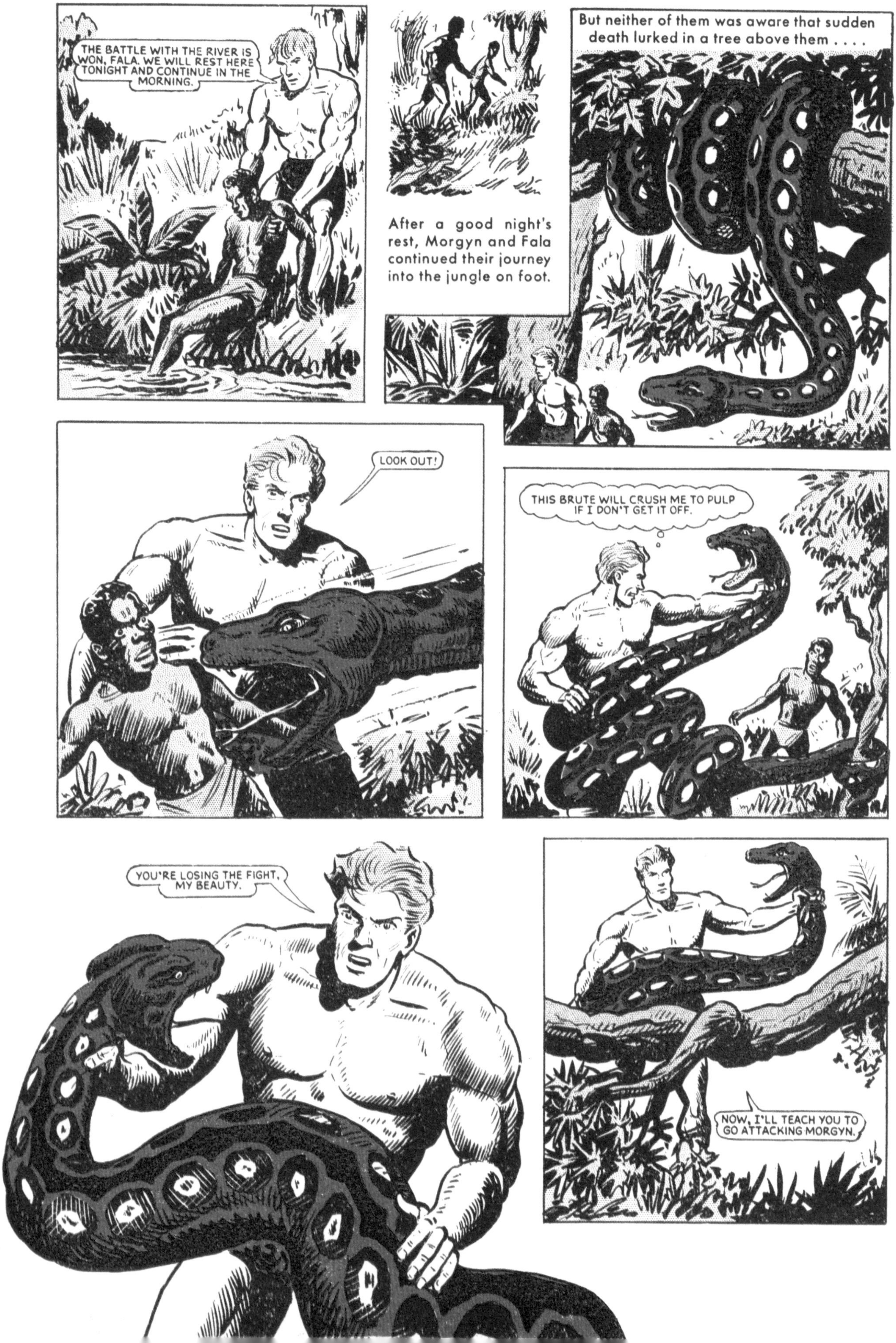
THE BATTLE WITH THE RIVER IS WON, FALA. WE WILL REST HERE TONIGHT AND CONTINUE IN THE MORNING.
After a good night's rest, Morgyn and Fala continued their journey into the jungle on foot.
But neither of them was aware that sudden death lurked in a tree above them . . . .
LOOK OUT!
THIS BRUTE WILL CRUSH ME TO PULP IF I DON'T GET IT OFF.
YOU'RE LOSING THE FIGHT, MY BEAUTY.
NOW, I'LL TEACH YOU TO GO ATTACKING MORGYN.

The village of the dead.

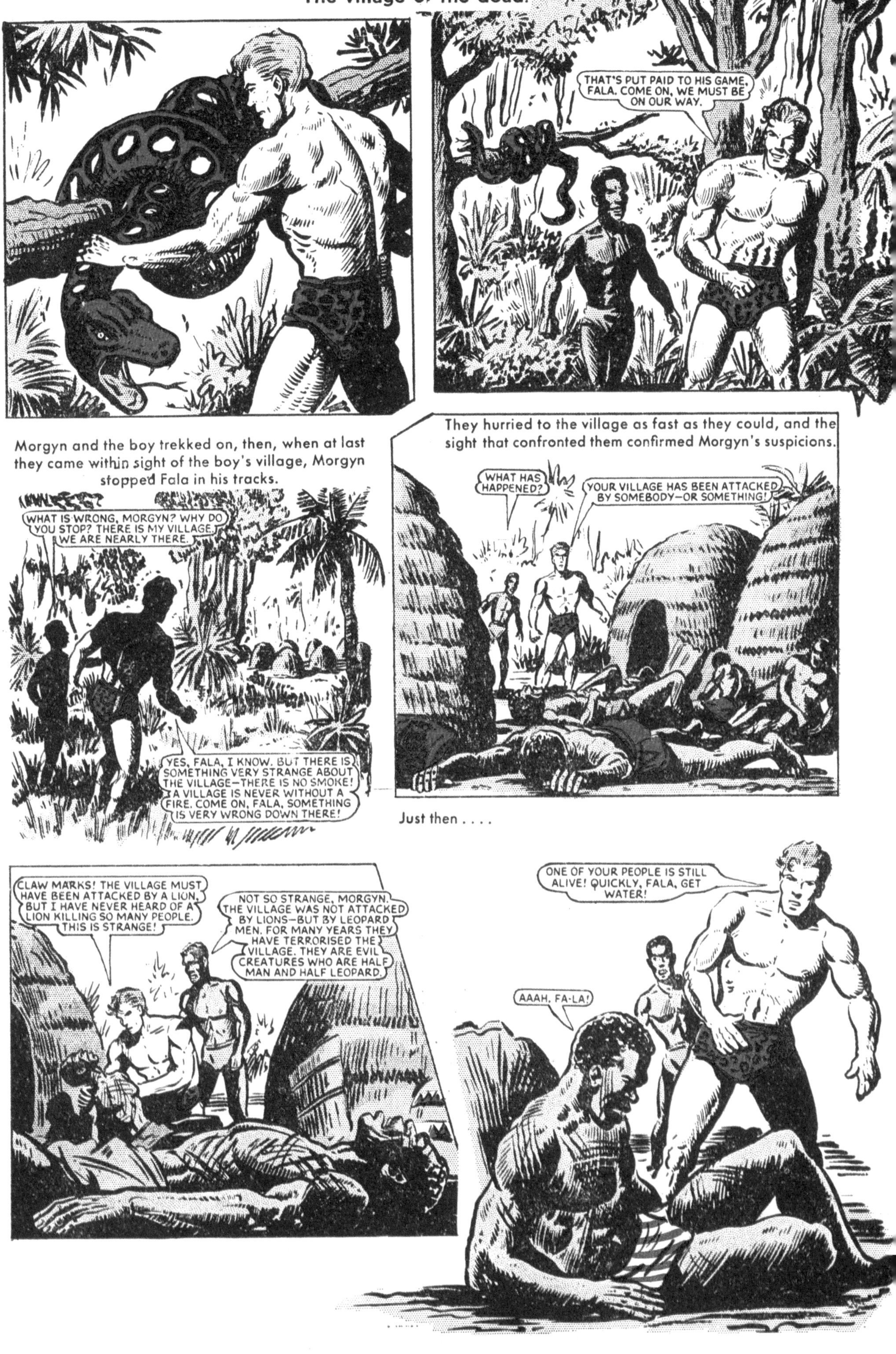
THAT'S PUT PAID TO HIS GAME, FALA. COME ON, WE MUST BE ON OUR WAY.
Morgyn and the boy trekked on, then, when at last they came within sight of the boy's village, Morgyn stopped Fala in his tracks.
WHAT IS WRONG, MORGYN? WHY DO YOU STOP? THERE IS MY VILLAGE. WE ARE NEARLY THERE.
YES, FALA, I KNOW. BUT THERE IS SOMETHING VERY STRANGE ABOUT THE VILLAGE—THERE IS NO SMOKE! A VILLAGE IS NEVER WITHOUT A FIRE. COME ON, FALA, SOMETHING IS VERY WRONG DOWN THERE!
They hurried to the village as fast as they could, and the sight that confronted them confirmed Morgyn's suspicions.
WHAT HAS HAPPENED?
YOUR VILLAGE HAS BEEN ATTACKED BY SOMEBODY—OR SOMETHING!
Just then . . . .
CLAW MARKS! THE VILLAGE MUST HAVE BEEN ATTACKED BY A LION. BUT I HAVE NEVER HEARD OF A LION KILLING SO MANY PEOPLE. THIS IS STRANGE!
NOT SO STRANGE, MORGYN. THE VILLAGE WAS NOT ATTACKED BY LIONS—BUT BY LEOPARD MEN. FOR MANY YEARS THEY HAVE TERRORISED THE VILLAGE. THEY ARE EVIL CREATURES WHO ARE HALF MAN AND HALF LEOPARD.
ONE OF YOUR PEOPLE IS STILL ALIVE! QUICKLY, FALA, GET WATER!
AAAH, FA-LA!

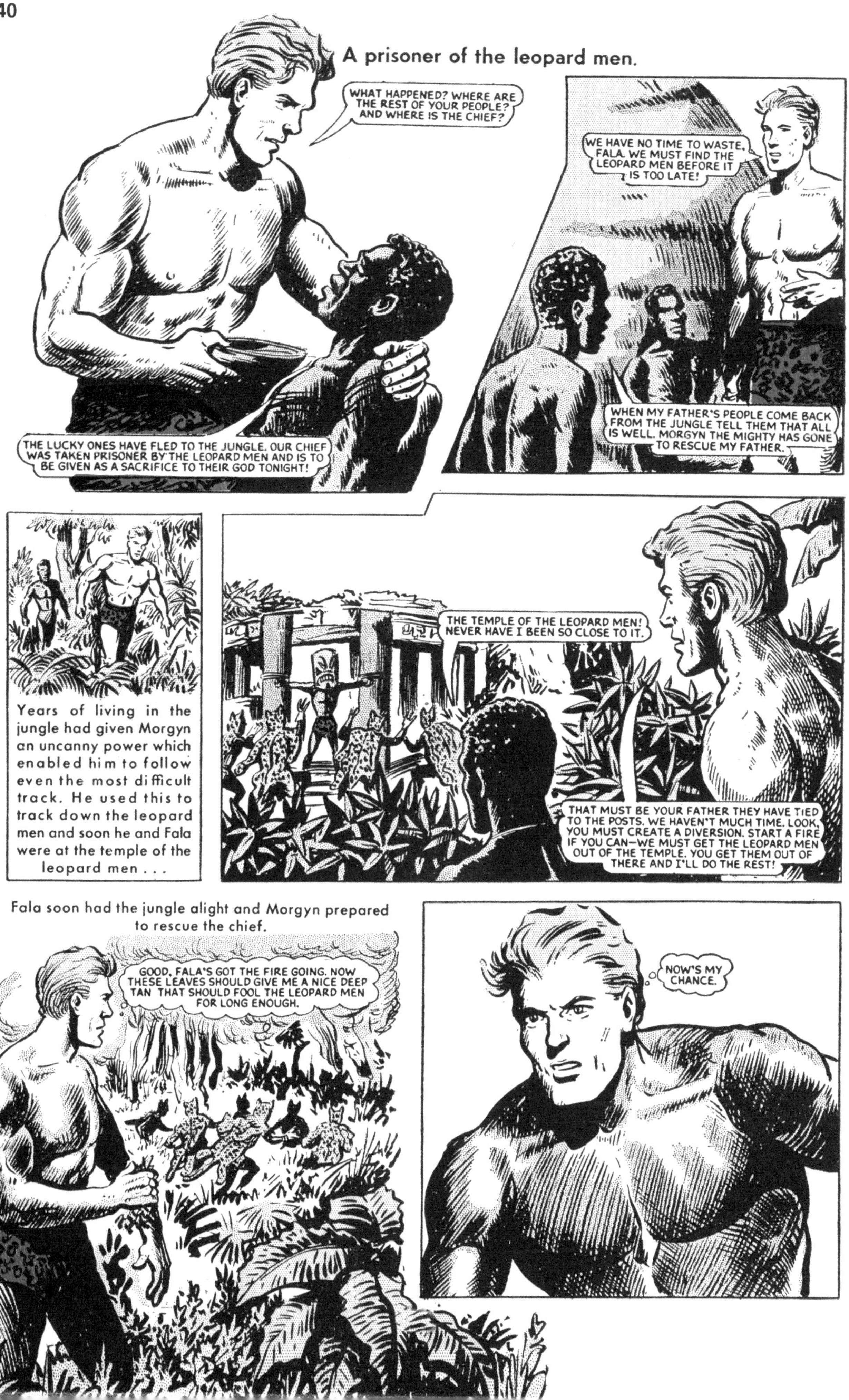
A prisoner of the leopard men.
WHAT HAPPENED? WHERE ARE THE REST OF YOUR PEOPLE? AND WHERE IS THE CHIEF?
THE LUCKY ONES HAVE FLED TO THE JUNGLE. OUR CHIEF WAS TAKEN PRISONER BY THE LEOPARD MEN AND IS TO BE GIVEN AS A SACRIFICE TO THEIR GOD TONIGHT!
WE HAVE NO TIME TO WASTE, FALA. WE MUST FIND THE LEOPARD MEN BEFORE IT IS TOO LATE!
WHEN MY FATHER'S PEOPLE COME BACK FROM THE JUNGLE TELL THEM THAT ALL IS WELL. MORGYN THE MIGHTY HAS GONE TO RESCUE MY FATHER.
Years of living in the jungle had given Morgyn an uncanny power which enabled him to follow even the most difficult track. He used this to track down the leopard men and soon he and Fala were at the temple of the leopard men . . .
THE TEMPLE OF THE LEOPARD MEN! NEVER HAVE I BEEN SO CLOSE TO IT.
THAT MUST BE YOUR FATHER THEY HAVE TIED TO THE POSTS. WE HAVEN'T MUCH TIME. LOOK, YOU MUST CREATE A DIVERSION. START A FIRE IF YOU CAN—WE MUST GET THE LEOPARD MEN OUT OF THE TEMPLE. YOU GET THEM OUT OF THERE AND I'LL DO THE REST!
Fala soon had the jungle alight and Morgyn prepared to rescue the chief.
GOOD, FALA'S GOT THE FIRE GOING. NOW THESE LEAVES SHOULD GIVE ME A NICE DEEP TAN THAT SHOULD FOOL THE LEOPARD MEN FOR LONG ENOUGH.
NOW'S MY CHANCE.

"And now you die!"

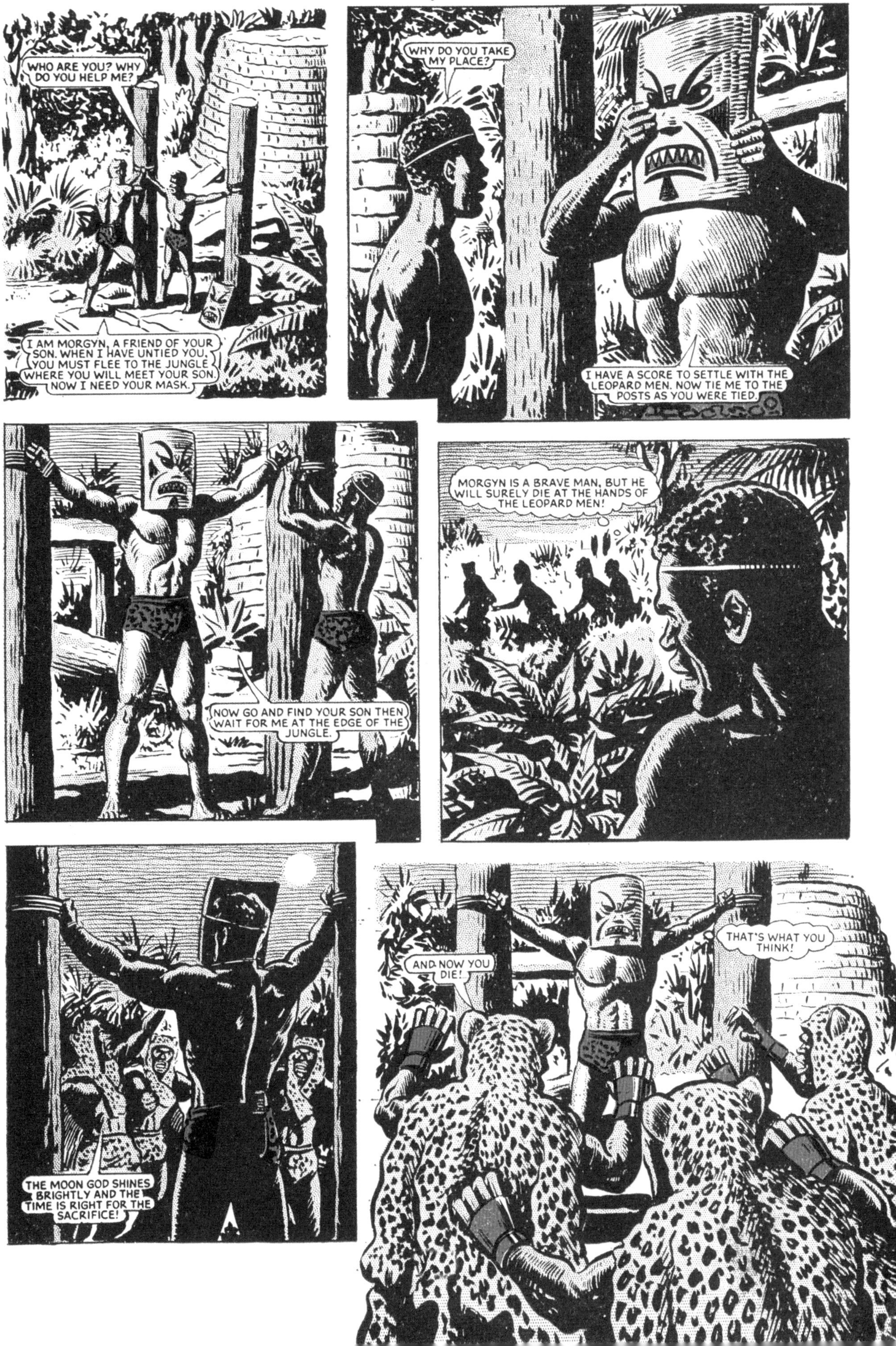
WHO ARE YOU? WHY DO YOU HELP ME?
I AM MORGYN, A FRIEND OF YOUR SON. WHEN I HAVE UNTIED YOU, YOU MUST FLEE TO THE JUNGLE WHERE YOU WILL MEET YOUR SON. NOW I NEED YOUR MASK.
WHY DO YOU TAKE MY PLACE?
I HAVE A SCORE TO SETTLE WITH THE LEOPARD MEN. NOW TIE ME TO THE POSTS AS YOU WERE TIED.
NOW GO AND FIND YOUR SON THEN WAIT FOR ME AT THE EDGE OF THE JUNGLE.
MORGYN IS A BRAVE MAN, BUT HE WILL SURELY DIE AT THE HANDS OF THE LEOPARD MEN!
THE MOON GOD SHINES BRIGHTLY AND THE TIME IS RIGHT FOR THE SACRIFICE!
AND NOW YOU DIE!
THAT'S WHAT YOU THINK!

Morgyn's revenge.

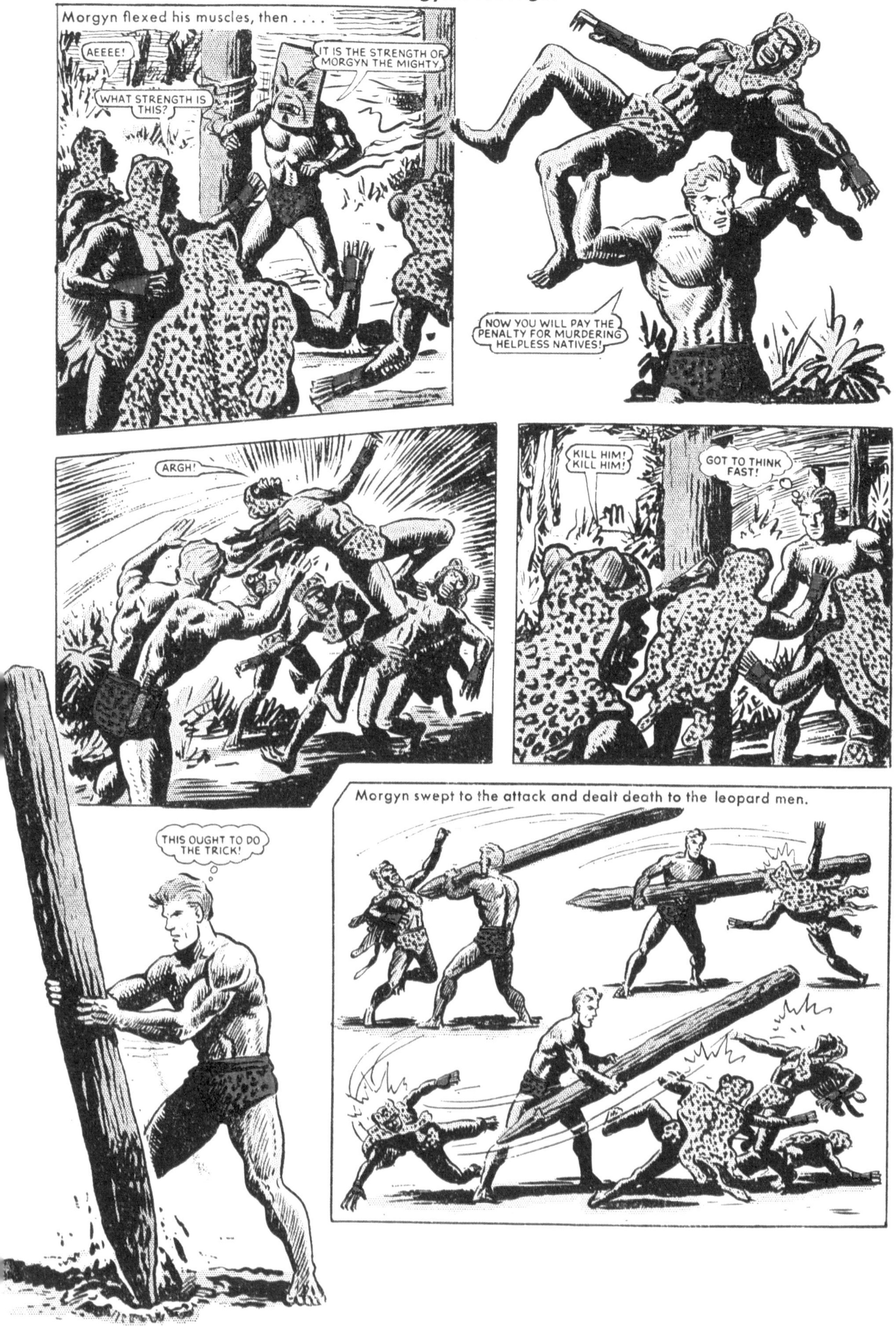
Morgyn flexed his muscles, then . . . .
AEEEE!
IT IS THE STRENGTH OF MORGYN THE MIGHTY.
WHAT STRENGTH IS THIS?
NOW YOU WILL PAY THE PENALTY FOR MURDERING HELPLESS NATIVES!
ARGH!
KILL HIM! KILL HIM!
GOT TO THINK FAST!
THIS OUGHT TO DO THE TRICK!
Morgyn swept to the attack and dealt death to the leopard men.

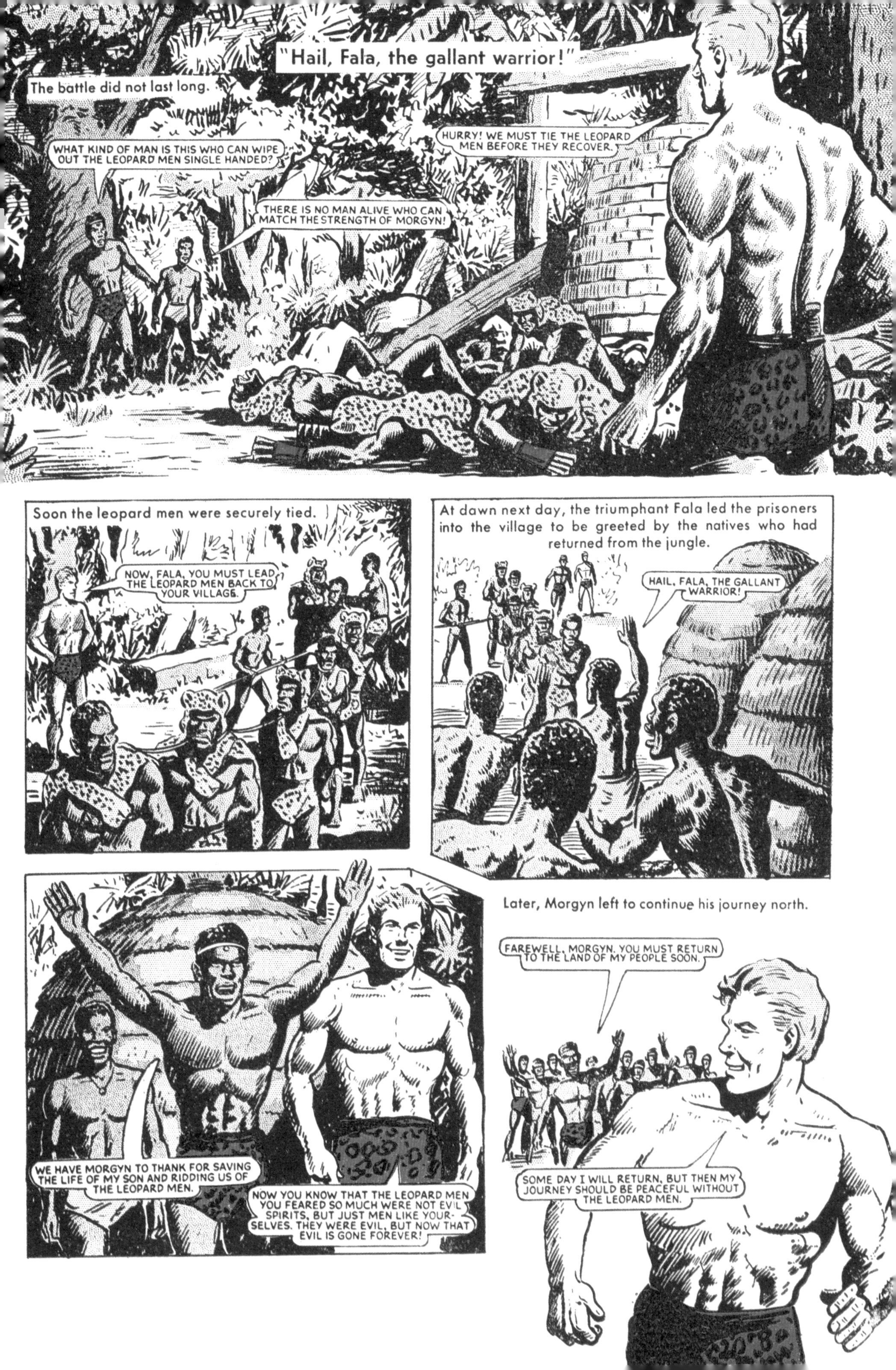
"Hail, Fala, the gallant warrior!"
The battle did not last long.
WHAT KIND OF MAN IS THIS WHO CAN WIPE OUT THE LEOPARD MEN SINGLE HANDED?
HURRY! WE MUST TIE THE LEOPARD MEN BEFORE THEY RECOVER.
THERE IS NO MAN ALIVE WHO CAN MATCH THE STRENGTH OF MORGYN!
Soon the leopard men were securely tied.
NOW, FALA, YOU MUST LEAD THE LEOPARD MEN BACK TO YOUR VILLAGE.
At dawn next day, the triumphant Fala led the prisoners into the village to be greeted by the natives who had returned from the jungle.
HAIL, FALA, THE GALLANT WARRIOR!
WE HAVE MORGYN TO THANK FOR SAVING THE LIFE OF MY SON AND RIDDING US OF THE LEOPARD MEN.
NOW YOU KNOW THAT THE LEOPARD MEN YOU FEARED SO MUCH WERE NOT EVIL SPIRITS, BUT JUST MEN LIKE YOUR-SELVES. THEY WERE EVIL, BUT NOW THAT EVIL IS GONE FOREVER!
Later, Morgyn left to continue his journey north.
FAREWELL, MORGYN. YOU MUST RETURN TO THE LAND OF MY PEOPLE SOON.
SOME DAY I WILL RETURN, BUT THEN MY JOURNEY SHOULD BE PEACEFUL WITHOUT THE LEOPARD MEN.

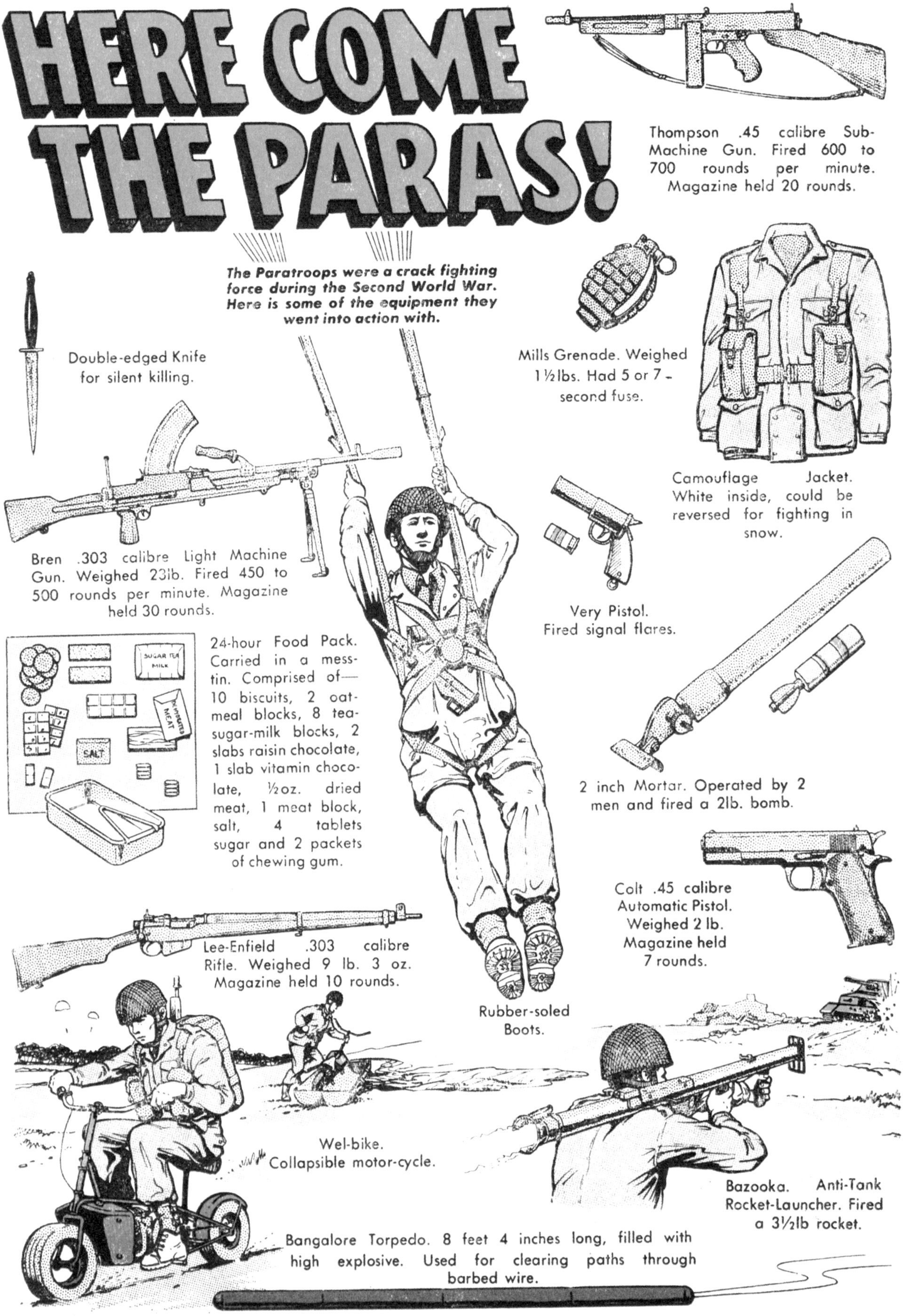
HERE COME THE PARAS!
The Paratroops were a crack fighting force during the Second World War. Here is some of the equipment they went into action with.
Thompson .45 calibre Sub-Machine Gun. Fired 600 to 700 rounds per minute. Magazine held 20 rounds.
Double-edged Knife for silent killing.
Mills Grenade. Weighed 1½ lbs. Had 5 or 7-second fuse.
Camouflage Jacket. White inside, could be reversed for fighting in snow.
Bren .303 calibre Light Machine Gun. Weighed 23lb. Fired 450 to 500 rounds per minute. Magazine held 30 rounds.
Very Pistol. Fired signal flares.
24-hour Food Pack. Carried in a mess-tin. Comprised of— 10 biscuits, 2 oatmeal blocks, 8 tea-sugar-milk blocks, 2 slabs raisin chocolate, 1 slab vitamin chocolate, ½ oz. dried meat, 1 meat block, salt, 4 tablets sugar and 2 packets of chewing gum.
SUGAR TEA MILK
MEAT
SALT
2 inch Mortar. Operated by 2 men and fired a 2lb. bomb.
Colt .45 calibre Automatic Pistol. Weighed 2 lb. Magazine held 7 rounds.
Lee-Enfield .303 calibre Rifle. Weighed 9 lb. 3 oz. Magazine held 10 rounds.
Rubber-soled Boots.
Wel-bike. Collapsible motor-cycle.
Bazooka. Anti-Tank Rocket-Launcher. Fired a 3½lb rocket.
Bangalore Torpedo. 8 feet 4 inches long, filled with high explosive. Used for clearing paths through barbed wire.

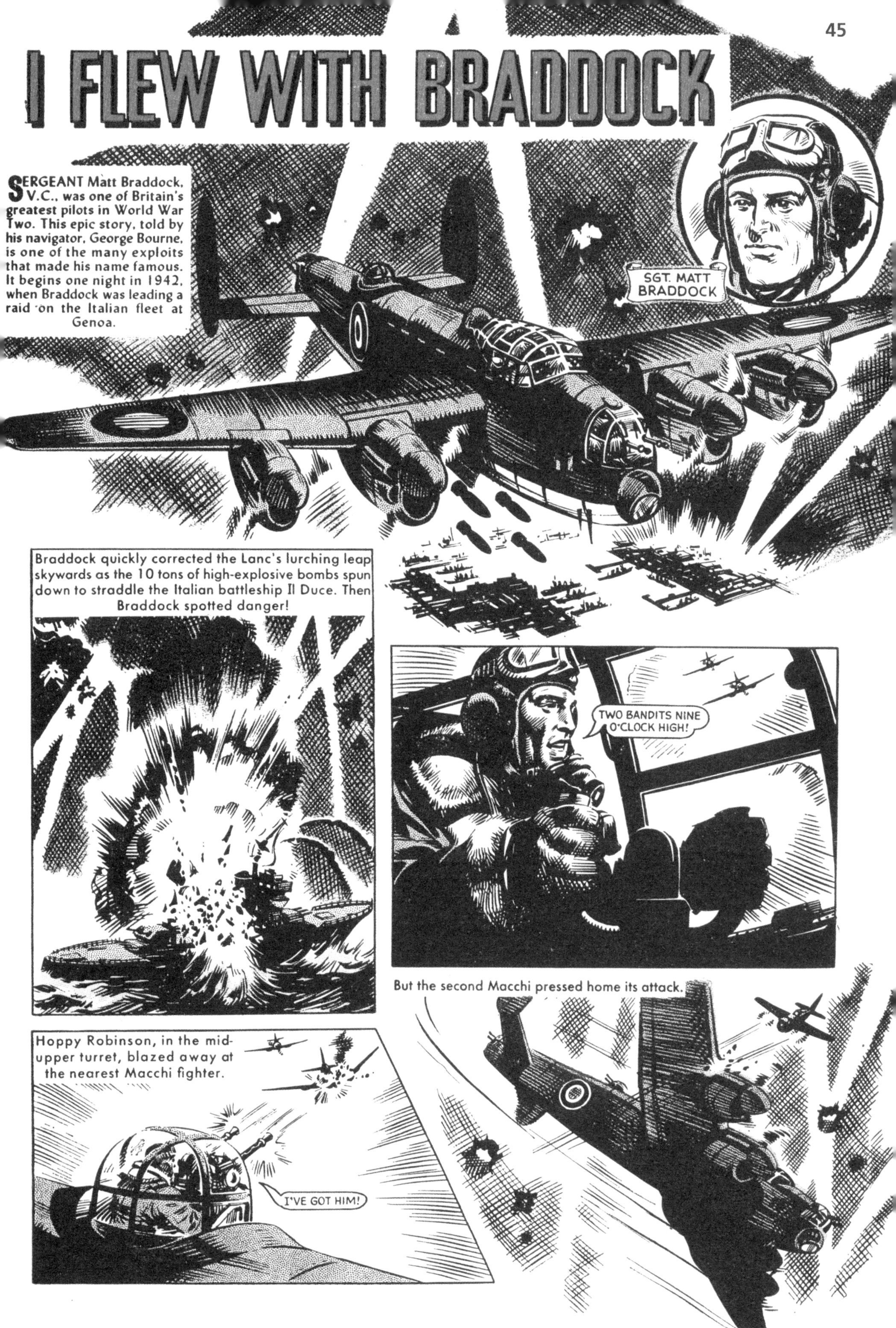
I FLEW WITH BRADDOCK
SERGEANT Matt Braddock, V.C., was one of Britain's greatest pilots in World War Two. This epic story, told by his navigator, George Bourne, is one of the many exploits that made his name famous. It begins one night in 1942, when Braddock was leading a raid on the Italian fleet at Genoa.
SGT. MATT BRADDOCK
Braddock quickly corrected the Lanc's lurching leap skywards as the 10 tons of high-explosive bombs spun down to straddle the Italian battleship Il Duce. Then Braddock spotted danger!
TWO BANDITS NINE O'CLOCK HIGH!
Hoppy Robinson, in the mid-upper turret, blazed away at the nearest Macchi fighter.
I'VE GOT HIM!
But the second Macchi pressed home its attack.

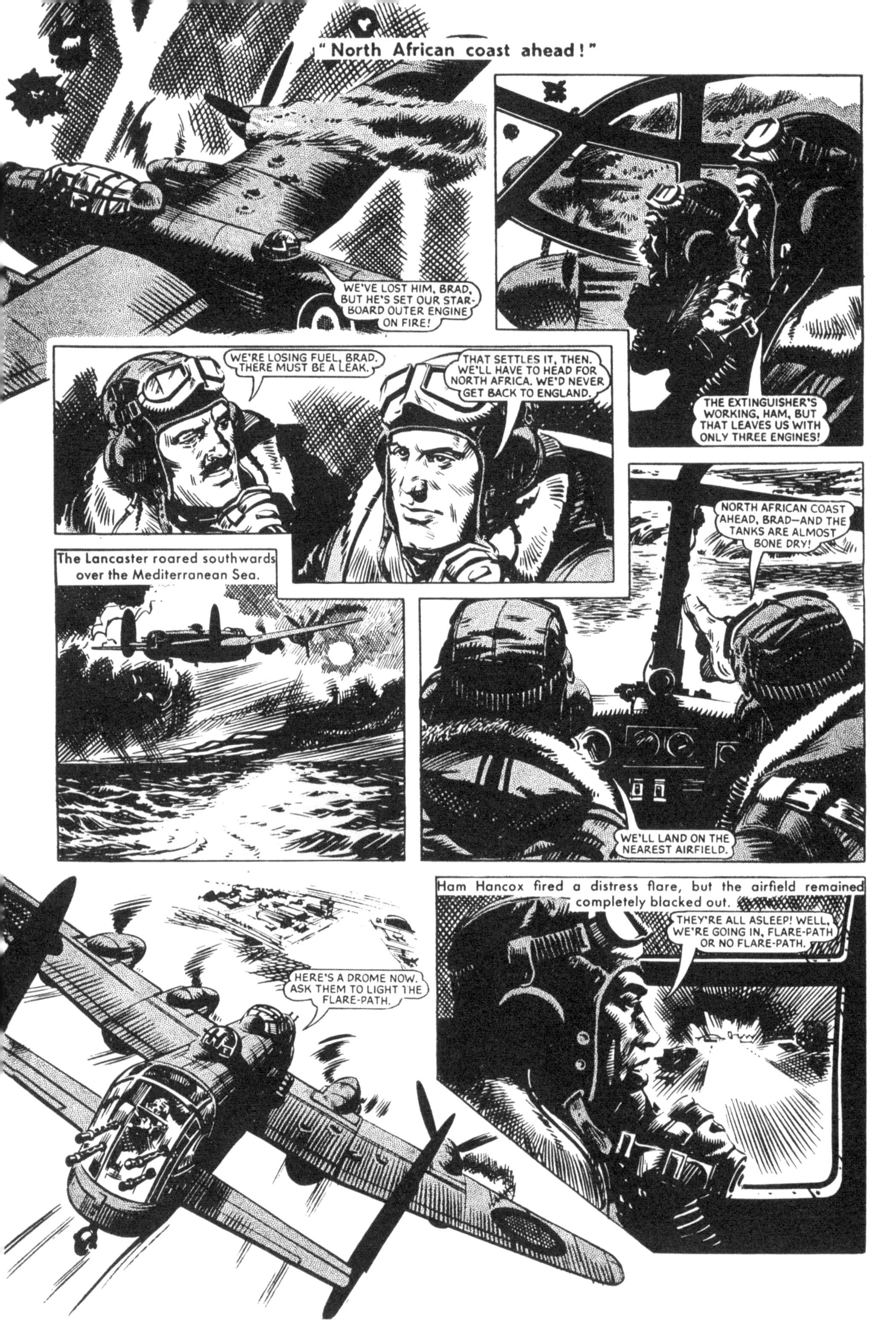
"North African coast ahead!"
WE'VE LOST HIM, BRAD, BUT HE'S SET OUR STARBOARD OUTER ENGINE ON FIRE!
THE EXTINGUISHER'S WORKING, HAM, BUT THAT LEAVES US WITH ONLY THREE ENGINES!
WE'RE LOSING FUEL, BRAD. THERE MUST BE A LEAK.
THAT SETTLES IT, THEN. WE'LL HAVE TO HEAD FOR NORTH AFRICA. WE'D NEVER GET BACK TO ENGLAND.
The Lancaster roared southwards over the Mediterranean Sea.
NORTH AFRICAN COAST AHEAD, BRAD—AND THE TANKS ARE ALMOST BONE DRY!
WE'LL LAND ON THE NEAREST AIRFIELD.
HERE'S A DROME NOW. ASK THEM TO LIGHT THE FLARE-PATH.
Ham Hancox fired a distress flare, but the airfield remained completely blacked out.
THEY'RE ALL ASLEEP! WELL, WE'RE GOING IN, FLARE-PATH OR NO FLARE-PATH.

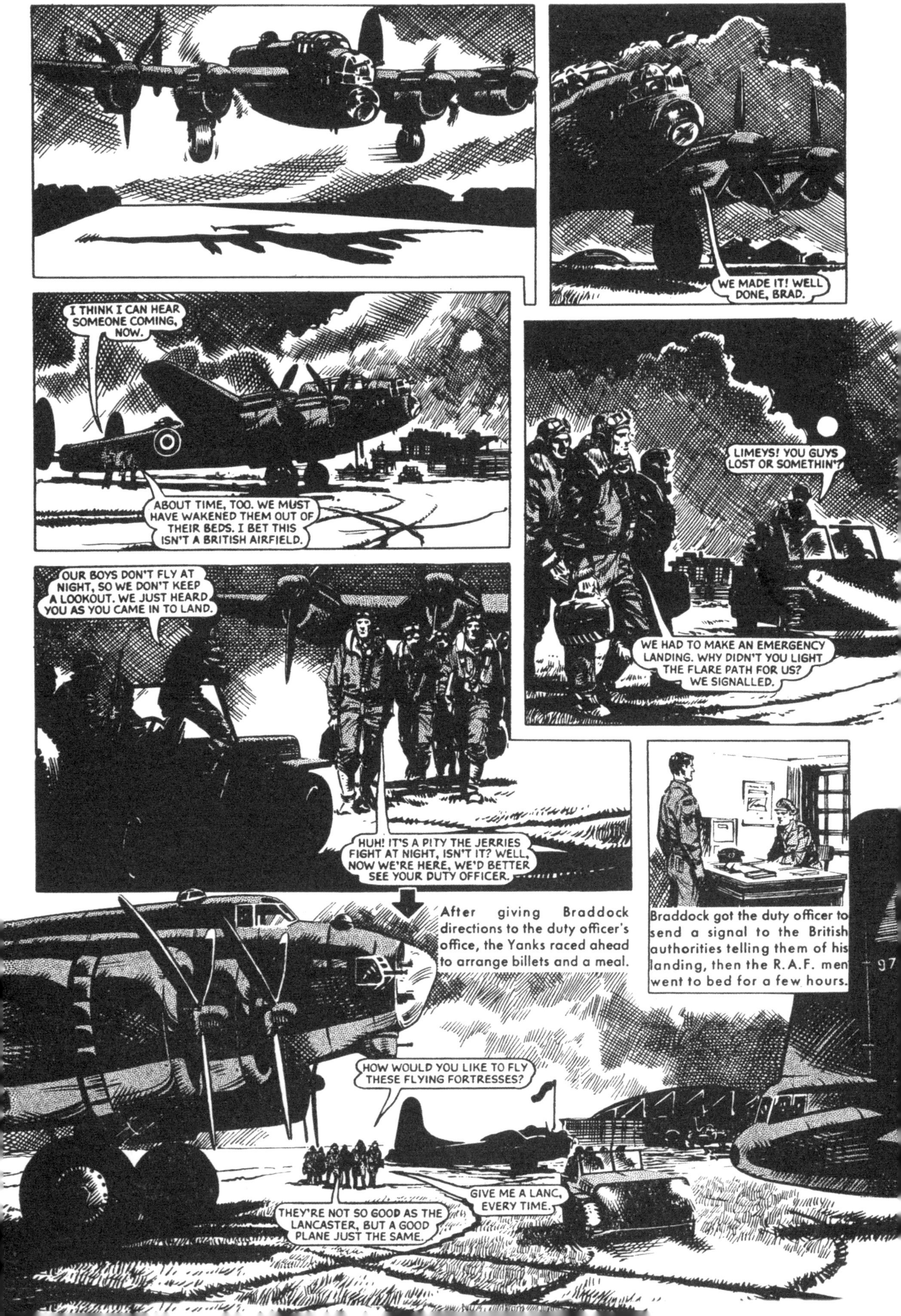
WE MADE IT! WELL DONE, BRAD.
I THINK I CAN HEAR SOMEONE COMING, NOW.
ABOUT TIME, TOO. WE MUST HAVE WAKENED THEM OUT OF THEIR BEDS. I BET THIS ISN'T A BRITISH AIRFIELD.
LIMEYS! YOU GUYS LOST OR SOMETHIN'?
WE HAD TO MAKE AN EMERGENCY LANDING. WHY DIDN'T YOU LIGHT THE FLARE PATH FOR US? WE SIGNALLED.
OUR BOYS DON'T FLY AT NIGHT, SO WE DON'T KEEP A LOOKOUT. WE JUST HEARD YOU AS YOU CAME IN TO LAND.
HUH! IT'S A PITY THE JERRIES FIGHT AT NIGHT, ISN'T IT? WELL, NOW WE'RE HERE, WE'D BETTER SEE YOUR DUTY OFFICER.
Braddock got the duty officer to send a signal to the British authorities telling them of his landing, then the R.A.F. men went to bed for a few hours.
After giving Braddock directions to the duty officer's office, the Yanks raced ahead to arrange billets and a meal.
HOW WOULD YOU LIKE TO FLY THESE FLYING FORTRESSES?
THEY'RE NOT SO GOOD AS THE LANCASTER, BUT A GOOD PLANE JUST THE SAME.
GIVE ME A LANC, EVERY TIME.

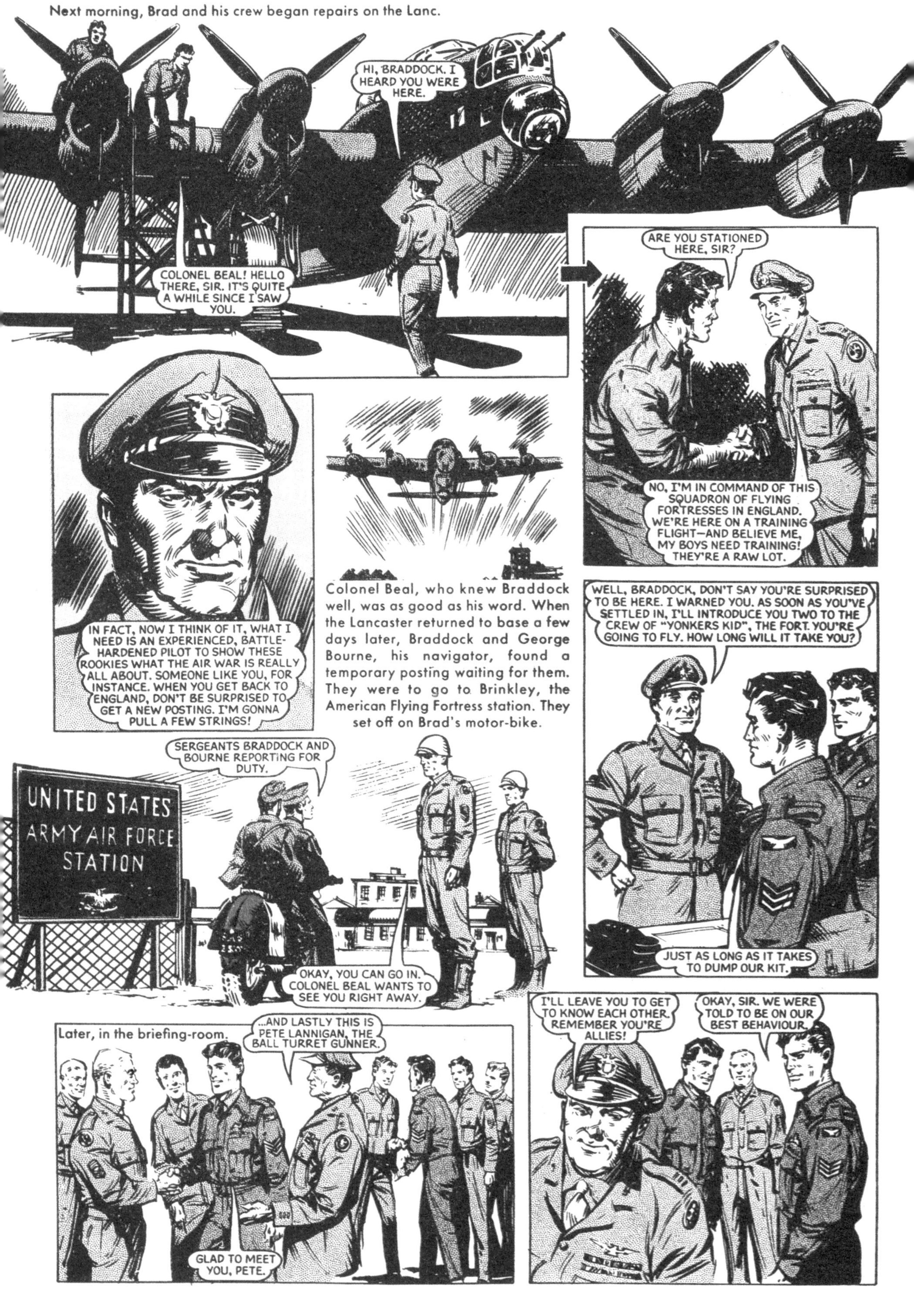
Next morning, Brad and his crew began repairs on the Lanc.
HI, BRADDOCK. I HEARD YOU WERE HERE.
COLONEL BEAL! HELLO THERE, SIR. IT'S QUITE A WHILE SINCE I SAW YOU.
ARE YOU STATIONED HERE, SIR?
NO, I'M IN COMMAND OF THIS SQUADRON OF FLYING FORTRESSES IN ENGLAND. WE'RE HERE ON A TRAINING FLIGHT—AND BELIEVE ME, MY BOYS NEED TRAINING! THEY'RE A RAW LOT.
IN FACT, NOW I THINK OF IT, WHAT I NEED IS AN EXPERIENCED, BATTLE-HARDENED PILOT TO SHOW THESE ROOKIES WHAT THE AIR WAR IS REALLY ALL ABOUT. SOMEONE LIKE YOU, FOR INSTANCE. WHEN YOU GET BACK TO ENGLAND, DON'T BE SURPRISED TO GET A NEW POSTING. I'M GONNA PULL A FEW STRINGS!
Colonel Beal, who knew Braddock well, was as good as his word. When the Lancaster returned to base a few days later, Braddock and George Bourne, his navigator, found a temporary posting waiting for them. They were to go to Brinkley, the American Flying Fortress station. They set off on Brad's motor-bike.
SERGEANTS BRADDOCK AND BOURNE REPORTING FOR DUTY.
UNITED STATES ARMY AIR FORCE STATION
OKAY, YOU CAN GO IN. COLONEL BEAL WANTS TO SEE YOU RIGHT AWAY.
WELL, BRADDOCK, DON'T SAY YOU'RE SURPRISED TO BE HERE. I WARNED YOU. AS SOON AS YOU'VE SETTLED IN, I'LL INTRODUCE YOU TWO TO THE CREW OF "YONKERS KID", THE FORT. YOU'RE GOING TO FLY. HOW LONG WILL IT TAKE YOU?
JUST AS LONG AS IT TAKES TO DUMP OUR KIT.
Later, in the briefing-room.
...AND LASTLY THIS IS PETE LANNIGAN, THE BALL TURRET GUNNER.
GLAD TO MEET YOU, PETE.
I'LL LEAVE YOU TO GET TO KNOW EACH OTHER. REMEMBER YOU'RE ALLIES!
OKAY, SIR. WE WERE TOLD TO BE ON OUR BEST BEHAVIOUR.

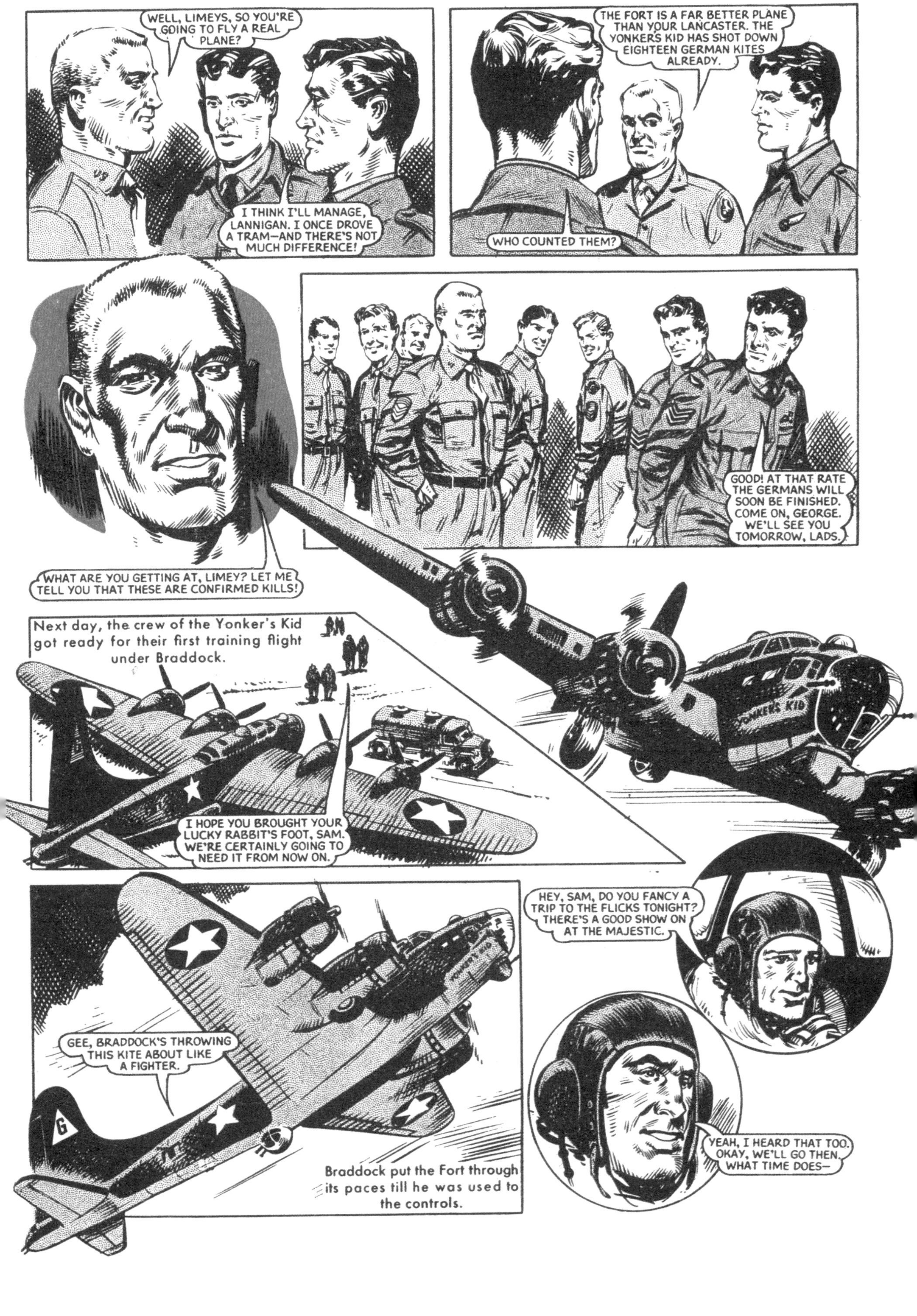
WELL, LIMEYS, SO YOU'RE GOING TO FLY A REAL PLANE?
I THINK I'LL MANAGE, LANNIGAN. I ONCE DROVE A TRAM—AND THERE'S NOT MUCH DIFFERENCE!
THE FORT IS A FAR BETTER PLANE THAN YOUR LANCASTER. THE YONKER'S KID HAS SHOT DOWN EIGHTEEN GERMAN KITES ALREADY.
WHO COUNTED THEM?
WHAT ARE YOU GETTING AT, LIMEY? LET ME TELL YOU THAT THESE ARE CONFIRMED KILLS!
GOOD! AT THAT RATE THE GERMANS WILL SOON BE FINISHED. COME ON, GEORGE. WE'LL SEE YOU TOMORROW, LADS.
YONKER'S KID
Next day, the crew of the Yonker's Kid got ready for their first training flight under Braddock.
I HOPE YOU BROUGHT YOUR LUCKY RABBIT'S FOOT, SAM. WE'RE CERTAINLY GOING TO NEED IT FROM NOW ON.
GEE, BRADDOCK'S THROWING THIS KITE ABOUT LIKE A FIGHTER.
Braddock put the Fort through its paces till he was used to the controls.
HEY, SAM, DO YOU FANCY A TRIP TO THE FLICKS TONIGHT? THERE'S A GOOD SHOW ON AT THE MAJESTIC.
YEAH, I HEARD THAT TOO. OKAY, WE'LL GO THEN. WHAT TIME DOES—

"This is where you get out, Lannigan!"

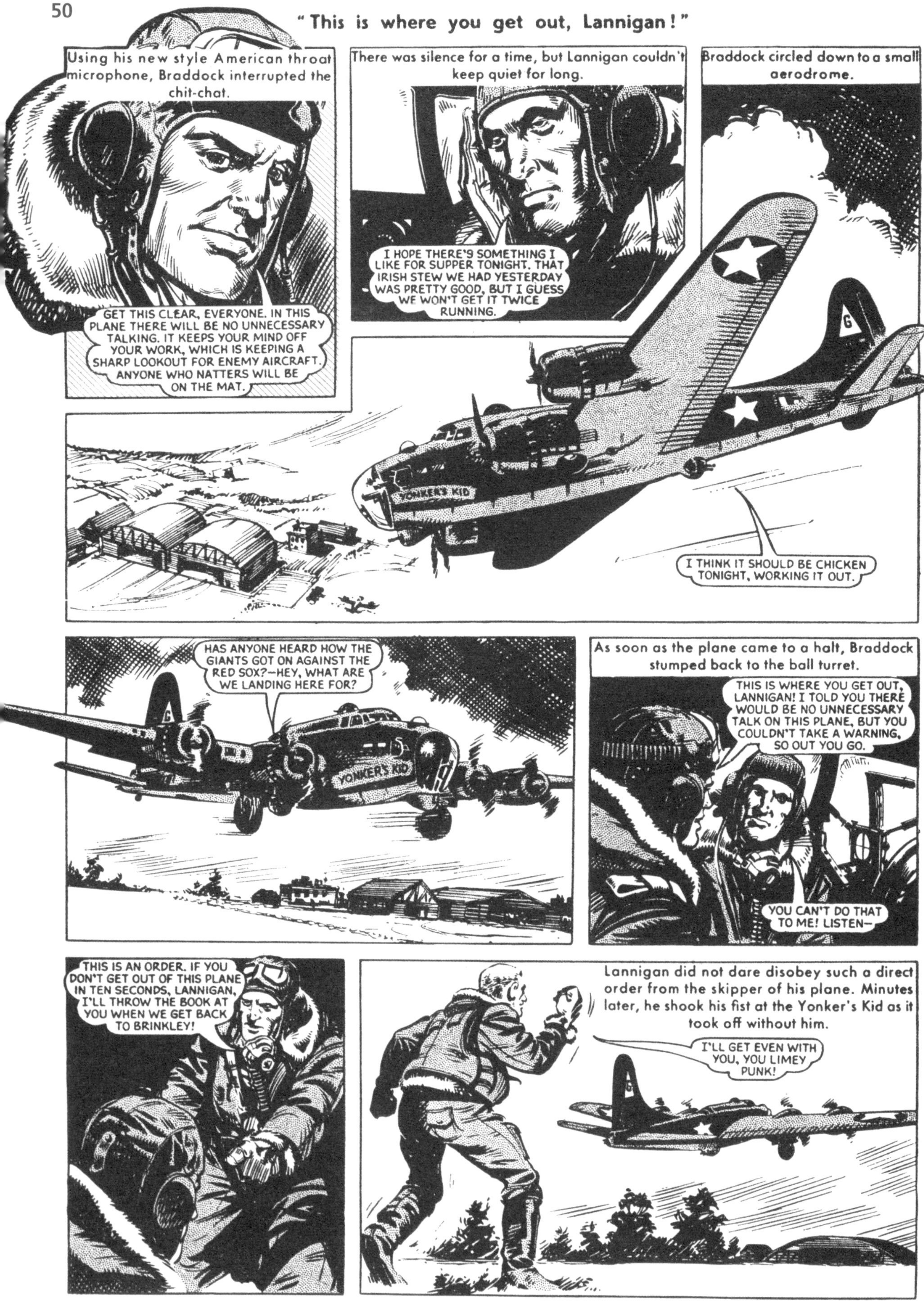
Using his new style American throat microphone, Braddock interrupted the chit-chat.
GET THIS CLEAR, EVERYONE. IN THIS PLANE THERE WILL BE NO UNNECESSARY TALKING. IT KEEPS YOUR MIND OFF YOUR WORK, WHICH IS KEEPING A SHARP LOOKOUT FOR ENEMY AIRCRAFT. ANYONE WHO NATTERS WILL BE ON THE MAT.
There was silence for a time, but Lannigan couldn't keep quiet for long.
I HOPE THERE'S SOMETHING I LIKE FOR SUPPER TONIGHT. THAT IRISH STEW WE HAD YESTERDAY WAS PRETTY GOOD, BUT I GUESS WE WON'T GET IT TWICE RUNNING.
Braddock circled down to a small aerodrome.
YONKER'S KID
I THINK IT SHOULD BE CHICKEN TONIGHT, WORKING IT OUT.
HAS ANYONE HEARD HOW THE GIANTS GOT ON AGAINST THE RED SOX?—HEY, WHAT ARE WE LANDING HERE FOR?
YONKER'S KID
As soon as the plane came to a halt, Braddock stumped back to the ball turret.
THIS IS WHERE YOU GET OUT, LANNIGAN! I TOLD YOU THERE WOULD BE NO UNNECESSARY TALK ON THIS PLANE, BUT YOU COULDN'T TAKE A WARNING, SO OUT YOU GO.
YOU CAN'T DO THAT TO ME! LISTEN—
THIS IS AN ORDER. IF YOU DON'T GET OUT OF THIS PLANE IN TEN SECONDS, LANNIGAN, I'LL THROW THE BOOK AT YOU WHEN WE GET BACK TO BRINKLEY!
Lannigan did not dare disobey such a direct order from the skipper of his plane. Minutes later, he shook his fist at the Yonker's Kid as it took off without him.
I'LL GET EVEN WITH YOU, YOU LIMEY PUNK!

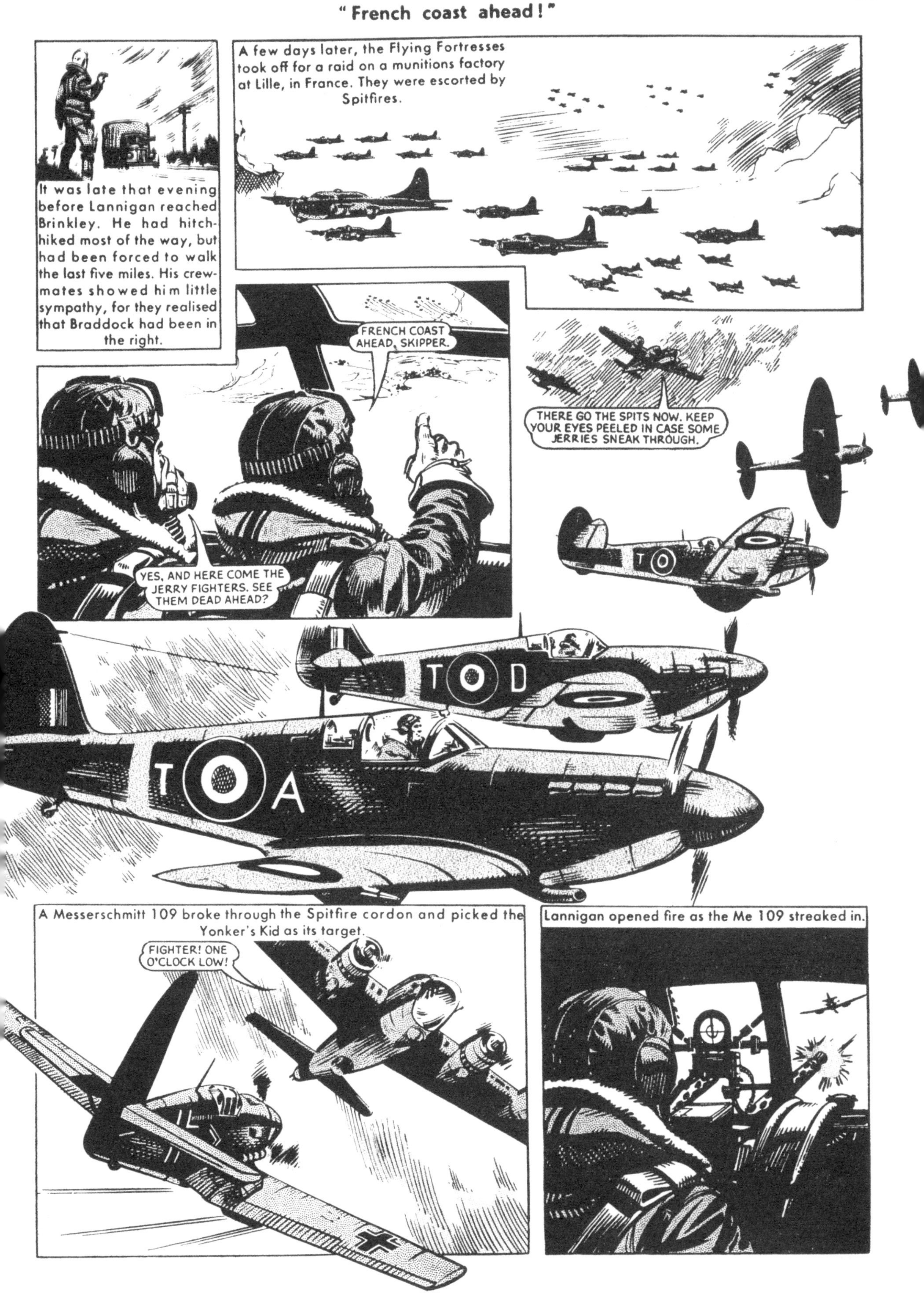
"French coast ahead!"
It was late that evening before Lannigan reached Brinkley. He had hitch-hiked most of the way, but had been forced to walk the last five miles. His crew-mates showed him little sympathy, for they realised that Braddock had been in the right.
A few days later, the Flying Fortresses took off for a raid on a munitions factory at Lille, in France. They were escorted by Spitfires.
FRENCH COAST AHEAD, SKIPPER.
YES, AND HERE COME THE JERRY FIGHTERS. SEE THEM DEAD AHEAD?
THERE GO THE SPITS NOW. KEEP YOUR EYES PEELED IN CASE SOME JERRIES SNEAK THROUGH.
TOD
TOA
A Messerschmitt 109 broke through the Spitfire cordon and picked the Yonker's Kid as its target.
FIGHTER! ONE O'CLOCK LOW!
Lannigan opened fire as the Me 109 streaked in.

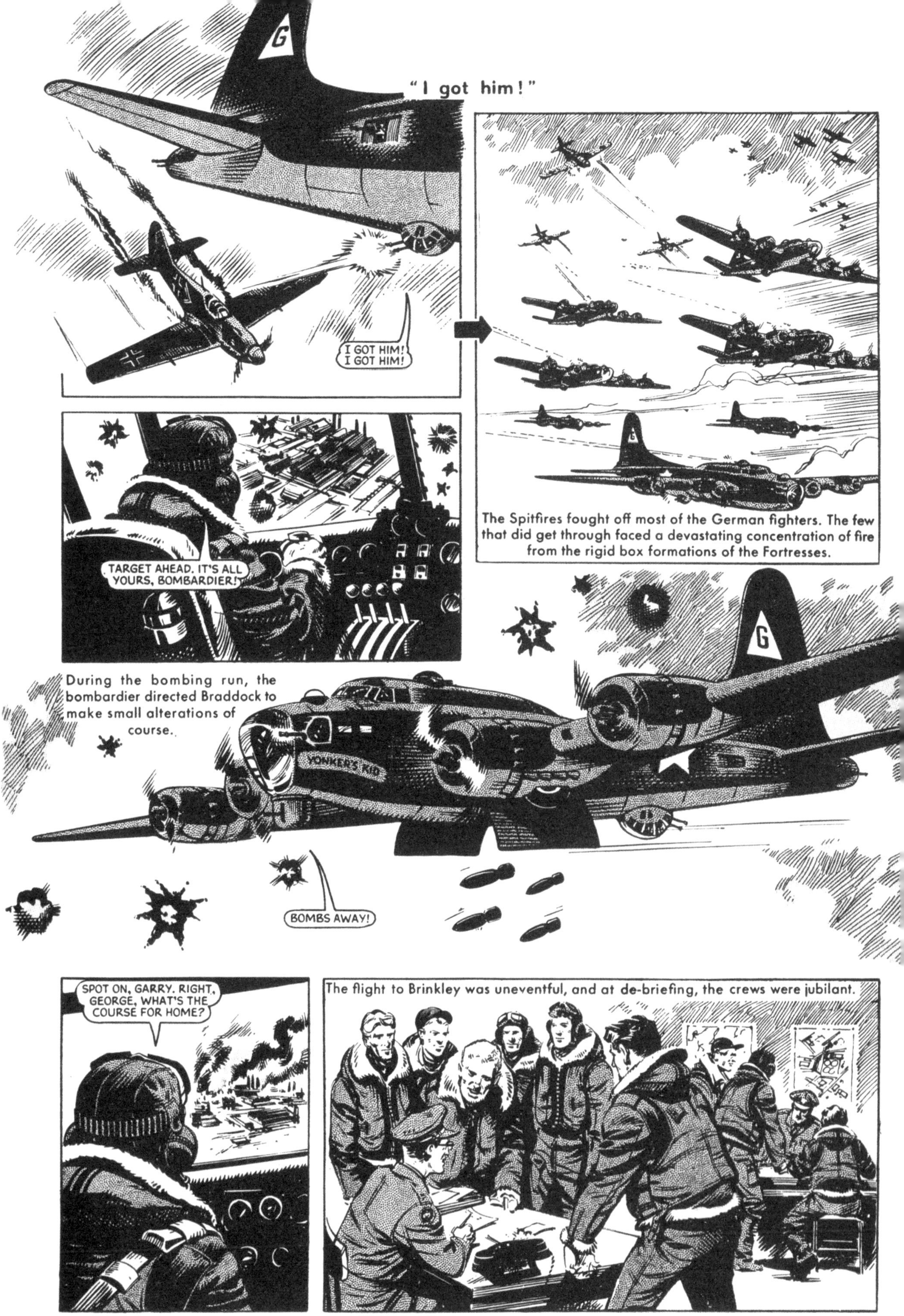
"I got him!"
I GOT HIM! I GOT HIM!
The Spitfires fought off most of the German fighters. The few that did get through faced a devastating concentration of fire from the rigid box formations of the Fortresses.
TARGET AHEAD. IT'S ALL YOURS, BOMBARDIER!
During the bombing run, the bombardier directed Braddock to make small alterations of course.
BOMBS AWAY!
SPOT ON, GARRY. RIGHT, GEORGE, WHAT'S THE COURSE FOR HOME?
The flight to Brinkley was uneventful, and at de-briefing, the crews were jubilant.

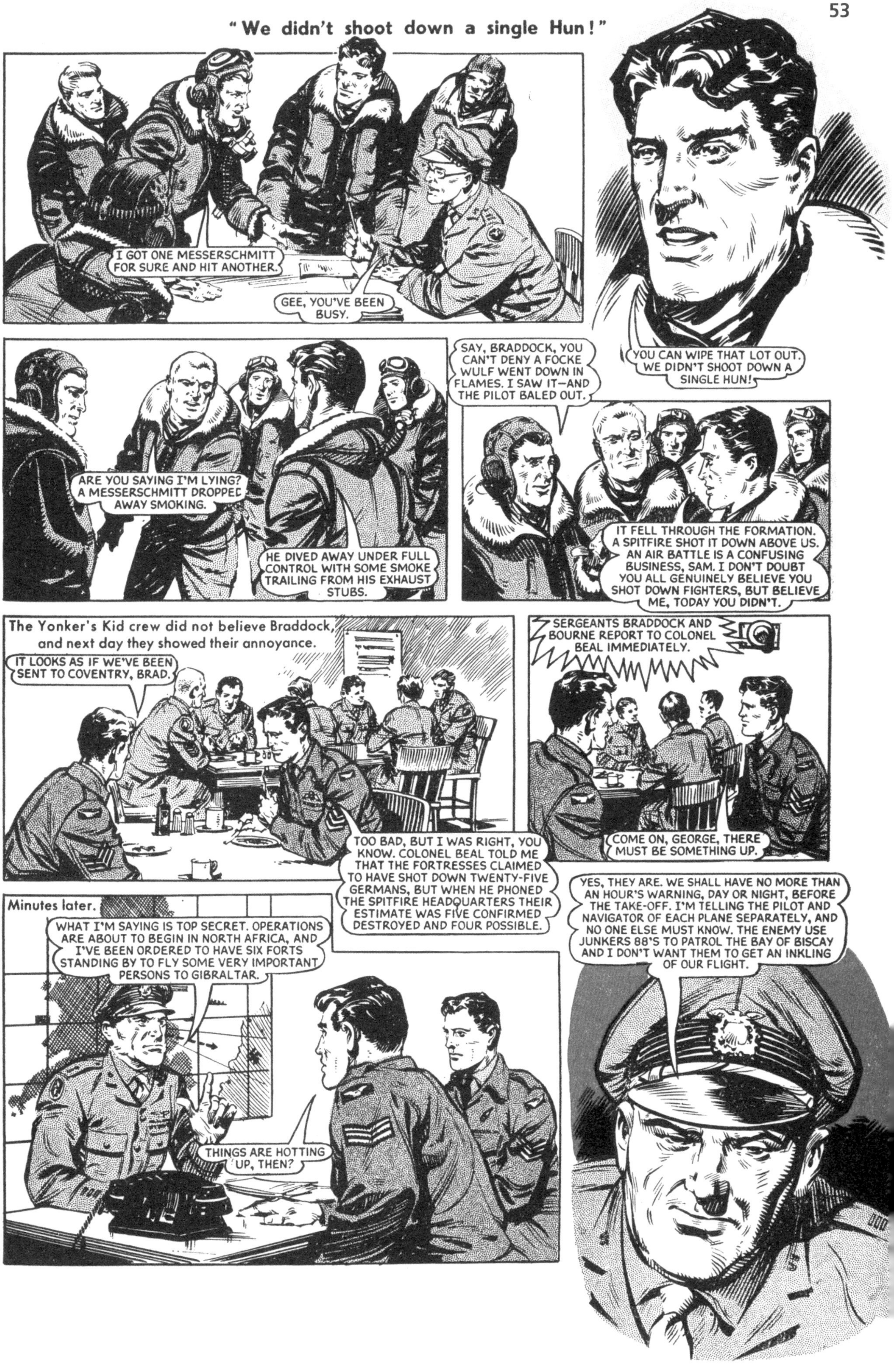
"We didn't shoot down a single Hun!"
I GOT ONE MESSERSCHMITT FOR SURE AND HIT ANOTHER.
GEE, YOU'VE BEEN BUSY.
YOU CAN WIPE THAT LOT OUT. WE DIDN'T SHOOT DOWN A SINGLE HUN!
ARE YOU SAYING I'M LYING? A MESSERSCHMITT DROPPED AWAY SMOKING.
HE DIVED AWAY UNDER FULL CONTROL WITH SOME SMOKE TRAILING FROM HIS EXHAUST STUBS.
SAY, BRADDOCK, YOU CAN'T DENY A FOCKE WULF WENT DOWN IN FLAMES. I SAW IT—AND THE PILOT BALED OUT.
IT FELL THROUGH THE FORMATION. A SPITFIRE SHOT IT DOWN ABOVE US. AN AIR BATTLE IS A CONFUSING BUSINESS, SAM. I DON'T DOUBT YOU ALL GENUINELY BELIEVE YOU SHOT DOWN FIGHTERS, BUT BELIEVE ME, TODAY YOU DIDN'T.
The Yonker's Kid crew did not believe Braddock, and next day they showed their annoyance.
IT LOOKS AS IF WE'VE BEEN SENT TO COVENTRY, BRAD.
TOO BAD, BUT I WAS RIGHT, YOU KNOW. COLONEL BEAL TOLD ME THAT THE FORTRESSES CLAIMED TO HAVE SHOT DOWN TWENTY-FIVE GERMANS, BUT WHEN HE PHONED THE SPITFIRE HEADQUARTERS THEIR ESTIMATE WAS FIVE CONFIRMED DESTROYED AND FOUR POSSIBLE.
SERGEANTS BRADDOCK AND BOURNE REPORT TO COLONEL BEAL IMMEDIATELY.
COME ON, GEORGE, THERE MUST BE SOMETHING UP.
Minutes later.
WHAT I'M SAYING IS TOP SECRET. OPERATIONS ARE ABOUT TO BEGIN IN NORTH AFRICA, AND I'VE BEEN ORDERED TO HAVE SIX FORTS STANDING BY TO FLY SOME VERY IMPORTANT PERSONS TO GIBRALTAR.
THINGS ARE HOTTING UP, THEN?
YES, THEY ARE. WE SHALL HAVE NO MORE THAN AN HOUR'S WARNING, DAY OR NIGHT, BEFORE THE TAKE-OFF. I'M TELLING THE PILOT AND NAVIGATOR OF EACH PLANE SEPARATELY, AND NO ONE ELSE MUST KNOW. THE ENEMY USE JUNKERS 88'S TO PATROL THE BAY OF BISCAY AND I DON'T WANT THEM TO GET AN INKLING OF OUR FLIGHT.

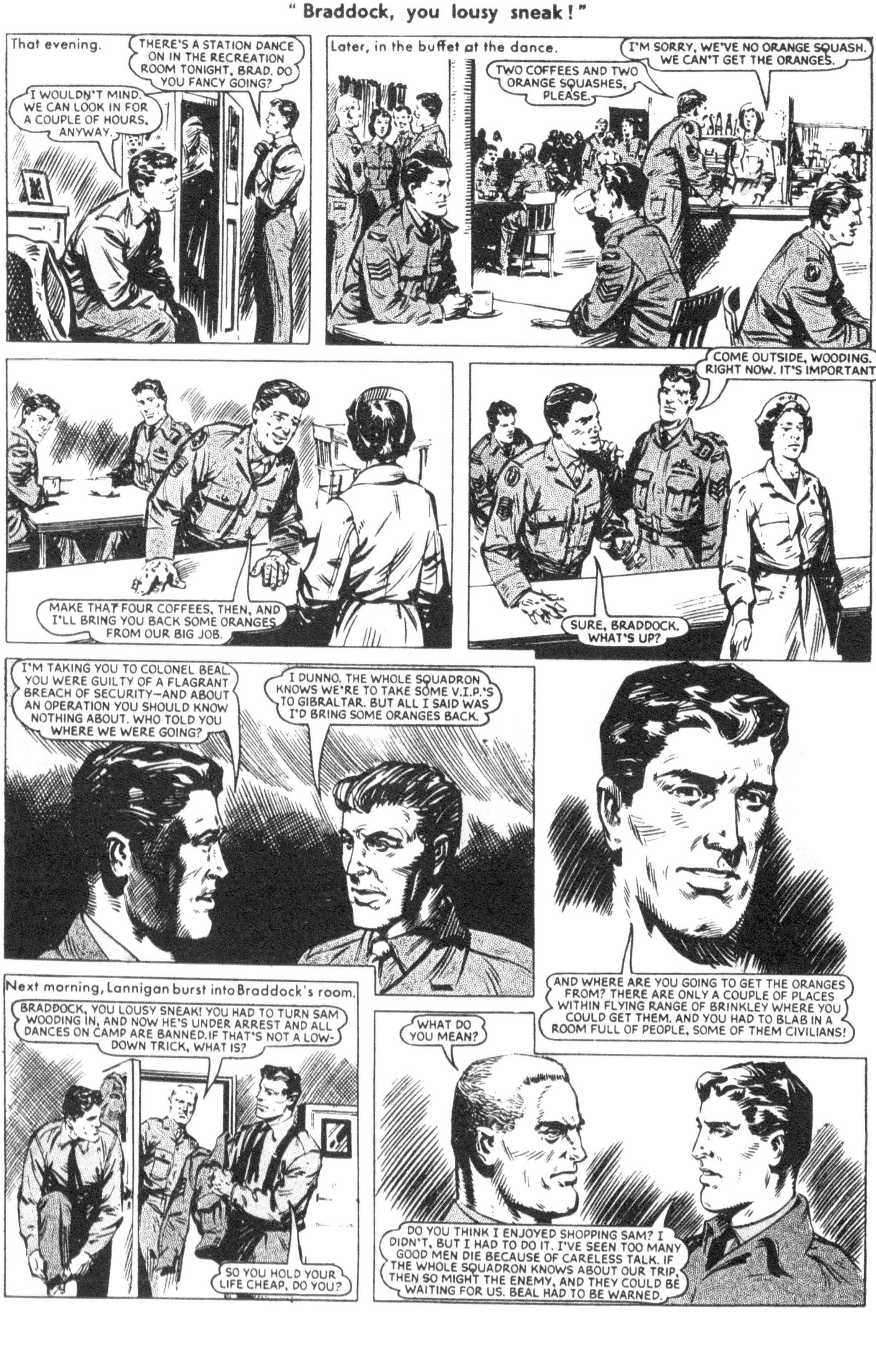
"Braddock, you lousy sneak!"
That evening.
THERE'S A STATION DANCE ON IN THE RECREATION ROOM TONIGHT, BRAD. DO YOU FANCY GOING?
I WOULDN'T MIND. WE CAN LOOK IN FOR A COUPLE OF HOURS, ANYWAY.
Later, in the buffet at the dance.
TWO COFFEES AND TWO ORANGE SQUASHES, PLEASE.
I'M SORRY, WE'VE NO ORANGE SQUASH. WE CAN'T GET THE ORANGES.
MAKE THAT FOUR COFFEES, THEN, AND I'LL BRING YOU BACK SOME ORANGES FROM OUR BIG JOB.
COME OUTSIDE, WOODING. RIGHT NOW. IT'S IMPORTANT.
SURE, BRADDOCK. WHAT'S UP?
I'M TAKING YOU TO COLONEL BEAL. YOU WERE GUILTY OF A FLAGRANT BREACH OF SECURITY—AND ABOUT AN OPERATION YOU SHOULD KNOW NOTHING ABOUT. WHO TOLD YOU WHERE WE WERE GOING?
I DUNNO. THE WHOLE SQUADRON KNOWS WE'RE TO TAKE SOME V.I.P.'S TO GIBRALTAR. BUT ALL I SAID WAS I'D BRING SOME ORANGES BACK.
AND WHERE ARE YOU GOING TO GET THE ORANGES FROM? THERE ARE ONLY A COUPLE OF PLACES WITHIN FLYING RANGE OF BRINKLEY WHERE YOU COULD GET THEM. AND YOU HAD TO BLAB IN A ROOM FULL OF PEOPLE, SOME OF THEM CIVILIANS!
Next morning, Lannigan burst into Braddock's room.
BRADDOCK, YOU LOUSY SNEAK! YOU HAD TO TURN SAM WOODING IN, AND NOW HE'S UNDER ARREST AND ALL DANCES ON CAMP ARE BANNED. IF THAT'S NOT A LOW-DOWN TRICK, WHAT IS?
SO YOU HOLD YOUR LIFE CHEAP, DO YOU?
WHAT DO YOU MEAN?
DO YOU THINK I ENJOYED SHOPPING SAM? I DIDN'T, BUT I HAD TO DO IT. I'VE SEEN TOO MANY GOOD MEN DIE BECAUSE OF CARELESS TALK. IF THE WHOLE SQUADRON KNOWS ABOUT OUR TRIP, THEN SO MIGHT THE ENEMY, AND THEY COULD BE WAITING FOR US. BEAL HAD TO BE WARNED.

"Bandit at nine o'clock!"

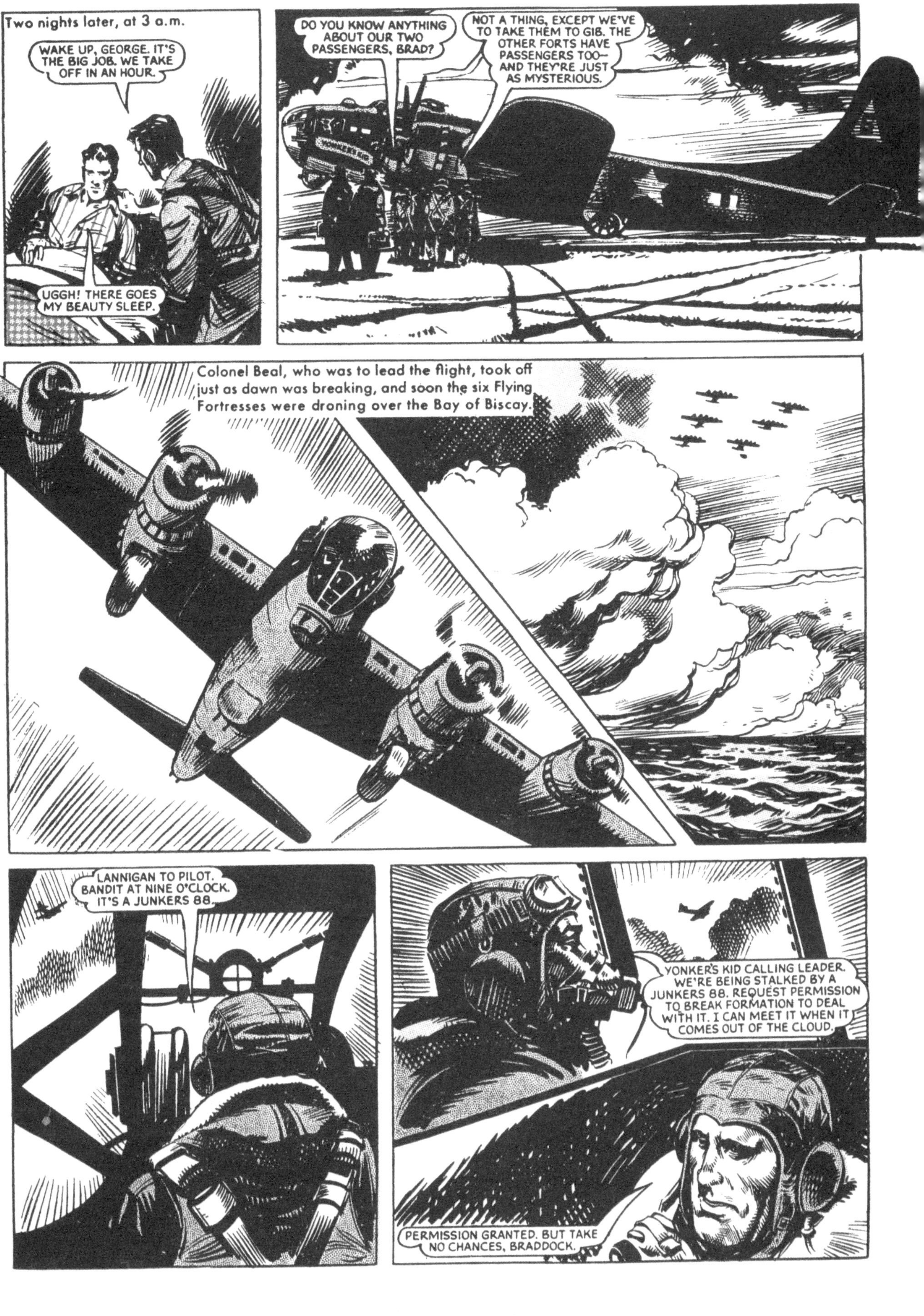
Two nights later, at 3 a.m.
WAKE UP, GEORGE. IT'S THE BIG JOB. WE TAKE OFF IN AN HOUR.
UGGH! THERE GOES MY BEAUTY SLEEP.
DO YOU KNOW ANYTHING ABOUT OUR TWO PASSENGERS, BRAD?
NOT A THING, EXCEPT WE'VE TO TAKE THEM TO GIB. THE OTHER FORTS HAVE PASSENGERS TOO— AND THEY'RE JUST AS MYSTERIOUS.
Colonel Beal, who was to lead the flight, took off just as dawn was breaking, and soon the six Flying Fortresses were droning over the Bay of Biscay.
LANNIGAN TO PILOT. BANDIT AT NINE O'CLOCK. IT'S A JUNKERS 88.
YONKER'S KID CALLING LEADER. WE'RE BEING STALKED BY A JUNKERS 88. REQUEST PERMISSION TO BREAK FORMATION TO DEAL WITH IT. I CAN MEET IT WHEN IT COMES OUT OF THE CLOUD.
PERMISSION GRANTED. BUT TAKE NO CHANCES, BRADDOCK.

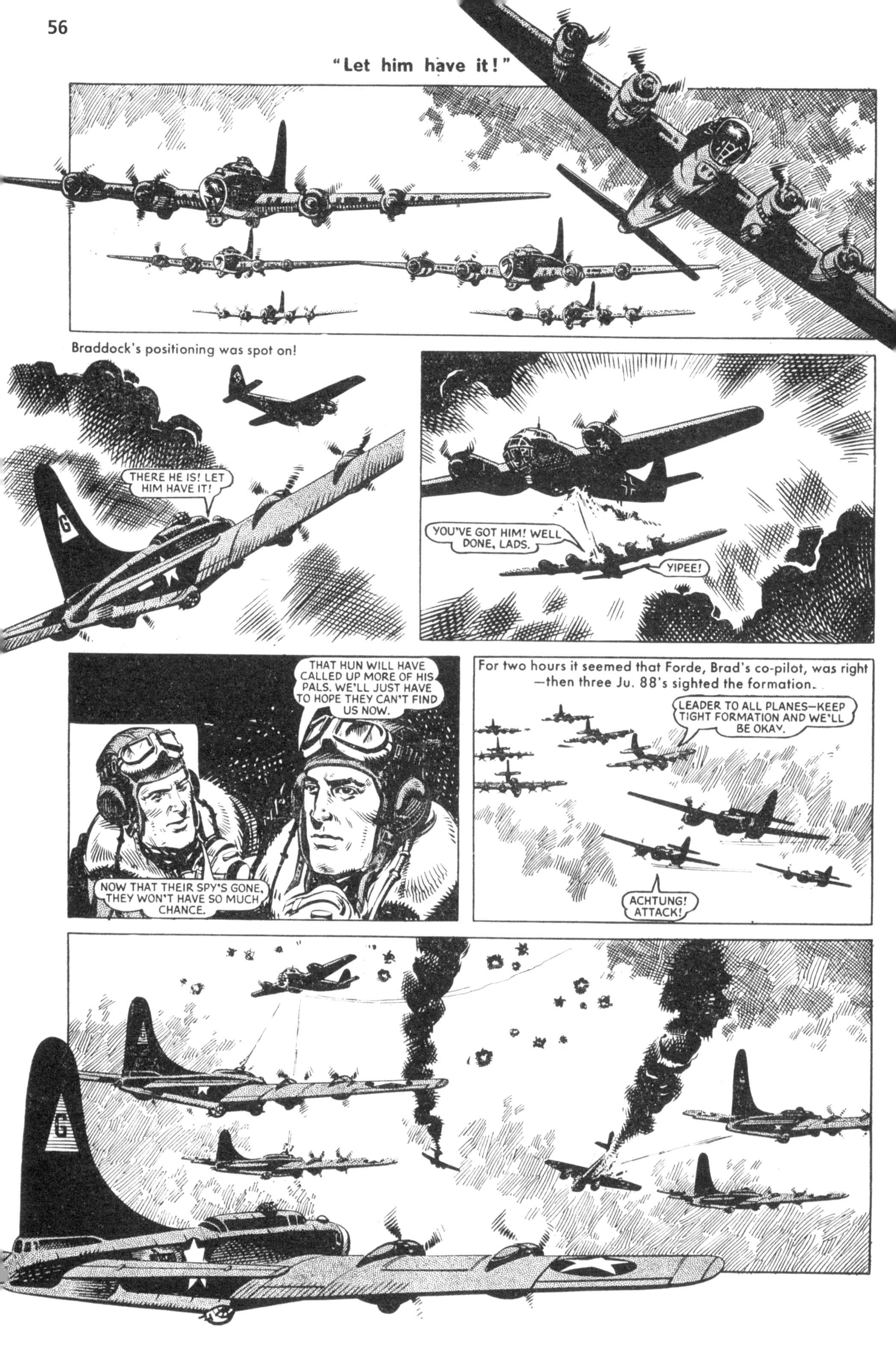
"Let him have it!"
Braddock's positioning was spot on!
THERE HE IS! LET HIM HAVE IT!
YOU'VE GOT HIM! WELL DONE, LADS.
YIPEE!
THAT HUN WILL HAVE CALLED UP MORE OF HIS PALS. WE'LL JUST HAVE TO HOPE THEY CAN'T FIND US NOW.
NOW THAT THEIR SPY'S GONE, THEY WON'T HAVE SO MUCH CHANCE.
For two hours it seemed that Forde, Brad's co-pilot, was right—then three Ju. 88's sighted the formation.
LEADER TO ALL PLANES—KEEP TIGHT FORMATION AND WE'LL BE OKAY.
ACHTUNG! ATTACK!

Mission accomplished!

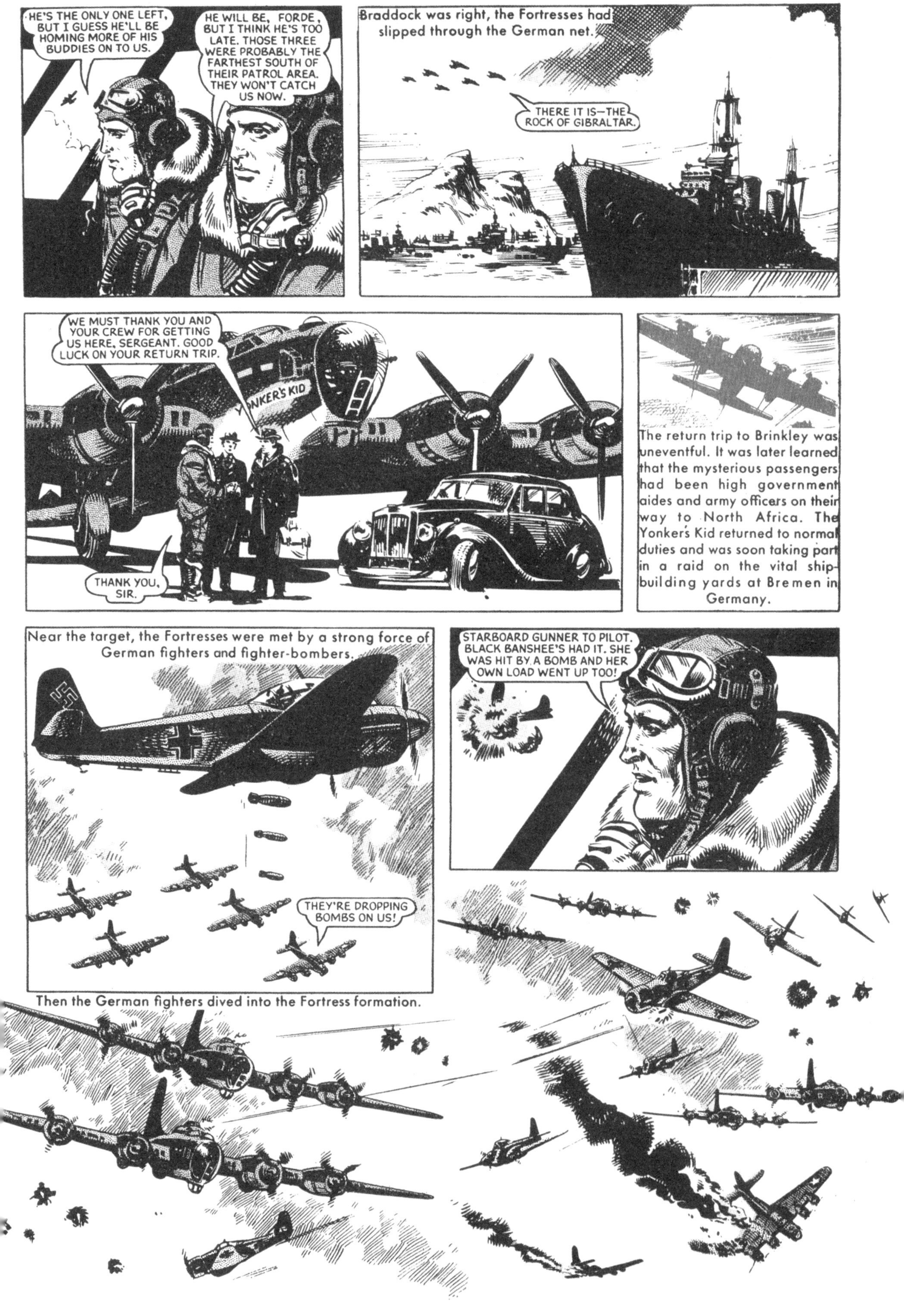
HE'S THE ONLY ONE LEFT, BUT I GUESS HE'LL BE HOMING MORE OF HIS BUDDIES ON TO US.
HE WILL BE, FORDE, BUT I THINK HE'S TOO LATE. THOSE THREE WERE PROBABLY THE FARTHEST SOUTH OF THEIR PATROL AREA. THEY WON'T CATCH US NOW.
Braddock was right, the Fortresses had slipped through the German net.
THERE IT IS—THE ROCK OF GIBRALTAR.
WE MUST THANK YOU AND YOUR CREW FOR GETTING US HERE, SERGEANT. GOOD LUCK ON YOUR RETURN TRIP.
YONKER'S KID
THANK YOU, SIR.
The return trip to Brinkley was uneventful. It was later learned that the mysterious passengers had been high government aides and army officers on their way to North Africa. The Yonker's Kid returned to normal duties and was soon taking part in a raid on the vital ship-building yards at Bremen in Germany.
Near the target, the Fortresses were met by a strong force of German fighters and fighter-bombers.
THEY'RE DROPPING BOMBS ON US!
STARBOARD GUNNER TO PILOT. BLACK BANSHEE'S HAD IT. SHE WAS HIT BY A BOMB AND HER OWN LOAD WENT UP TOO!
Then the German fighters dived into the Fortress formation.

"Bombs away!"

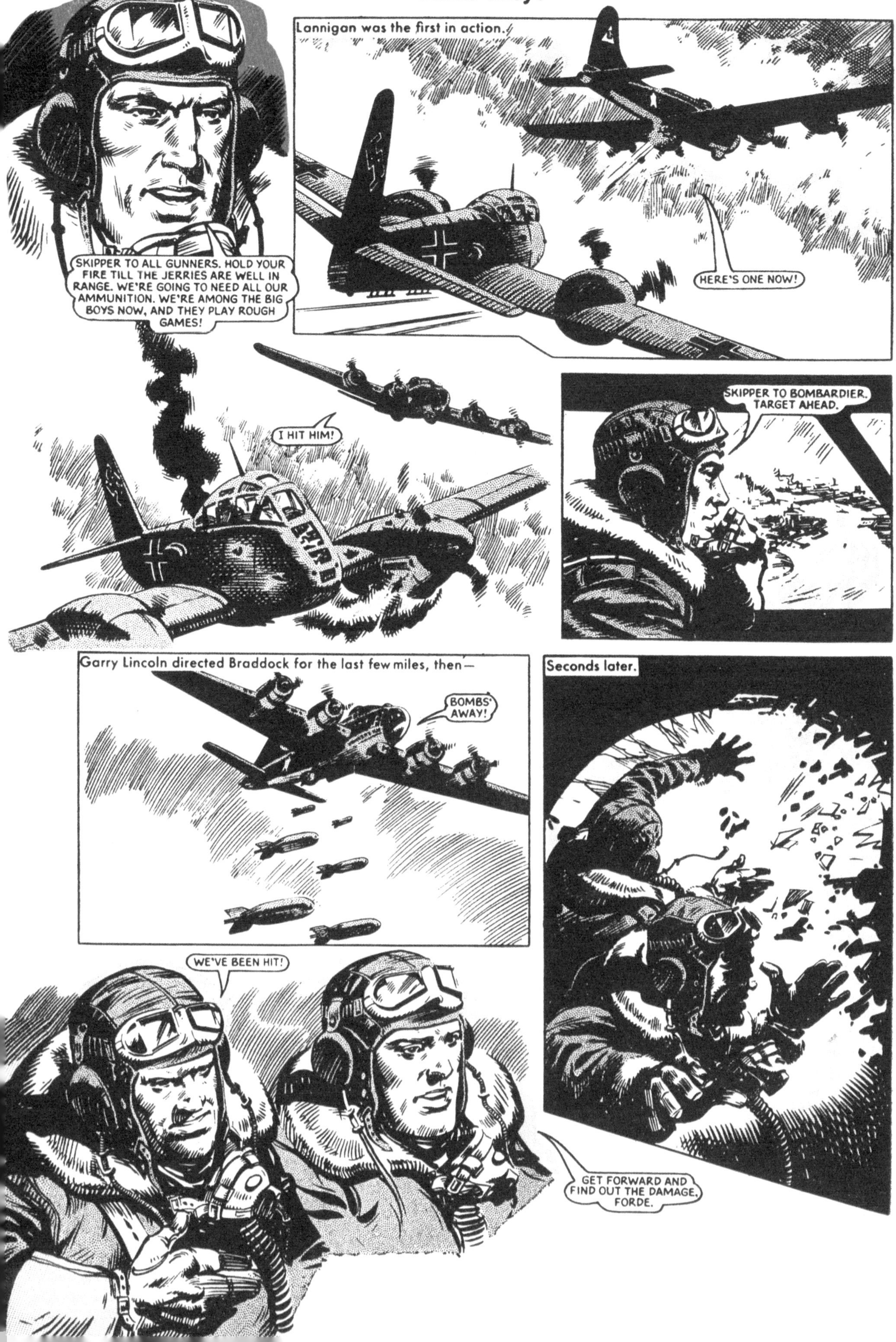
SKIPPER TO ALL GUNNERS. HOLD YOUR FIRE TILL THE JERRIES ARE WELL IN RANGE. WE'RE GOING TO NEED ALL OUR AMMUNITION. WE'RE AMONG THE BIG BOYS NOW, AND THEY PLAY ROUGH GAMES!
Lannigan was the first in action.
HERE'S ONE NOW!
I HIT HIM!
SKIPPER TO BOMBARDIER. TARGET AHEAD.
Garry Lincoln directed Braddock for the last few miles, then—
BOMBS' AWAY!
Seconds later.
WE'VE BEEN HIT!
GET FORWARD AND FIND OUT THE DAMAGE, FORDE.

"The port outer engine has copped it!"

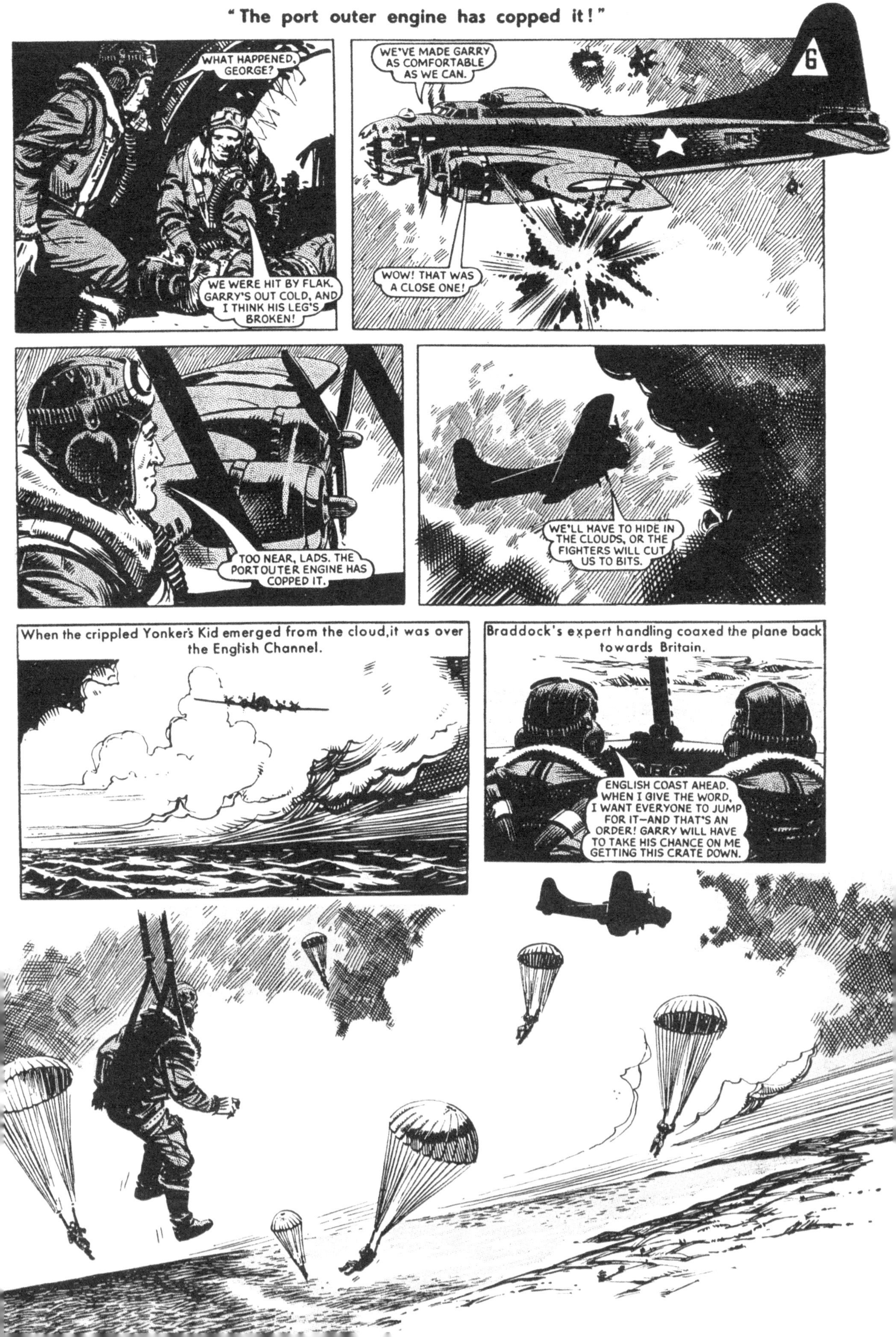

WHAT HAPPENED, GEORGE?
WE WERE HIT BY FLAK. GARRY'S OUT COLD, AND I THINK HIS LEG'S BROKEN!
WE'VE MADE GARRY AS COMFORTABLE AS WE CAN.
WOW! THAT WAS A CLOSE ONE!
TOO NEAR, LADS. THE PORT OUTER ENGINE HAS COPPED IT.
WE'LL HAVE TO HIDE IN THE CLOUDS, OR THE FIGHTERS WILL CUT US TO BITS.
When the crippled Yonker's Kid emerged from the cloud, it was over the English Channel.
Braddock's expert handling coaxed the plane back towards Britain.
ENGLISH COAST AHEAD. WHEN I GIVE THE WORD, I WANT EVERYONE TO JUMP FOR IT—AND THAT'S AN ORDER! GARRY WILL HAVE TO TAKE HIS CHANCE ON ME GETTING THIS CRATE DOWN.

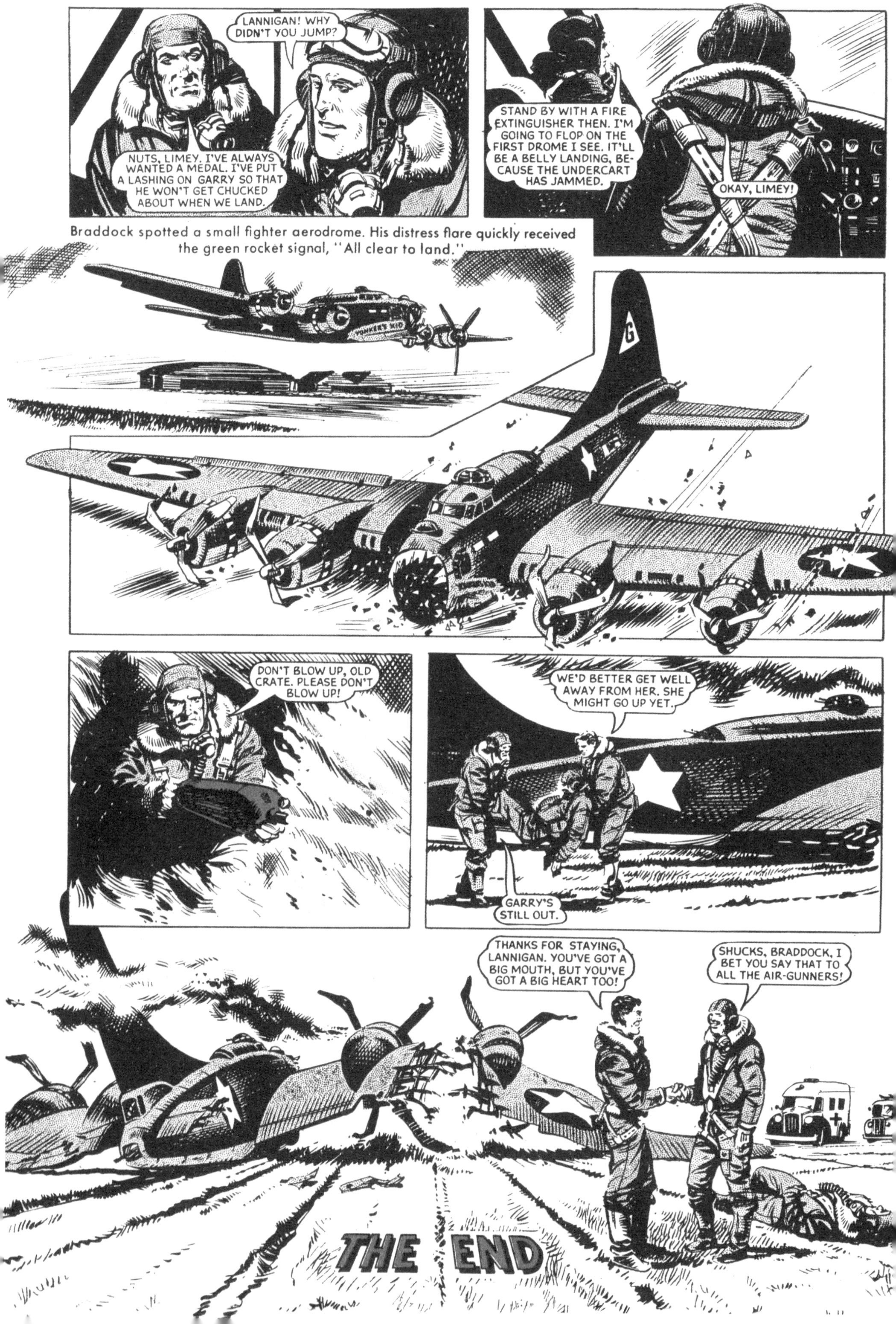
LANNIGAN! WHY DIDN'T YOU JUMP?
NUTS, LIMEY. I'VE ALWAYS WANTED A MEDAL. I'VE PUT A LASHING ON GARRY SO THAT HE WON'T GET CHUCKED ABOUT WHEN WE LAND.
STAND BY WITH A FIRE EXTINGUISHER THEN. I'M GOING TO FLOP ON THE FIRST DROME I SEE. IT'LL BE A BELLY LANDING, BECAUSE THE UNDERCART HAS JAMMED.
OKAY, LIMEY!
Braddock spotted a small fighter aerodrome. His distress flare quickly received the green rocket signal, "All clear to land."
DON'T BLOW UP, OLD CRATE. PLEASE DON'T BLOW UP!
WE'D BETTER GET WELL AWAY FROM HER. SHE MIGHT GO UP YET.
GARRY'S STILL OUT.
THANKS FOR STAYING, LANNIGAN. YOU'VE GOT A BIG MOUTH, BUT YOU'VE GOT A BIG HEART TOO!
SHUCKS, BRADDOCK, I BET YOU SAY THAT TO ALL THE AIR-GUNNERS!
THE END

THE LANCER LAUGHED LAST!

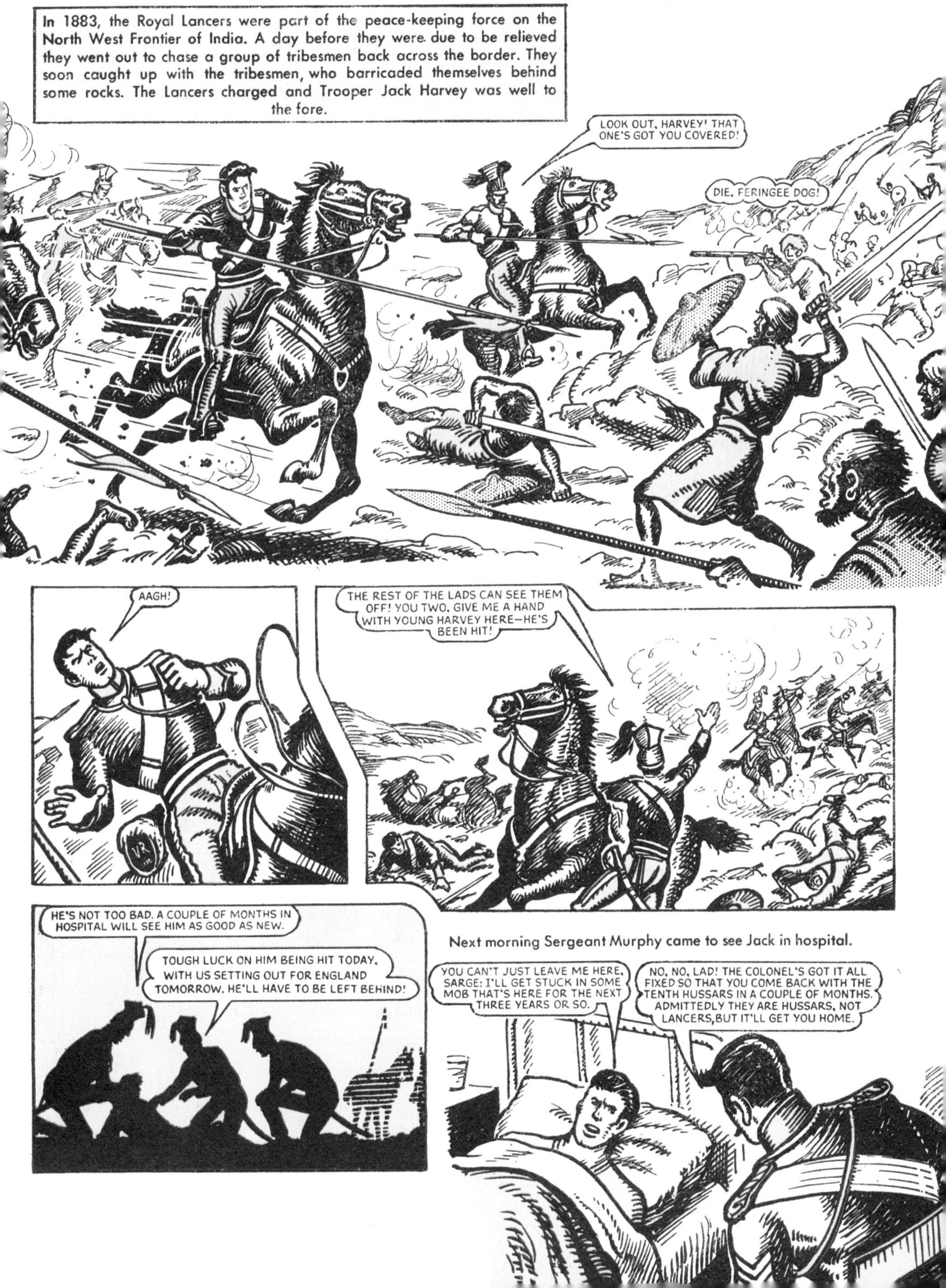

In 1883, the Royal Lancers were part of the peace-keeping force on the North West Frontier of India. A day before they were due to be relieved they went out to chase a group of tribesmen back across the border. They soon caught up with the tribesmen, who barricaded themselves behind some rocks. The Lancers charged and Trooper Jack Harvey was well to the fore.
LOOK OUT, HARVEY! THAT ONE'S GOT YOU COVERED!
DIE, FERINGEE DOG!
AAGH!
THE REST OF THE LADS CAN SEE THEM OFF! YOU TWO, GIVE ME A HAND WITH YOUNG HARVEY HERE—HE'S BEEN HIT!
HE'S NOT TOO BAD. A COUPLE OF MONTHS IN HOSPITAL WILL SEE HIM AS GOOD AS NEW.
TOUGH LUCK ON HIM BEING HIT TODAY, WITH US SETTING OUT FOR ENGLAND TOMORROW. HE'LL HAVE TO BE LEFT BEHIND!
Next morning Sergeant Murphy came to see Jack in hospital.
YOU CAN'T JUST LEAVE ME HERE, SARGE: I'LL GET STUCK IN SOME MOB THAT'S HERE FOR THE NEXT THREE YEARS OR SO.
NO, NO, LAD! THE COLONEL'S GOT IT ALL FIXED SO THAT YOU COME BACK WITH THE TENTH HUSSARS IN A COUPLE OF MONTHS. ADMITTEDLY THEY ARE HUSSARS, NOT LANCERS, BUT IT'LL GET YOU HOME.

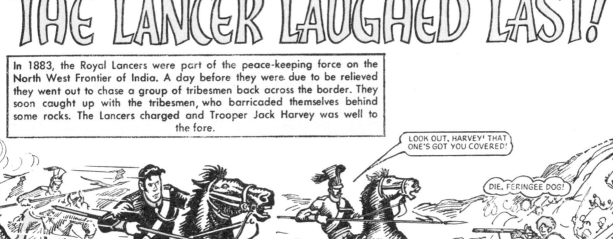

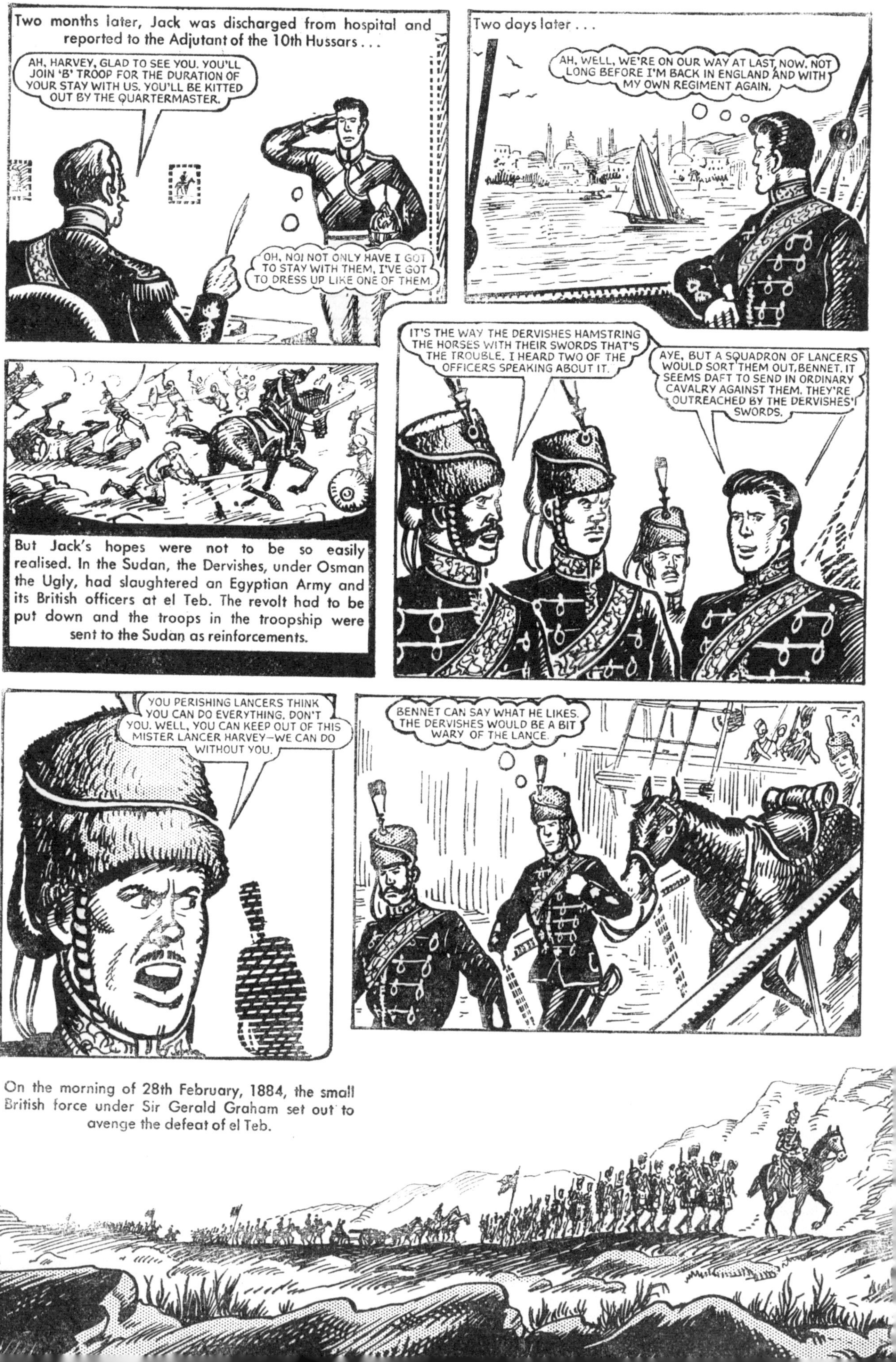
Two months later, Jack was discharged from hospital and reported to the Adjutant of the 10th Hussars . . .
AH, HARVEY, GLAD TO SEE YOU. YOU'LL JOIN 'B' TROOP FOR THE DURATION OF YOUR STAY WITH US. YOU'LL BE KITTED OUT BY THE QUARTERMASTER.
OH, NO! NOT ONLY HAVE I GOT TO STAY WITH THEM, I'VE GOT TO DRESS UP LIKE ONE OF THEM.
Two days later . . .
AH, WELL, WE'RE ON OUR WAY AT LAST, NOW. NOT LONG BEFORE I'M BACK IN ENGLAND AND WITH MY OWN REGIMENT AGAIN.
But Jack's hopes were not to be so easily realised. In the Sudan, the Dervishes, under Osman the Ugly, had slaughtered an Egyptian Army and its British officers at el Teb. The revolt had to be put down and the troops in the troopship were sent to the Sudan as reinforcements.
IT'S THE WAY THE DERVISHES HAMSTRING THE HORSES WITH THEIR SWORDS THAT'S THE TROUBLE. I HEARD TWO OF THE OFFICERS SPEAKING ABOUT IT.
AYE, BUT A SQUADRON OF LANCERS WOULD SORT THEM OUT, BENNET. IT SEEMS DAFT TO SEND IN ORDINARY CAVALRY AGAINST THEM. THEY'RE OUTREACHED BY THE DERVISHES' SWORDS.
YOU PERISHING LANCERS THINK YOU CAN DO EVERYTHING, DON'T YOU. WELL, YOU CAN KEEP OUT OF THIS MISTER LANCER HARVEY—WE CAN DO WITHOUT YOU.
BENNET CAN SAY WHAT HE LIKES. THE DERVISHES WOULD BE A BIT WARY OF THE LANCE.
On the morning of 28th February, 1884, the small British force under Sir Gerald Graham set out to avenge the defeat of el Teb.

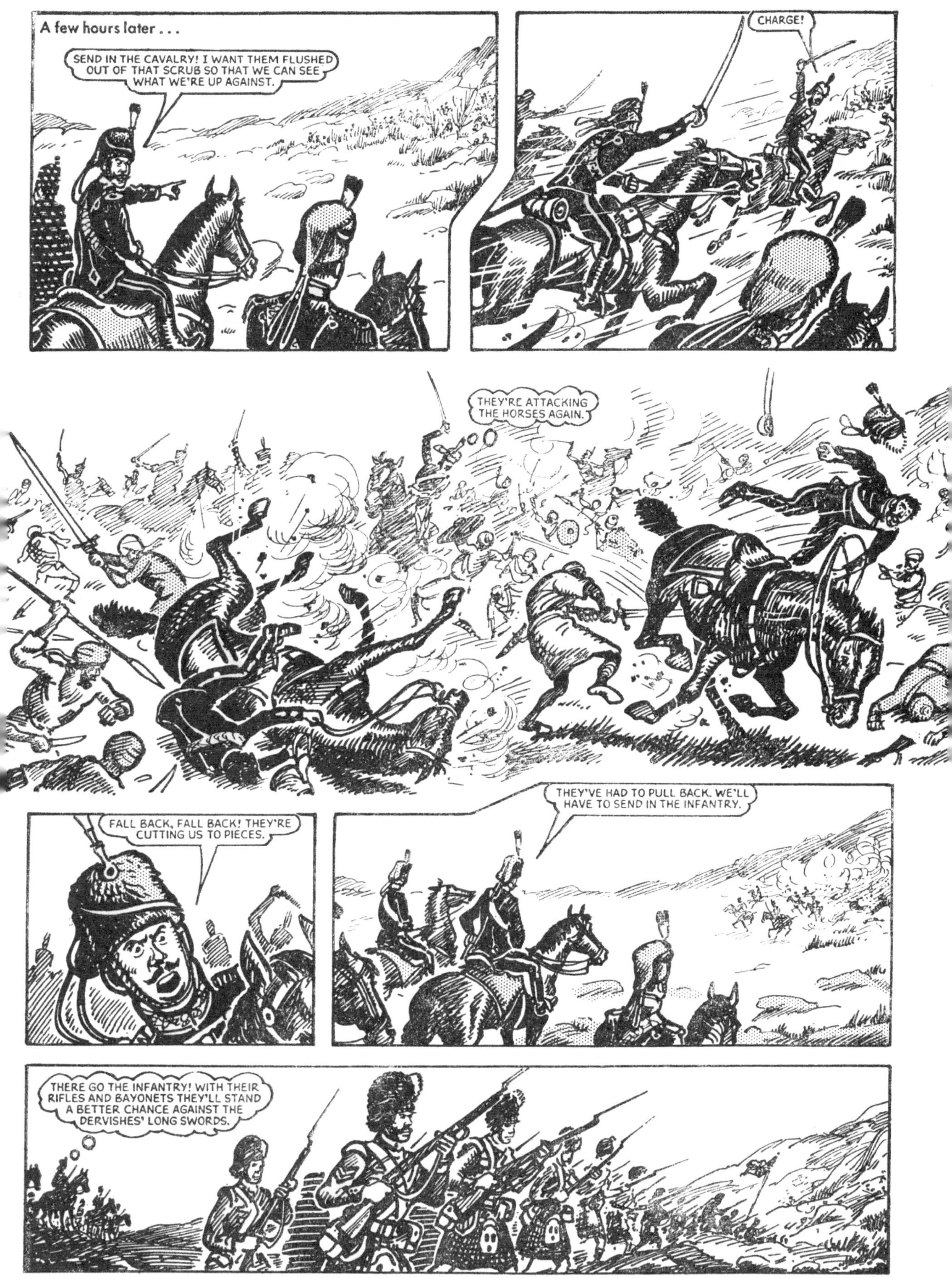
A few hours later . . .
SEND IN THE CAVALRY! I WANT THEM FLUSHED OUT OF THAT SCRUB SO THAT WE CAN SEE WHAT WE'RE UP AGAINST.
CHARGE!
THEY'RE ATTACKING THE HORSES AGAIN.
FALL BACK, FALL BACK! THEY'RE CUTTING US TO PIECES.
THEY'VE HAD TO PULL BACK. WE'LL HAVE TO SEND IN THE INFANTRY.
THERE GO THE INFANTRY! WITH THEIR RIFLES AND BAYONETS THEY'LL STAND A BETTER CHANCE AGAINST THE DERVISHES' LONG SWORDS.

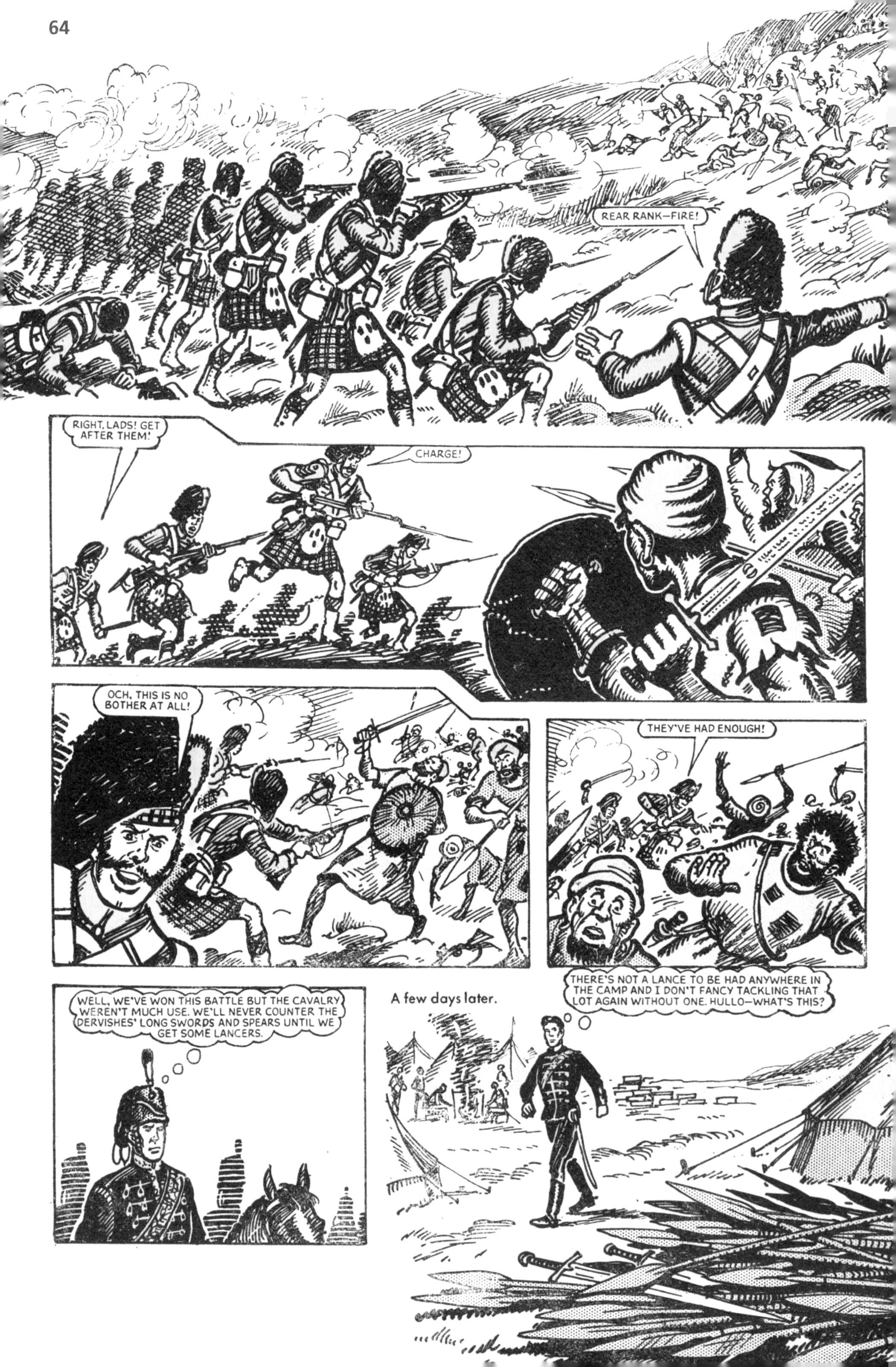
REAR RANK—FIRE!
RIGHT, LADS! GET AFTER THEM!
CHARGE!
OCH, THIS IS NO BOTHER AT ALL!
THEY'VE HAD ENOUGH!
WELL, WE'VE WON THIS BATTLE BUT THE CAVALRY WEREN'T MUCH USE. WE'LL NEVER COUNTER THE DERVISHES' LONG SWORDS AND SPEARS UNTIL WE GET SOME LANCERS.
A few days later.
THERE'S NOT A LANCE TO BE HAD ANYWHERE IN THE CAMP AND I DON'T FANCY TACKLING THAT LOT AGAIN WITHOUT ONE. HULLO—WHAT'S THIS?

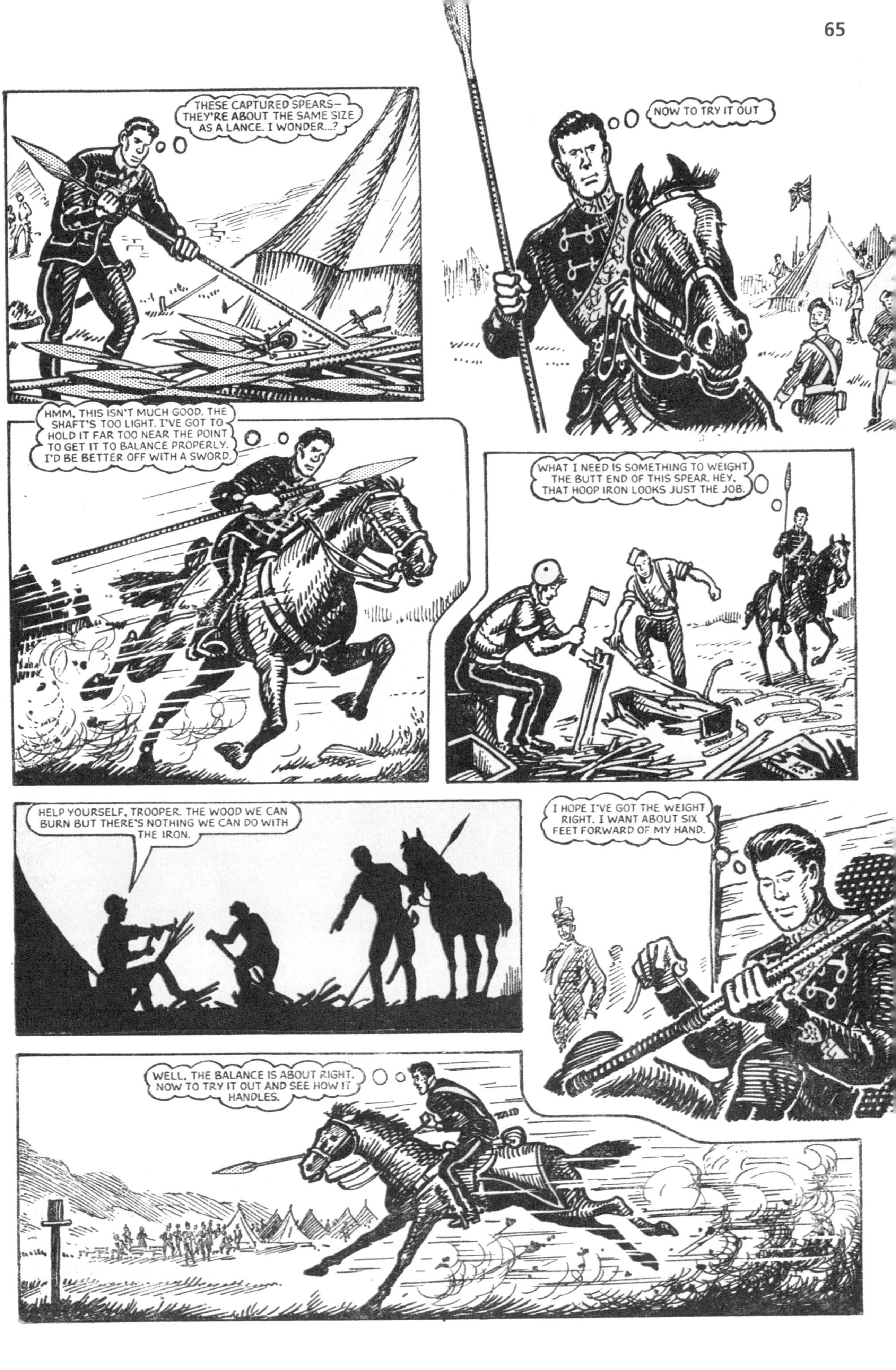
THESE CAPTURED SPEARS— THEY'RE ABOUT THE SAME SIZE AS A LANCE. I WONDER...?
NOW TO TRY IT OUT
HMM, THIS ISN'T MUCH GOOD. THE SHAFT'S TOO LIGHT. I'VE GOT TO HOLD IT FAR TOO NEAR THE POINT TO GET IT TO BALANCE PROPERLY. I'D BE BETTER OFF WITH A SWORD.
WHAT I NEED IS SOMETHING TO WEIGHT THE BUTT END OF THIS SPEAR. HEY, THAT HOOP IRON LOOKS JUST THE JOB.
HELP YOURSELF, TROOPER. THE WOOD WE CAN BURN BUT THERE'S NOTHING WE CAN DO WITH THE IRON.
I HOPE I'VE GOT THE WEIGHT RIGHT. I WANT ABOUT SIX FEET FORWARD OF MY HAND.
WELL, THE BALANCE IS ABOUT RIGHT. NOW TO TRY IT OUT AND SEE HOW IT HANDLES.

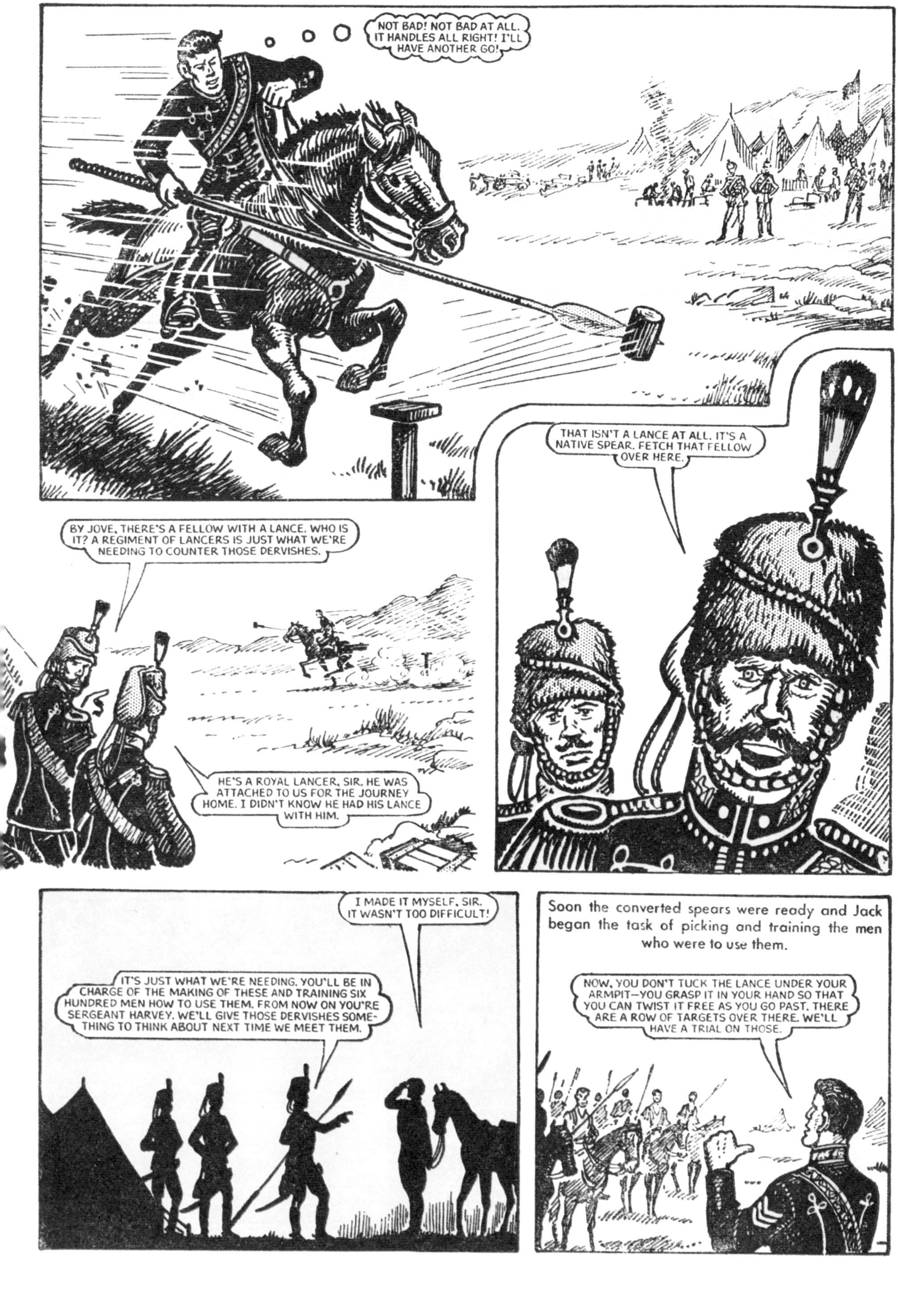
NOT BAD! NOT BAD AT ALL. IT HANDLES ALL RIGHT! I'LL HAVE ANOTHER GO!
BY JOVE, THERE'S A FELLOW WITH A LANCE. WHO IS IT? A REGIMENT OF LANCERS IS JUST WHAT WE'RE NEEDING TO COUNTER THOSE DERVISHES.
HE'S A ROYAL LANCER, SIR. HE WAS ATTACHED TO US FOR THE JOURNEY HOME. I DIDN'T KNOW HE HAD HIS LANCE WITH HIM.
THAT ISN'T A LANCE AT ALL. IT'S A NATIVE SPEAR. FETCH THAT FELLOW OVER HERE.
I MADE IT MYSELF, SIR. IT WASN'T TOO DIFFICULT!
IT'S JUST WHAT WE'RE NEEDING. YOU'LL BE IN CHARGE OF THE MAKING OF THESE AND TRAINING SIX HUNDRED MEN HOW TO USE THEM. FROM NOW ON YOU'RE SERGEANT HARVEY. WE'LL GIVE THOSE DERVISHES SOME-THING TO THINK ABOUT NEXT TIME WE MEET THEM.
Soon the converted spears were ready and Jack began the task of picking and training the men who were to use them.
NOW, YOU DON'T TUCK THE LANCE UNDER YOUR ARMPIT—YOU GRASP IT IN YOUR HAND SO THAT YOU CAN TWIST IT FREE AS YOU GO PAST. THERE ARE A ROW OF TARGETS OVER THERE. WE'LL HAVE A TRIAL ON THOSE.

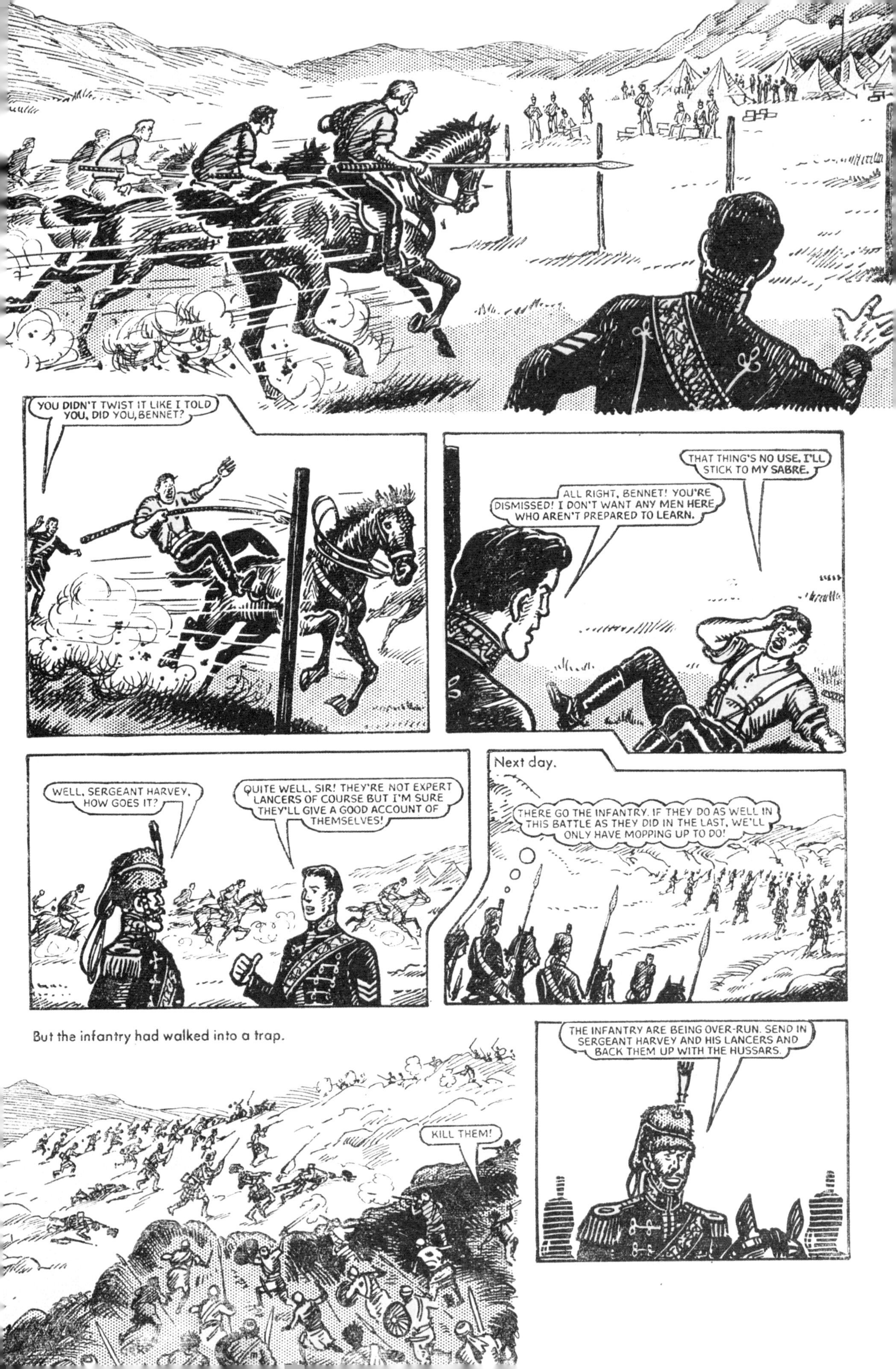
YOU DIDN'T TWIST IT LIKE I TOLD YOU, DID YOU, BENNET?
THAT THING'S NO USE. I'LL STICK TO MY SABRE.
ALL RIGHT, BENNET! YOU'RE DISMISSED! I DON'T WANT ANY MEN HERE WHO AREN'T PREPARED TO LEARN.
WELL, SERGEANT HARVEY, HOW GOES IT?
QUITE WELL, SIR! THEY'RE NOT EXPERT LANCERS OF COURSE BUT I'M SURE THEY'LL GIVE A GOOD ACCOUNT OF THEMSELVES!
Next day.
THERE GO THE INFANTRY. IF THEY DO AS WELL IN THIS BATTLE AS THEY DID IN THE LAST, WE'LL ONLY HAVE MOPPING UP TO DO!
But the infantry had walked into a trap.
KILL THEM!
THE INFANTRY ARE BEING OVER-RUN. SEND IN SERGEANT HARVEY AND HIS LANCERS AND BACK THEM UP WITH THE HUSSARS.

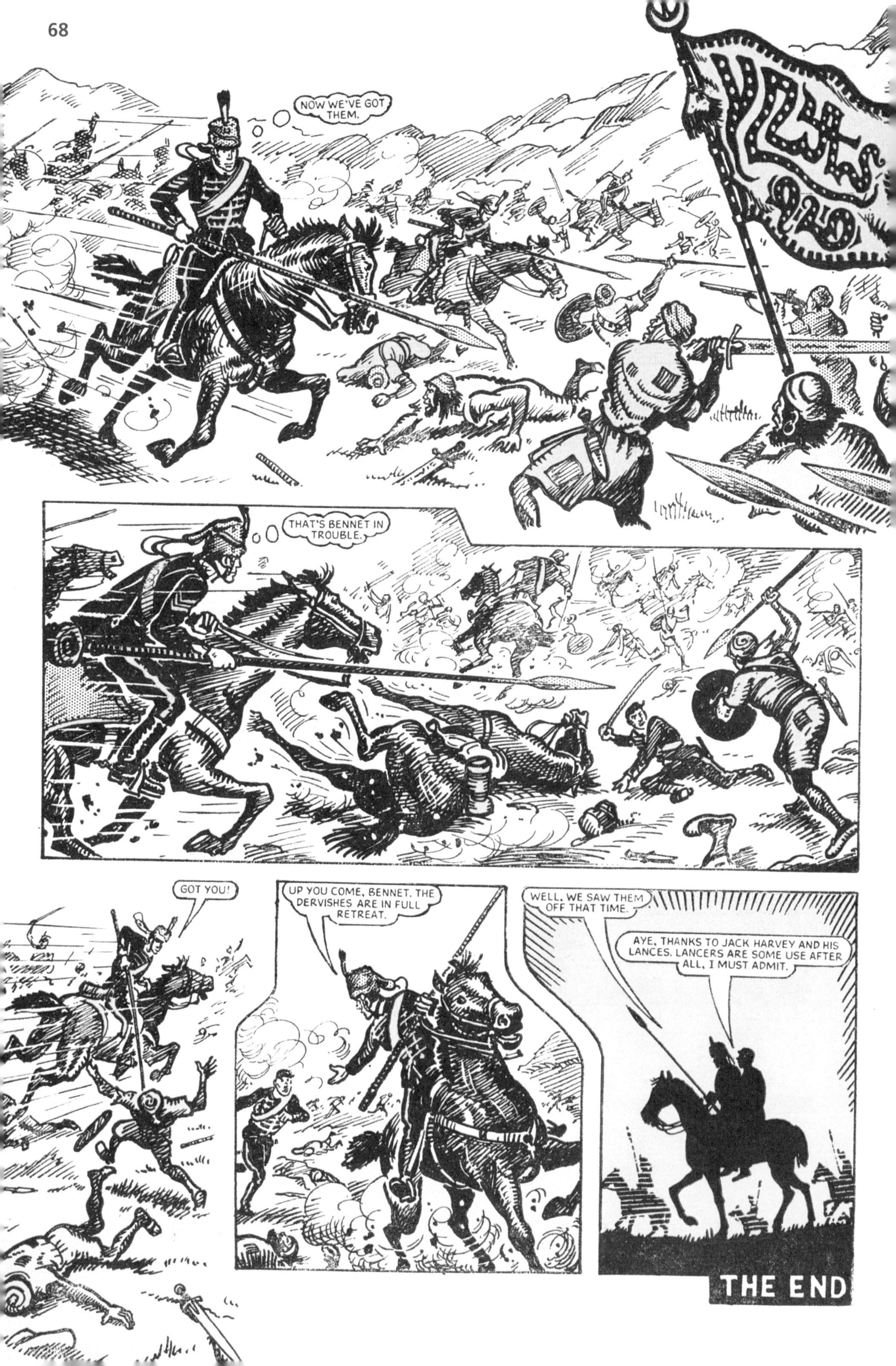
NOW WE'VE GOT THEM.
THAT'S BENNET IN TROUBLE.
GOT YOU!
UP YOU COME, BENNET. THE DERVISHES ARE IN FULL RETREAT.
WELL, WE SAW THEM OFF THAT TIME.
AYE, THANKS TO JACK HARVEY AND HIS LANCES. LANCERS ARE SOME USE AFTER ALL, I MUST ADMIT.
THE END

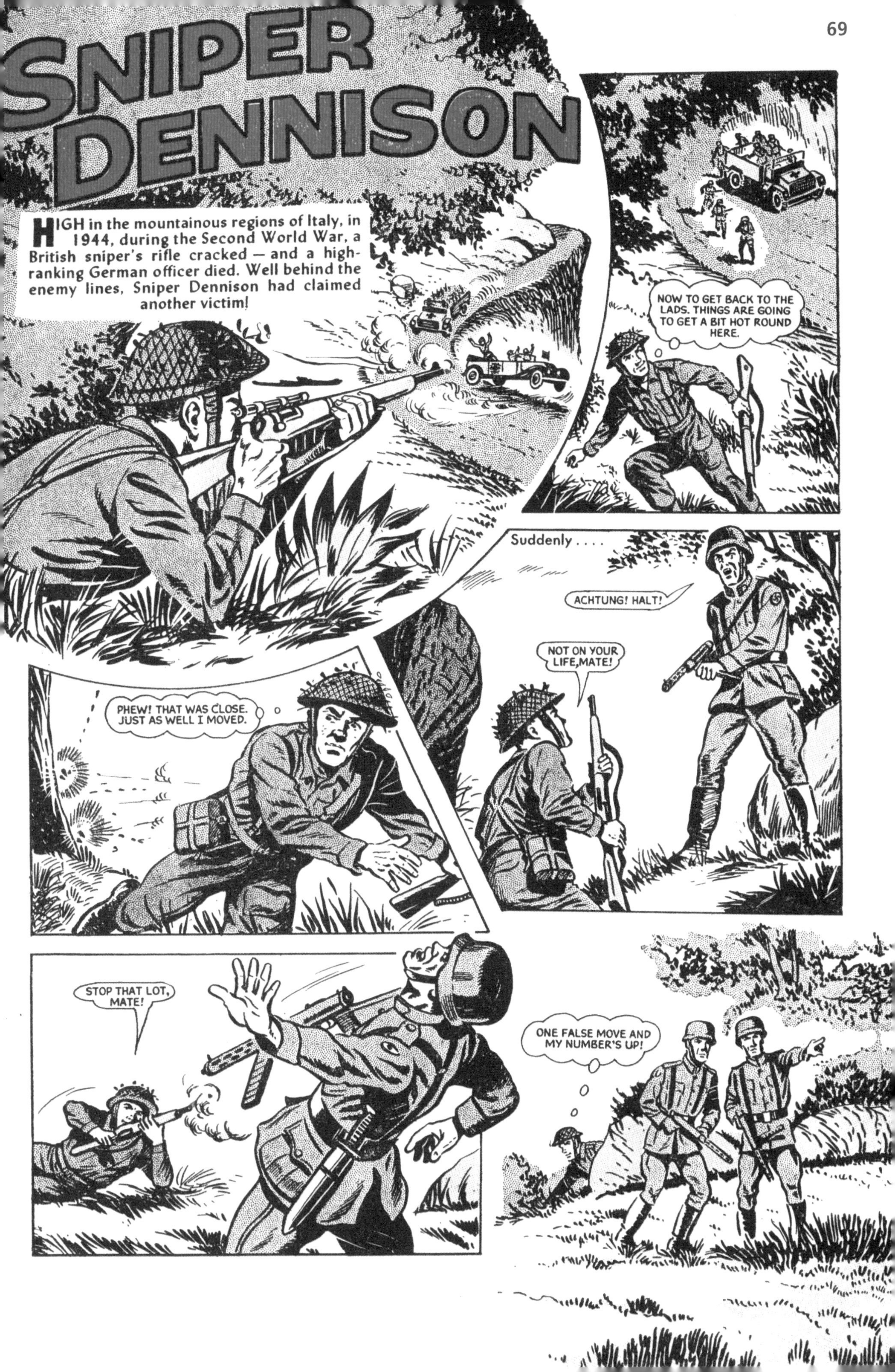
SNIPER DENNISON
HIGH in the mountainous regions of Italy, in 1944, during the Second World War, a British sniper's rifle cracked — and a high-ranking German officer died. Well behind the enemy lines, Sniper Dennison had claimed another victim!
NOW TO GET BACK TO THE LADS. THINGS ARE GOING TO GET A BIT HOT ROUND HERE.
PHEW! THAT WAS CLOSE. JUST AS WELL I MOVED.
Suddenly . . . .
ACHTUNG! HALT!
NOT ON YOUR LIFE, MATE!
STOP THAT LOT, MATE!
ONE FALSE MOVE AND MY NUMBER'S UP!

Behind the German lines!

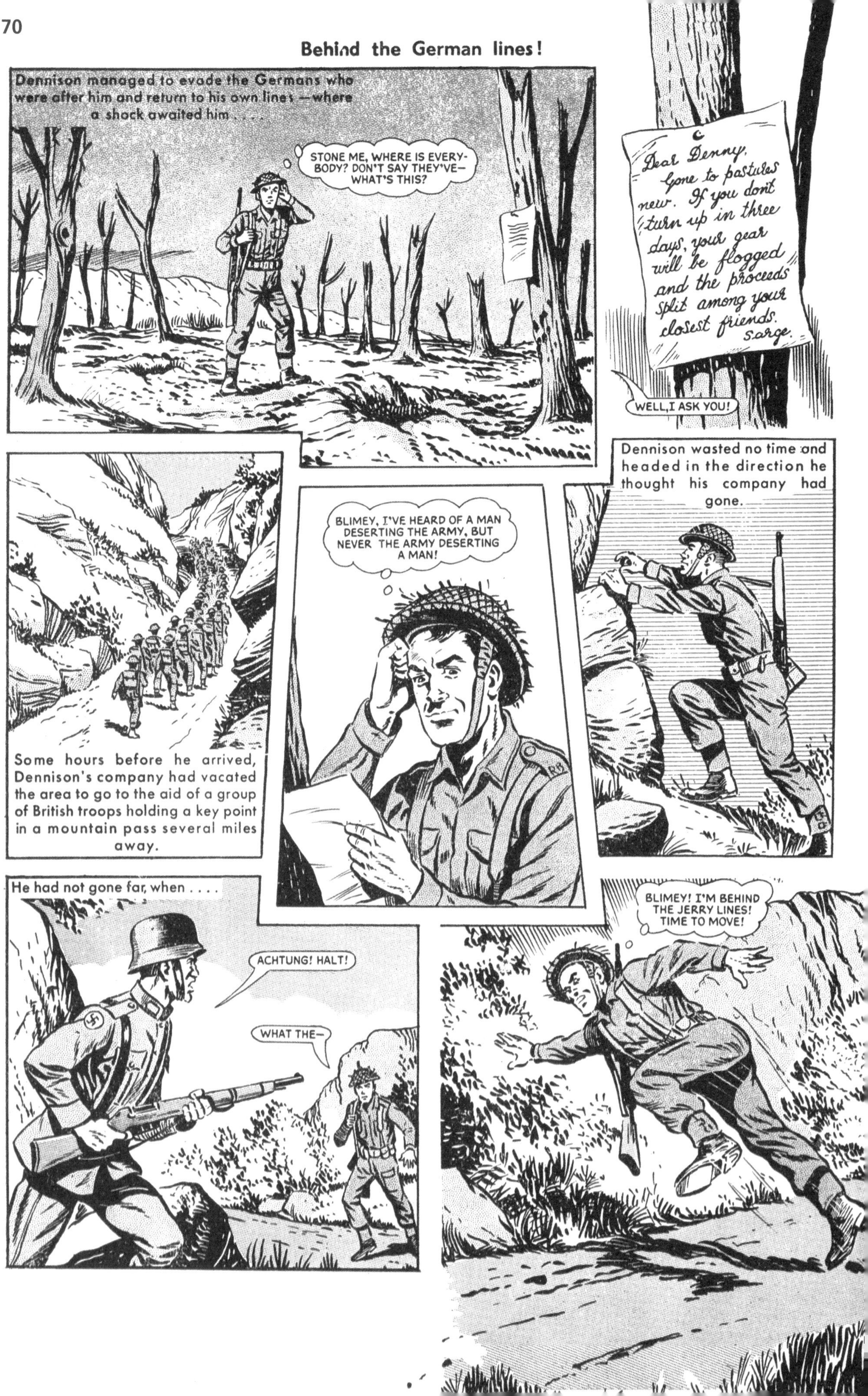
Dennison managed to evade the Germans who were after him and return to his own lines — where a shock awaited him . . . .
STONE ME, WHERE IS EVERY-BODY? DON'T SAY THEY'VE— WHAT'S THIS?
Dear Denny, Gone to pastules new. If you dont turn up in three days, your gear will be flogged and the proceeds split among your closest friends. Sarge.
WELL, I ASK YOU!
Some hours before he arrived, Dennison's company had vacated the area to go to the aid of a group of British troops holding a key point in a mountain pass several miles away.
BLIMEY, I'VE HEARD OF A MAN DESERTING THE ARMY, BUT NEVER THE ARMY DESERTING A MAN!
Dennison wasted no time and headed in the direction he thought his company had gone.
He had not gone far, when . . . .
ACHTUNG! HALT!
WHAT THE—
BLIMEY! I'M BEHIND THE JERRY LINES! TIME TO MOVE!

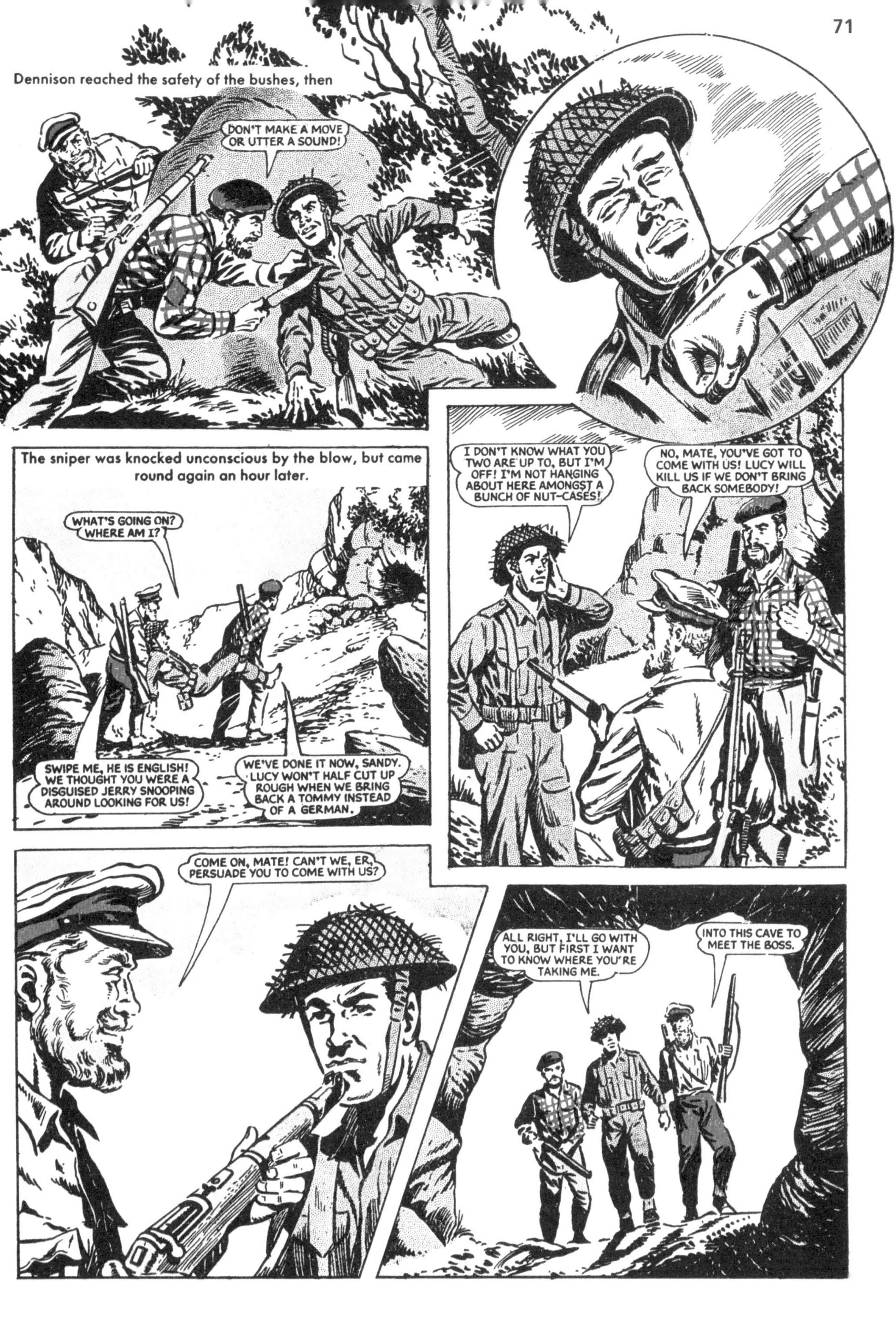
Dennison reached the safety of the bushes, then
DON'T MAKE A MOVE OR UTTER A SOUND!
The sniper was knocked unconscious by the blow, but came round again an hour later.
WHAT'S GOING ON? WHERE AM I?
SWIPE ME, HE IS ENGLISH! WE THOUGHT YOU WERE A DISGUISED JERRY SNOOPING AROUND LOOKING FOR US!
WE'VE DONE IT NOW, SANDY. LUCY WON'T HALF CUT UP ROUGH WHEN WE BRING BACK A TOMMY INSTEAD OF A GERMAN.
I DON'T KNOW WHAT YOU TWO ARE UP TO, BUT I'M OFF! I'M NOT HANGING ABOUT HERE AMONGST A BUNCH OF NUT-CASES!
NO, MATE, YOU'VE GOT TO COME WITH US! LUCY WILL KILL US IF WE DON'T BRING BACK SOMEBODY!
COME ON, MATE! CAN'T WE, ER, PERSUADE YOU TO COME WITH US?
ALL RIGHT, I'LL GO WITH YOU, BUT FIRST I WANT TO KNOW WHERE YOU'RE TAKING ME.
INTO THIS CAVE TO MEET THE BOSS.

The underground arsenal.

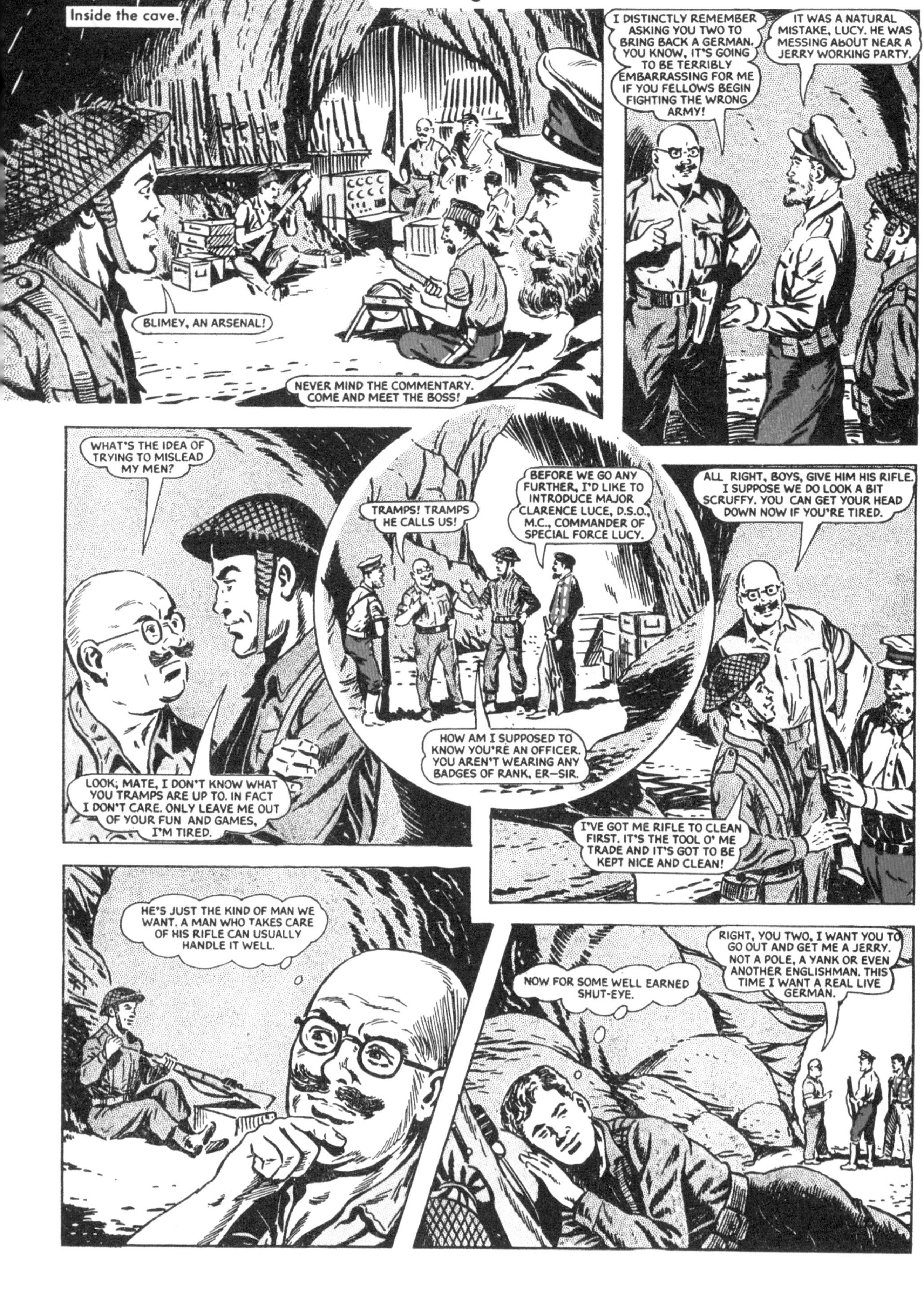
Inside the cave.
BLIMEY, AN ARSENAL!
NEVER MIND THE COMMENTARY. COME AND MEET THE BOSS!
I DISTINCTLY REMEMBER ASKING YOU TWO TO BRING BACK A GERMAN. YOU KNOW, IT'S GOING TO BE TERRIBLY EMBARRASSING FOR ME IF YOU FELLOWS BEGIN FIGHTING THE WRONG ARMY!
IT WAS A NATURAL MISTAKE, LUCY. HE WAS MESSING ABOUT NEAR A JERRY WORKING PARTY.
WHAT'S THE IDEA OF TRYING TO MISLEAD MY MEN?
LOOK, MATE, I DON'T KNOW WHAT YOU TRAMPS ARE UP TO. IN FACT I DON'T CARE. ONLY LEAVE ME OUT OF YOUR FUN AND GAMES, I'M TIRED.
TRAMPS! TRAMPS HE CALLS US!
BEFORE WE GO ANY FURTHER, I'D LIKE TO INTRODUCE MAJOR CLARENCE LUCE, D.S.O., M.C., COMMANDER OF SPECIAL FORCE LUCY.
HOW AM I SUPPOSED TO KNOW YOU'RE AN OFFICER. YOU AREN'T WEARING ANY BADGES OF RANK, ER—SIR.
ALL RIGHT, BOYS, GIVE HIM HIS RIFLE. I SUPPOSE WE DO LOOK A BIT SCRUFFY. YOU CAN GET YOUR HEAD DOWN NOW IF YOU'RE TIRED.
I'VE GOT ME RIFLE TO CLEAN FIRST. IT'S THE TOOL O' ME TRADE AND IT'S GOT TO BE KEPT NICE AND CLEAN!
HE'S JUST THE KIND OF MAN WE WANT. A MAN WHO TAKES CARE OF HIS RIFLE CAN USUALLY HANDLE IT WELL.
NOW FOR SOME WELL EARNED SHUT-EYE.
RIGHT, YOU TWO, I WANT YOU TO GO OUT AND GET ME A JERRY. NOT A POLE, A YANK OR EVEN ANOTHER ENGLISHMAN. THIS TIME I WANT A REAL LIVE GERMAN.

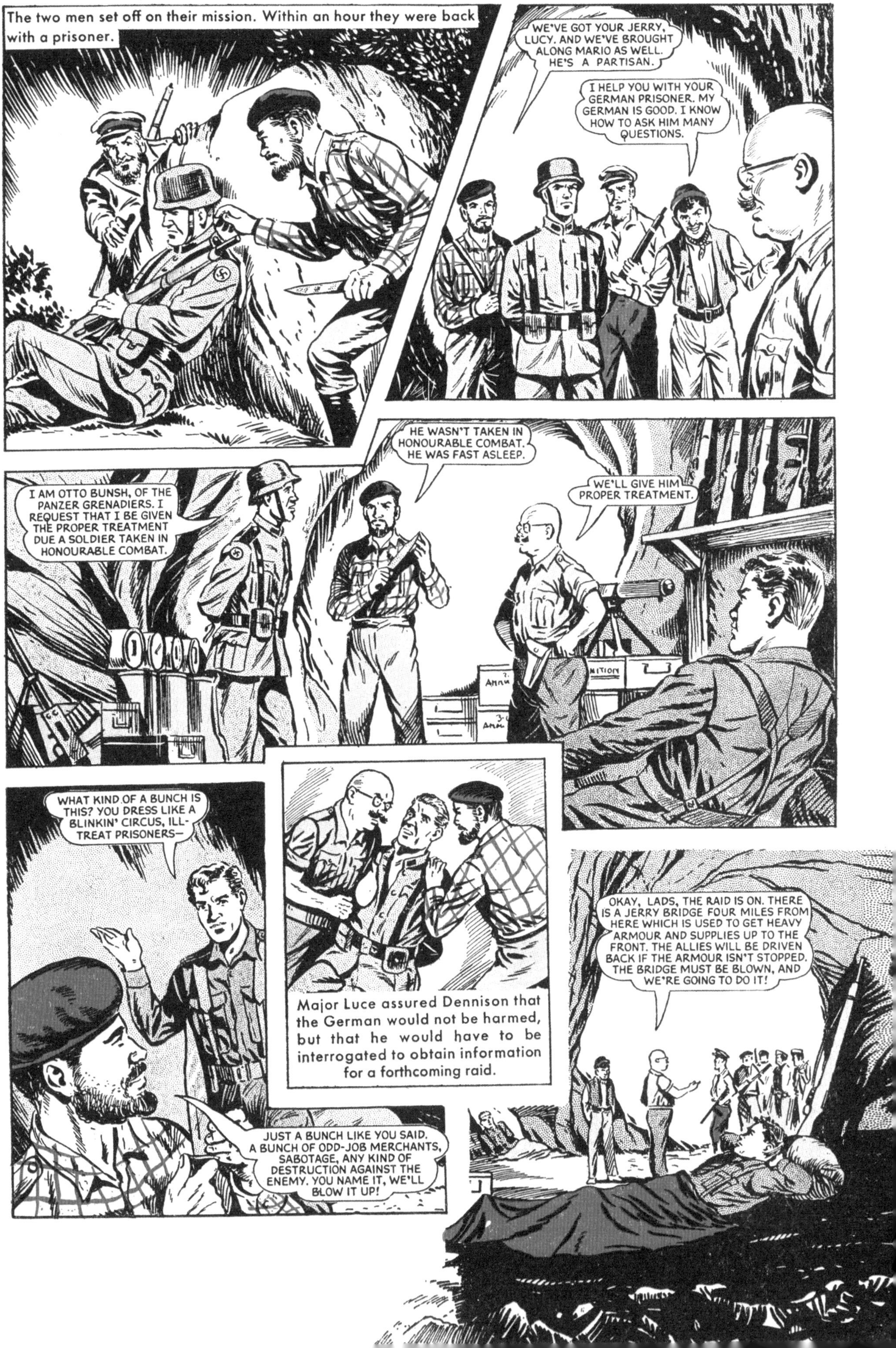
The two men set off on their mission. Within an hour they were back with a prisoner.
WE'VE GOT YOUR JERRY, LUCY. AND WE'VE BROUGHT ALONG MARIO AS WELL. HE'S A PARTISAN.
I HELP YOU WITH YOUR GERMAN PRISONER. MY GERMAN IS GOOD. I KNOW HOW TO ASK HIM MANY QUESTIONS.
I AM OTTO BUNSH, OF THE PANZER GRENADIERS. I REQUEST THAT I BE GIVEN THE PROPER TREATMENT DUE A SOLDIER TAKEN IN HONOURABLE COMBAT.
HE WASN'T TAKEN IN HONOURABLE COMBAT. HE WAS FAST ASLEEP.
WE'LL GIVE HIM PROPER TREATMENT.
WHAT KIND OF A BUNCH IS THIS? YOU DRESS LIKE A BLINKIN' CIRCUS, ILL-TREAT PRISONERS—
JUST A BUNCH LIKE YOU SAID. A BUNCH OF ODD-JOB MERCHANTS, SABOTAGE, ANY KIND OF DESTRUCTION AGAINST THE ENEMY. YOU NAME IT, WE'LL BLOW IT UP!
Major Luce assured Dennison that the German would not be harmed, but that he would have to be interrogated to obtain information for a forthcoming raid.
OKAY, LADS, THE RAID IS ON. THERE IS A JERRY BRIDGE FOUR MILES FROM HERE WHICH IS USED TO GET HEAVY ARMOUR AND SUPPLIES UP TO THE FRONT. THE ALLIES WILL BE DRIVEN BACK IF THE ARMOUR ISN'T STOPPED. THE BRIDGE MUST BE BLOWN, AND WE'RE GOING TO DO IT!

A traitor in the camp!

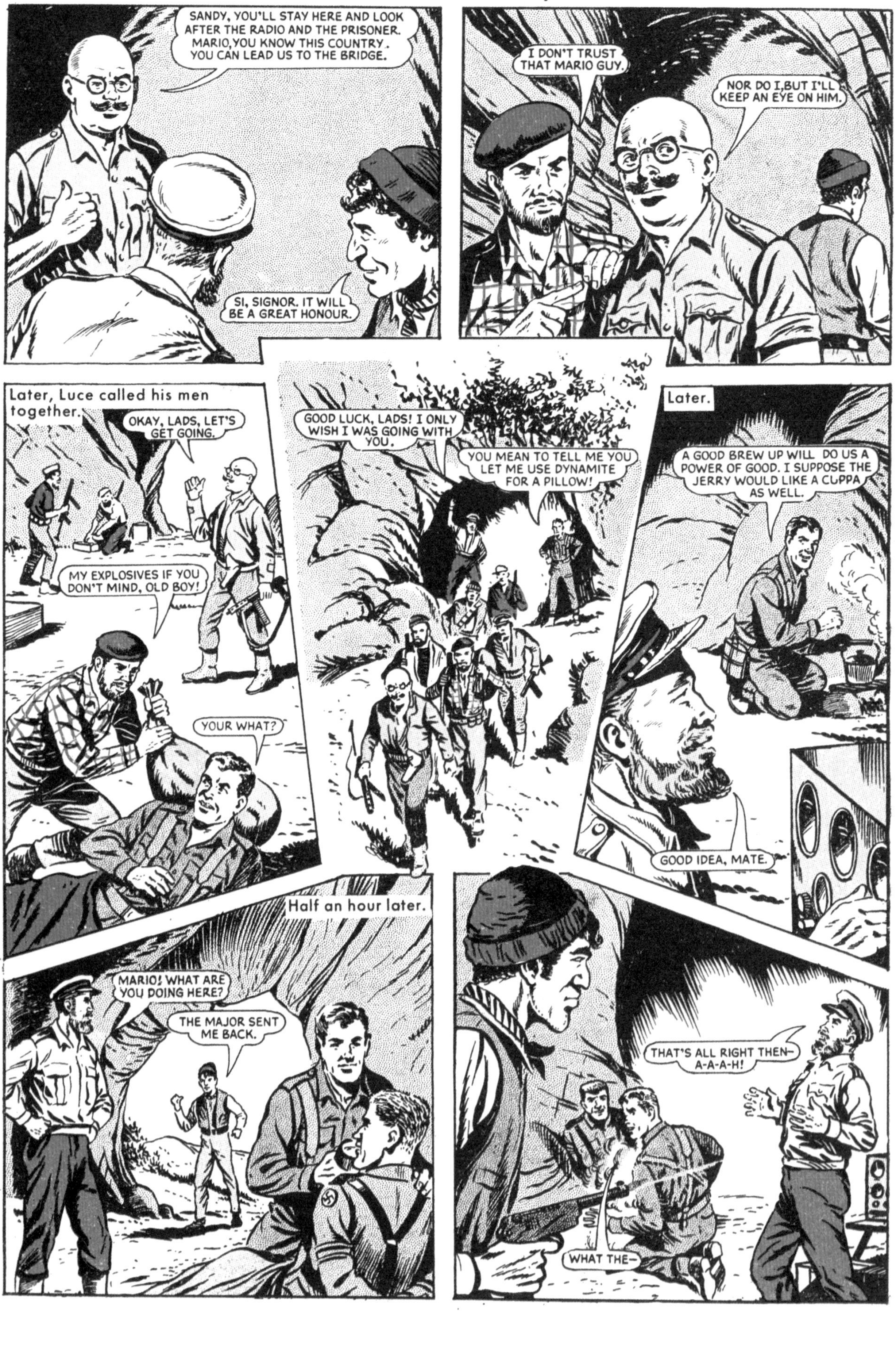
SANDY, YOU'LL STAY HERE AND LOOK AFTER THE RADIO AND THE PRISONER. MARIO, YOU KNOW THIS COUNTRY. YOU CAN LEAD US TO THE BRIDGE.
SI, SIGNOR. IT WILL BE A GREAT HONOUR.
I DON'T TRUST THAT MARIO GUY.
NOR DO I, BUT I'LL KEEP AN EYE ON HIM.
Later, Luce called his men together.
OKAY, LADS, LET'S GET GOING.
MY EXPLOSIVES IF YOU DON'T MIND, OLD BOY!
YOUR WHAT?
GOOD LUCK, LADS! I ONLY WISH I WAS GOING WITH YOU.
YOU MEAN TO TELL ME YOU LET ME USE DYNAMITE FOR A PILLOW!
Later.
A GOOD BREW UP WILL DO US A POWER OF GOOD. I SUPPOSE THE JERRY WOULD LIKE A CUPPA AS WELL.
GOOD IDEA, MATE.
Half an hour later.
MARIO! WHAT ARE YOU DOING HERE?
THE MAJOR SENT ME BACK.
THAT'S ALL RIGHT THEN— A-A-A-H!
WHAT THE—

"Still alive, Englishman?"

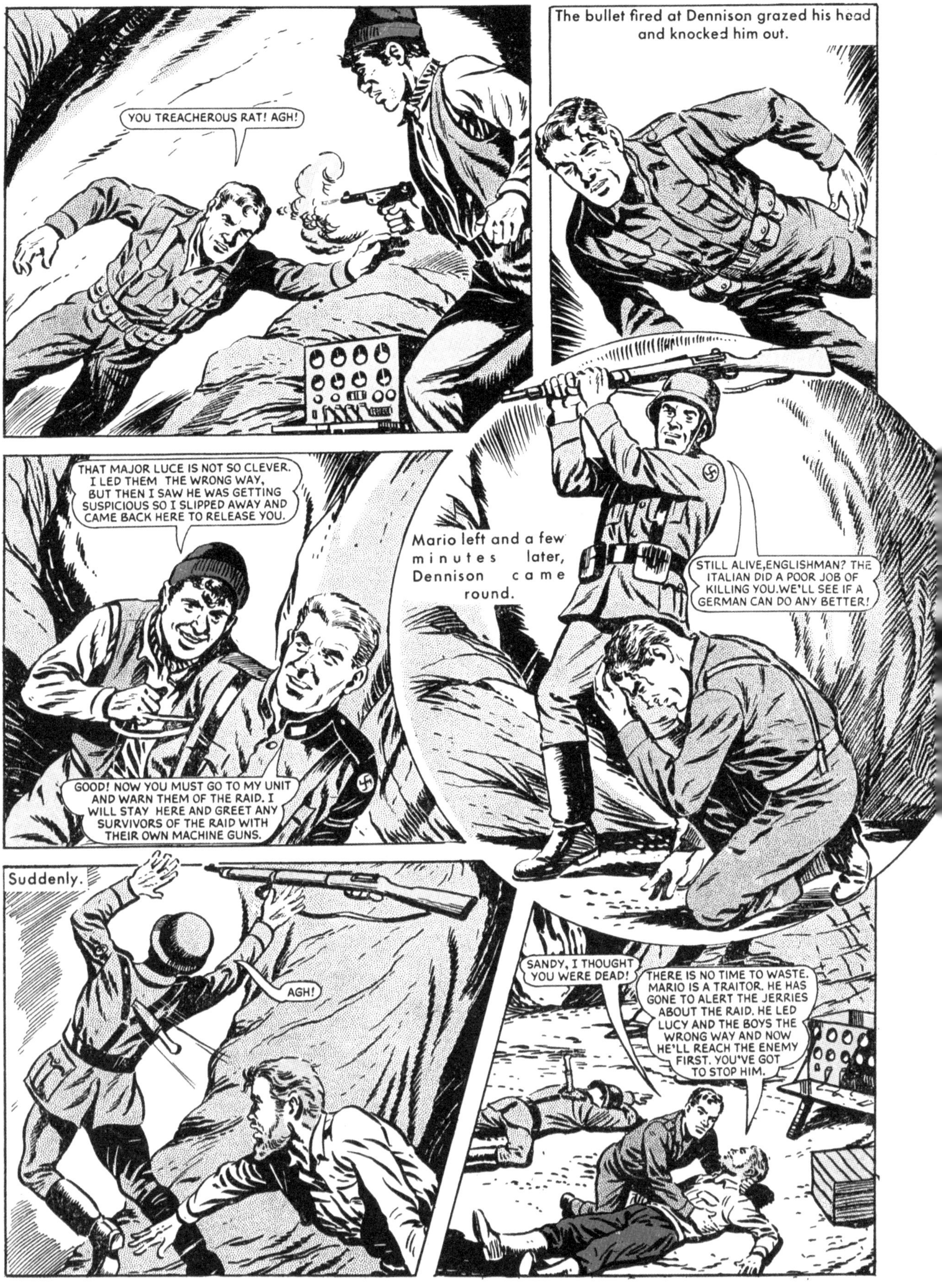
YOU TREACHEROUS RAT! AGH!
The bullet fired at Dennison grazed his head and knocked him out.
THAT MAJOR LUCE IS NOT SO CLEVER. I LED THEM THE WRONG WAY, BUT THEN I SAW HE WAS GETTING SUSPICIOUS SO I SLIPPED AWAY AND CAME BACK HERE TO RELEASE YOU.
GOOD! NOW YOU MUST GO TO MY UNIT AND WARN THEM OF THE RAID. I WILL STAY HERE AND GREET ANY SURVIVORS OF THE RAID WITH THEIR OWN MACHINE GUNS.
Mario left and a few minutes later, Dennison came round.
STILL ALIVE,ENGLISHMAN? THE ITALIAN DID A POOR JOB OF KILLING YOU.WE'LL SEE IF A GERMAN CAN DO ANY BETTER!
Suddenly.
AGH!
SANDY, I THOUGHT YOU WERE DEAD!
THERE IS NO TIME TO WASTE. MARIO IS A TRAITOR. HE HAS GONE TO ALERT THE JERRIES ABOUT THE RAID. HE LED LUCY AND THE BOYS THE WRONG WAY AND NOW HE'LL REACH THE ENEMY FIRST. YOU'VE GOT TO STOP HIM.

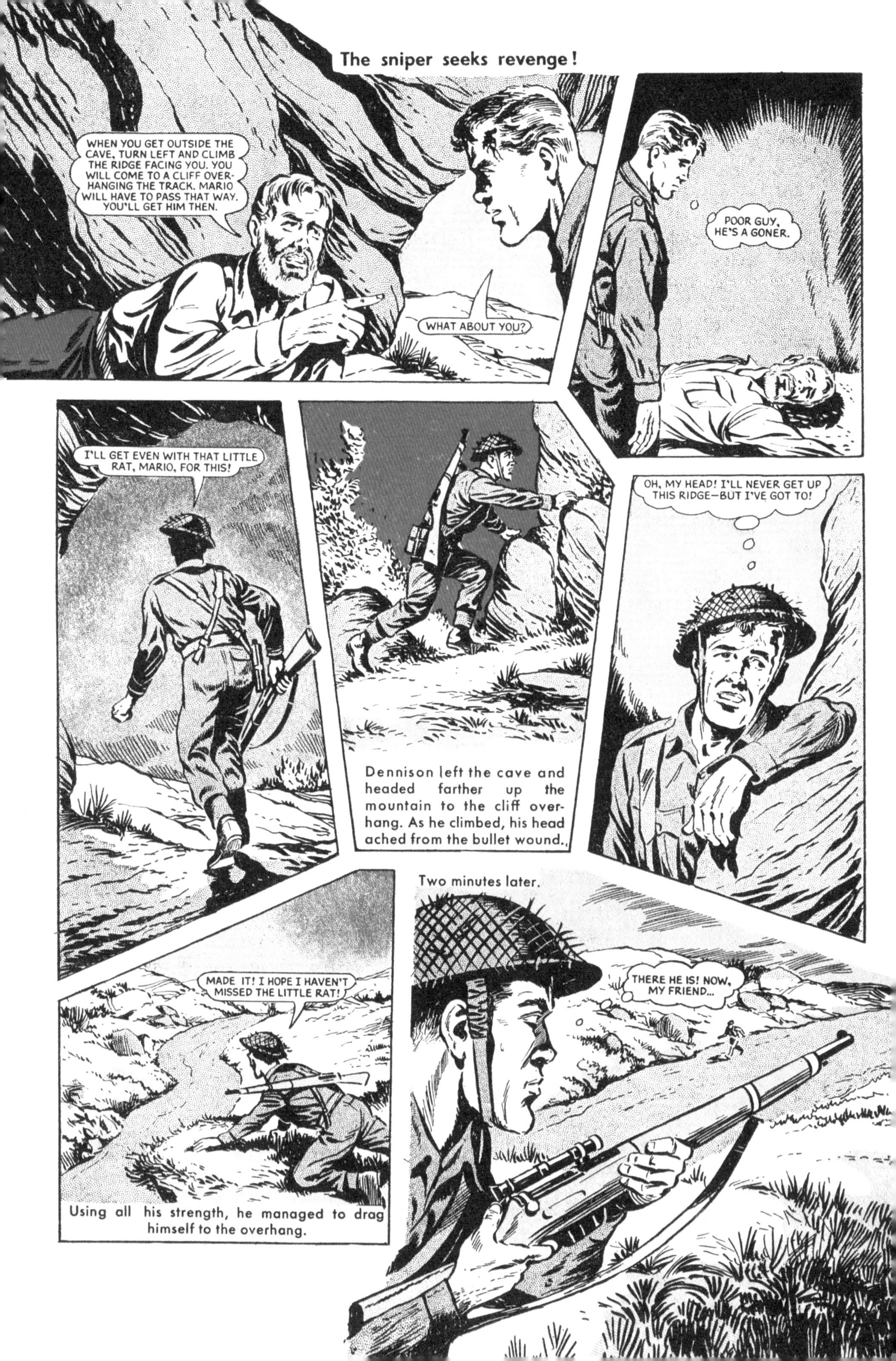

The sniper seeks revenge!
WHEN YOU GET OUTSIDE THE CAVE, TURN LEFT AND CLIMB THE RIDGE FACING YOU. YOU WILL COME TO A CLIFF OVER-HANGING THE TRACK. MARIO WILL HAVE TO PASS THAT WAY. YOU'LL GET HIM THEN.
WHAT ABOUT YOU?
POOR GUY, HE'S A GONER.
I'LL GET EVEN WITH THAT LITTLE RAT, MARIO, FOR THIS!
Dennison left the cave and headed farther up the mountain to the cliff over-hang. As he climbed, his head ached from the bullet wound.
OH, MY HEAD! I'LL NEVER GET UP THIS RIDGE—BUT I'VE GOT TO!
MADE IT! I HOPE I HAVEN'T MISSED THE LITTLE RAT!
Using all his strength, he managed to drag himself to the overhang.
Two minutes later.
THERE HE IS! NOW, MY FRIEND...

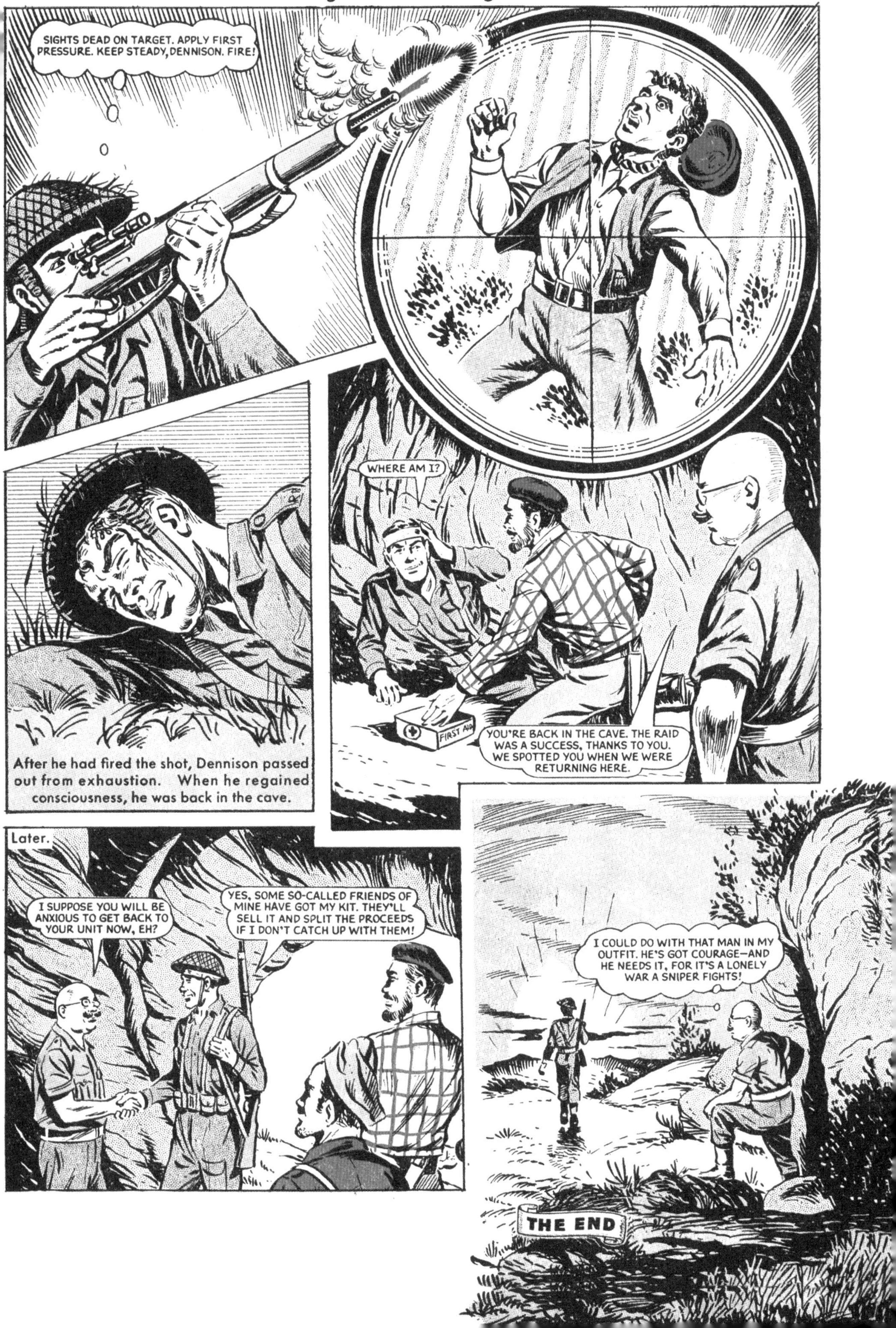
SIGHTS DEAD ON TARGET. APPLY FIRST PRESSURE. KEEP STEADY, DENNISON. FIRE!
After he had fired the shot, Dennison passed out from exhaustion. When he regained consciousness, he was back in the cave.
WHERE AM I?
FIRST AID
YOU'RE BACK IN THE CAVE. THE RAID WAS A SUCCESS, THANKS TO YOU. WE SPOTTED YOU WHEN WE WERE RETURNING HERE.
Later.
I SUPPOSE YOU WILL BE ANXIOUS TO GET BACK TO YOUR UNIT NOW, EH?
YES, SOME SO-CALLED FRIENDS OF MINE HAVE GOT MY KIT. THEY'LL SELL IT AND SPLIT THE PROCEEDS IF I DON'T CATCH UP WITH THEM!
I COULD DO WITH THAT MAN IN MY OUTFIT. HE'S GOT COURAGE—AND HE NEEDS IT, FOR IT'S A LONELY WAR A SNIPER FIGHTS!
THE END

BUILD A BATTLE GUN

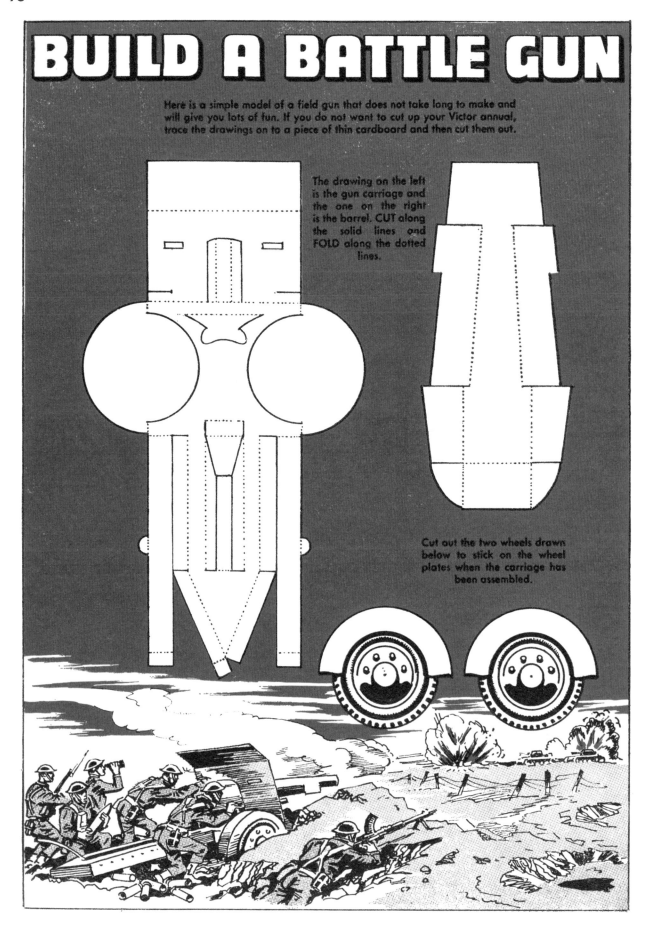

Here is a simple model of a field gun that does not take long to make and will give you lots of fun. If you do not want to cut up your Victor annual, trace the drawings on to a piece of thin cardboard and then cut them out.

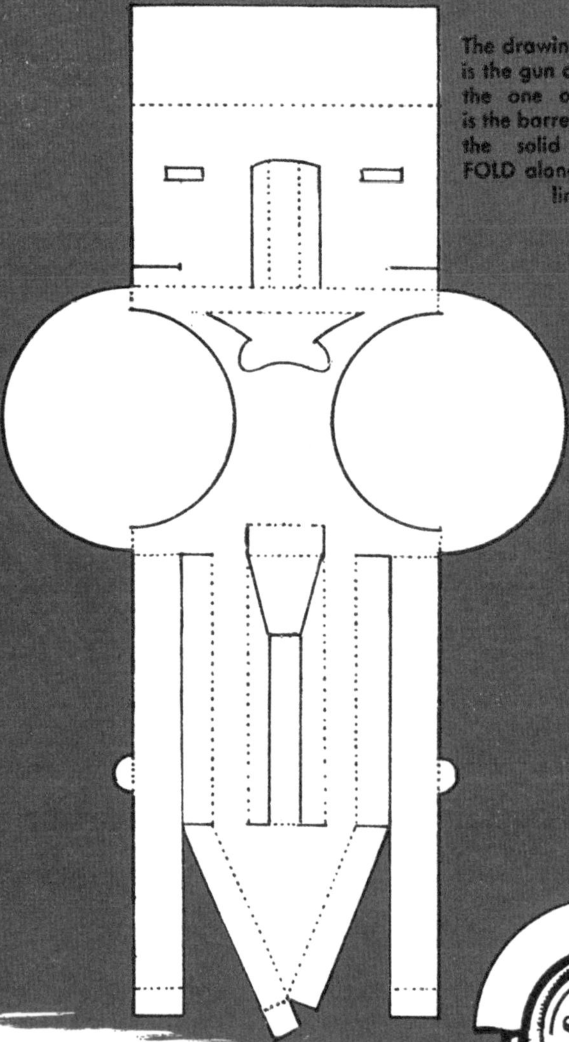

The drawing on the left is the gun carriage and the one on the right is the barrel. CUT along the solid lines and FOLD along the dotted lines.

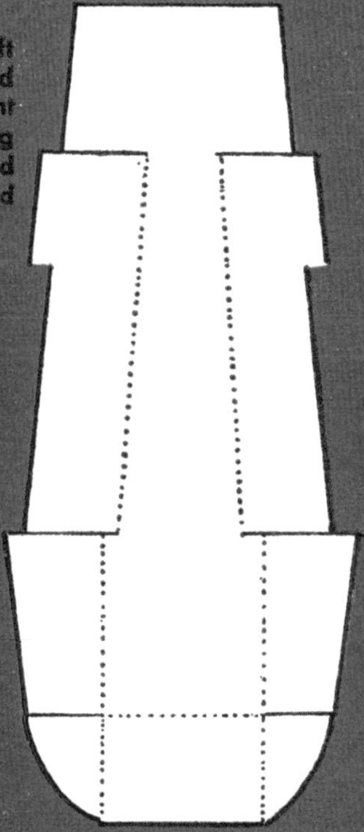

Cut out the two wheels drawn below to stick on the wheel plates when the carriage has been assembled.

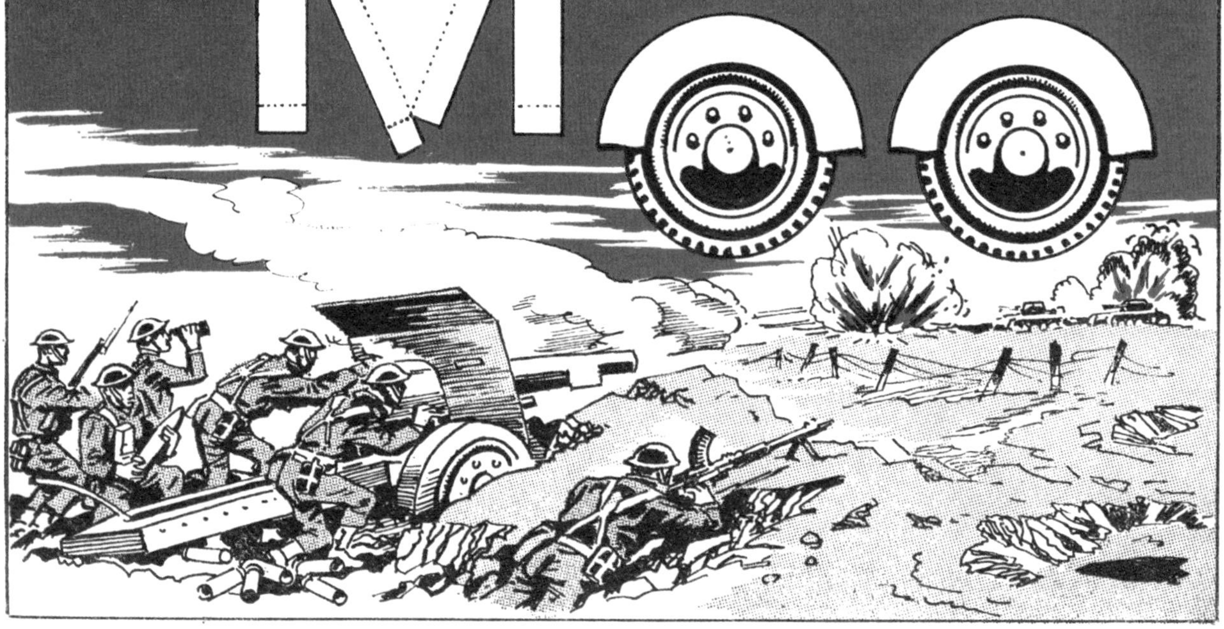

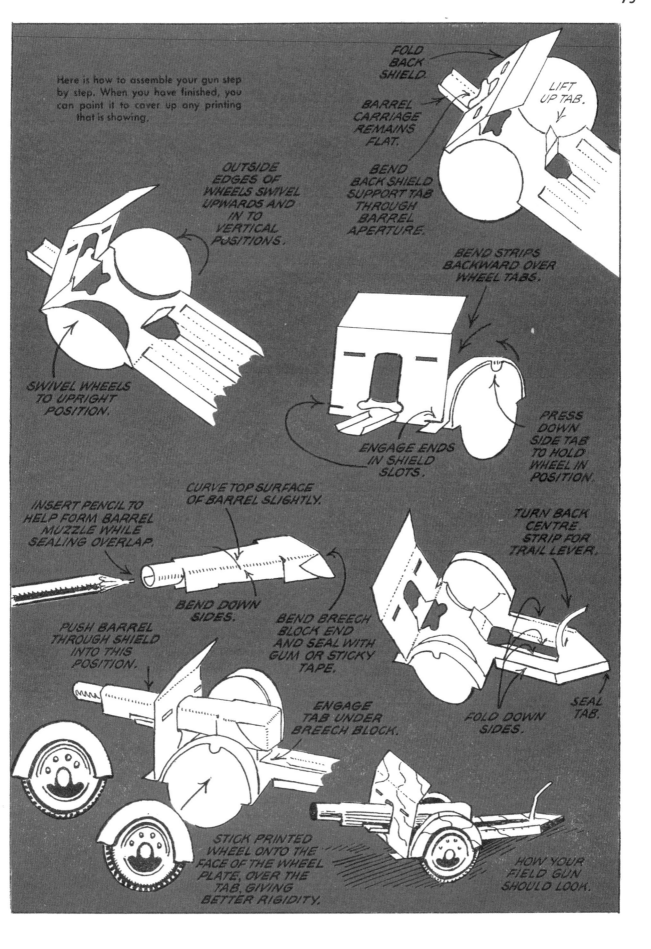

Here is how to assemble your gun step by step. When you have finished, you can paint it to cover up any printing that is showing.

FOLD BACK SHIELD.

LIFT UP TAB.

BARREL CARRIAGE REMAINS FLAT.

BEND BACK SHIELD SUPPORT TAB THROUGH BARREL APERTURE.

OUTSIDE EDGES OF WHEELS SWIVEL UPWARDS AND IN TO VERTICAL POSITIONS.

BEND STRIPS BACKWARD OVER WHEEL TABS.

SWIVEL WHEELS TO UPRIGHT POSITION.

ENGAGE ENDS IN SHIELD SLOTS.

PRESS DOWN SIDE TAB TO HOLD WHEEL IN POSITION.

CURVE TOP SURFACE OF BARREL SLIGHTLY.

INSERT PENCIL TO HELP FORM BARREL MUZZLE WHILE SEALING OVERLAP.

TURN BACK CENTRE STRIP FOR TRAIL LEVER.

BEND DOWN SIDES.

BEND BREECH BLOCK END AND SEAL WITH GUM OR STICKY TAPE.

PUSH BARREL THROUGH SHIELD INTO THIS POSITION.

ENGAGE TAB UNDER BREECH BLOCK.

FOLD DOWN SIDES.

SEAL TAB.

STICK PRINTED WHEEL ONTO THE FACE OF THE WHEEL PLATE, OVER THE TAB, GIVING BETTER RIGIDITY.

HOW YOUR FIELD GUN SHOULD LOOK.

GAMES THEY USED TO PLAY

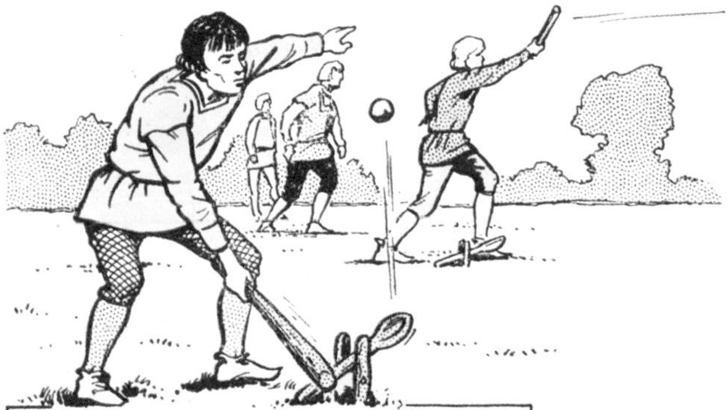

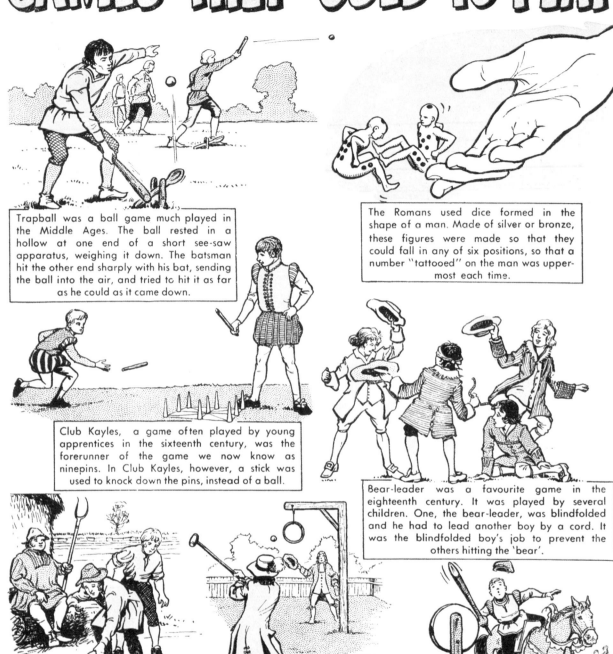

Trapball was a ball game much played in the Middle Ages. The ball rested in a hollow at one end of a short see-saw apparatus, weighing it down. The batsman hit the other end sharply with his bat, sending the ball into the air, and tried to hit it as far as he could as it came down.

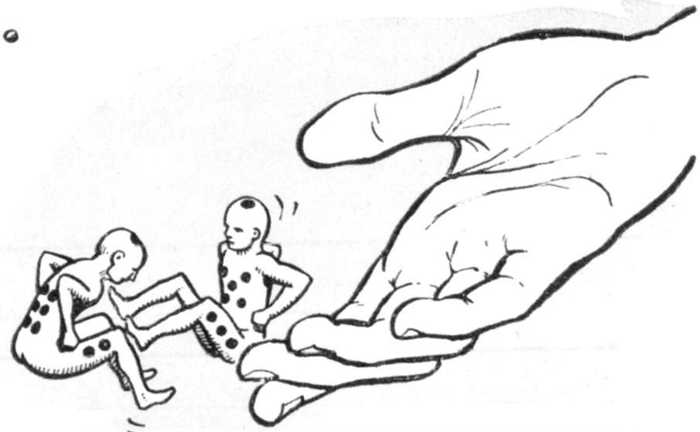

The Romans used dice formed in the shape of a man. Made of silver or bronze, these figures were made so that they could fall in any of six positions, so that a number "tattooed" on the man was uppermost each time.

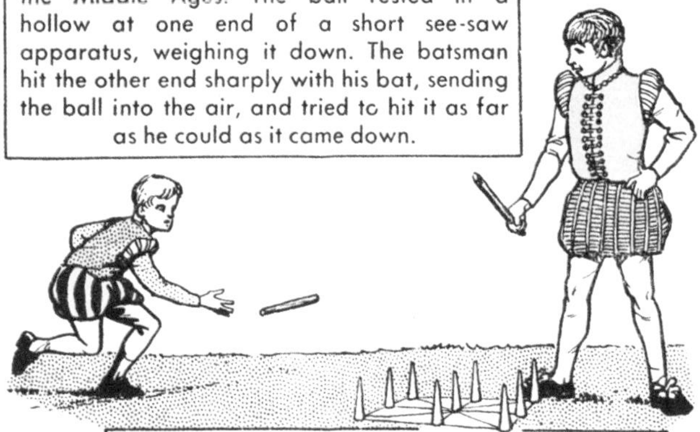

Club Kayles, a game often played by young apprentices in the sixteenth century, was the forerunner of the game we now know as ninepins. In Club Kayles, however, a stick was used to knock down the pins, instead of a ball.

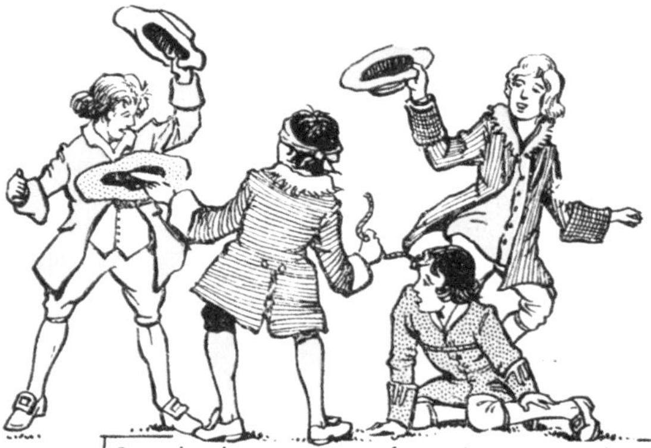

Bear-leader was a favourite game in the eighteenth century. It was played by several children. One, the bear-leader, was blindfolded and he had to lead another boy by a cord. It was the blindfolded boy's job to prevent the others hitting the 'bear'.

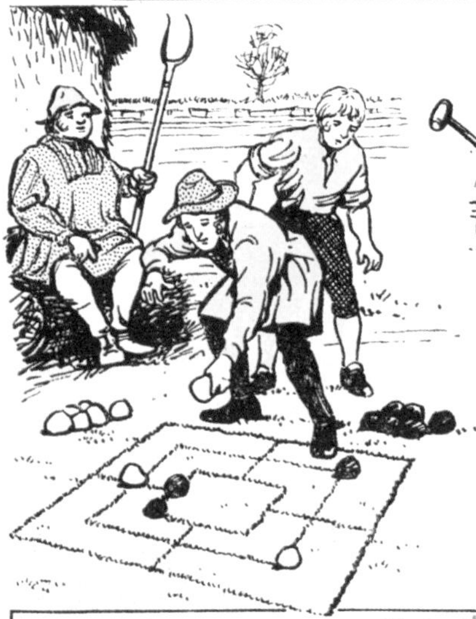

Nine Men's Morris was an old English game played with black and white pebbles. Each player tried to get three of his nine men into a line; he could then remove from the board one of his opponent's men. When one player was left with only two men the game was over.

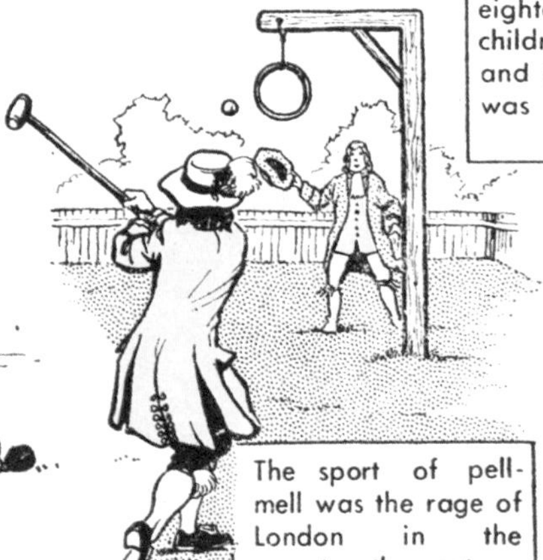

The sport of pell-mell was the rage of London in the seventeenth century. In this game, a box-wood ball was driven through a metal ring with a long-handled wooden hammer like a croquet mallet.

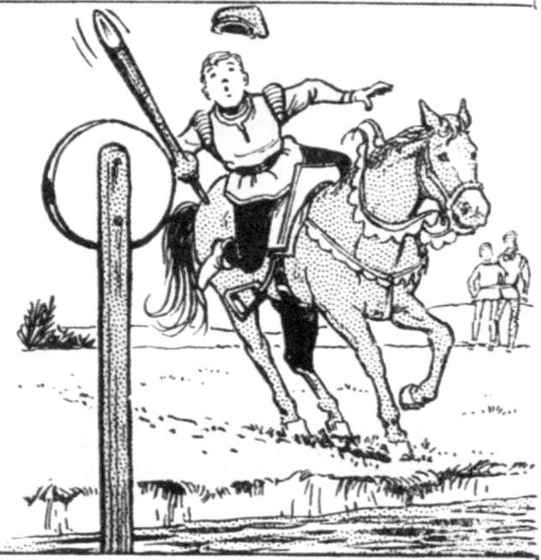

In 'water quintains' a pole with a target attached to it was fixed in a river bed. Any competitor whose lance missed its mark lost his balance and fell into the water.

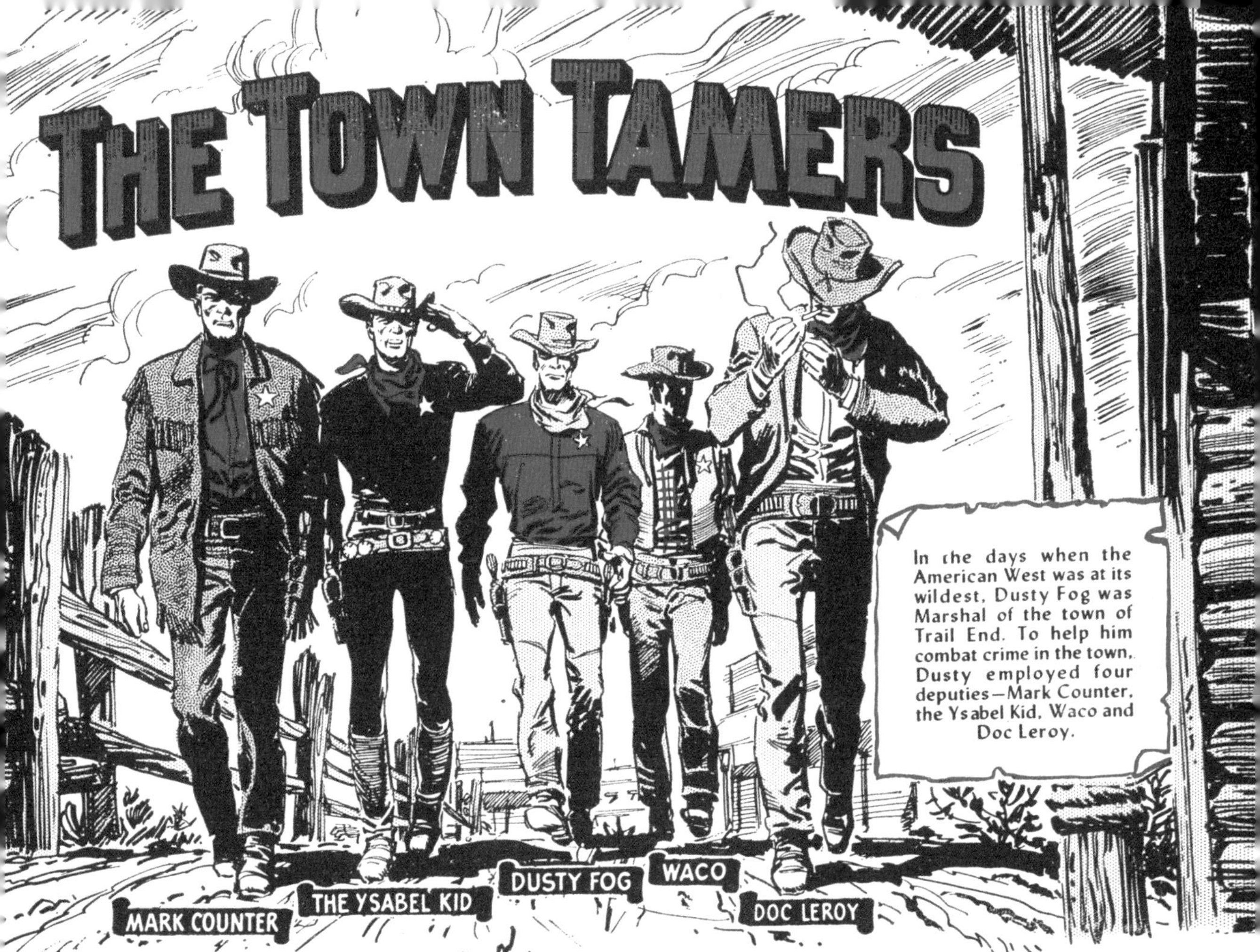
THE TOWN TAMERS
In the days when the American West was at its wildest, Dusty Fog was Marshal of the town of Trail End. To help him combat crime in the town, Dusty employed four deputies—Mark Counter, the Ysabel Kid, Waco and Doc Leroy.
MARK COUNTER
THE YSABEL KID
DUSTY FOG
WACO
DOC LEROY

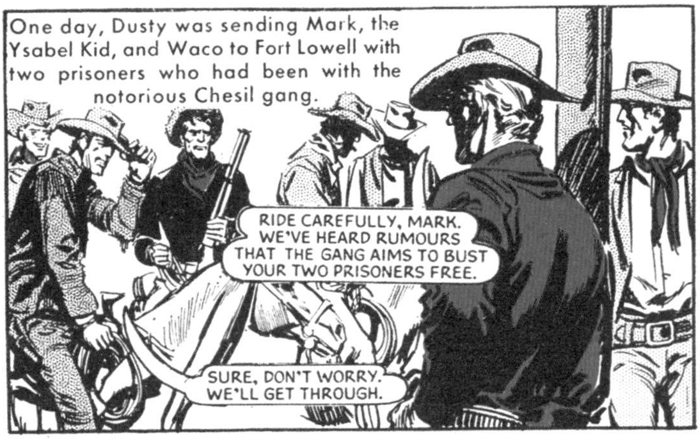
One day, Dusty was sending Mark, the Ysabel Kid, and Waco to Fort Lowell with two prisoners who had been with the notorious Chesil gang.
RIDE CAREFULLY, MARK. WE'VE HEARD RUMOURS THAT THE GANG AIMS TO BUST YOUR TWO PRISONERS FREE.
SURE, DON'T WORRY. WE'LL GET THROUGH.

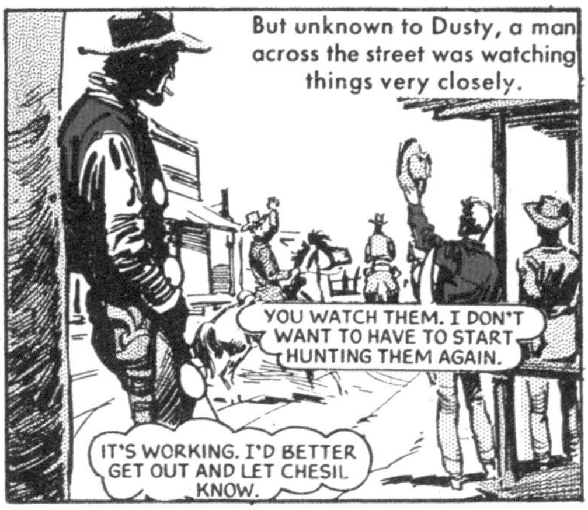
But unknown to Dusty, a man across the street was watching things very closely.
YOU WATCH THEM. I DON'T WANT TO HAVE TO START HUNTING THEM AGAIN.
IT'S WORKING. I'D BETTER GET OUT AND LET CHESIL KNOW.

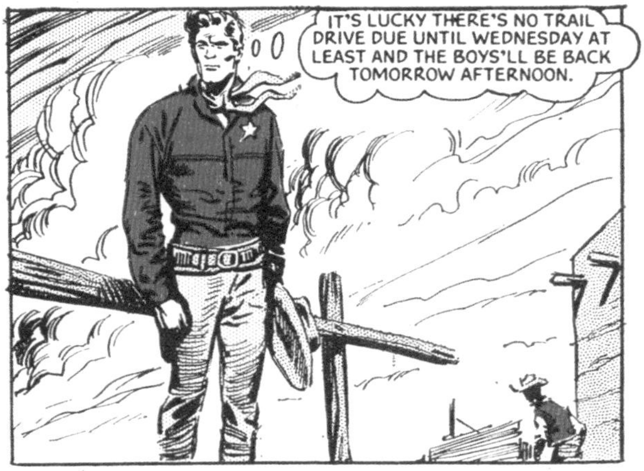
IT'S LUCKY THERE'S NO TRAIL DRIVE DUE UNTIL WEDNESDAY AT LEAST AND THE BOYS'LL BE BACK TOMORROW AFTERNOON.

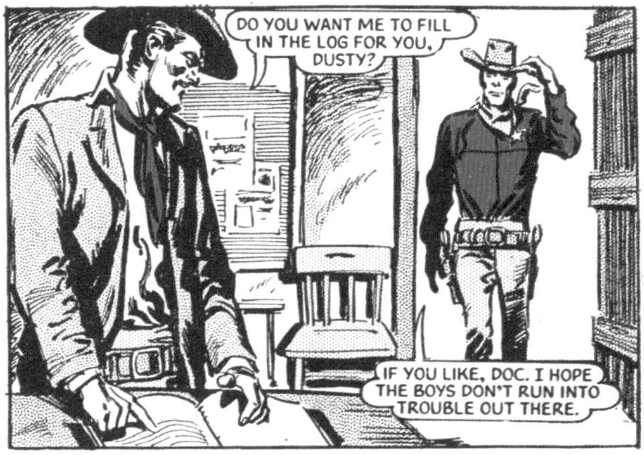
DO YOU WANT ME TO FILL IN THE LOG FOR YOU, DUSTY?
IF YOU LIKE, DOC. I HOPE THE BOYS DON'T RUN INTO TROUBLE OUT THERE.

"He's real fast with a gun!"

Later, a couple of miles outside Trail End, where the Chesil gang was in hiding.

CHESIL, WADE'S COMIN'!

I HOPE HE'S GOT THE WORD I WANT.

COUNTER RODE OUT WITH THE YSABEL KID AND WACO, BOSS, TAKING THE PRISONERS.

I THOUGHT DUSTY FOG WOULD SEND ALL THREE. THAT WAS WHY I STARTED THE RUMOUR ABOUT A RESCUE ATTEMPT.

WHEN DO WE HIT THE CATTLEMAN'S BANK, BOSS?

LATE ON TONIGHT, JACKIE, AFTER THE REST OF MY PLAN'S BEEN WORKED. THE BANKER WILL BE WORKING LATE. HE ALWAYS DOES ON MONDAYS. NOW GET YOUR HORSES AND WE'LL RIDE.

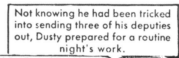

Not knowing he had been tricked into sending three of his deputies out, Dusty prepared for a routine night's work.

IS THAT LAMP FILLED, DOC? I DON'T WANT TO HAVE IT GOING OUT WHEN WE NEED IT ON.

I JUST FILLED ALL OF THEM THIS AFTERNOON. I'M GOING TO MAKE MY ROUNDS NOW.

I SAW MAJOR GALT EARLIER. HE WAS COMPLAINING ABOUT ME SENDING THREE DEPUTIES OUT OF TOWN. HE SAYS WE MIGHT HAVE TROUBLE NOW I'M SHORT HANDED.

HE'D LIKE THERE TO BE TROUBLE. THEN HE COULD FIRE US AND START HIS OLD CROOKED GAMES AGAIN.

SURE HE'D LIKE IT. SO WATCH YOURSELF!

YOU KNOW ME, REAL CAREFUL ALL THE TIME. DON'T LET ANYBODY STEAL THE JAIL WHILE I'M OUT.

Doc left to do his rounds, but a surprise was in store for him . . .

HERE HE COMES NOW, SNELL.

WATCH HIM, JONER, HE'S REAL FAST WITH A GUN!

"There's trouble in here!"

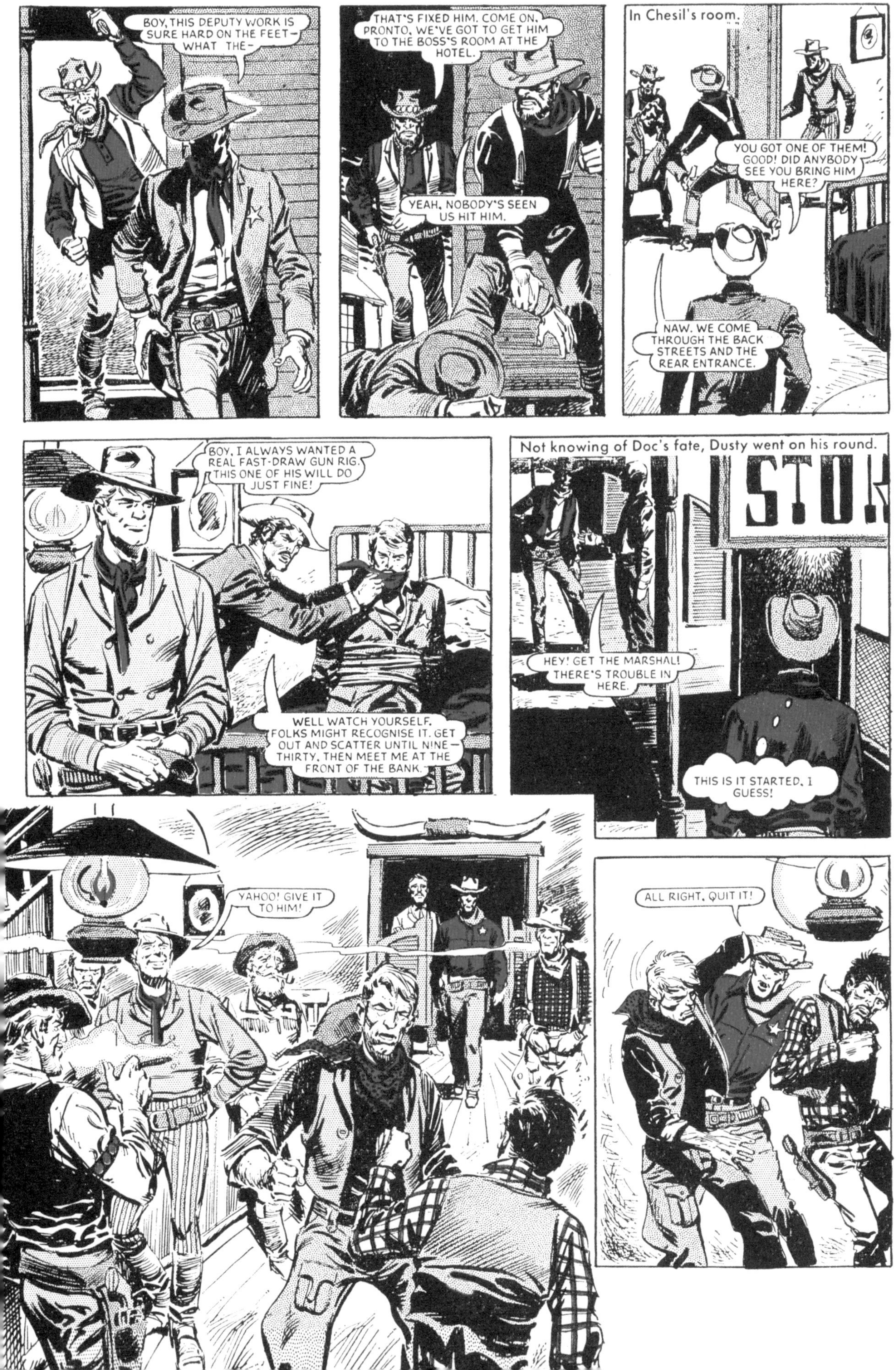
BOY, THIS DEPUTY WORK IS SURE HARD ON THE FEET– WHAT THE–
THAT'S FIXED HIM. COME ON, PRONTO. WE'VE GOT TO GET HIM TO THE BOSS'S ROOM AT THE HOTEL.
YEAH, NOBODY'S SEEN US HIT HIM.
In Chesil's room.
YOU GOT ONE OF THEM! GOOD! DID ANYBODY SEE YOU BRING HIM HERE?
NAW. WE COME THROUGH THE BACK STREETS AND THE REAR ENTRANCE.
BOY, I ALWAYS WANTED A REAL FAST-DRAW GUN RIG. THIS ONE OF HIS WILL DO JUST FINE!
WELL WATCH YOURSELF. FOLKS MIGHT RECOGNISE IT. GET OUT AND SCATTER UNTIL NINE-THIRTY, THEN MEET ME AT THE FRONT OF THE BANK.
Not knowing of Doc's fate, Dusty went on his round.
STOR
HEY! GET THE MARSHAL! THERE'S TROUBLE IN HERE.
THIS IS IT STARTED, I GUESS!
YAHOO! GIVE IT TO HIM!
ALL RIGHT, QUIT IT!

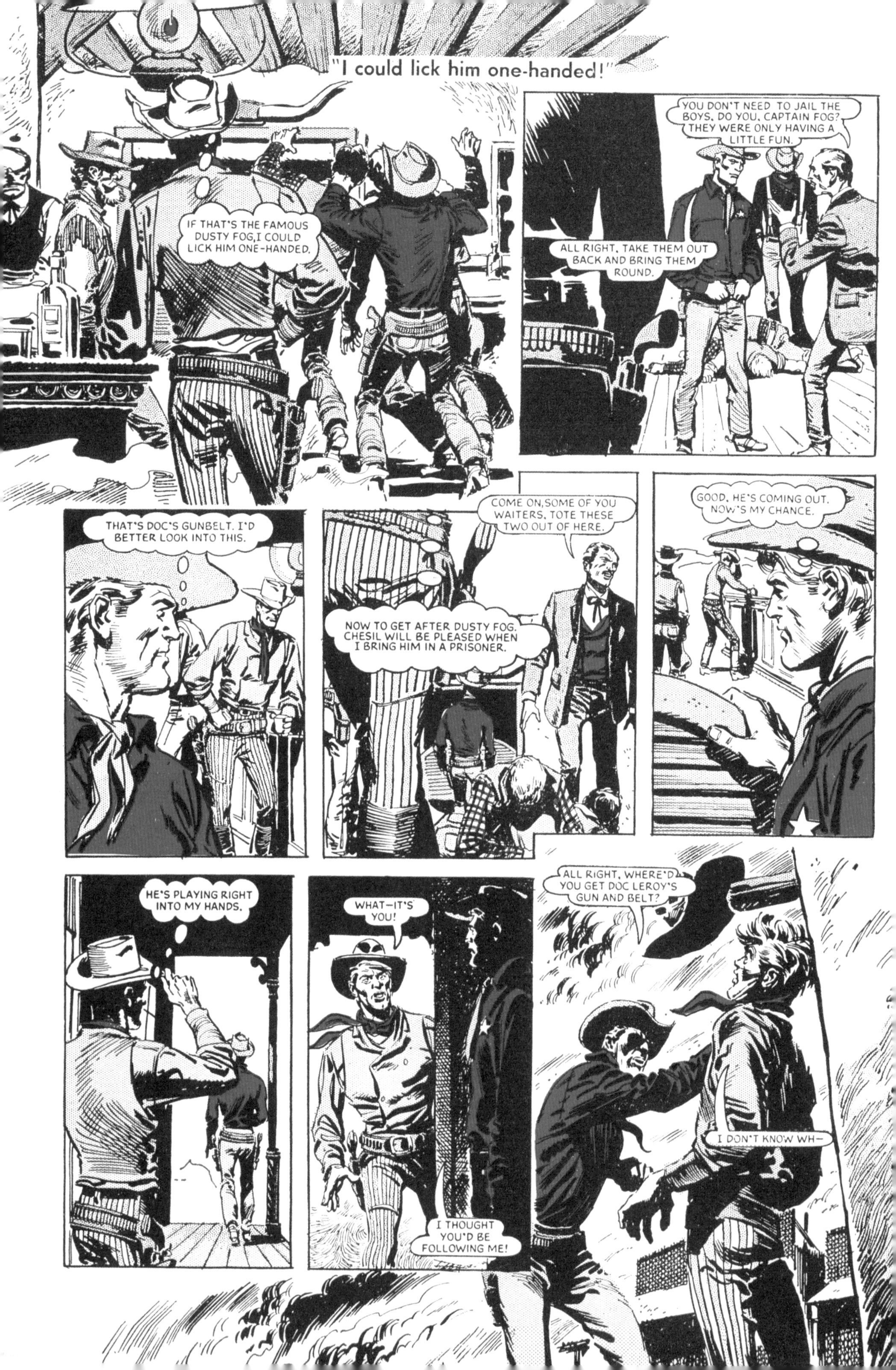
"I could lick him one-handed!"
IF THAT'S THE FAMOUS DUSTY FOG, I COULD LICK HIM ONE-HANDED.
YOU DON'T NEED TO JAIL THE BOYS, DO YOU, CAPTAIN FOG? THEY WERE ONLY HAVING A LITTLE FUN.
ALL RIGHT, TAKE THEM OUT BACK AND BRING THEM ROUND.
THAT'S DOC'S GUNBELT. I'D BETTER LOOK INTO THIS.
COME ON, SOME OF YOU WAITERS, TOTE THESE TWO OUT OF HERE.
NOW TO GET AFTER DUSTY FOG. CHESIL WILL BE PLEASED WHEN I BRING HIM IN A PRISONER.
GOOD, HE'S COMING OUT. NOW'S MY CHANCE.
HE'S PLAYING RIGHT INTO MY HANDS.
WHAT—IT'S YOU!
I THOUGHT YOU'D BE FOLLOWING ME!
ALL RIGHT, WHERE'D YOU GET DOC LEROY'S GUN AND BELT?
I DON'T KNOW WH—

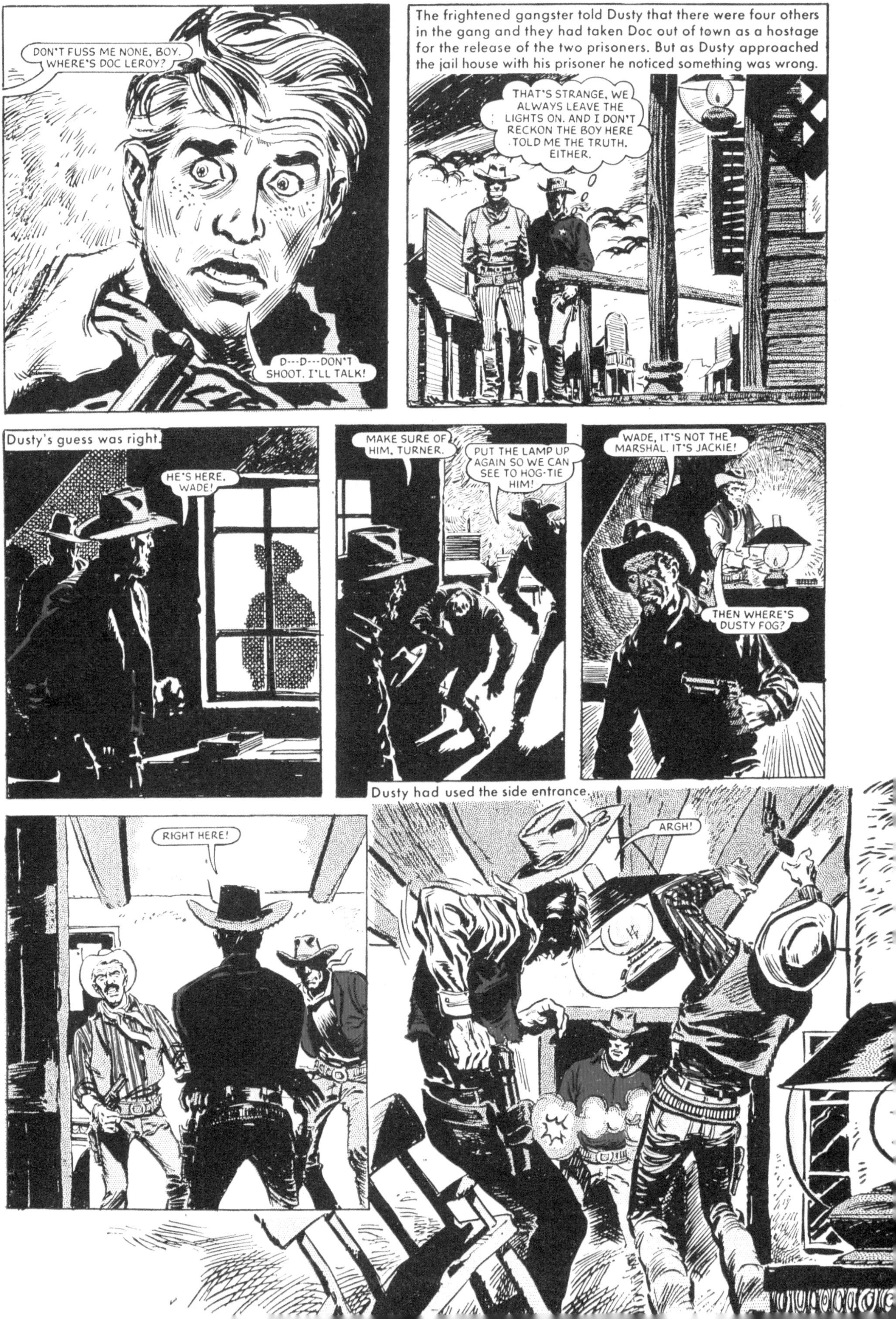
DON'T FUSS ME NONE, BOY. WHERE'S DOC LEROY?
D---D---DON'T SHOOT. I'LL TALK!
The frightened gangster told Dusty that there were four others in the gang and they had taken Doc out of town as a hostage for the release of the two prisoners. But as Dusty approached the jail house with his prisoner he noticed something was wrong.
THAT'S STRANGE, WE ALWAYS LEAVE THE LIGHTS ON. AND I DON'T RECKON THE BOY HERE TOLD ME THE TRUTH, EITHER.
Dusty's guess was right.
HE'S HERE, WADE!
MAKE SURE OF HIM, TURNER.
PUT THE LAMP UP AGAIN SO WE CAN SEE TO HOG-TIE HIM!
WADE, IT'S NOT THE MARSHAL. IT'S JACKIE!
THEN WHERE'S DUSTY FOG?
Dusty had used the side entrance.
RIGHT HERE!
ARGH!

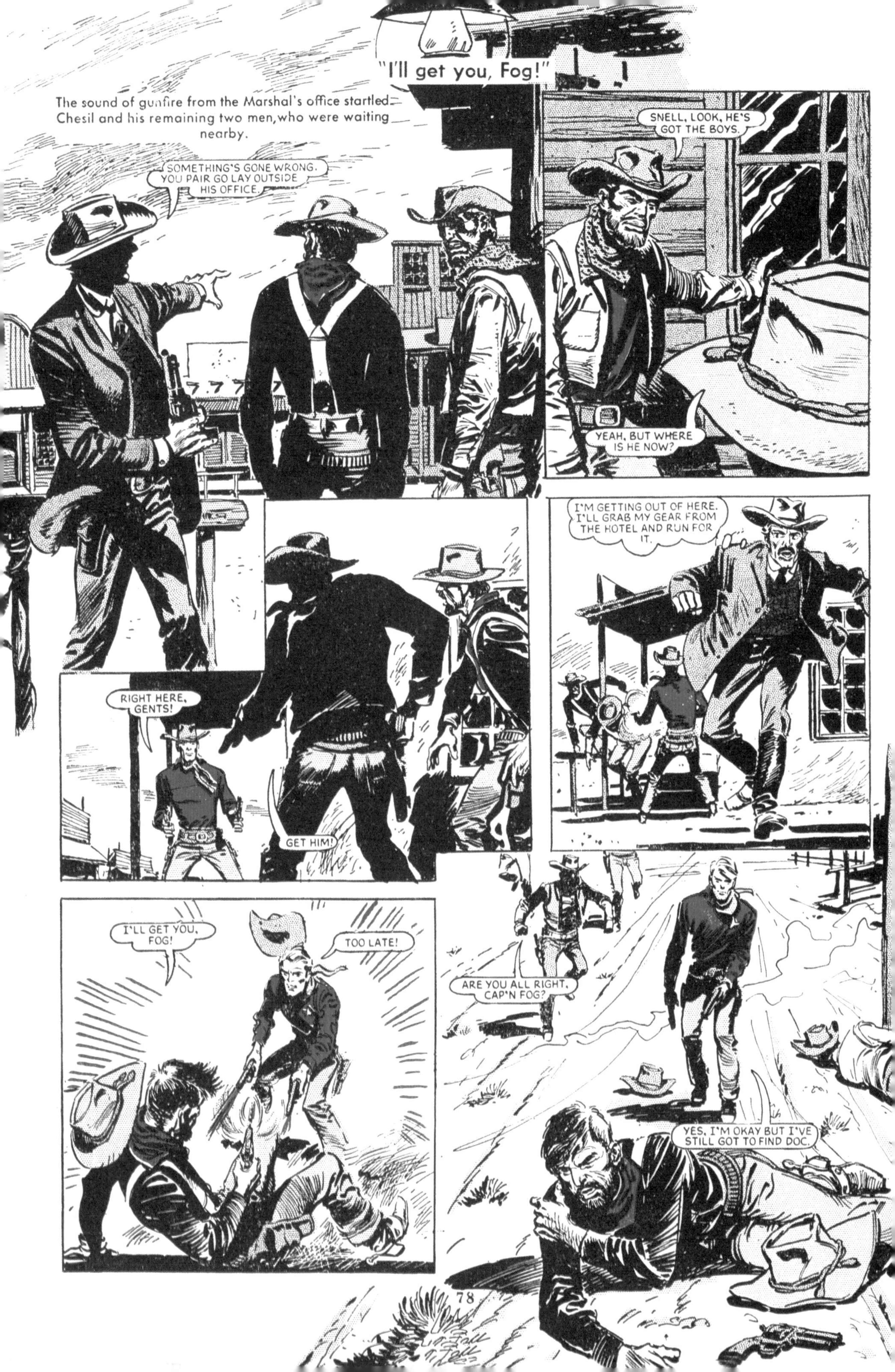

"I'll get you, Fog!"
The sound of gunfire from the Marshal's office startled Chesil and his remaining two men, who were waiting nearby.
SOMETHING'S GONE WRONG. YOU PAIR GO LAY OUTSIDE HIS OFFICE.
SNELL, LOOK, HE'S GOT THE BOYS.
YEAH, BUT WHERE IS HE NOW?
RIGHT HERE, GENTS!
GET HIM!
I'M GETTING OUT OF HERE. I'LL GRAB MY GEAR FROM THE HOTEL AND RUN FOR IT.
I'LL GET YOU, FOG!
TOO LATE!
ARE YOU ALL RIGHT, CAP'N FOG?
YES, I'M OKAY BUT I'VE STILL GOT TO FIND DOC.

A surprise for Chesil.

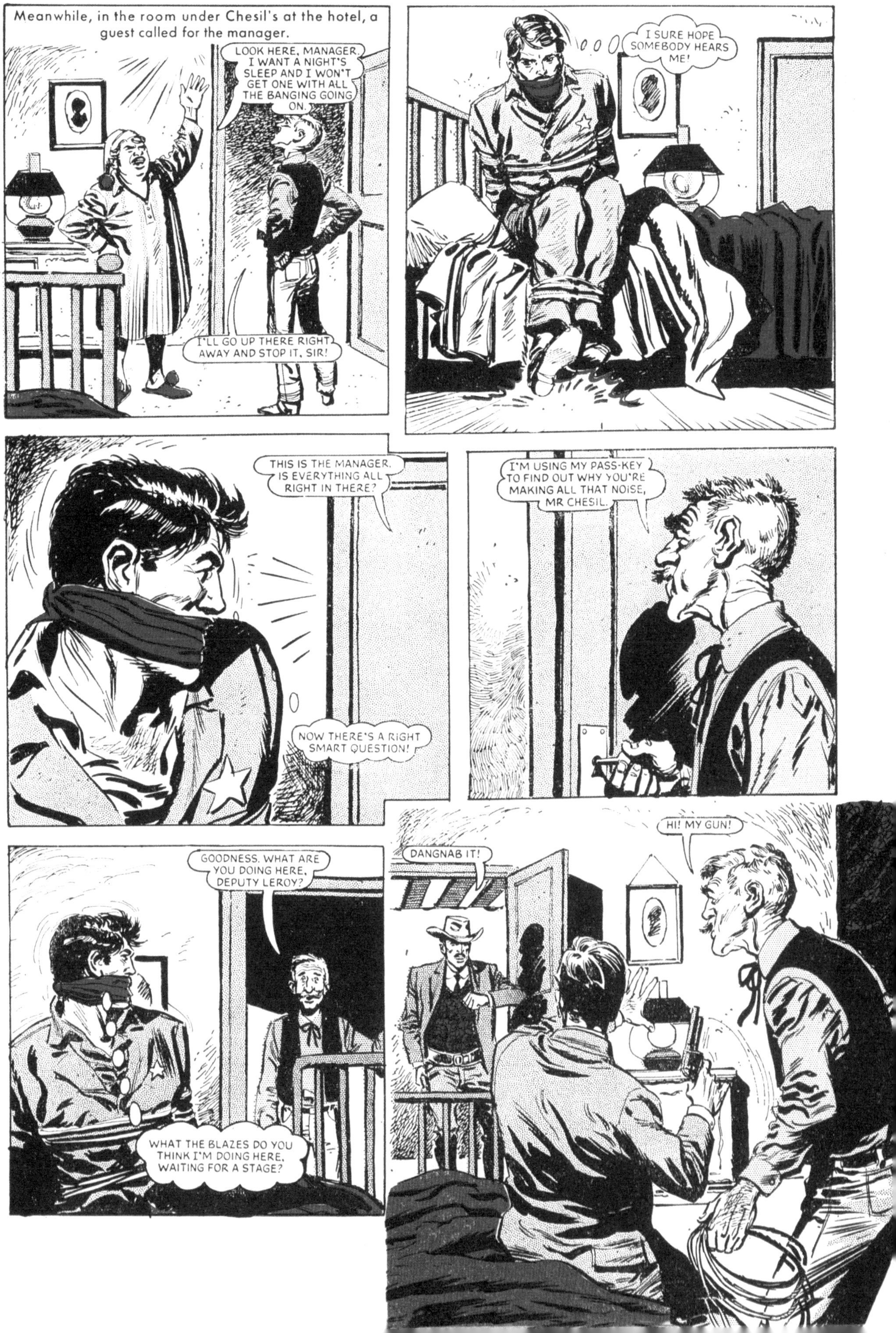
Meanwhile, in the room under Chesil's at the hotel, a guest called for the manager.
LOOK HERE, MANAGER, I WANT A NIGHT'S SLEEP AND I WON'T GET ONE WITH ALL THE BANGING GOING ON.
I'LL GO UP THERE RIGHT AWAY AND STOP IT, SIR!
I SURE HOPE SOMEBODY HEARS ME!
THIS IS THE MANAGER. IS EVERYTHING ALL RIGHT IN THERE?
NOW THERE'S A RIGHT SMART QUESTION!
I'M USING MY PASS-KEY TO FIND OUT WHY YOU'RE MAKING ALL THAT NOISE, MR CHESIL.
GOODNESS. WHAT ARE YOU DOING HERE, DEPUTY LEROY?
WHAT THE BLAZES DO YOU THINK I'M DOING HERE, WAITING FOR A STAGE?
DANGNAB IT!
HI! MY GUN!

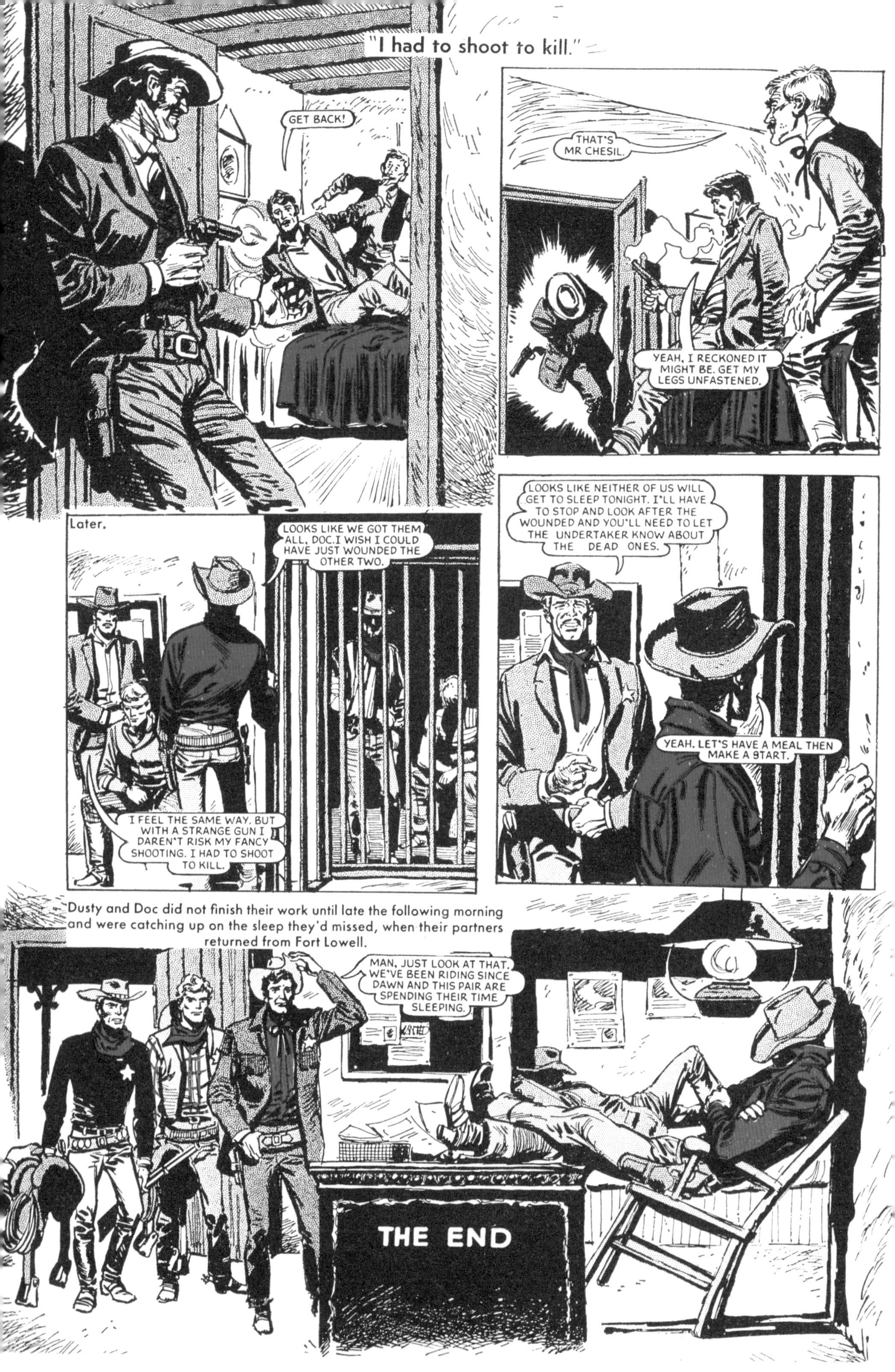

"I had to shoot to kill."
GET BACK!
THAT'S MR CHESIL.
YEAH, I RECKONED IT MIGHT BE. GET MY LEGS UNFASTENED.
Later.
LOOKS LIKE WE GOT THEM ALL, DOC. I WISH I COULD HAVE JUST WOUNDED THE OTHER TWO.
I FEEL THE SAME WAY. BUT WITH A STRANGE GUN I DAREN'T RISK MY FANCY SHOOTING. I HAD TO SHOOT TO KILL.
LOOKS LIKE NEITHER OF US WILL GET TO SLEEP TONIGHT. I'LL HAVE TO STOP AND LOOK AFTER THE WOUNDED AND YOU'LL NEED TO LET THE UNDERTAKER KNOW ABOUT THE DEAD ONES.
YEAH. LET'S HAVE A MEAL THEN MAKE A START.
Dusty and Doc did not finish their work until late the following morning and were catching up on the sleep they'd missed, when their partners returned from Fort Lowell.
MAN, JUST LOOK AT THAT. WE'VE BEEN RIDING SINCE DAWN AND THIS PAIR ARE SPENDING THEIR TIME SLEEPING.
THE END

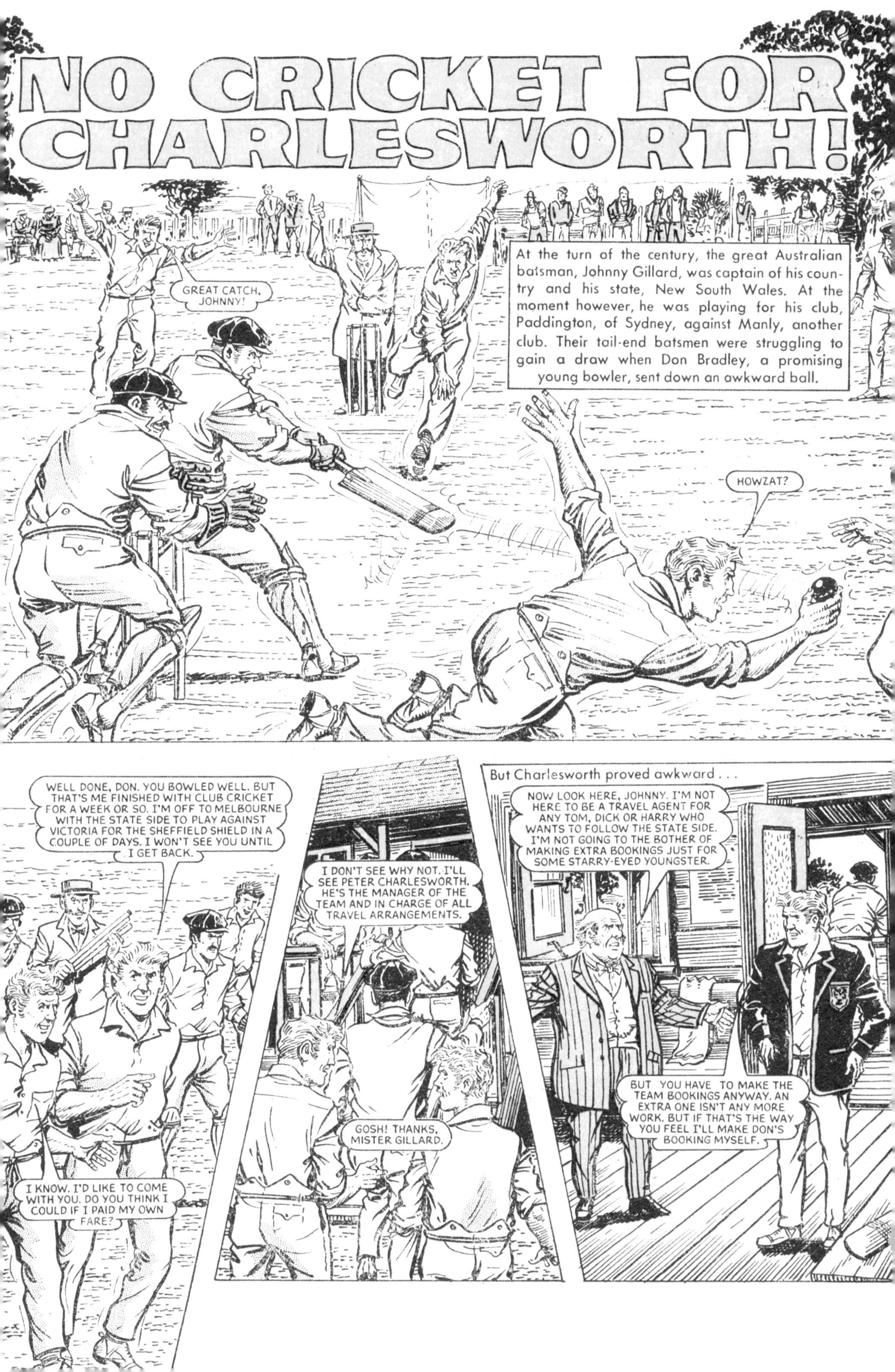
NO CRICKET FOR CHARLESWORTH!
At the turn of the century, the great Australian batsman, Johnny Gillard, was captain of his country and his state, New South Wales. At the moment however, he was playing for his club, Paddington, of Sydney, against Manly, another club. Their tail-end batsmen were struggling to gain a draw when Don Bradley, a promising young bowler, sent down an awkward ball.
GREAT CATCH, JOHNNY!
HOWZAT?
WELL DONE, DON. YOU BOWLED WELL. BUT THAT'S ME FINISHED WITH CLUB CRICKET FOR A WEEK OR SO. I'M OFF TO MELBOURNE WITH THE STATE SIDE TO PLAY AGAINST VICTORIA FOR THE SHEFFIELD SHIELD IN A COUPLE OF DAYS. I WON'T SEE YOU UNTIL I GET BACK.
I KNOW. I'D LIKE TO COME WITH YOU. DO YOU THINK I COULD IF I PAID MY OWN FARE?
I DON'T SEE WHY NOT. I'LL SEE PETER CHARLESWORTH. HE'S THE MANAGER OF THE TEAM AND IN CHARGE OF ALL TRAVEL ARRANGEMENTS.
GOSH! THANKS, MISTER GILLARD.
But Charlesworth proved awkward . . .
NOW LOOK HERE, JOHNNY. I'M NOT HERE TO BE A TRAVEL AGENT FOR ANY TOM, DICK OR HARRY WHO WANTS TO FOLLOW THE STATE SIDE. I'M NOT GOING TO THE BOTHER OF MAKING EXTRA BOOKINGS JUST FOR SOME STARRY-EYED YOUNGSTER.
BUT YOU HAVE TO MAKE THE TEAM BOOKINGS ANYWAY. AN EXTRA ONE ISN'T ANY MORE WORK. BUT IF THAT'S THE WAY YOU FEEL I'LL MAKE DON'S BOOKING MYSELF.

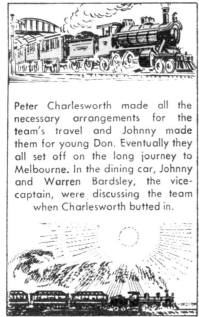

Peter Charlesworth made all the necessary arrangements for the team's travel and Johnny made them for young Don. Eventually they all set off on the long journey to Melbourne. In the dining car, Johnny and Warren Bardsley, the vice-captain, were discussing the team when Charlesworth butted in.

I TAKE IT YOUNG DOCTOR ARMITAGE WILL BE PLAYING. HE'S A PROMISING SPIN BOWLER, YOU KNOW.

I KNOW HE'S A PROMISING SPIN BOWLER BUT HE WON'T BE PLAYING. THE TEAM HAS BEEN PICKED AND HE IS TWELFTH MAN.

NOW HALF A MINUTE. HERE ARE THE REGULATIONS. IT SAYS THAT IF CAPTAIN AND VICE-CAPTAIN DISAGREE THEY MUST REFER TO THE MANAGER. IF EITHER IS UNABLE TO ACT THE MANAGER SHALL TAKE HIS PLACE.

BUT WARREN AND I DO AGREE AND WE HAVE ACTED. DOC ARMITAGE IS TWELFTH MAN. WE'RE HAPPY ABOUT IT AND SO IS HE. HE REALISES HE WAS ONLY BROUGHT ALONG AS TWELFTH MAN TO GIVE HIM THE EXPERIENCE.

THAT MAN GIVES ME A PAIN IN THE TONSILS!

DON'T LET IT WORRY YOU, JOHNNY. LET'S GO AND GET SOME SHUT-EYE.

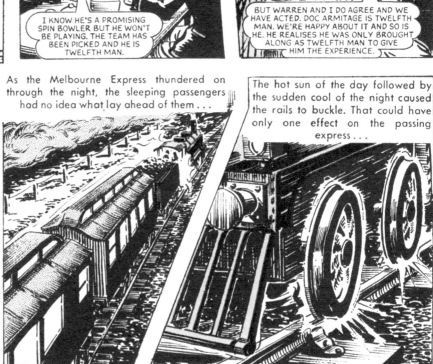

As the Melbourne Express thundered on through the night, the sleeping passengers had no idea what lay ahead of them...

The hot sun of the day followed by the sudden cool of the night caused the rails to buckle. That could have only one effect on the passing express...

WHAT HAPPENED? WHAT'S GOING ON?

DERAILMENT, THAT'S WHAT!

HAVE YOU SEEN ANY OF THE OTHER TEAM MEMBERS, DOC?

I'VE SEEN ONE OR TWO OF THEM ABOUT NURSING THE ODD BRUISE. FORTUNATELY THE TRAIN STAYED UPRIGHT SO CASUALTIES AREN'T BAD.

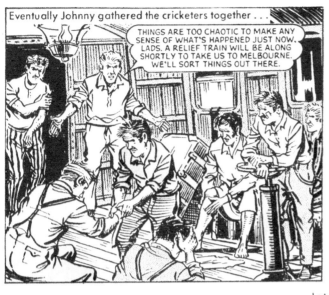

Eventually Johnny gathered the cricketers together . . .

THINGS ARE TOO CHAOTIC TO MAKE ANY SENSE OF WHAT'S HAPPENED JUST NOW, LADS. A RELIEF TRAIN WILL BE ALONG SHORTLY TO TAKE US TO MELBOURNE. WE'LL SORT THINGS OUT THERE.

Some time later at Melbourne station

WHO ARE THEY? THEY LOOK A RIGHT BUNCH OF CROCKS.

THAT'S THE NEW SOUTH WALES CRICKET TEAM. I'D RECOGNISE JOHNNY GILLARD ANYWHERE.

I SUGGEST YOU ALL TRY TO GET SOME REST UNTIL LUNCHTIME. THEN I'LL GET DOC ARMITAGE TO EXAMINE YOU THOROUGHLY AND WE'LL DECIDE THEN WHO'S FIT TO PLAY.

Later—

ONLY NINE OF THE SELECTED TEAM COULD POSSIBLY PLAY, JOHNNY. EVEN SOME OF THEM WOULD BE BETTER TO GIVE THE GAME A MISS. PETER CHARLESWORTH IS OKAY, I'M OKAY AND YOUNG DON IS OKAY.

RIGHT, DOC. IT LOOKS LIKE YOU AND DON WILL BE PLAYING FOR THE STATE TEAM. NOW I'M GOING SWIMMING. ARE YOU COMING?

LOOK AT THESE BOOTS! I DIDN'T HAVE TIME TO CLEAN THE MUCK OFF THEM AFTER THE LAST GAME.

I HAVE A WIRE BRUSH I'LL LET YOU HAVE. THAT SHOULD MAKE SHORT WORK OF THE MESS.

THANKS. I'LL DO IT ON THE BEACH.

AH, THERE YOU ARE, GILLARD. I WANT TO SEE YOU ABOUT TOMORROW'S TEAM. IT'S A GOOD JOB I BROUGHT MY FLANNELS WITH ME. I CAN BORROW BOOTS BUT GETTING FLANNELS TO FIT IS A BIT DIFFICULT.

I CAN BELIEVE THAT! BUT WHAT'S ALL THIS ABOUT?

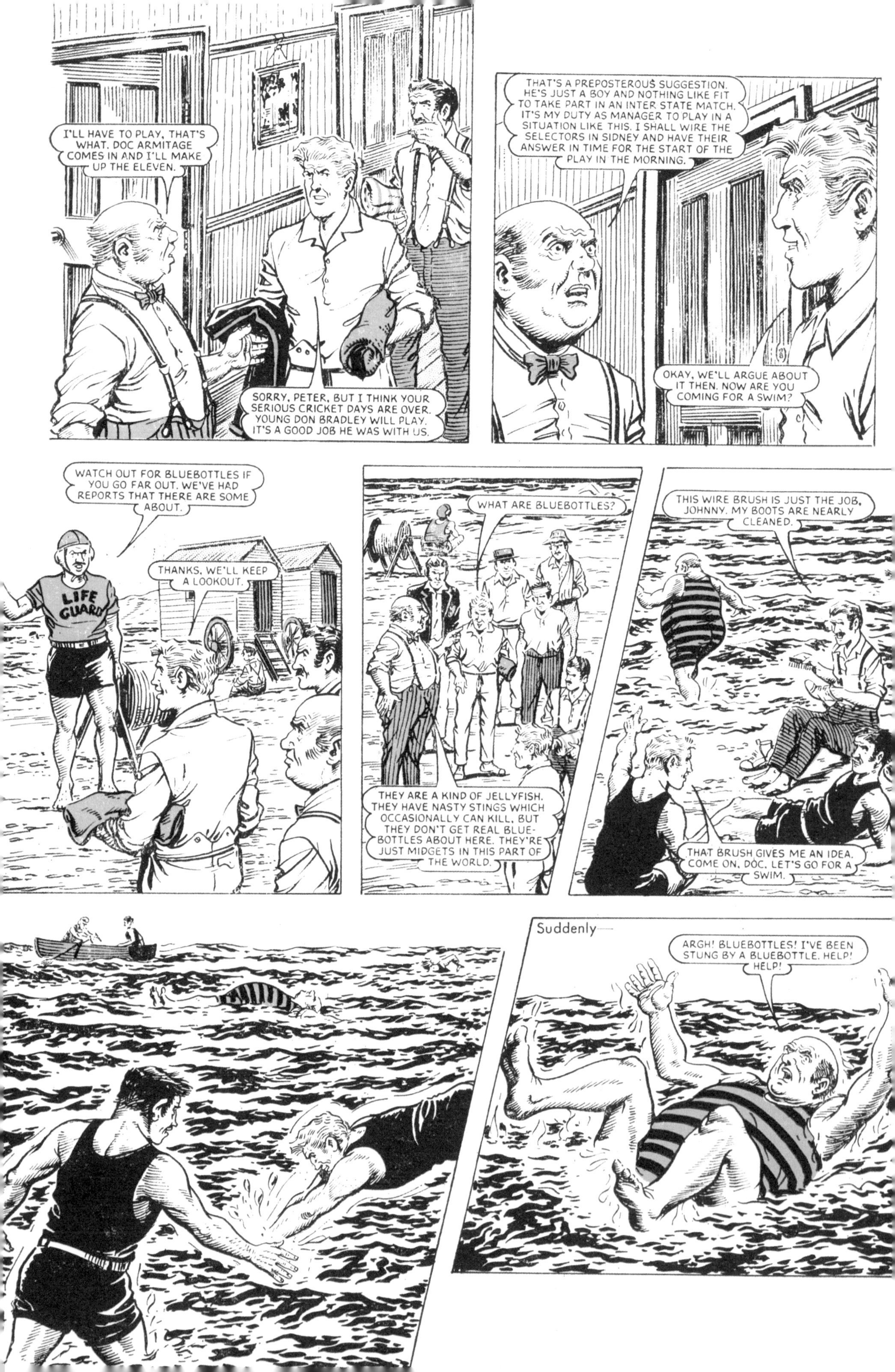
I'LL HAVE TO PLAY, THAT'S WHAT. DOC ARMITAGE COMES IN AND I'LL MAKE UP THE ELEVEN.
SORRY, PETER, BUT I THINK YOUR SERIOUS CRICKET DAYS ARE OVER. YOUNG DON BRADLEY WILL PLAY. IT'S A GOOD JOB HE WAS WITH US.
THAT'S A PREPOSTEROUS SUGGESTION. HE'S JUST A BOY AND NOTHING LIKE FIT TO TAKE PART IN AN INTER STATE MATCH. IT'S MY DUTY AS MANAGER TO PLAY IN A SITUATION LIKE THIS. I SHALL WIRE THE SELECTORS IN SIDNEY AND HAVE THEIR ANSWER IN TIME FOR THE START OF THE PLAY IN THE MORNING.
OKAY, WE'LL ARGUE ABOUT IT THEN. NOW ARE YOU COMING FOR A SWIM?
WATCH OUT FOR BLUEBOTTLES IF YOU GO FAR OUT. WE'VE HAD REPORTS THAT THERE ARE SOME ABOUT.
LIFE GUARD
THANKS. WE'LL KEEP A LOOKOUT.
WHAT ARE BLUEBOTTLES?
THEY ARE A KIND OF JELLYFISH. THEY HAVE NASTY STINGS WHICH OCCASIONALLY CAN KILL, BUT THEY DON'T GET REAL BLUE-BOTTLES ABOUT HERE. THEY'RE JUST MIDGETS IN THIS PART OF THE WORLD.
THIS WIRE BRUSH IS JUST THE JOB, JOHNNY. MY BOOTS ARE NEARLY CLEANED.
THAT BRUSH GIVES ME AN IDEA. COME ON, DOC. LET'S GO FOR A SWIM.
Suddenly—
ARGH! BLUEBOTTLES! I'VE BEEN STUNG BY A BLUEBOTTLE. HELP! HELP!

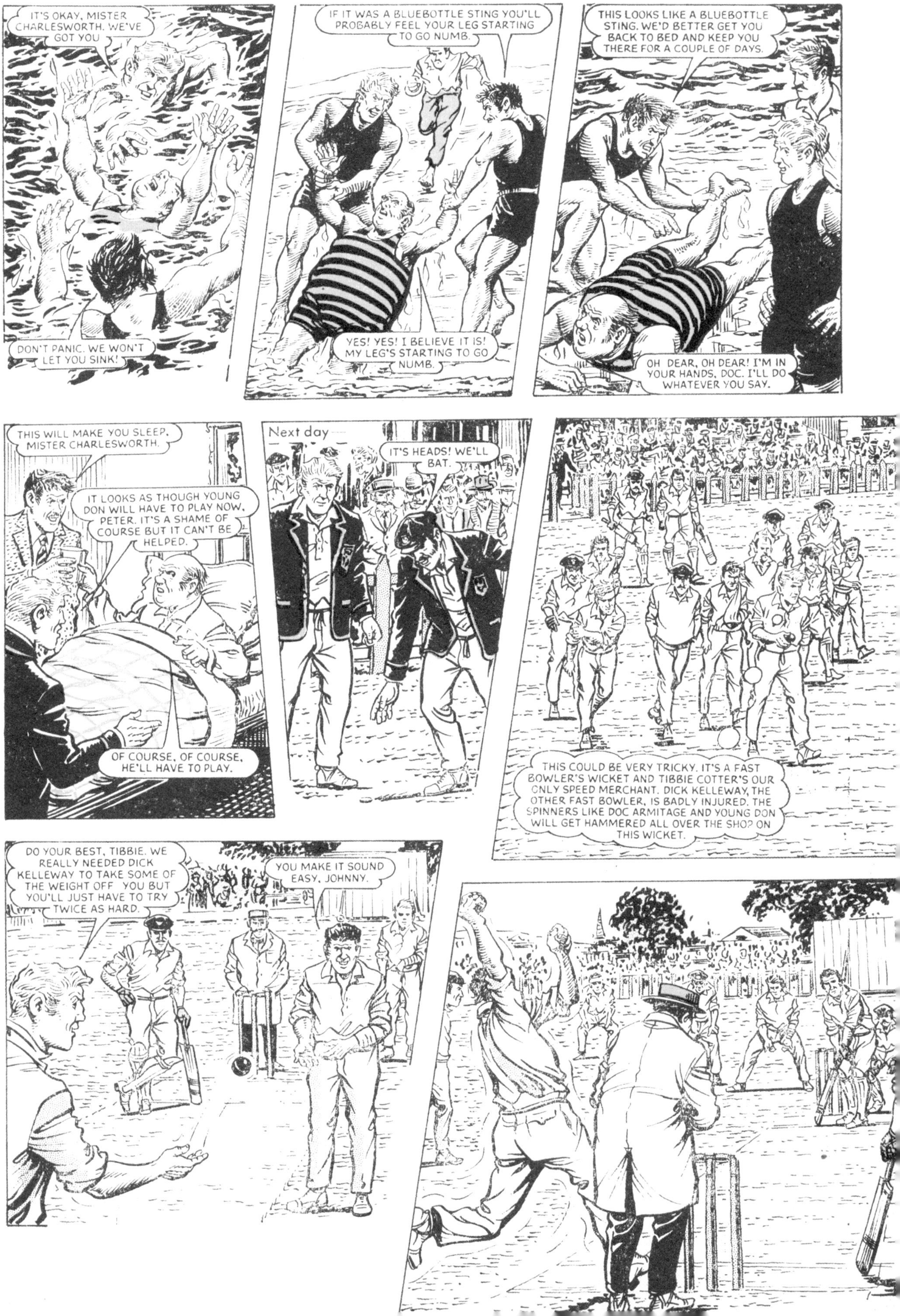

IT'S OKAY, MISTER CHARLESWORTH. WE'VE GOT YOU
DON'T PANIC. WE WON'T LET YOU SINK!
IF IT WAS A BLUEBOTTLE STING YOU'LL PROBABLY FEEL YOUR LEG STARTING TO GO NUMB.
YES! YES! I BELIEVE IT IS! MY LEG'S STARTING TO GO NUMB.
THIS LOOKS LIKE A BLUEBOTTLE STING. WE'D BETTER GET YOU BACK TO BED AND KEEP YOU THERE FOR A COUPLE OF DAYS.
OH DEAR, OH DEAR! I'M IN YOUR HANDS, DOC. I'LL DO WHATEVER YOU SAY.
THIS WILL MAKE YOU SLEEP, MISTER CHARLESWORTH.
IT LOOKS AS THOUGH YOUNG DON WILL HAVE TO PLAY NOW, PETER. IT'S A SHAME OF COURSE BUT IT CAN'T BE HELPED.
OF COURSE, OF COURSE, HE'LL HAVE TO PLAY.
Next day
IT'S HEADS! WE'LL BAT.
THIS COULD BE VERY TRICKY. IT'S A FAST BOWLER'S WICKET AND TIBBIE COTTER'S OUR ONLY SPEED MERCHANT. DICK KELLEWAY, THE OTHER FAST BOWLER, IS BADLY INJURED. THE SPINNERS LIKE DOC ARMITAGE AND YOUNG DON WILL GET HAMMERED ALL OVER THE SHOP ON THIS WICKET.
DO YOUR BEST, TIBBIE. WE REALLY NEEDED DICK KELLEWAY TO TAKE SOME OF THE WEIGHT OFF YOU BUT YOU'LL JUST HAVE TO TRY TWICE AS HARD.
YOU MAKE IT SOUND EASY, JOHNNY.

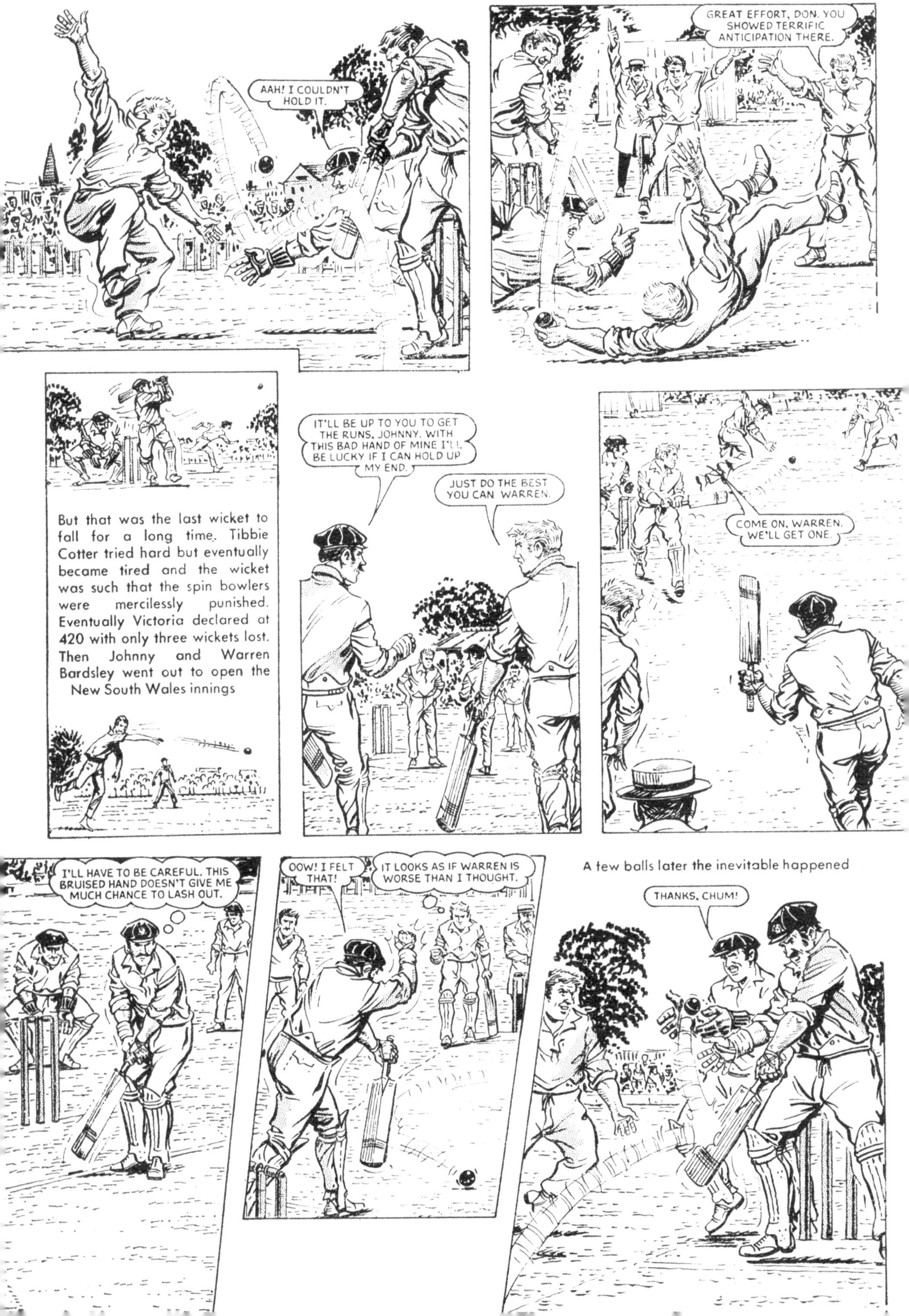
AAH! I COULDN'T HOLD IT.
GREAT EFFORT, DON. YOU SHOWED TERRIFIC ANTICIPATION THERE.
But that was the last wicket to fall for a long time. Tibbie Cotter tried hard but eventually became tired and the wicket was such that the spin bowlers were mercilessly punished. Eventually Victoria declared at 420 with only three wickets lost. Then Johnny and Warren Bardsley went out to open the New South Wales innings
IT'LL BE UP TO YOU TO GET THE RUNS, JOHNNY. WITH THIS BAD HAND OF MINE I'LL BE LUCKY IF I CAN HOLD UP MY END.
JUST DO THE BEST YOU CAN WARREN.
COME ON, WARREN. WE'LL GET ONE.
I'LL HAVE TO BE CAREFUL. THIS BRUISED HAND DOESN'T GIVE ME MUCH CHANCE TO LASH OUT.
OOW! I FELT THAT!
IT LOOKS AS IF WARREN IS WORSE THAN I THOUGHT.
A few balls later the inevitable happened
THANKS, CHUM!

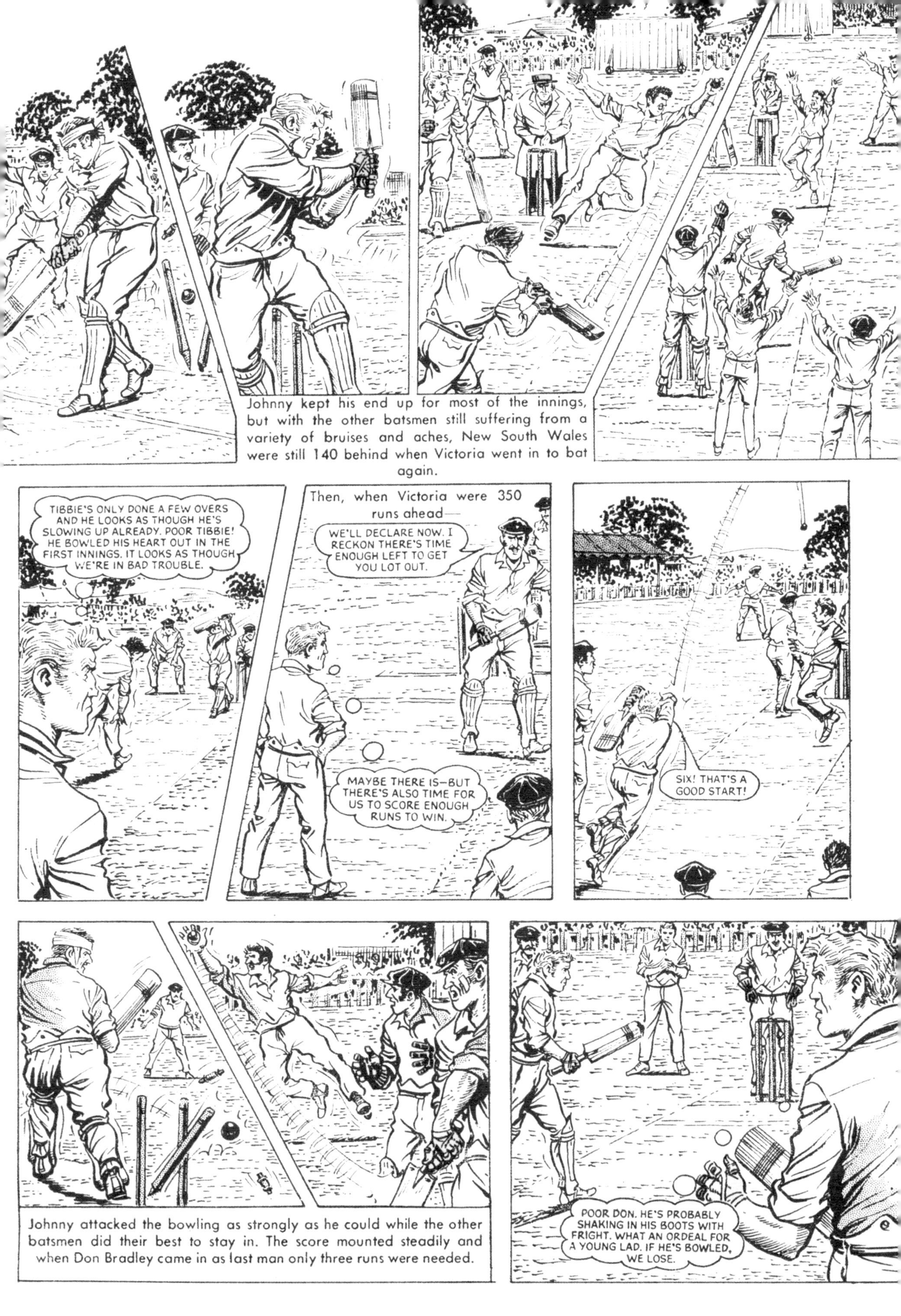
Johnny kept his end up for most of the innings, but with the other batsmen still suffering from a variety of bruises and aches, New South Wales were still 140 behind when Victoria went in to bat again.
TIBBIE'S ONLY DONE A FEW OVERS AND HE LOOKS AS THOUGH HE'S SLOWING UP ALREADY. POOR TIBBIE! HE BOWLED HIS HEART OUT IN THE FIRST INNINGS. IT LOOKS AS THOUGH WE'RE IN BAD TROUBLE.
Then, when Victoria were 350 runs ahead—
WE'LL DECLARE NOW. I RECKON THERE'S TIME ENOUGH LEFT TO GET YOU LOT OUT.
MAYBE THERE IS—BUT THERE'S ALSO TIME FOR US TO SCORE ENOUGH RUNS TO WIN.
SIX! THAT'S A GOOD START!
Johnny attacked the bowling as strongly as he could while the other batsmen did their best to stay in. The score mounted steadily and when Don Bradley came in as last man only three runs were needed.
POOR DON. HE'S PROBABLY SHAKING IN HIS BOOTS WITH FRIGHT. WHAT AN ORDEAL FOR A YOUNG LAD. IF HE'S BOWLED, WE LOSE.

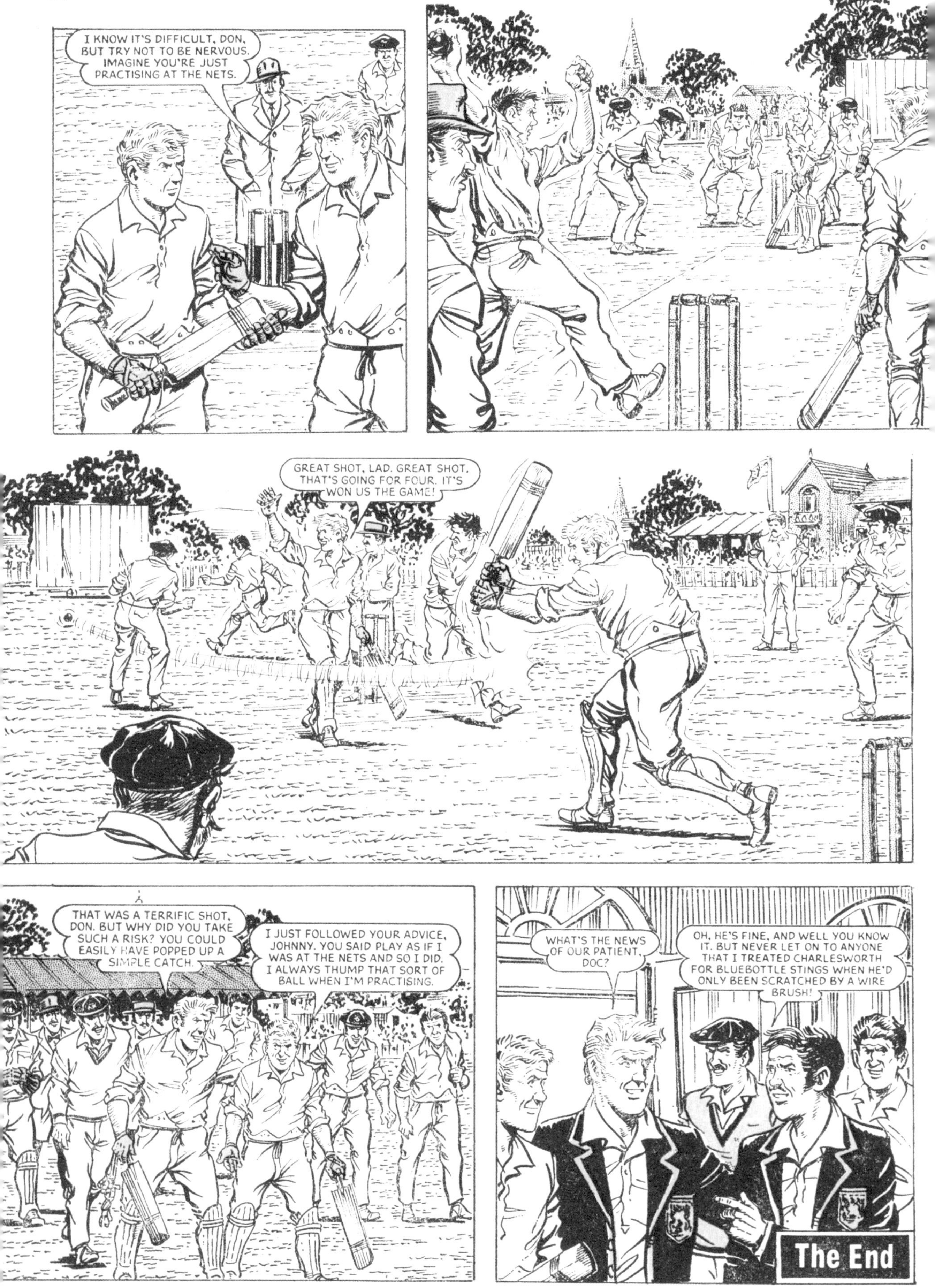
I KNOW IT'S DIFFICULT, DON, BUT TRY NOT TO BE NERVOUS. IMAGINE YOU'RE JUST PRACTISING AT THE NETS.
GREAT SHOT, LAD. GREAT SHOT. THAT'S GOING FOR FOUR. IT'S WON US THE GAME!
THAT WAS A TERRIFIC SHOT, DON. BUT WHY DID YOU TAKE SUCH A RISK? YOU COULD EASILY HAVE POPPED UP A SIMPLE CATCH.
I JUST FOLLOWED YOUR ADVICE, JOHNNY. YOU SAID PLAY AS IF I WAS AT THE NETS AND SO I DID. I ALWAYS THUMP THAT SORT OF BALL WHEN I'M PRACTISING.
WHAT'S THE NEWS OF OUR PATIENT, DOC?
OH, HE'S FINE, AND WELL YOU KNOW IT. BUT NEVER LET ON TO ANYONE THAT I TREATED CHARLESWORTH FOR BLUEBOTTLE STINGS WHEN HE'D ONLY BEEN SCRATCHED BY A WIRE BRUSH!
The End

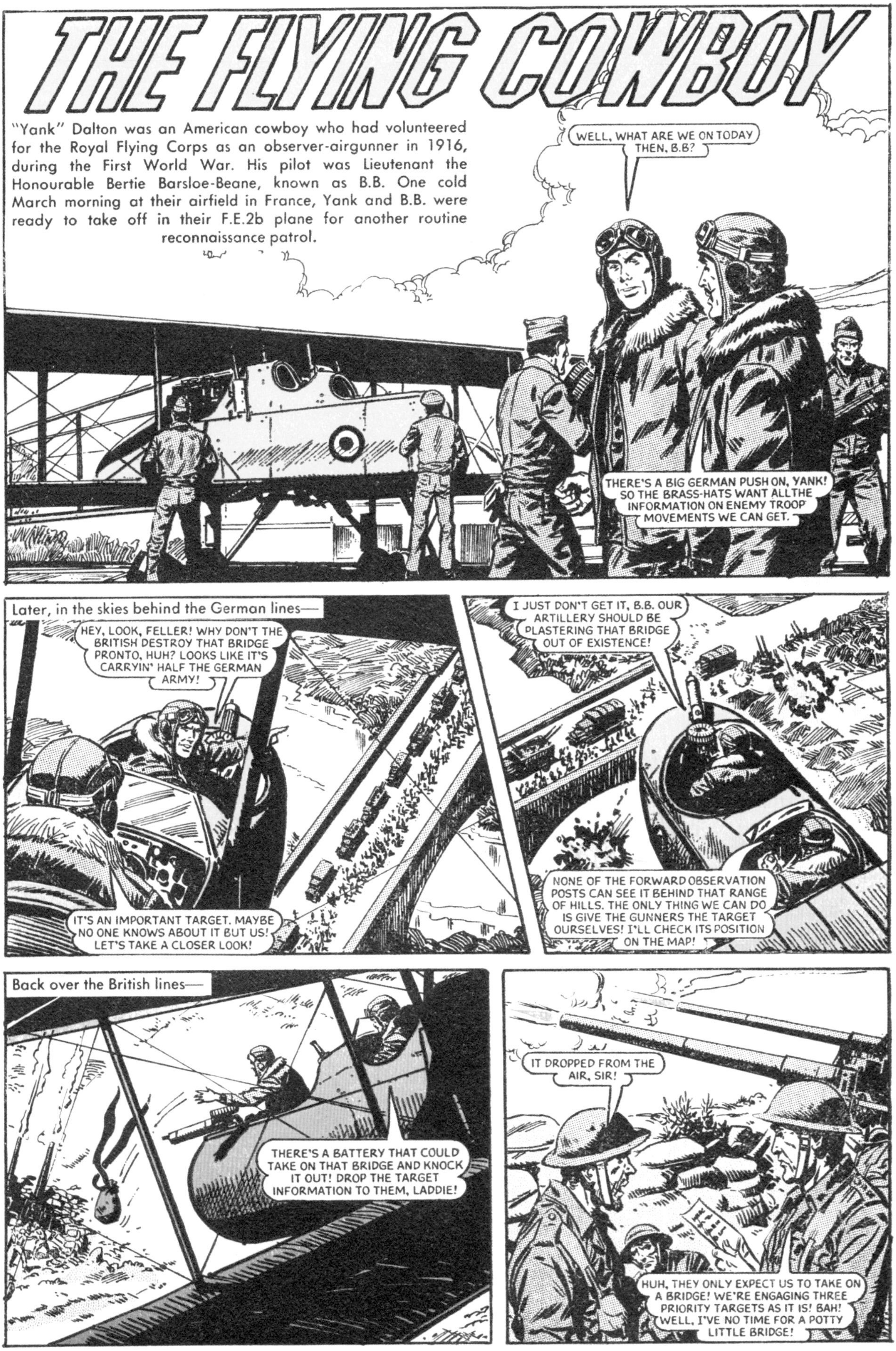
THE FLYING COWBOY
"Yank" Dalton was an American cowboy who had volunteered for the Royal Flying Corps as an observer-airgunner in 1916, during the First World War. His pilot was Lieutenant the Honourable Bertie Barsloe-Beane, known as B.B. One cold March morning at their airfield in France, Yank and B.B. were ready to take off in their F.E.2b plane for another routine reconnaissance patrol.
WELL, WHAT ARE WE ON TODAY THEN, B.B?
THERE'S A BIG GERMAN PUSH ON, YANK! SO THE BRASS-HATS WANT ALL THE INFORMATION ON ENEMY TROOP MOVEMENTS WE CAN GET.
Later, in the skies behind the German lines—
HEY, LOOK, FELLER! WHY DON'T THE BRITISH DESTROY THAT BRIDGE PRONTO, HUH? LOOKS LIKE IT'S CARRYIN' HALF THE GERMAN ARMY!
IT'S AN IMPORTANT TARGET. MAYBE NO ONE KNOWS ABOUT IT BUT US! LET'S TAKE A CLOSER LOOK!
I JUST DON'T GET IT, B.B. OUR ARTILLERY SHOULD BE PLASTERING THAT BRIDGE OUT OF EXISTENCE!
NONE OF THE FORWARD OBSERVATION POSTS CAN SEE IT BEHIND THAT RANGE OF HILLS. THE ONLY THING WE CAN DO IS GIVE THE GUNNERS THE TARGET OURSELVES! I'LL CHECK ITS POSITION ON THE MAP!
Back over the British lines—
THERE'S A BATTERY THAT COULD TAKE ON THAT BRIDGE AND KNOCK IT OUT! DROP THE TARGET INFORMATION TO THEM, LADDIE!
IT DROPPED FROM THE AIR, SIR!
HUH, THEY ONLY EXPECT US TO TAKE ON A BRIDGE! WE'RE ENGAGING THREE PRIORITY TARGETS AS IT IS! BAH! WELL, I'VE NO TIME FOR A POTTY LITTLE BRIDGE!

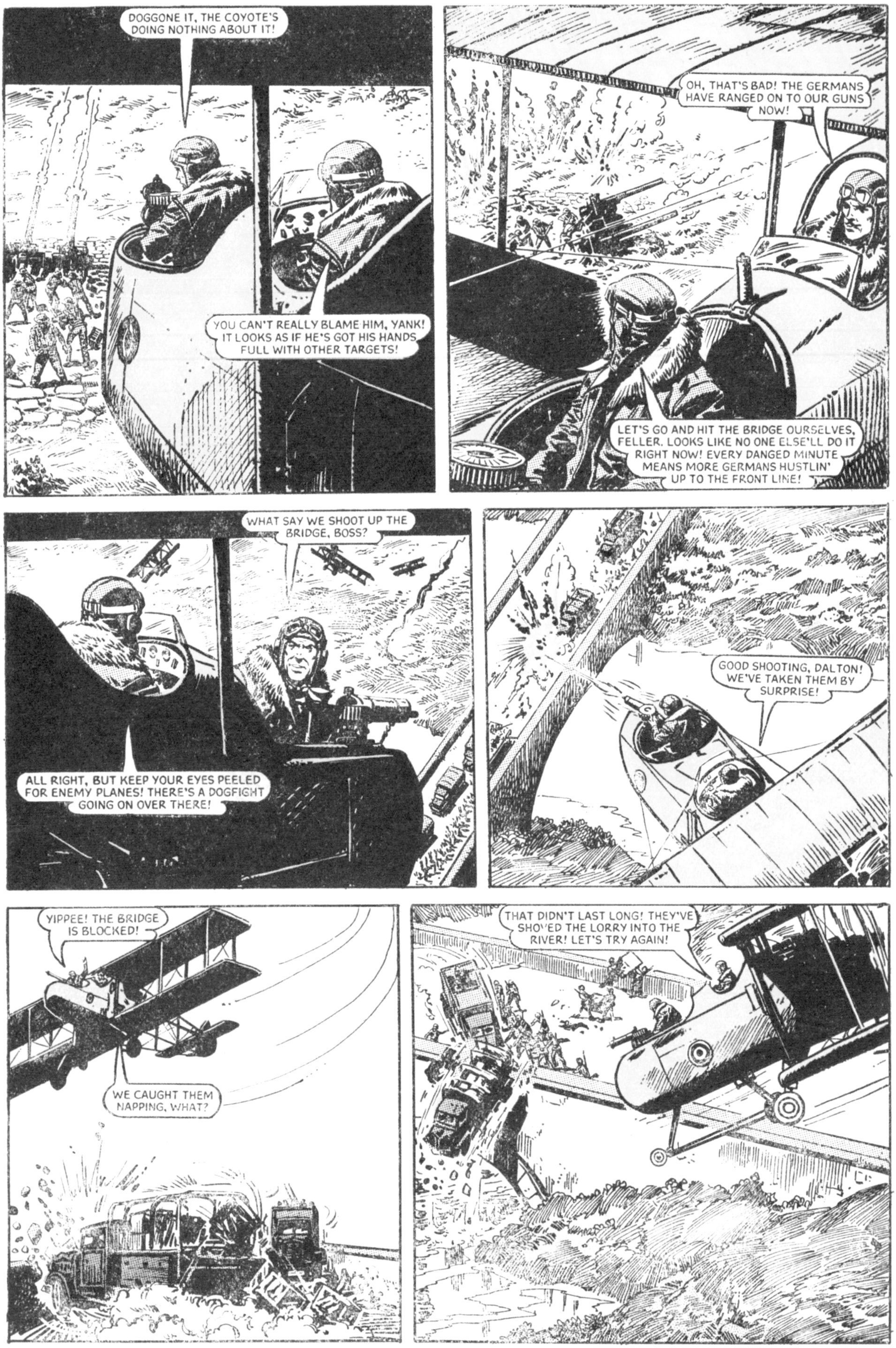
DOGGONE IT, THE COYOTE'S DOING NOTHING ABOUT IT!
YOU CAN'T REALLY BLAME HIM, YANK! IT LOOKS AS IF HE'S GOT HIS HANDS FULL WITH OTHER TARGETS!
OH, THAT'S BAD! THE GERMANS HAVE RANGED ON TO OUR GUNS NOW!
LET'S GO AND HIT THE BRIDGE OURSELVES, FELLER. LOOKS LIKE NO ONE ELSE'LL DO IT RIGHT NOW! EVERY DANGED MINUTE MEANS MORE GERMANS HUSTLIN' UP TO THE FRONT LINE!
WHAT SAY WE SHOOT UP THE BRIDGE, BOSS?
ALL RIGHT, BUT KEEP YOUR EYES PEELED FOR ENEMY PLANES! THERE'S A DOGFIGHT GOING ON OVER THERE!
GOOD SHOOTING, DALTON! WE'VE TAKEN THEM BY SURPRISE!
YIPPEE! THE BRIDGE IS BLOCKED!
WE CAUGHT THEM NAPPING, WHAT?
THAT DIDN'T LAST LONG! THEY'VE SHOVED THE LORRY INTO THE RIVER! LET'S TRY AGAIN!

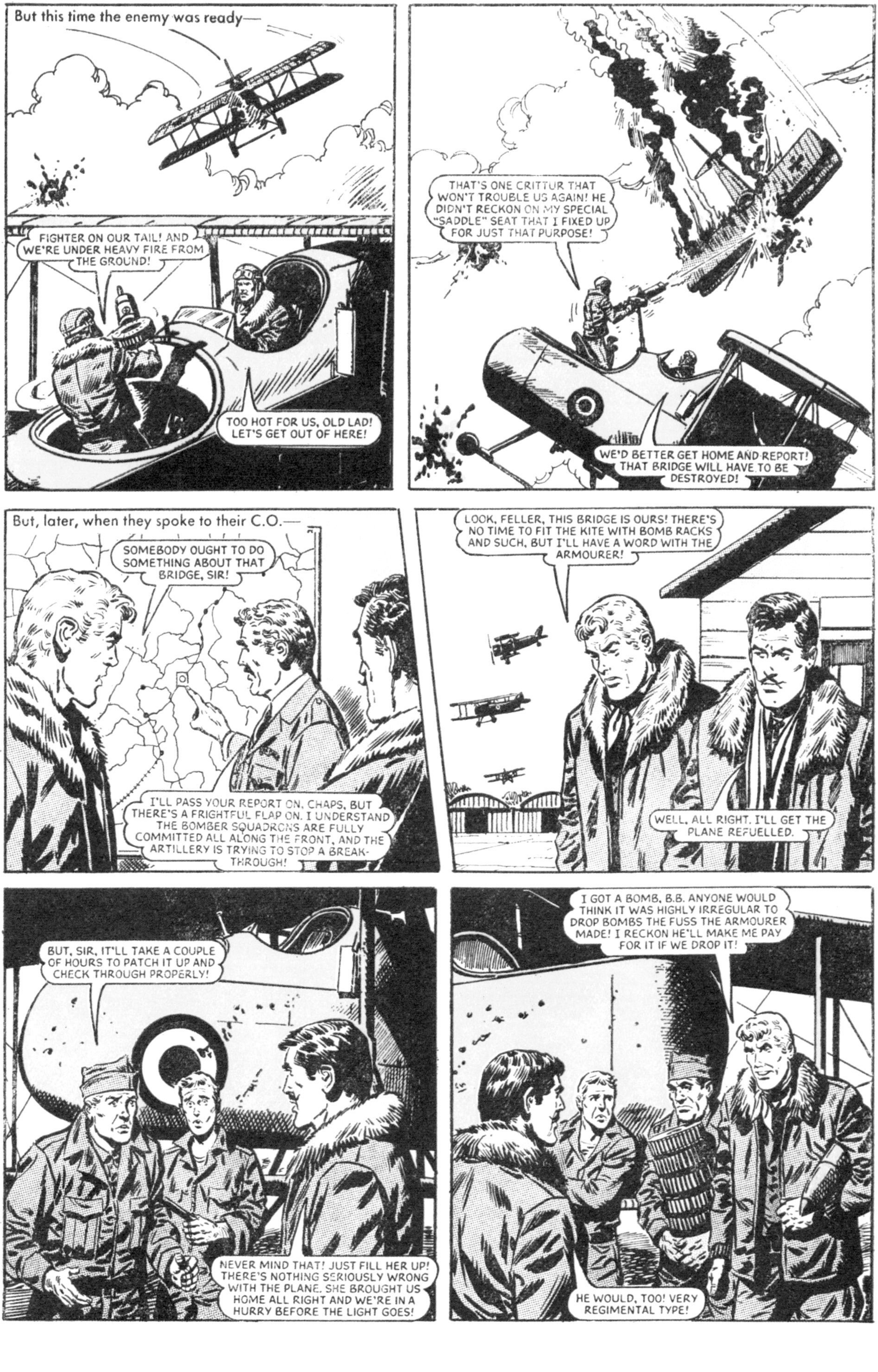
But this time the enemy was ready—
FIGHTER ON OUR TAIL! AND WE'RE UNDER HEAVY FIRE FROM THE GROUND!
TOO HOT FOR US, OLD LAD! LET'S GET OUT OF HERE!
THAT'S ONE CRITTUR THAT WON'T TROUBLE US AGAIN! HE DIDN'T RECKON ON MY SPECIAL "SADDLE" SEAT THAT I FIXED UP FOR JUST THAT PURPOSE!
WE'D BETTER GET HOME AND REPORT! THAT BRIDGE WILL HAVE TO BE DESTROYED!
But, later, when they spoke to their C.O.—
SOMEBODY OUGHT TO DO SOMETHING ABOUT THAT BRIDGE, SIR!
I'LL PASS YOUR REPORT ON, CHAPS, BUT THERE'S A FRIGHTFUL FLAP ON. I UNDERSTAND THE BOMBER SQUADRONS ARE FULLY COMMITTED ALL ALONG THE FRONT, AND THE ARTILLERY IS TRYING TO STOP A BREAK-THROUGH!
LOOK, FELLER, THIS BRIDGE IS OURS! THERE'S NO TIME TO FIT THE KITE WITH BOMB RACKS AND SUCH, BUT I'LL HAVE A WORD WITH THE ARMOURER!
WELL, ALL RIGHT. I'LL GET THE PLANE REFUELLED.
BUT, SIR, IT'LL TAKE A COUPLE OF HOURS TO PATCH IT UP AND CHECK THROUGH PROPERLY!
NEVER MIND THAT! JUST FILL HER UP! THERE'S NOTHING SERIOUSLY WRONG WITH THE PLANE. SHE BROUGHT US HOME ALL RIGHT AND WE'RE IN A HURRY BEFORE THE LIGHT GOES!
I GOT A BOMB, B.B. ANYONE WOULD THINK IT WAS HIGHLY IRREGULAR TO DROP BOMBS THE FUSS THE ARMOURER MADE! I RECKON HE'LL MAKE ME PAY FOR IT IF WE DROP IT!
HE WOULD, TOO! VERY REGIMENTAL TYPE!

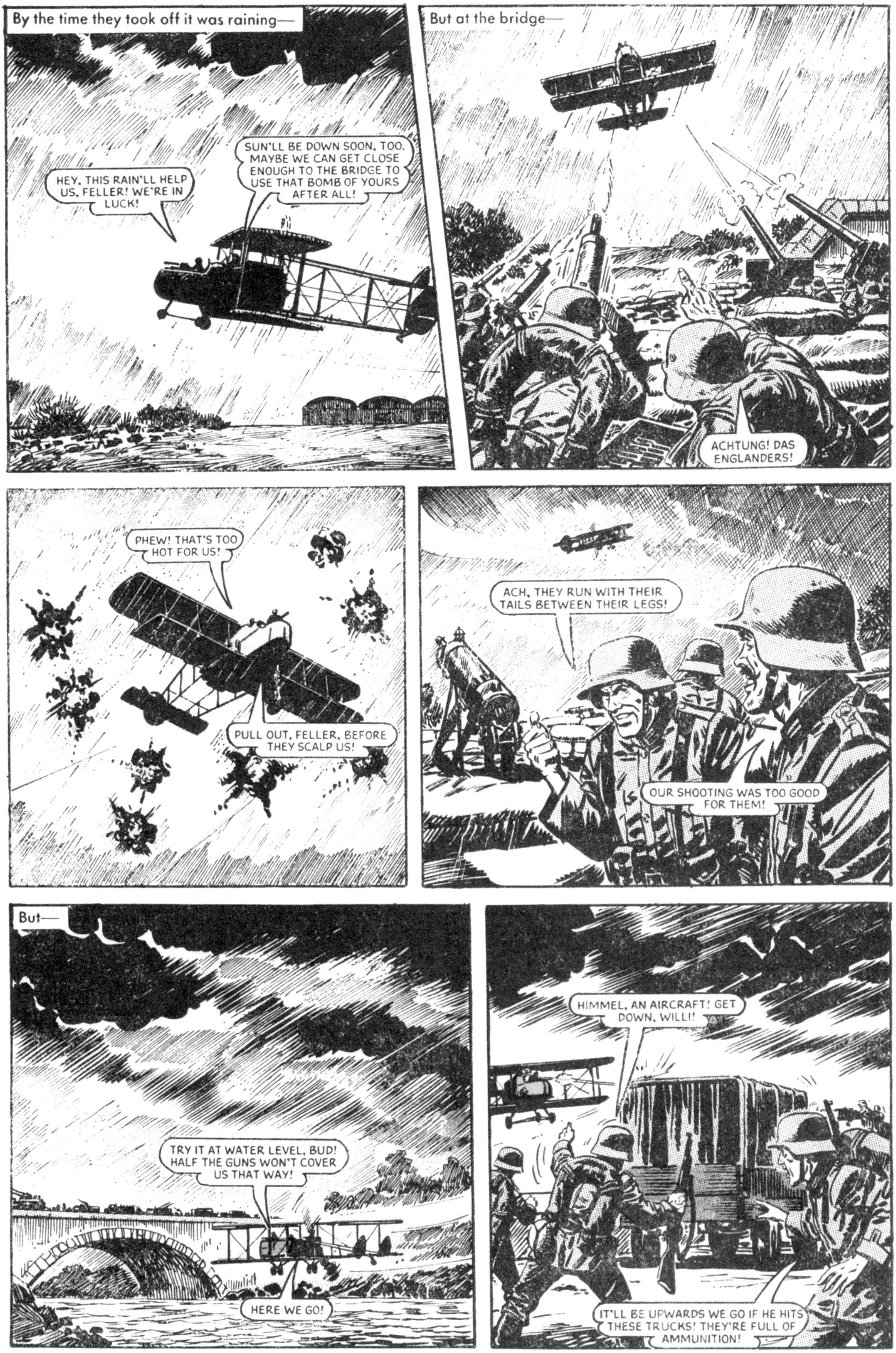
By the time they took off it was raining—
HEY, THIS RAIN'LL HELP US, FELLER! WE'RE IN LUCK!
SUN'LL BE DOWN SOON, TOO. MAYBE WE CAN GET CLOSE ENOUGH TO THE BRIDGE TO USE THAT BOMB OF YOURS AFTER ALL!
But at the bridge—
ACHTUNG! DAS ENGLANDERS!
PHEW! THAT'S TOO HOT FOR US!
PULL OUT, FELLER, BEFORE THEY SCALP US!
ACH, THEY RUN WITH THEIR TAILS BETWEEN THEIR LEGS!
OUR SHOOTING WAS TOO GOOD FOR THEM!
But—
TRY IT AT WATER LEVEL, BUD! HALF THE GUNS WON'T COVER US THAT WAY!
HERE WE GO!
HIMMEL, AN AIRCRAFT! GET DOWN, WILLI!
IT'LL BE UPWARDS WE GO IF HE HITS THESE TRUCKS! THEY'RE FULL OF AMMUNITION!

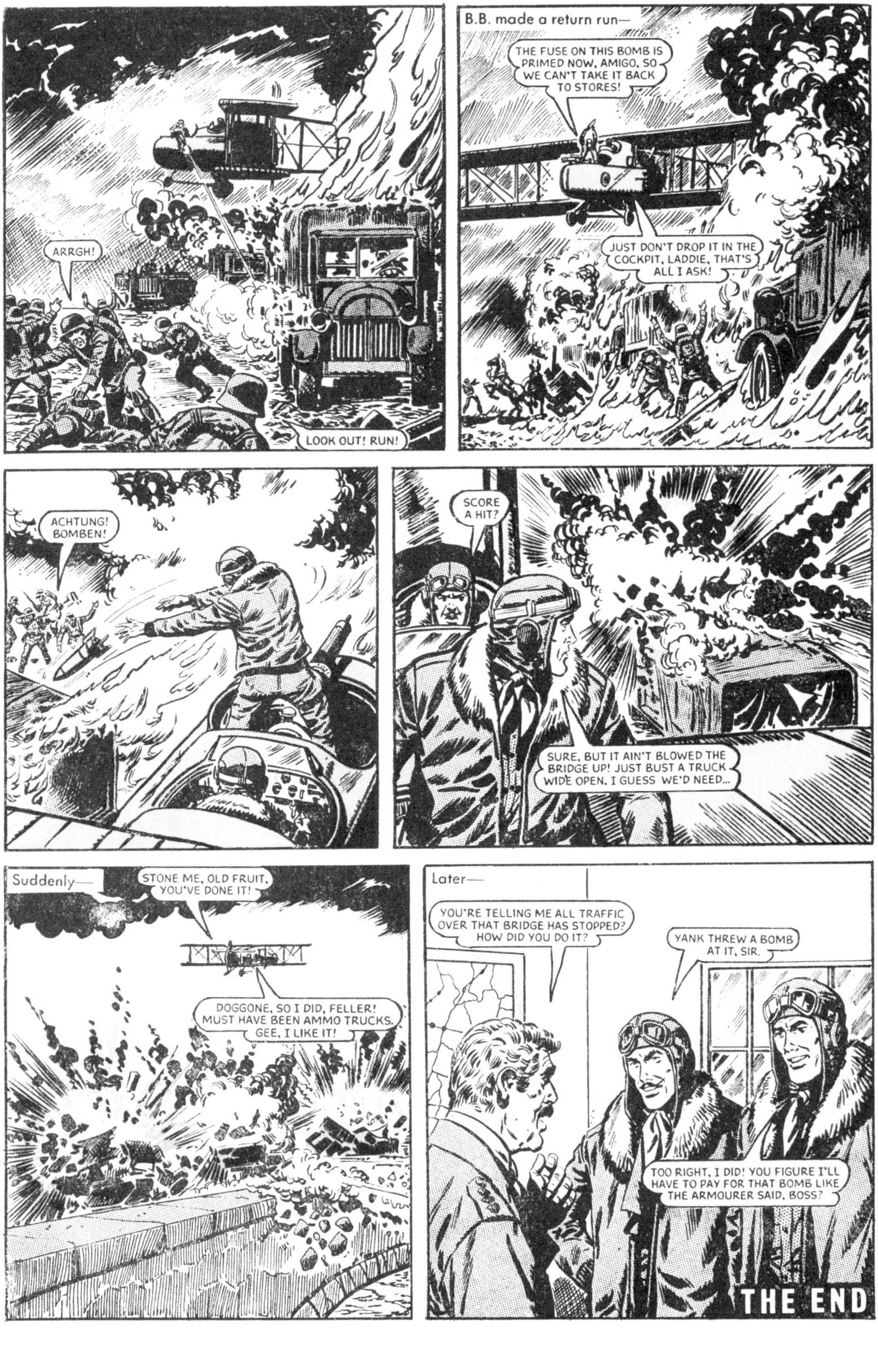
ARRGH!
LOOK OUT! RUN!
B.B. made a return run—
THE FUSE ON THIS BOMB IS PRIMED NOW, AMIGO, SO WE CAN'T TAKE IT BACK TO STORES!
JUST DON'T DROP IT IN THE COCKPIT, LADDIE, THAT'S ALL I ASK!
ACHTUNG! BOMBEN!
SCORE A HIT?
SURE, BUT IT AIN'T BLOWED THE BRIDGE UP! JUST BUST A TRUCK WIDE OPEN. I GUESS WE'D NEED...
Suddenly—
STONE ME, OLD FRUIT, YOU'VE DONE IT!
DOGGONE, SO I DID, FELLER! MUST HAVE BEEN AMMO TRUCKS. GEE, I LIKE IT!
Later—
YOU'RE TELLING ME ALL TRAFFIC OVER THAT BRIDGE HAS STOPPED? HOW DID YOU DO IT?
YANK THREW A BOMB AT IT, SIR.
TOO RIGHT, I DID! YOU FIGURE I'LL HAVE TO PAY FOR THAT BOMB LIKE THE ARMOURER SAID, BOSS?
THE END

ODD CARS

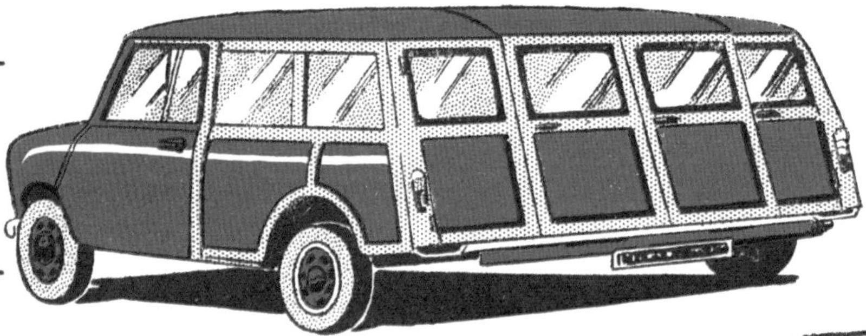

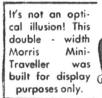

It's not an optical illusion! This double - width Morris Mini-Traveller was built for display purposes only.

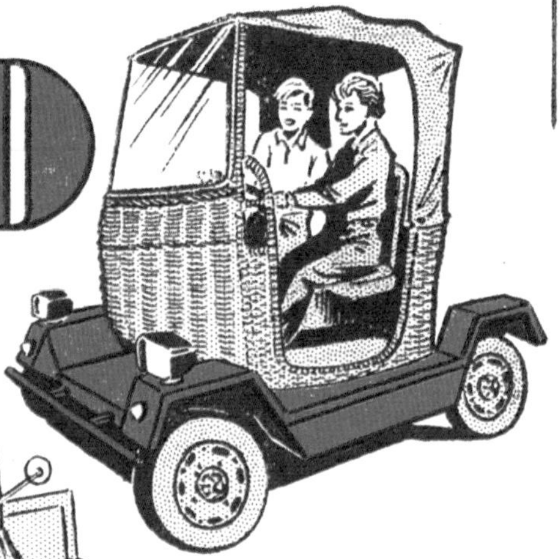

This novel basket weave car is powered by a 24-volt battery.

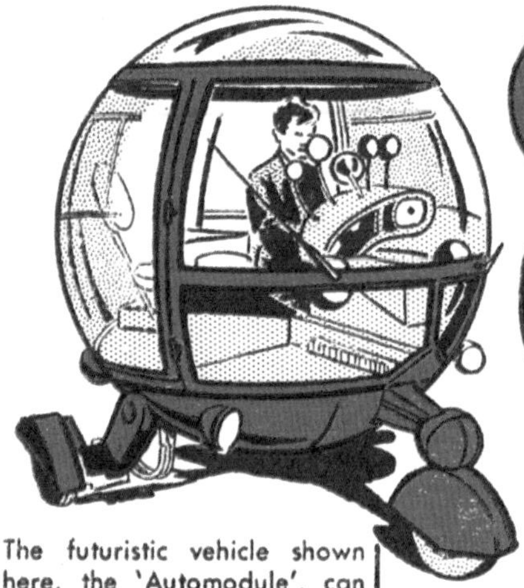

The futuristic vehicle shown here, the 'Automodule', can run in any direction due to a unique arrangement of its steering system.

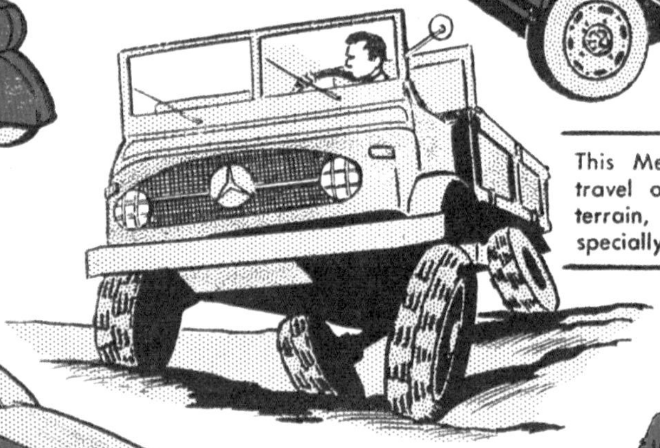

This Mercedes Unimog can travel over the roughest of terrain, thanks to its specially designed suspension.

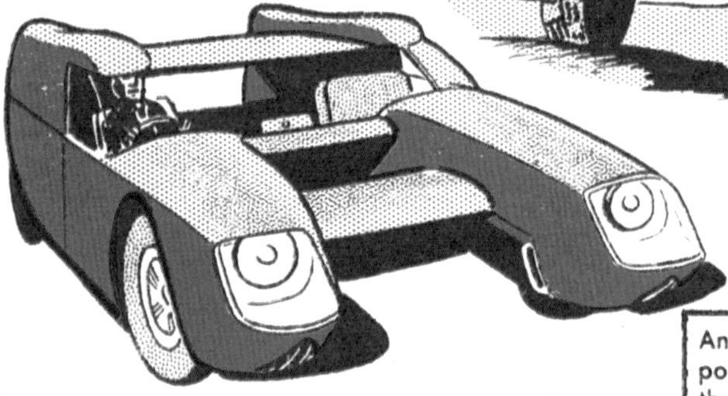

This unusual catamaran-shaped sports-car, the 'Silver Fox', was built in Italy.

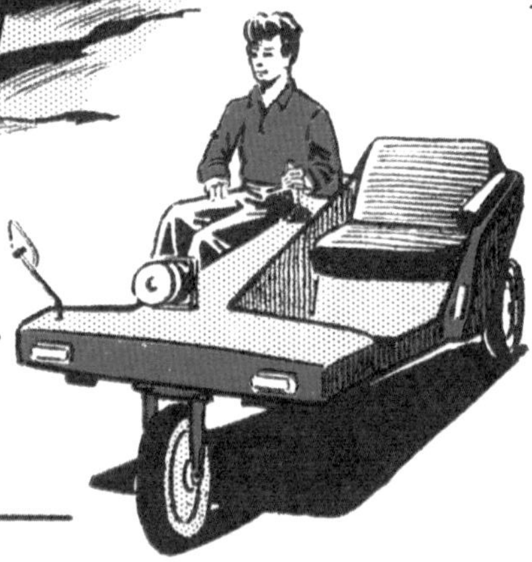

Another electrically-powered car—a three wheeler intended for use as a city runabout.

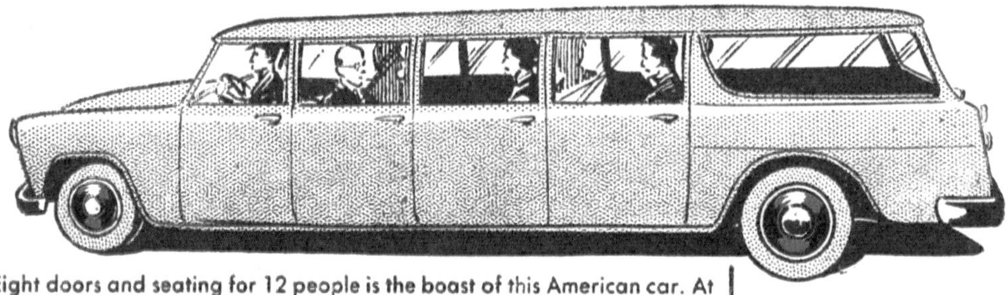

Eight doors and seating for 12 people is the boast of this American car. At 22 ft. 5 ¾ inches, the Checker Aerocar is the world's longest modern car.

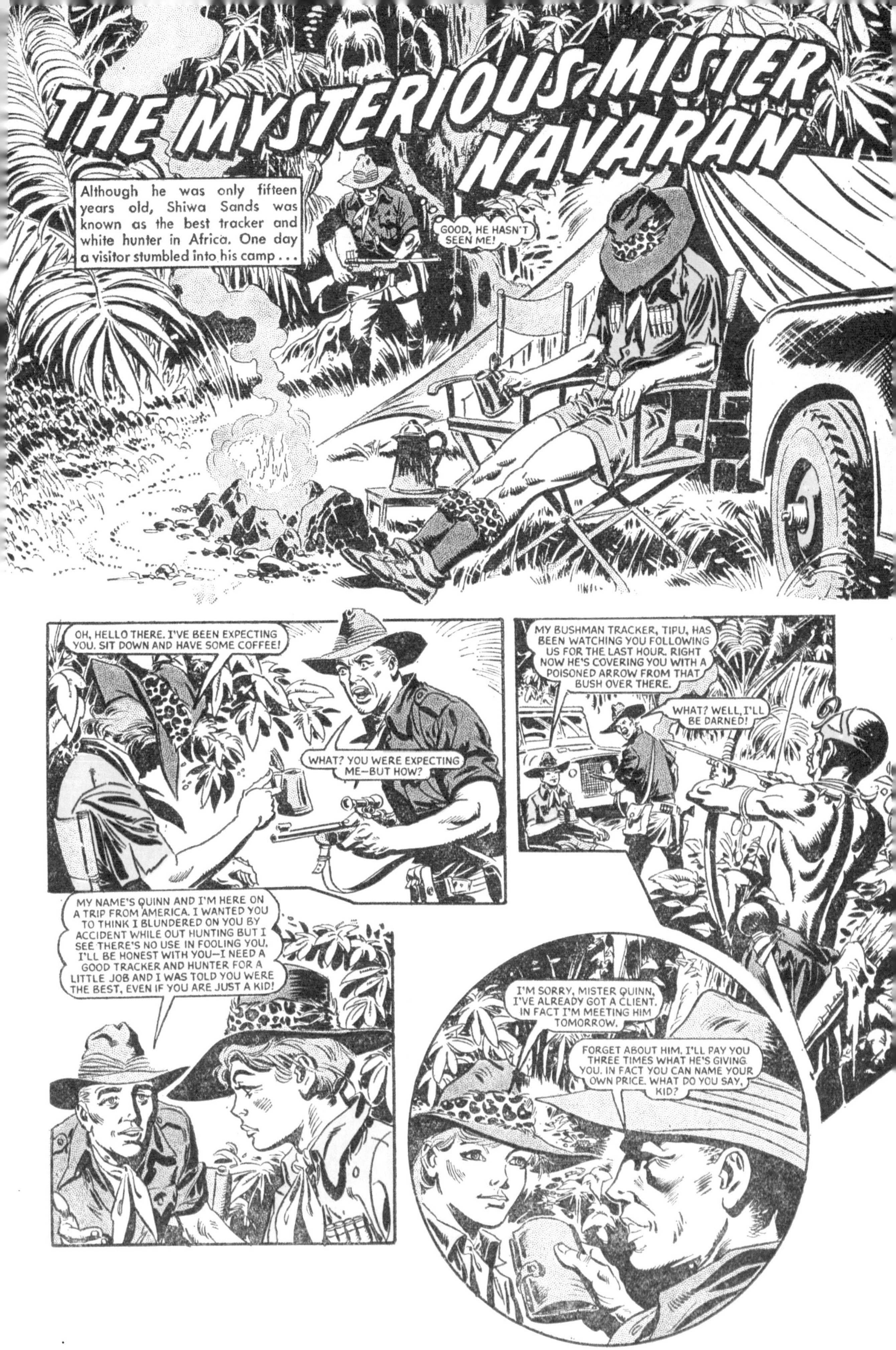
THE MYSTERIOUS MISTER NAVARAN
Although he was only fifteen years old, Shiwa Sands was known as the best tracker and white hunter in Africa. One day a visitor stumbled into his camp . . .
GOOD, HE HASN'T SEEN ME!
OH, HELLO THERE. I'VE BEEN EXPECTING YOU. SIT DOWN AND HAVE SOME COFFEE!
WHAT? YOU WERE EXPECTING ME—BUT HOW?
MY BUSHMAN TRACKER, TIPU, HAS BEEN WATCHING YOU FOLLOWING US FOR THE LAST HOUR. RIGHT NOW HE'S COVERING YOU WITH A POISONED ARROW FROM THAT BUSH OVER THERE.
WHAT? WELL, I'LL BE DARNED!
MY NAME'S QUINN AND I'M HERE ON A TRIP FROM AMERICA. I WANTED YOU TO THINK I BLUNDERED ON YOU BY ACCIDENT WHILE OUT HUNTING BUT I SEE THERE'S NO USE IN FOOLING YOU. I'LL BE HONEST WITH YOU—I NEED A GOOD TRACKER AND HUNTER FOR A LITTLE JOB AND I WAS TOLD YOU WERE THE BEST, EVEN IF YOU ARE JUST A KID!
I'M SORRY, MISTER QUINN. I'VE ALREADY GOT A CLIENT. IN FACT I'M MEETING HIM TOMORROW.
FORGET ABOUT HIM. I'LL PAY YOU THREE TIMES WHAT HE'S GIVING YOU. IN FACT YOU CAN NAME YOUR OWN PRICE. WHAT DO YOU SAY, KID?

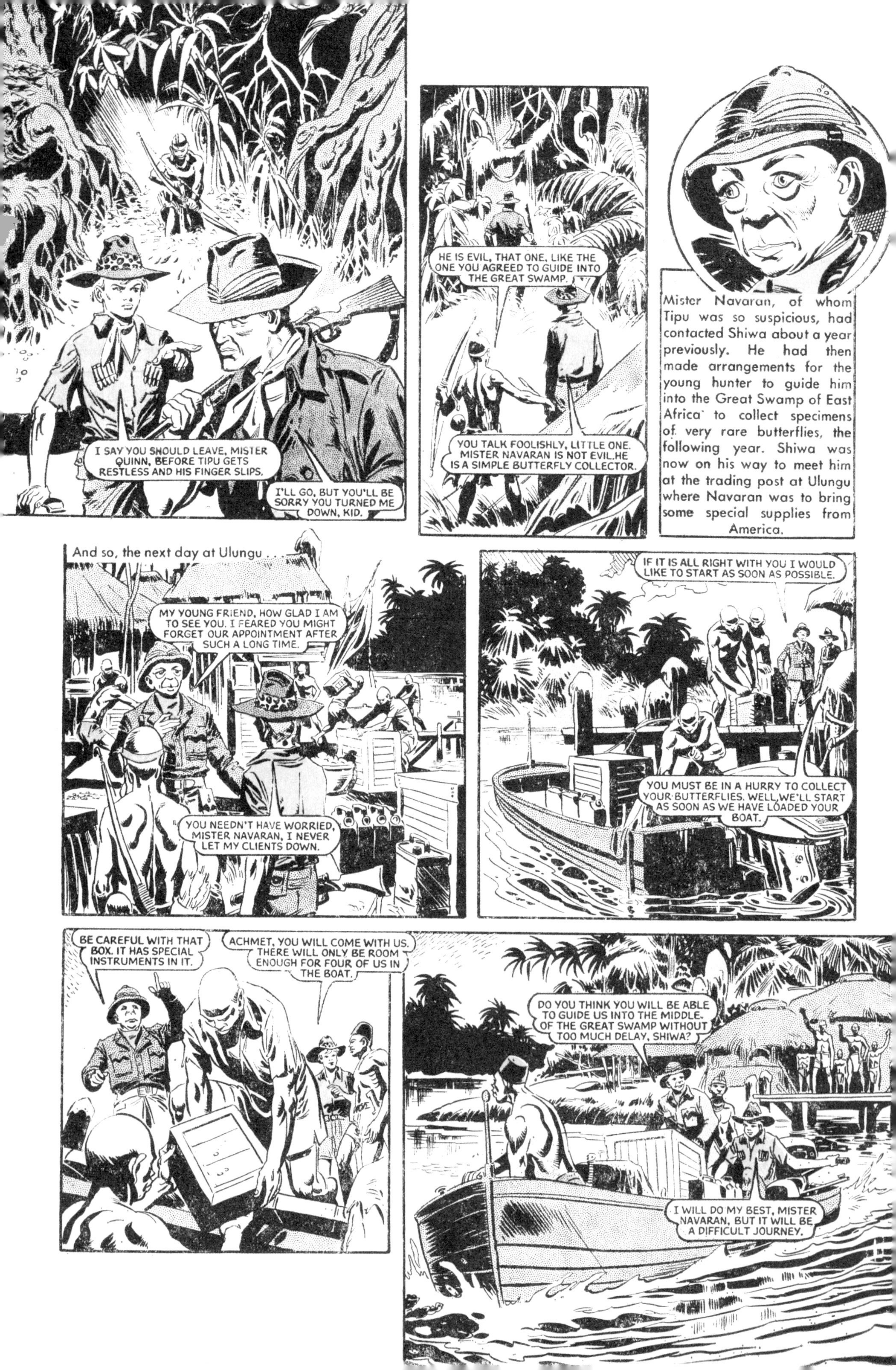
I SAY YOU SHOULD LEAVE, MISTER QUINN, BEFORE TIPU GETS RESTLESS AND HIS FINGER SLIPS.
I'LL GO, BUT YOU'LL BE SORRY YOU TURNED ME DOWN, KID.
HE IS EVIL, THAT ONE, LIKE THE ONE YOU AGREED TO GUIDE INTO THE GREAT SWAMP.
YOU TALK FOOLISHLY, LITTLE ONE. MISTER NAVARAN IS NOT EVIL. HE IS A SIMPLE BUTTERFLY COLLECTOR.
Mister Navaran, of whom Tipu was so suspicious, had contacted Shiwa about a year previously. He had then made arrangements for the young hunter to guide him into the Great Swamp of East Africa to collect specimens of very rare butterflies, the following year. Shiwa was now on his way to meet him at the trading post at Ulungu where Navaran was to bring some special supplies from America.
And so, the next day at Ulungu . . .
MY YOUNG FRIEND, HOW GLAD I AM TO SEE YOU. I FEARED YOU MIGHT FORGET OUR APPOINTMENT AFTER SUCH A LONG TIME.
YOU NEEDN'T HAVE WORRIED, MISTER NAVARAN, I NEVER LET MY CLIENTS DOWN.
IF IT IS ALL RIGHT WITH YOU I WOULD LIKE TO START AS SOON AS POSSIBLE.
YOU MUST BE IN A HURRY TO COLLECT YOUR BUTTERFLIES. WELL, WE'LL START AS SOON AS WE HAVE LOADED YOUR BOAT.
BE CAREFUL WITH THAT BOX. IT HAS SPECIAL INSTRUMENTS IN IT.
ACHMET, YOU WILL COME WITH US. THERE WILL ONLY BE ROOM ENOUGH FOR FOUR OF US IN THE BOAT.
DO YOU THINK YOU WILL BE ABLE TO GUIDE US INTO THE MIDDLE OF THE GREAT SWAMP WITHOUT TOO MUCH DELAY, SHIWA?
I WILL DO MY BEST, MISTER NAVARAN, BUT IT WILL BE A DIFFICULT JOURNEY.

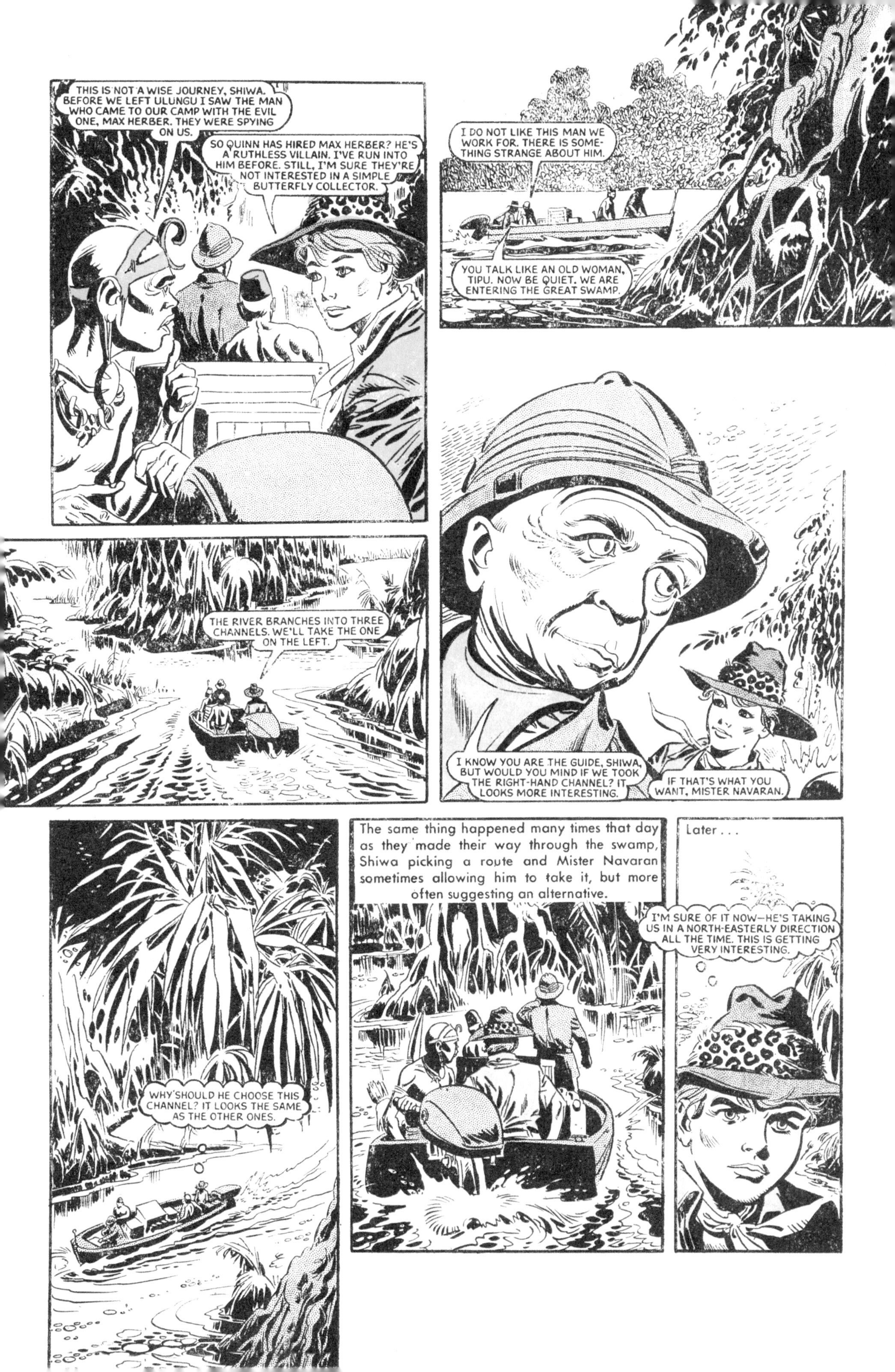
THIS IS NOT A WISE JOURNEY, SHIWA. BEFORE WE LEFT ULUNGU I SAW THE MAN WHO CAME TO OUR CAMP WITH THE EVIL ONE, MAX HERBER. THEY WERE SPYING ON US.
SO QUINN HAS HIRED MAX HERBER? HE'S A RUTHLESS VILLAIN. I'VE RUN INTO HIM BEFORE. STILL, I'M SURE THEY'RE NOT INTERESTED IN A SIMPLE BUTTERFLY COLLECTOR.
I DO NOT LIKE THIS MAN WE WORK FOR. THERE IS SOMETHING STRANGE ABOUT HIM.
YOU TALK LIKE AN OLD WOMAN, TIPU. NOW BE QUIET. WE ARE ENTERING THE GREAT SWAMP.
THE RIVER BRANCHES INTO THREE CHANNELS. WE'LL TAKE THE ONE ON THE LEFT.
I KNOW YOU ARE THE GUIDE, SHIWA, BUT WOULD YOU MIND IF WE TOOK THE RIGHT-HAND CHANNEL? IT LOOKS MORE INTERESTING.
IF THAT'S WHAT YOU WANT, MISTER NAVARAN.
WHY SHOULD HE CHOOSE THIS CHANNEL? IT LOOKS THE SAME AS THE OTHER ONES.
The same thing happened many times that day as they made their way through the swamp, Shiwa picking a route and Mister Navaran sometimes allowing him to take it, but more often suggesting an alternative.
Later . . .
I'M SURE OF IT NOW—HE'S TAKING US IN A NORTH-EASTERLY DIRECTION ALL THE TIME. THIS IS GETTING VERY INTERESTING.

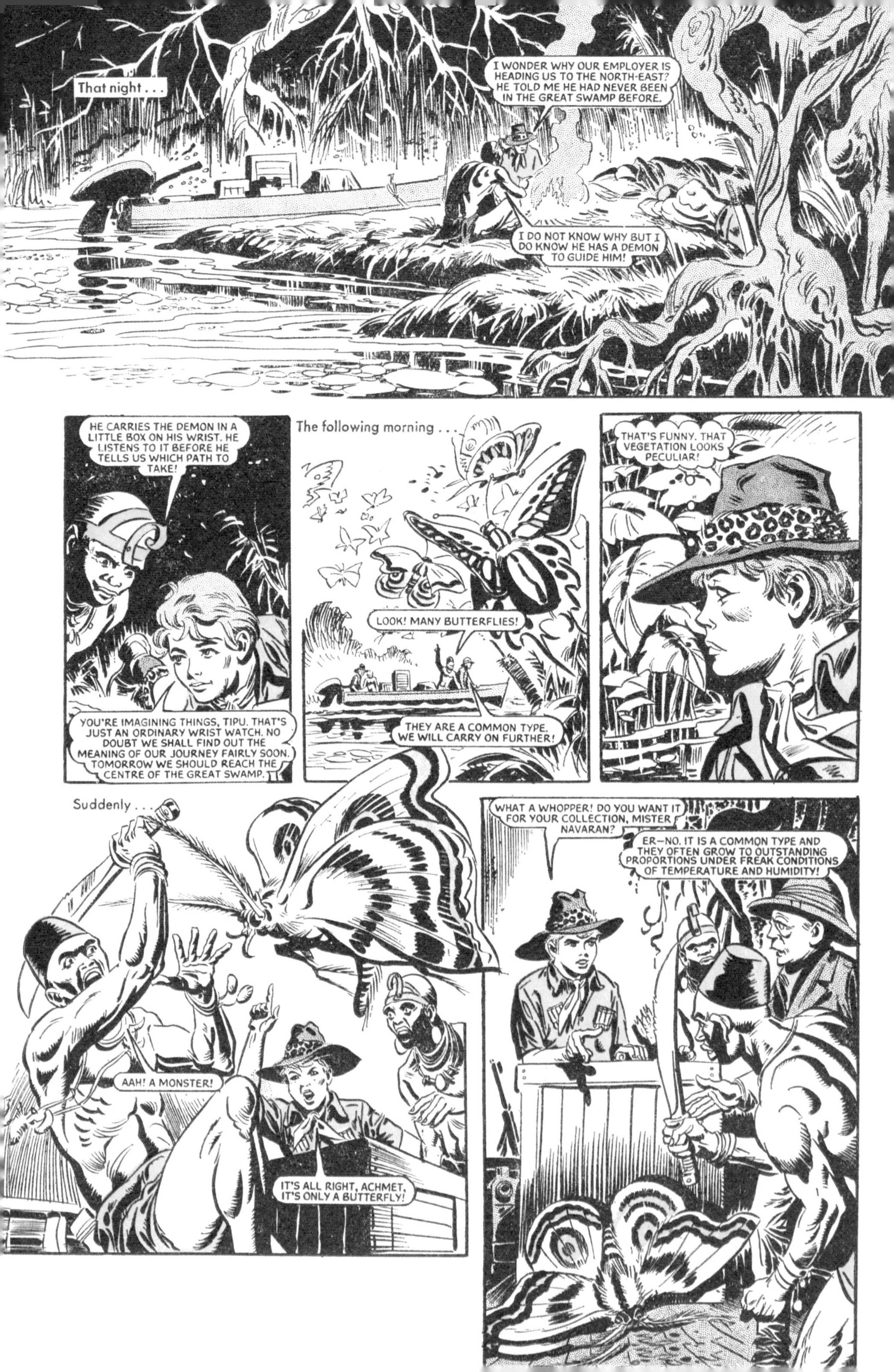
That night . . .
I WONDER WHY OUR EMPLOYER IS HEADING US TO THE NORTH-EAST? HE TOLD ME HE HAD NEVER BEEN IN THE GREAT SWAMP BEFORE.
I DO NOT KNOW WHY BUT I DO KNOW HE HAS A DEMON TO GUIDE HIM!
HE CARRIES THE DEMON IN A LITTLE BOX ON HIS WRIST. HE LISTENS TO IT BEFORE HE TELLS US WHICH PATH TO TAKE!
YOU'RE IMAGINING THINGS, TIPU. THAT'S JUST AN ORDINARY WRIST WATCH. NO DOUBT WE SHALL FIND OUT THE MEANING OF OUR JOURNEY FAIRLY SOON. TOMORROW WE SHOULD REACH THE CENTRE OF THE GREAT SWAMP.
The following morning . . .
LOOK! MANY BUTTERFLIES!
THEY ARE A COMMON TYPE. WE WILL CARRY ON FURTHER!
THAT'S FUNNY. THAT VEGETATION LOOKS PECULIAR!
Suddenly . . .
AAH! A MONSTER!
IT'S ALL RIGHT, ACHMET, IT'S ONLY A BUTTERFLY!
WHAT A WHOPPER! DO YOU WANT IT FOR YOUR COLLECTION, MISTER NAVARAN?
ER—NO. IT IS A COMMON TYPE AND THEY OFTEN GROW TO OUTSTANDING PROPORTIONS UNDER FREAK CONDITIONS OF TEMPERATURE AND HUMIDITY!

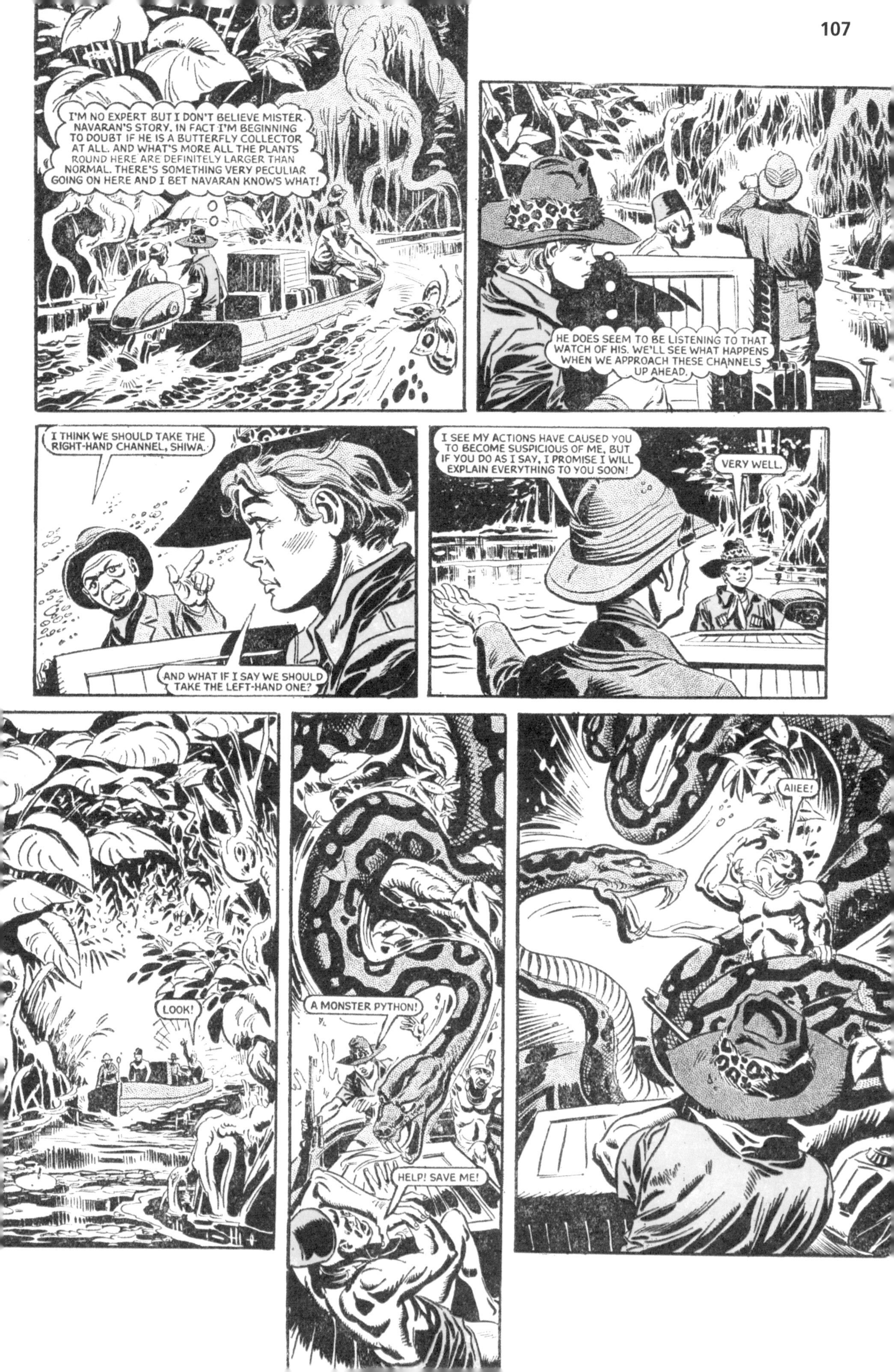
I'M NO EXPERT BUT I DON'T BELIEVE MISTER NAVARAN'S STORY. IN FACT I'M BEGINNING TO DOUBT IF HE IS A BUTTERFLY COLLECTOR AT ALL. AND WHAT'S MORE ALL THE PLANTS ROUND HERE ARE DEFINITELY LARGER THAN NORMAL. THERE'S SOMETHING VERY PECULIAR GOING ON HERE AND I BET NAVARAN KNOWS WHAT!
HE DOES SEEM TO BE LISTENING TO THAT WATCH OF HIS. WE'LL SEE WHAT HAPPENS WHEN WE APPROACH THESE CHANNELS UP AHEAD.
I THINK WE SHOULD TAKE THE RIGHT-HAND CHANNEL, SHIWA.
AND WHAT IF I SAY WE SHOULD TAKE THE LEFT-HAND ONE?
I SEE MY ACTIONS HAVE CAUSED YOU TO BECOME SUSPICIOUS OF ME, BUT IF YOU DO AS I SAY, I PROMISE I WILL EXPLAIN EVERYTHING TO YOU SOON!
VERY WELL.
LOOK!
A MONSTER PYTHON!
HELP! SAVE ME!
AIIEE!

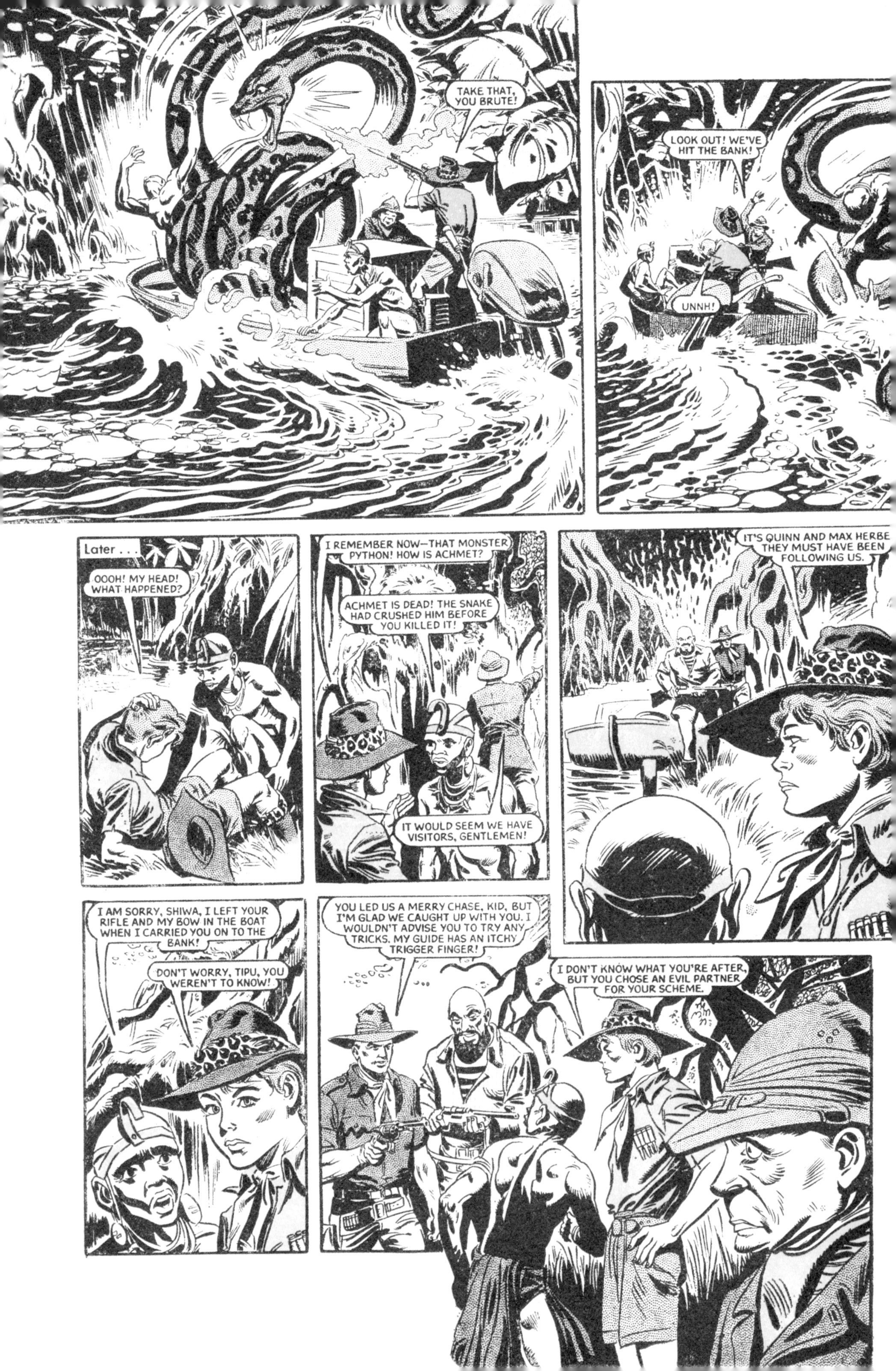
TAKE THAT, YOU BRUTE!
LOOK OUT! WE'VE HIT THE BANK!
UNNH!
Later . . .
OOOH! MY HEAD! WHAT HAPPENED?
I REMEMBER NOW—THAT MONSTER PYTHON! HOW IS ACHMET?
ACHMET IS DEAD! THE SNAKE HAD CRUSHED HIM BEFORE YOU KILLED IT!
IT WOULD SEEM WE HAVE VISITORS, GENTLEMEN!
IT'S QUINN AND MAX HERBE THEY MUST HAVE BEEN FOLLOWING US.
I AM SORRY, SHIWA, I LEFT YOUR RIFLE AND MY BOW IN THE BOAT WHEN I CARRIED YOU ON TO THE BANK!
DON'T WORRY, TIPU, YOU WEREN'T TO KNOW!
YOU LED US A MERRY CHASE, KID, BUT I'M GLAD WE CAUGHT UP WITH YOU. I WOULDN'T ADVISE YOU TO TRY ANY TRICKS. MY GUIDE HAS AN ITCHY TRIGGER FINGER!
I DON'T KNOW WHAT YOU'RE AFTER, BUT YOU CHOSE AN EVIL PARTNER FOR YOUR SCHEME.

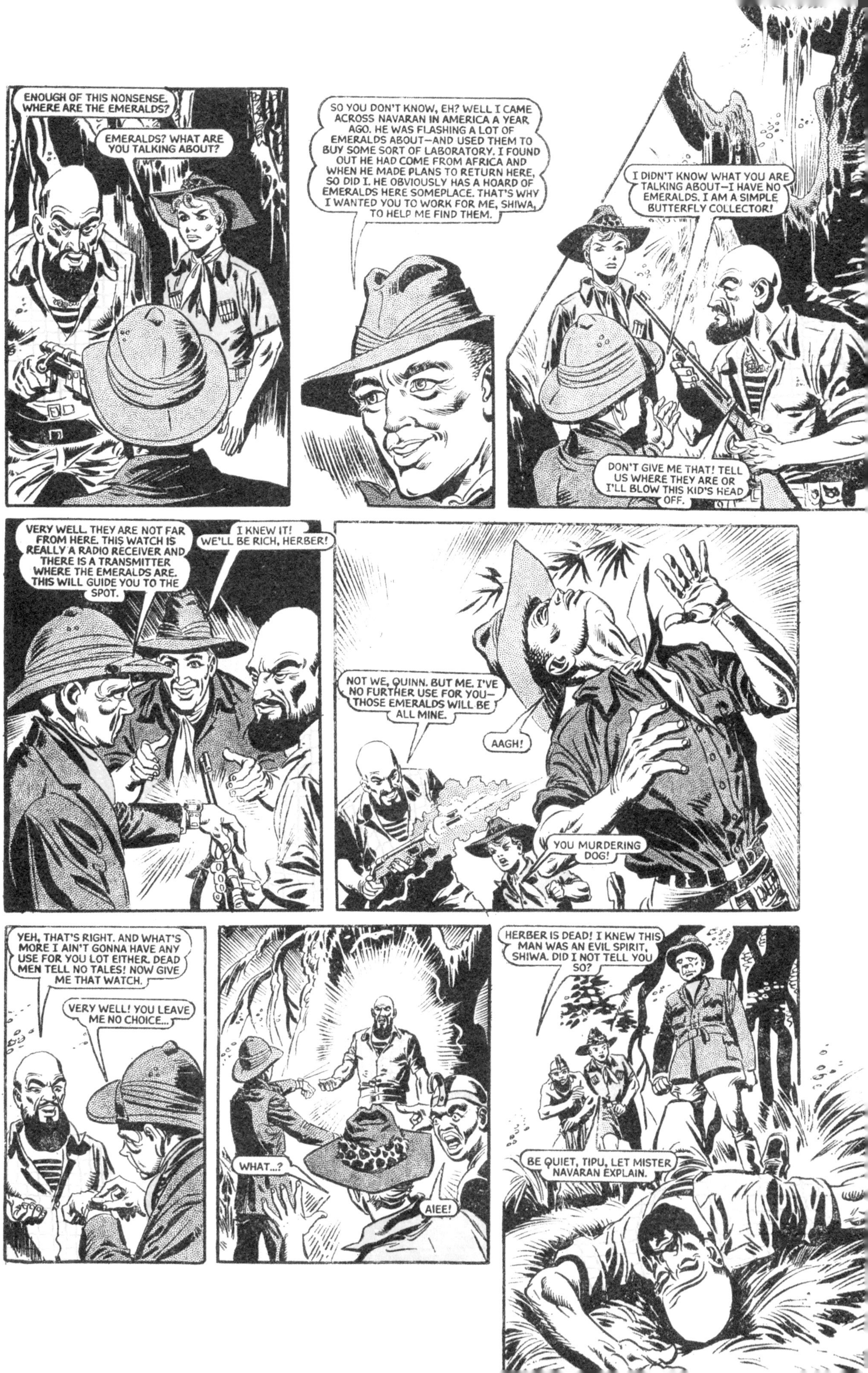
ENOUGH OF THIS NONSENSE. WHERE ARE THE EMERALDS?
EMERALDS? WHAT ARE YOU TALKING ABOUT?
SO YOU DON'T KNOW, EH? WELL I CAME ACROSS NAVARAN IN AMERICA A YEAR AGO. HE WAS FLASHING A LOT OF EMERALDS ABOUT—AND USED THEM TO BUY SOME SORT OF LABORATORY. I FOUND OUT HE HAD COME FROM AFRICA AND WHEN HE MADE PLANS TO RETURN HERE, SO DID I. HE OBVIOUSLY HAS A HOARD OF EMERALDS HERE SOMEPLACE. THAT'S WHY I WANTED YOU TO WORK FOR ME, SHIWA, TO HELP ME FIND THEM.
I DIDN'T KNOW WHAT YOU ARE TALKING ABOUT—I HAVE NO EMERALDS. I AM A SIMPLE BUTTERFLY COLLECTOR!
DON'T GIVE ME THAT! TELL US WHERE THEY ARE OR I'LL BLOW THIS KID'S HEAD OFF.
VERY WELL. THEY ARE NOT FAR FROM HERE. THIS WATCH IS REALLY A RADIO RECEIVER AND THERE IS A TRANSMITTER WHERE THE EMERALDS ARE. THIS WILL GUIDE YOU TO THE SPOT.
I KNEW IT! WE'LL BE RICH, HERBER!
NOT WE, QUINN. BUT ME. I'VE NO FURTHER USE FOR YOU—THOSE EMERALDS WILL BE ALL MINE.
AAGH!
YOU MURDERING DOG!
YEH, THAT'S RIGHT. AND WHAT'S MORE I AIN'T GONNA HAVE ANY USE FOR YOU LOT EITHER. DEAD MEN TELL NO TALES! NOW GIVE ME THAT WATCH.
VERY WELL! YOU LEAVE ME NO CHOICE...
WHAT...?
AIEE!
HERBER IS DEAD! I KNEW THIS MAN WAS AN EVIL SPIRIT, SHIWA. DID I NOT TELL YOU SO?
BE QUIET, TIPU, LET MISTER NAVARAN EXPLAIN.

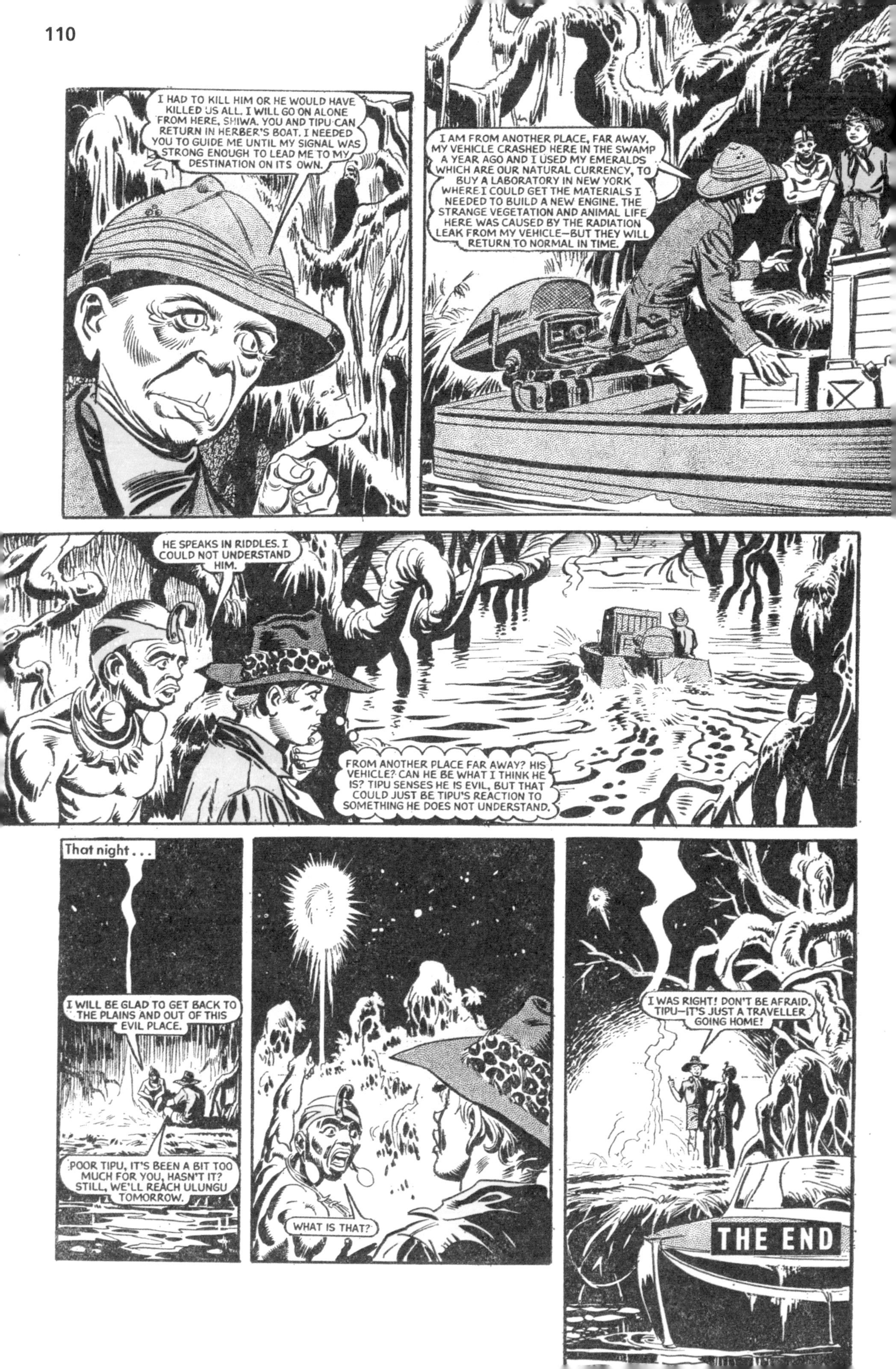
I HAD TO KILL HIM OR HE WOULD HAVE KILLED US ALL. I WILL GO ON ALONE FROM HERE, SHIWA. YOU AND TIPU CAN RETURN IN HERBER'S BOAT. I NEEDED YOU TO GUIDE ME UNTIL MY SIGNAL WAS STRONG ENOUGH TO LEAD ME TO MY DESTINATION ON ITS OWN.
I AM FROM ANOTHER PLACE, FAR AWAY. MY VEHICLE CRASHED HERE IN THE SWAMP A YEAR AGO AND I USED MY EMERALDS WHICH ARE OUR NATURAL CURRENCY, TO BUY A LABORATORY IN NEW YORK WHERE I COULD GET THE MATERIALS I NEEDED TO BUILD A NEW ENGINE. THE STRANGE VEGETATION AND ANIMAL LIFE HERE WAS CAUSED BY THE RADIATION LEAK FROM MY VEHICLE—BUT THEY WILL RETURN TO NORMAL IN TIME.
HE SPEAKS IN RIDDLES. I COULD NOT UNDERSTAND HIM.
FROM ANOTHER PLACE FAR AWAY? HIS VEHICLE? CAN HE BE WHAT I THINK HE IS? TIPU SENSES HE IS EVIL, BUT THAT COULD JUST BE TIPU'S REACTION TO SOMETHING HE DOES NOT UNDERSTAND.
That night . . .
I WILL BE GLAD TO GET BACK TO THE PLAINS AND OUT OF THIS EVIL PLACE.
POOR TIPU, IT'S BEEN A BIT TOO MUCH FOR YOU, HASN'T IT? STILL, WE'LL REACH ULUNGU TOMORROW.
WHAT IS THAT?
I WAS RIGHT! DON'T BE AFRAID, TIPU—IT'S JUST A TRAVELLER GOING HOME!
THE END

It's brains versus brawn when manager, Sam Barnham, steers United into a Cup Final!

COME AWAY THE UNITED

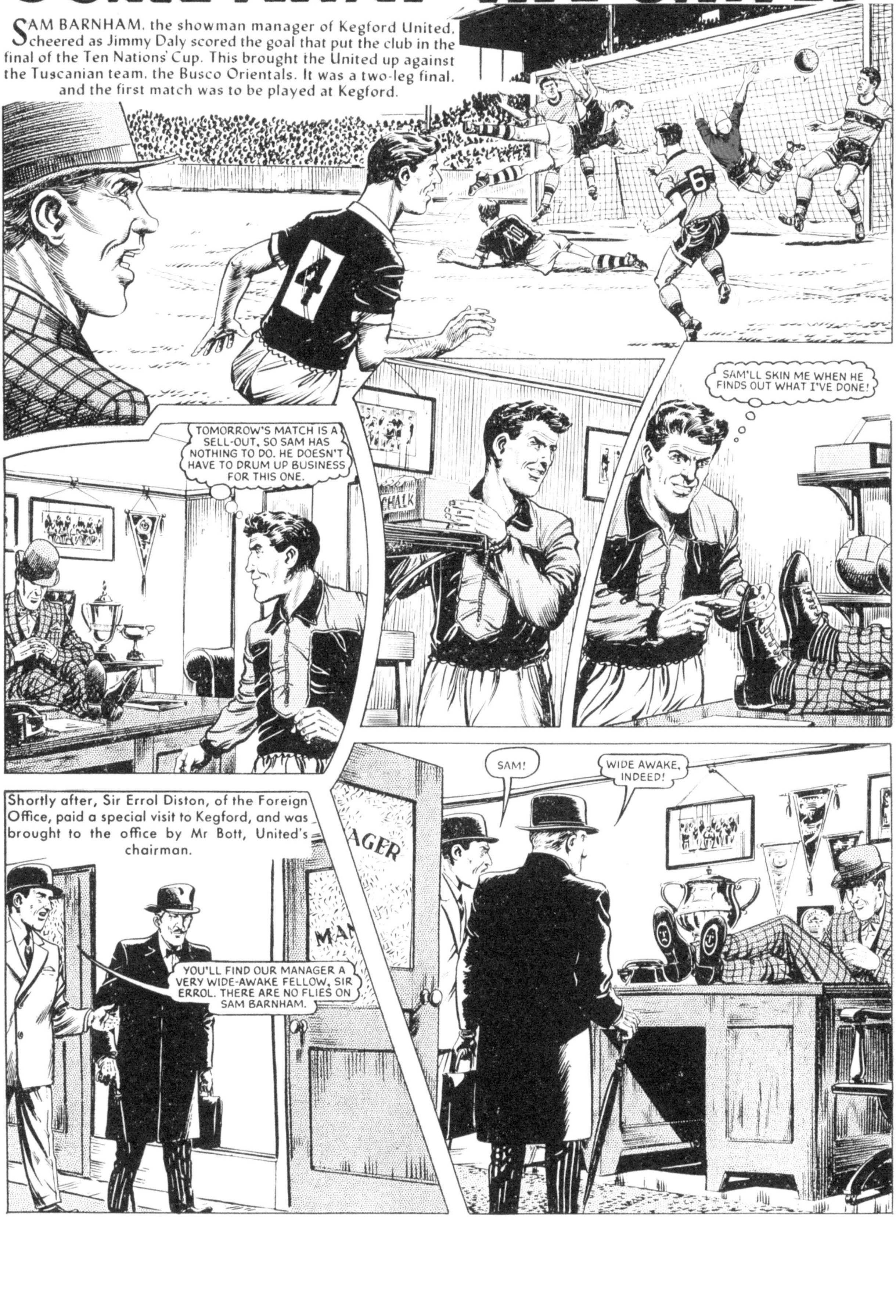
SAM BARNHAM, the showman manager of Kegford United, cheered as Jimmy Daly scored the goal that put the club in the final of the Ten Nations' Cup. This brought the United up against the Tuscanian team, the Busco Orientals. It was a two-leg final, and the first match was to be played at Kegford.
TOMORROW'S MATCH IS A SELL-OUT, SO SAM HAS NOTHING TO DO. HE DOESN'T HAVE TO DRUM UP BUSINESS FOR THIS ONE.
CHALK
SAM'LL SKIN ME WHEN HE FINDS OUT WHAT I'VE DONE!
Shortly after, Sir Errol Diston, of the Foreign Office, paid a special visit to Kegford, and was brought to the office by Mr Bott, United's chairman.
YOU'LL FIND OUR MANAGER A VERY WIDE-AWAKE FELLOW, SIR ERROL. THERE ARE NO FLIES ON SAM BARNHAM.
SAM!
WIDE AWAKE, INDEED!

Deadshot Daly shoots for "sausages"!

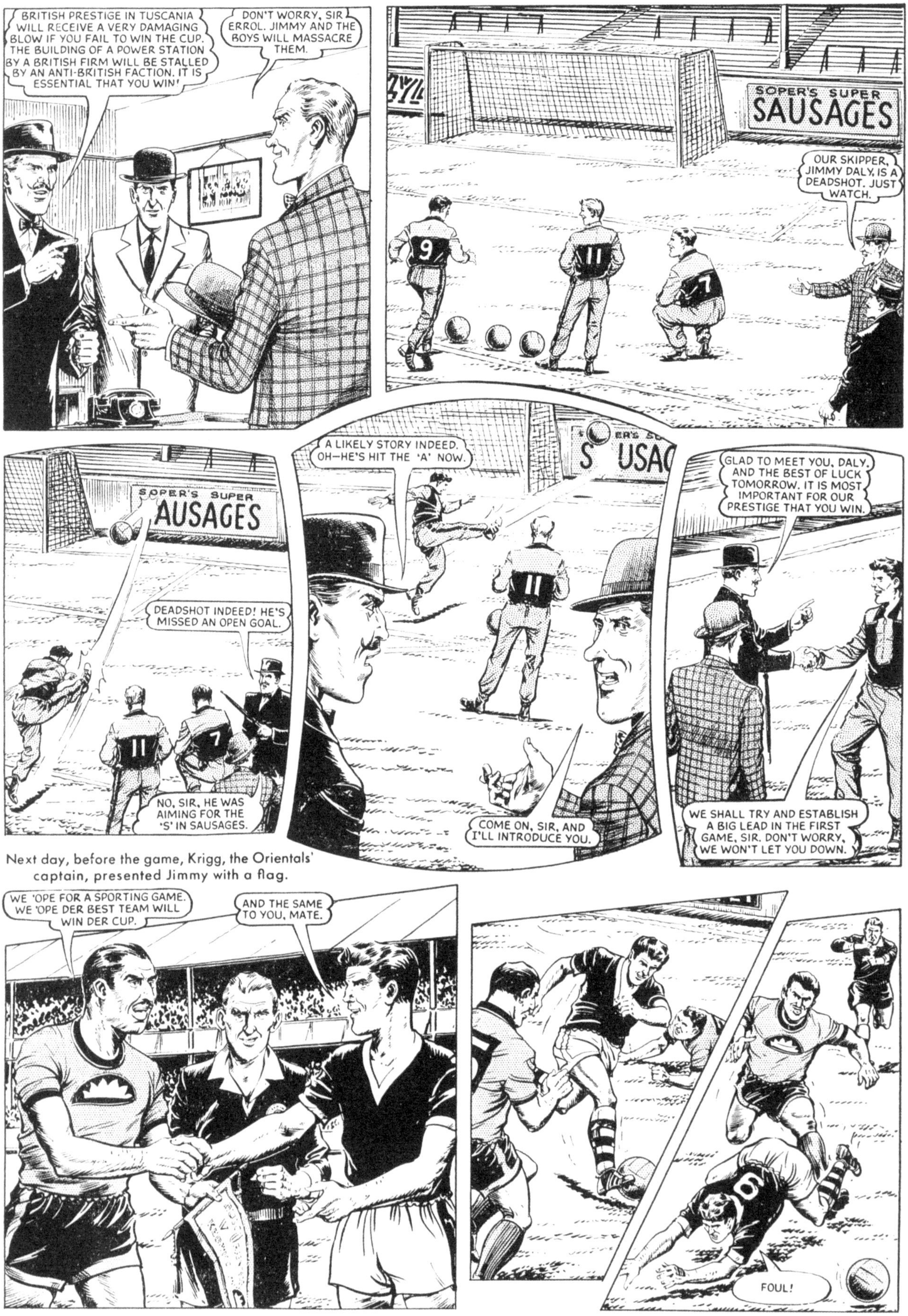
BRITISH PRESTIGE IN TUSCANIA WILL RECEIVE A VERY DAMAGING BLOW IF YOU FAIL TO WIN THE CUP. THE BUILDING OF A POWER STATION BY A BRITISH FIRM WILL BE STALLED BY AN ANTI-BRITISH FACTION. IT IS ESSENTIAL THAT YOU WIN!
DON'T WORRY, SIR ERROL. JIMMY AND THE BOYS WILL MASSACRE THEM.
SOPER'S SUPER SAUSAGES
OUR SKIPPER, JIMMY DALY, IS A DEADSHOT. JUST WATCH.
SOPER'S SUPER SAUSAGES
DEADSHOT INDEED! HE'S MISSED AN OPEN GOAL.
NO, SIR, HE WAS AIMING FOR THE 'S' IN SAUSAGES.
A LIKELY STORY INDEED. OH—HE'S HIT THE 'A' NOW.
COME ON, SIR, AND I'LL INTRODUCE YOU.
GLAD TO MEET YOU, DALY, AND THE BEST OF LUCK TOMORROW. IT IS MOST IMPORTANT FOR OUR PRESTIGE THAT YOU WIN.
WE SHALL TRY AND ESTABLISH A BIG LEAD IN THE FIRST GAME, SIR. DON'T WORRY, WE WON'T LET YOU DOWN.
Next day, before the game, Krigg, the Orientals' captain, presented Jimmy with a flag.
WE 'OPE FOR A SPORTING GAME. WE 'OPE DER BEST TEAM WILL WIN DER CUP.
AND THE SAME TO YOU, MATE.
FOUL!

Rough stuff from the Busco bashers!

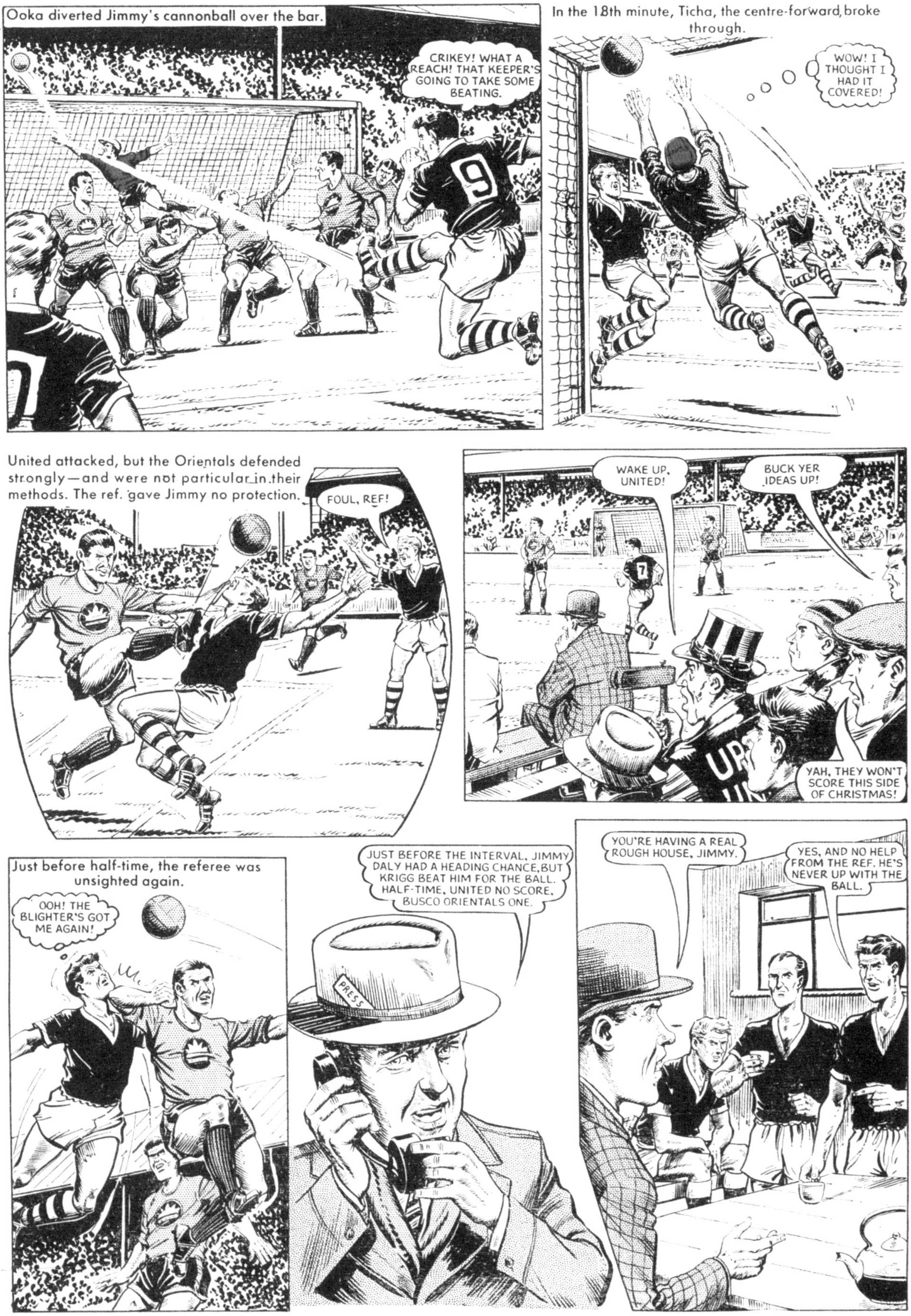
Ooka diverted Jimmy's cannonball over the bar.
CRIKEY! WHAT A REACH! THAT KEEPER'S GOING TO TAKE SOME BEATING.
In the 18th minute, Ticha, the centre-forward, broke through.
WOW! I THOUGHT I HAD IT COVERED!
United attacked, but the Orientals defended strongly—and were not particular in their methods. The ref. gave Jimmy no protection.
FOUL, REF!
WAKE UP, UNITED!
BUCK YER IDEAS UP!
YAH, THEY WON'T SCORE THIS SIDE OF CHRISTMAS!
Just before half-time, the referee was unsighted again.
OOH! THE BLIGHTER'S GOT ME AGAIN!
JUST BEFORE THE INTERVAL, JIMMY DALY HAD A HEADING CHANCE, BUT KRIGG BEAT HIM FOR THE BALL. HALF-TIME, UNITED NO SCORE, BUSCO ORIENTALS ONE.
PRESS
YOU'RE HAVING A REAL ROUGH HOUSE, JIMMY.
YES, AND NO HELP FROM THE REF. HE'S NEVER UP WITH THE BALL.

The last kick counts.

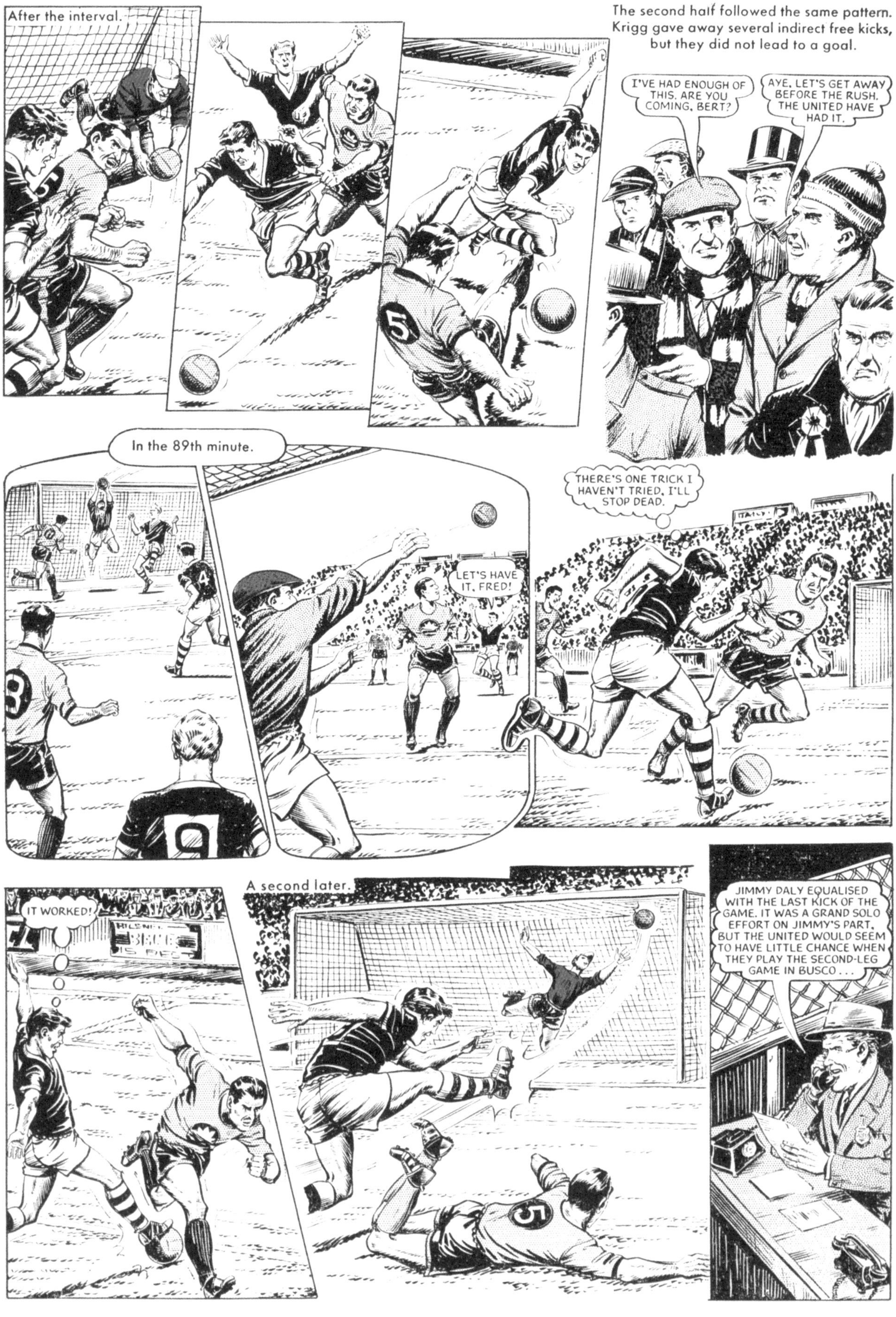
After the interval.
The second half followed the same pattern. Krigg gave away several indirect free kicks, but they did not lead to a goal.
I'VE HAD ENOUGH OF THIS. ARE YOU COMING, BERT?
AYE, LET'S GET AWAY BEFORE THE RUSH. THE UNITED HAVE HAD IT.
In the 89th minute.
LET'S HAVE IT, FRED!
THERE'S ONE TRICK I HAVEN'T TRIED. I'LL STOP DEAD.
IT WORKED!
A second later.
JIMMY DALY EQUALISED WITH THE LAST KICK OF THE GAME. IT WAS A GRAND SOLO EFFORT ON JIMMY'S PART, BUT THE UNITED WOULD SEEM TO HAVE LITTLE CHANCE WHEN THEY PLAY THE SECOND-LEG GAME IN BUSCO . . .

Fair play for Jimmy Daly!

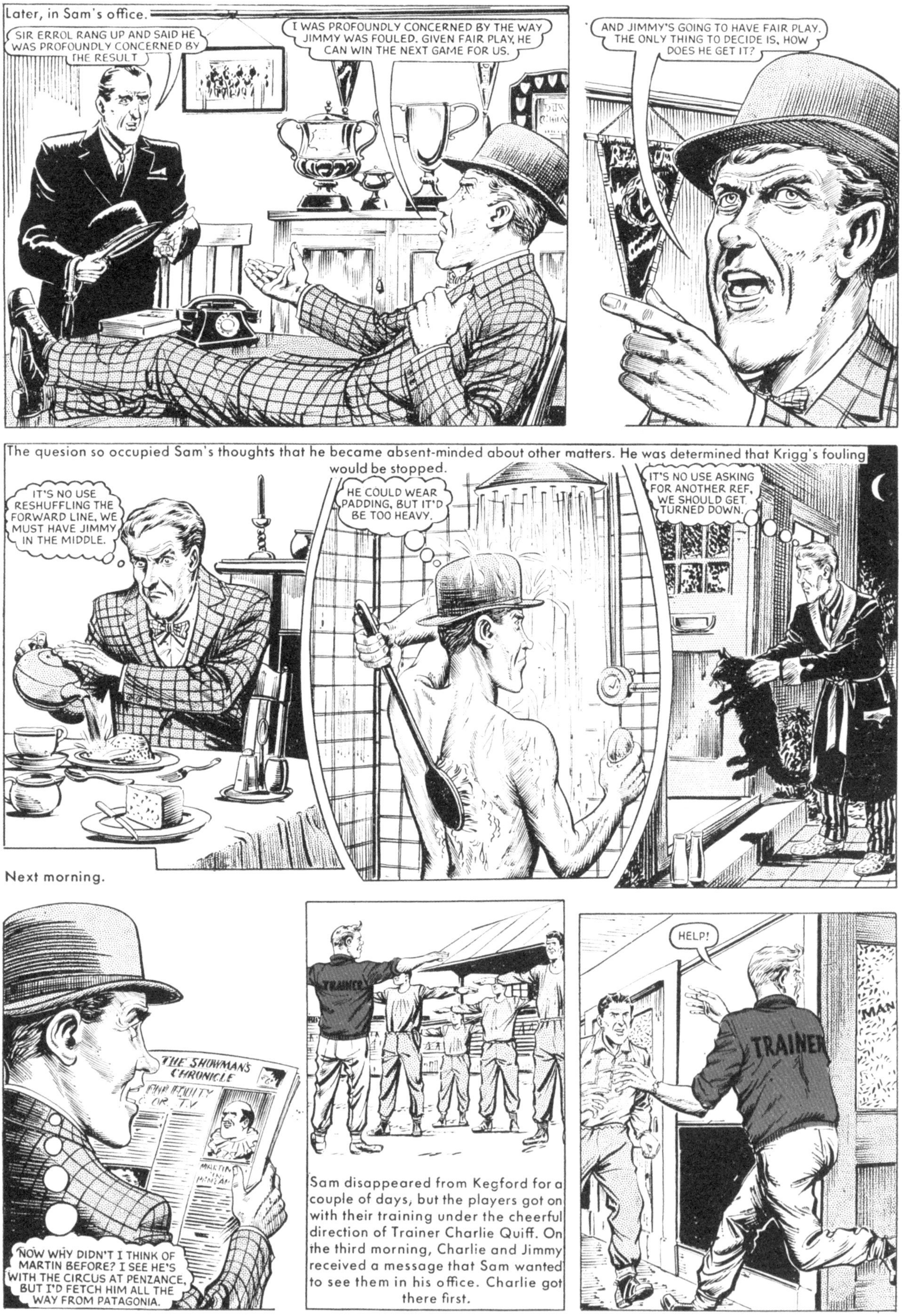
Later, in Sam's office.
SIR ERROL RANG UP AND SAID HE WAS PROFOUNDLY CONCERNED BY THE RESULT
I WAS PROFOUNDLY CONCERNED BY THE WAY JIMMY WAS FOULED. GIVEN FAIR PLAY, HE CAN WIN THE NEXT GAME FOR US.
AND JIMMY'S GOING TO HAVE FAIR PLAY. THE ONLY THING TO DECIDE IS, HOW DOES HE GET IT?
The quesion so occupied Sam's thoughts that he became absent-minded about other matters. He was determined that Krigg's fouling would be stopped.
IT'S NO USE RESHUFFLING THE FORWARD LINE, WE MUST HAVE JIMMY IN THE MIDDLE.
HE COULD WEAR PADDING, BUT IT'D BE TOO HEAVY.
IT'S NO USE ASKING FOR ANOTHER REF, WE SHOULD GET TURNED DOWN.
Next morning.
THE SHOWMAN'S CHRONICLE
NOW WHY DIDN'T I THINK OF MARTIN BEFORE? I SEE HE'S WITH THE CIRCUS AT PENZANCE, BUT I'D FETCH HIM ALL THE WAY FROM PATAGONIA.
TRAINER
Sam disappeared from Kegford for a couple of days, but the players got on with their training under the cheerful direction of Trainer Charlie Quiff. On the third morning, Charlie and Jimmy received a message that Sam wanted to see them in his office. Charlie got there first.
HELP!
TRAINER

Sam Barnham's monkey business.

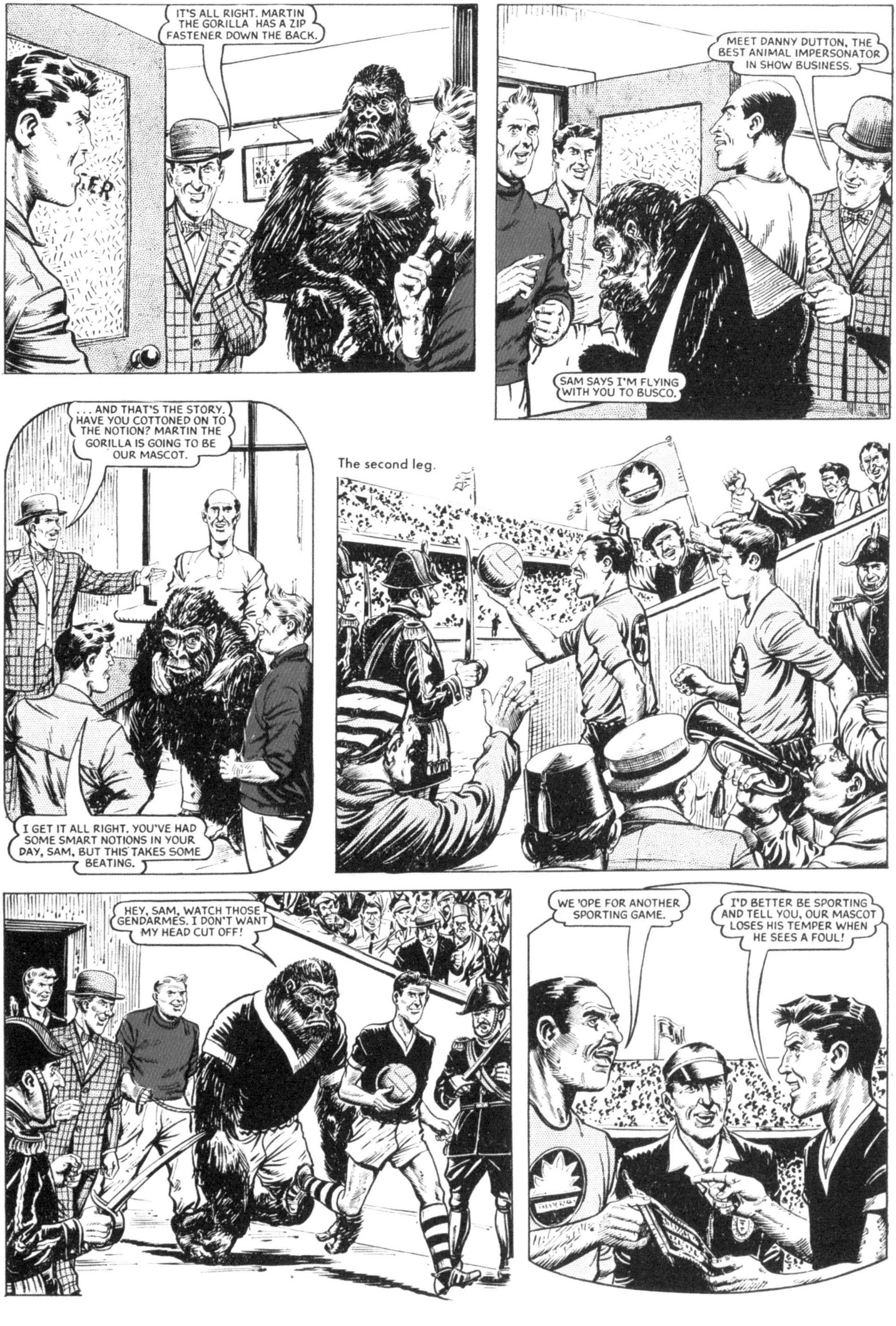
IT'S ALL RIGHT. MARTIN THE GORILLA HAS A ZIP FASTENER DOWN THE BACK.
MEET DANNY DUTTON, THE BEST ANIMAL IMPERSONATOR IN SHOW BUSINESS.
SAM SAYS I'M FLYING WITH YOU TO BUSCO.
. . . AND THAT'S THE STORY. HAVE YOU COTTONED ON TO THE NOTION? MARTIN THE GORILLA IS GOING TO BE OUR MASCOT.
I GET IT ALL RIGHT. YOU'VE HAD SOME SMART NOTIONS IN YOUR DAY, SAM, BUT THIS TAKES SOME BEATING.
The second leg.
HEY, SAM, WATCH THOSE GENDARMES. I DON'T WANT MY HEAD CUT OFF!
WE 'OPE FOR ANOTHER SPORTING GAME.
I'D BETTER BE SPORTING AND TELL YOU, OUR MASCOT LOSES HIS TEMPER WHEN HE SEES A FOUL!

"Martin is watching you!"

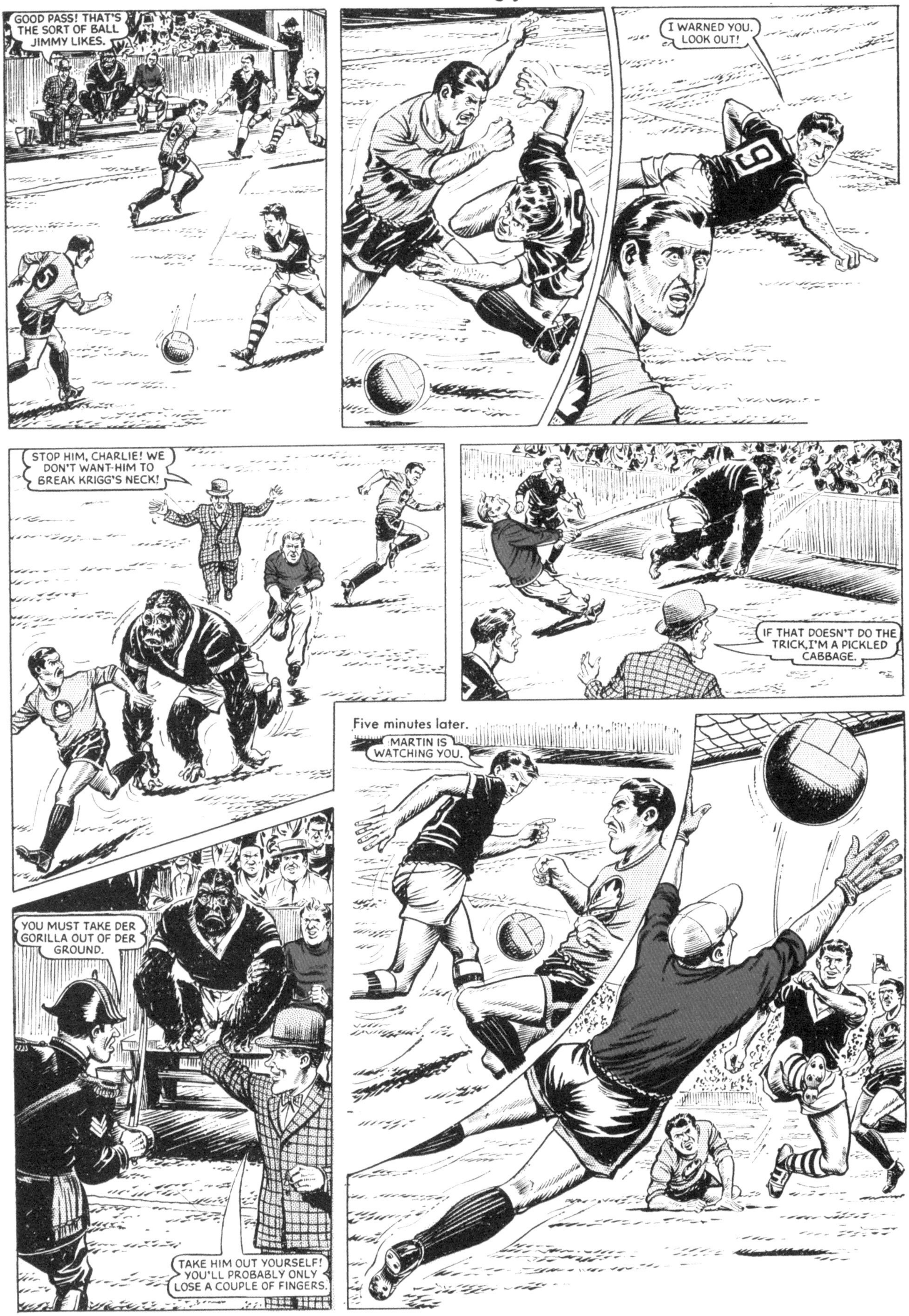
GOOD PASS! THAT'S THE SORT OF BALL JIMMY LIKES.
I WARNED YOU. LOOK OUT!
STOP HIM, CHARLIE! WE DON'T WANT-HIM TO BREAK KRIGG'S NECK!
IF THAT DOESN'T DO THE TRICK,I'M A PICKLED CABBAGE.
YOU MUST TAKE DER GORILLA OUT OF DER GROUND.
TAKE HIM OUT YOURSELF! YOU'LL PROBABLY ONLY LOSE A COUPLE OF FINGERS.
Five minutes later.
MARTIN IS WATCHING YOU.

The deadly head of Jimmy Daly!

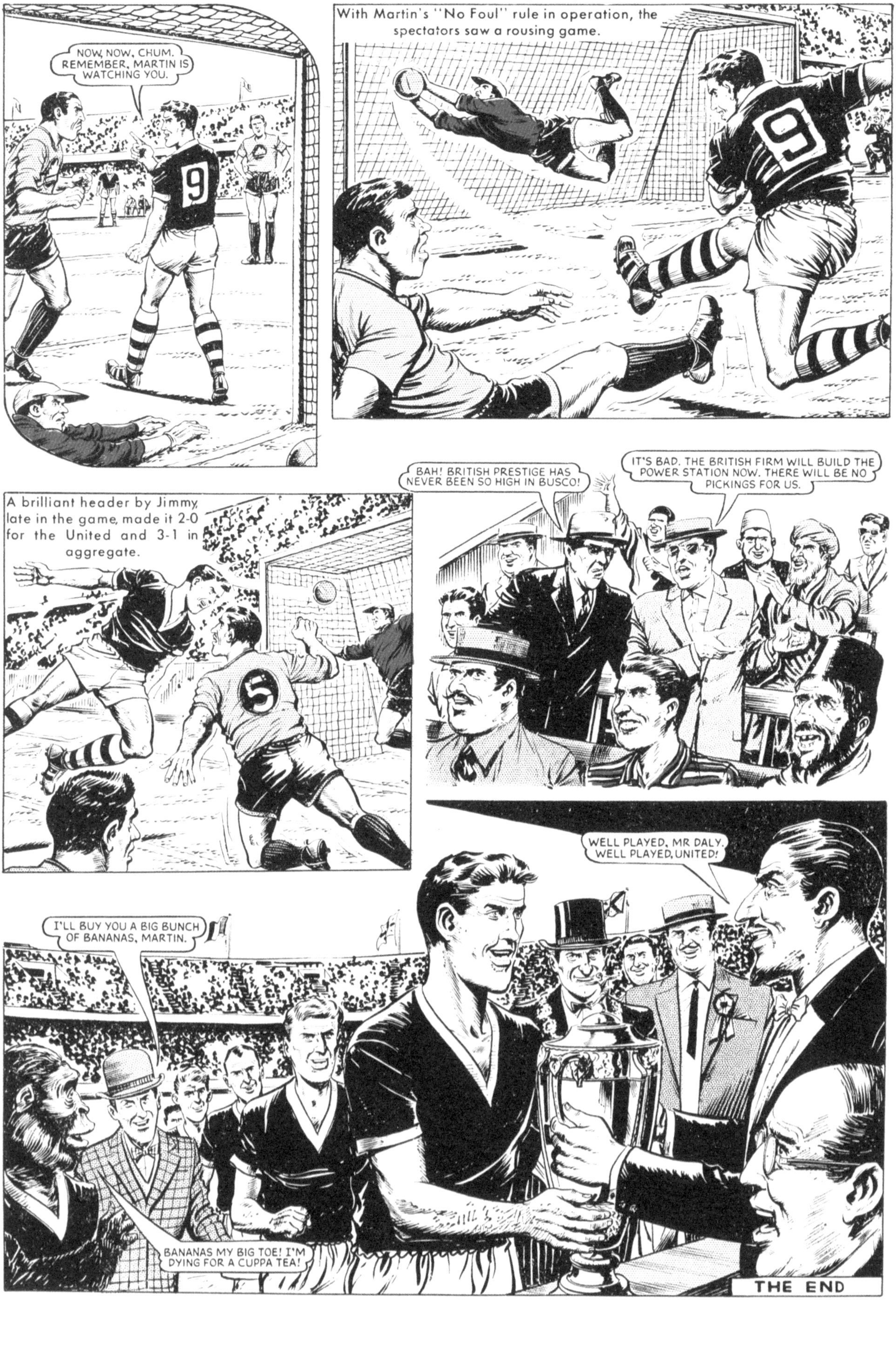
NOW, NOW, CHUM. REMEMBER, MARTIN IS WATCHING YOU.
With Martin's "No Foul" rule in operation, the spectators saw a rousing game.
A brilliant header by Jimmy, late in the game, made it 2-0 for the United and 3-1 in aggregate.
BAH! BRITISH PRESTIGE HAS NEVER BEEN SO HIGH IN BUSCO!
IT'S BAD. THE BRITISH FIRM WILL BUILD THE POWER STATION NOW. THERE WILL BE NO PICKINGS FOR US.
I'LL BUY YOU A BIG BUNCH OF BANANAS, MARTIN.
BANANAS MY BIG TOE! I'M DYING FOR A CUPPA TEA!
WELL PLAYED, MR DALY. WELL PLAYED, UNITED!
THE END

THE SLEEPING TIGER

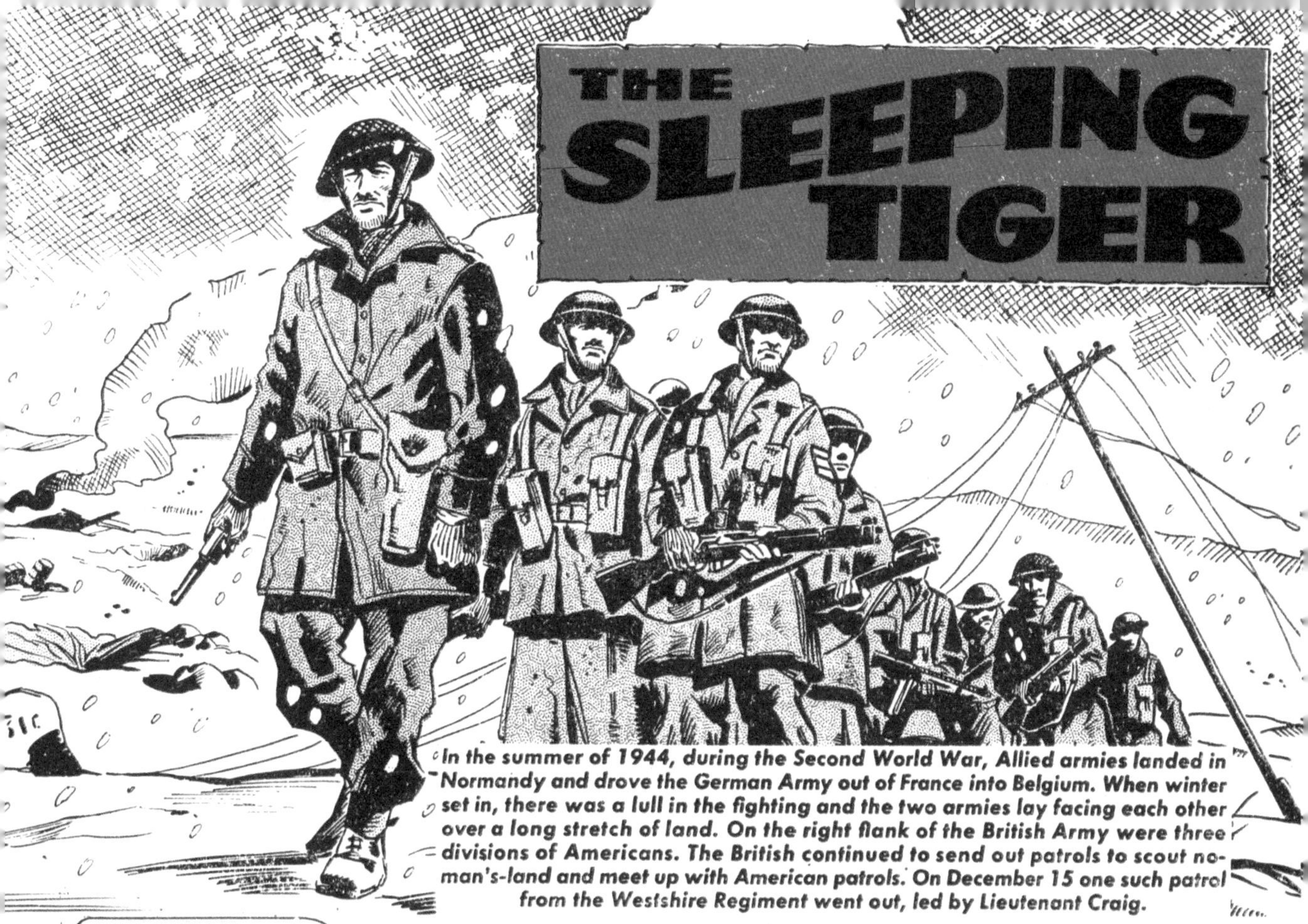
THE SLEEPING TIGER
In the summer of 1944, during the Second World War, Allied armies landed in Normandy and drove the German Army out of France into Belgium. When winter set in, there was a lull in the fighting and the two armies lay facing each other over a long stretch of land. On the right flank of the British Army were three divisions of Americans. The British continued to send out patrols to scout no-man's-land and meet up with American patrols. On December 15 one such patrol from the Westshire Regiment went out, led by Lieutenant Craig.

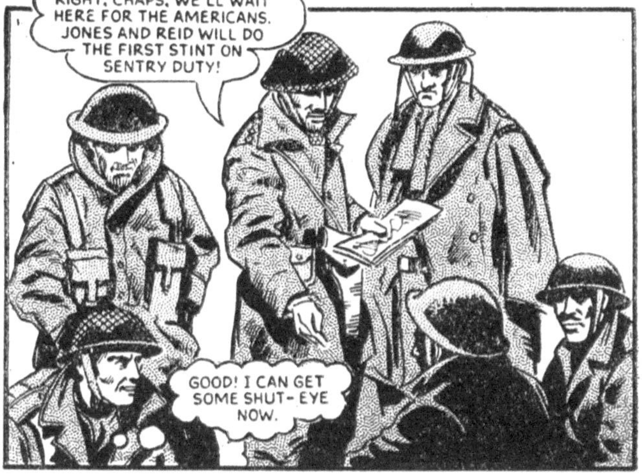
RIGHT, CHAPS, WE'LL WAIT HERE FOR THE AMERICANS. JONES AND REID WILL DO THE FIRST STINT ON SENTRY DUTY!
GOOD! I CAN GET SOME SHUT-EYE NOW.

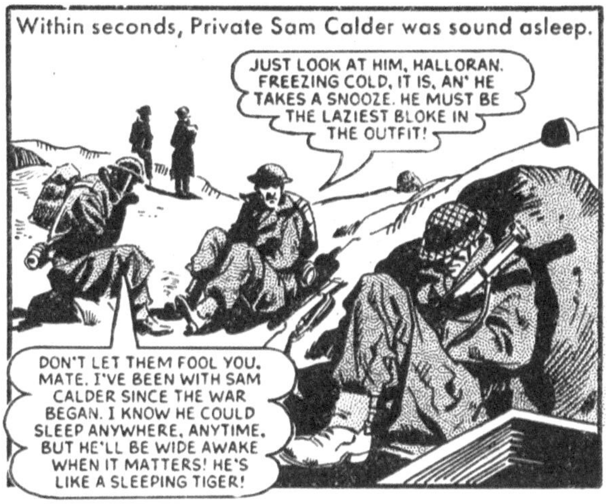
Within seconds, Private Sam Calder was sound asleep.
JUST LOOK AT HIM, HALLORAN. FREEZING COLD, IT IS, AN' HE TAKES A SNOOZE. HE MUST BE THE LAZIEST BLOKE IN THE OUTFIT!
DON'T LET THEM FOOL YOU, MATE. I'VE BEEN WITH SAM CALDER SINCE THE WAR BEGAN. I KNOW HE COULD SLEEP ANYWHERE, ANYTIME, BUT HE'LL BE WIDE AWAKE WHEN IT MATTERS! HE'S LIKE A SLEEPING TIGER!

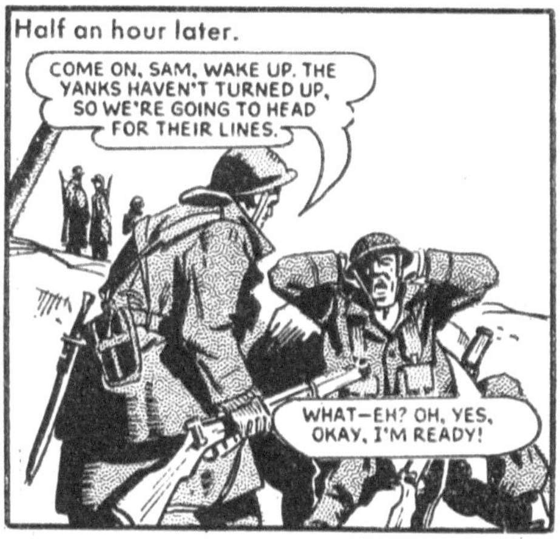
Half an hour later.
COME ON, SAM, WAKE UP. THE YANKS HAVEN'T TURNED UP, SO WE'RE GOING TO HEAD FOR THEIR LINES.
WHAT—EH? OH, YES, OKAY, I'M READY!

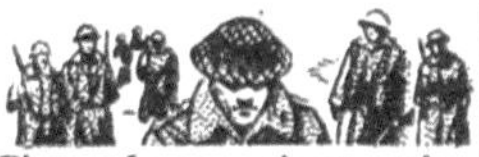

The fact that the Americans had not turned up at the rendezvous point was not unusual. The Americans thought that the Germans were now too weak to launch an attack and therefore did not always bother with reconnaissance patrols. The British forces were more cautious.

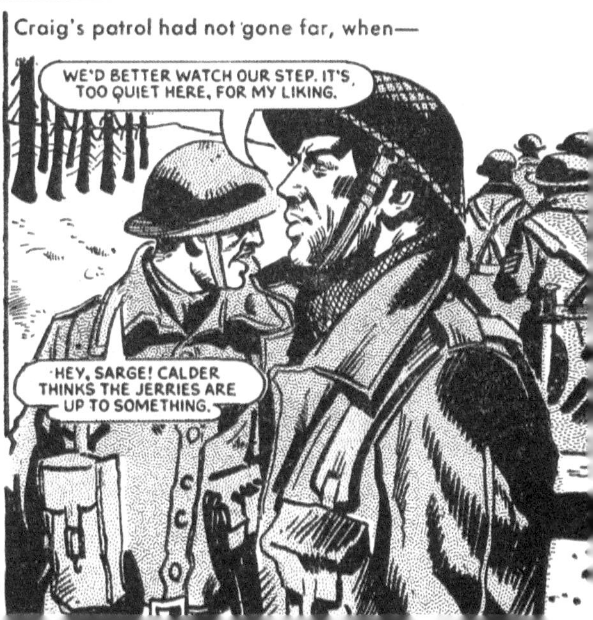
Craig's patrol had not gone far, when—
WE'D BETTER WATCH OUR STEP. IT'S TOO QUIET HERE, FOR MY LIKING.
HEY, SARGE! CALDER THINKS THE JERRIES ARE UP TO SOMETHING.

"Those blokes ain't Yanks—they're Germans!"

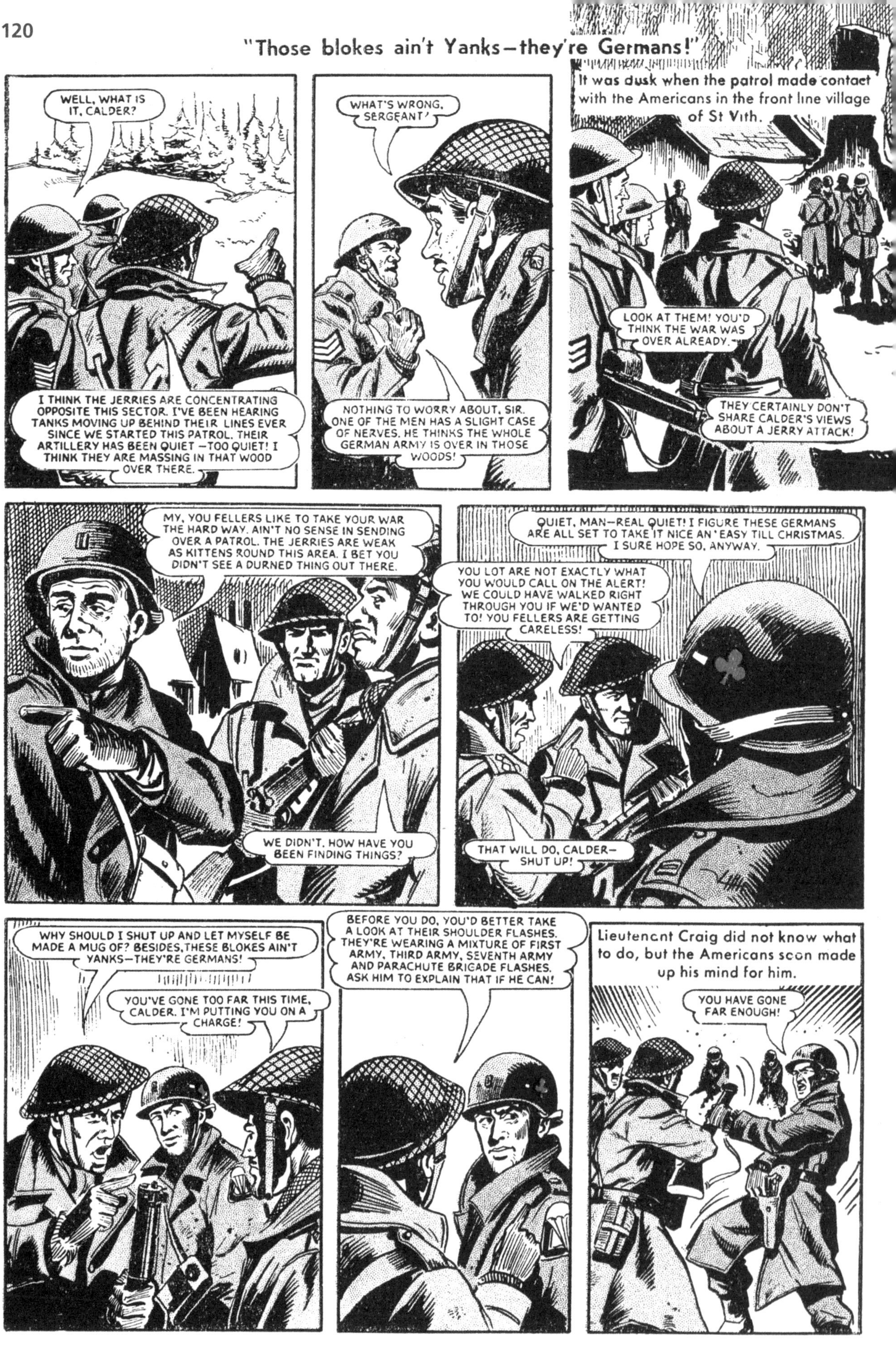
WELL, WHAT IS IT, CALDER?
I THINK THE JERRIES ARE CONCENTRATING OPPOSITE THIS SECTOR. I'VE BEEN HEARING TANKS MOVING UP BEHIND THEIR LINES EVER SINCE WE STARTED THIS PATROL. THEIR ARTILLERY HAS BEEN QUIET —TOO QUIET! I THINK THEY ARE MASSING IN THAT WOOD OVER THERE.
WHAT'S WRONG, SERGEANT?
NOTHING TO WORRY ABOUT, SIR. ONE OF THE MEN HAS A SLIGHT CASE OF NERVES. HE THINKS THE WHOLE GERMAN ARMY IS OVER IN THOSE WOODS!
It was dusk when the patrol made contact with the Americans in the front line village of St Vith.
LOOK AT THEM! YOU'D THINK THE WAR WAS OVER ALREADY.
THEY CERTAINLY DON'T SHARE CALDER'S VIEWS ABOUT A JERRY ATTACK!
MY, YOU FELLERS LIKE TO TAKE YOUR WAR THE HARD WAY. AIN'T NO SENSE IN SENDING OVER A PATROL. THE JERRIES ARE WEAK AS KITTENS ROUND THIS AREA. I BET YOU DIDN'T SEE A DURNED THING OUT THERE.
WE DIDN'T. HOW HAVE YOU BEEN FINDING THINGS?
QUIET, MAN—REAL QUIET! I FIGURE THESE GERMANS ARE ALL SET TO TAKE IT NICE AN' EASY TILL CHRISTMAS. I SURE HOPE SO, ANYWAY.
YOU LOT ARE NOT EXACTLY WHAT YOU WOULD CALL ON THE ALERT! WE COULD HAVE WALKED RIGHT THROUGH YOU IF WE'D WANTED TO! YOU FELLERS ARE GETTING CARELESS!
THAT WILL DO, CALDER—SHUT UP!
WHY SHOULD I SHUT UP AND LET MYSELF BE MADE A MUG OF? BESIDES, THESE BLOKES AIN'T YANKS—THEY'RE GERMANS!
YOU'VE GONE TOO FAR THIS TIME, CALDER. I'M PUTTING YOU ON A CHARGE!
BEFORE YOU DO, YOU'D BETTER TAKE A LOOK AT THEIR SHOULDER FLASHES. THEY'RE WEARING A MIXTURE OF FIRST ARMY, THIRD ARMY, SEVENTH ARMY AND PARACHUTE BRIGADE FLASHES. ASK HIM TO EXPLAIN THAT IF HE CAN!
Lieutenant Craig did not know what to do, but the Americans soon made up his mind for him.
YOU HAVE GONE FAR ENOUGH!

"Let 'em have it, lads!"

LET 'EM HAVE IT, LADS!

THE LIEUTENANT'S COPPED IT!

LET'S GET OUT OF HERE. THERE ARE TOO MANY FOR US!

THE REST OF THE LADS HAVE HAD IT. WE'D BEST PUT AS MUCH GROUND AS WE CAN BETWEEN US AND THESE JERRIES!

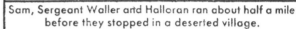

Sam, Sergeant Waller and Halloran ran about half a mile before they stopped in a deserted village.

WE'RE CLEAR OF THEM NOW. WE'LL STAY HERE FOR THE NIGHT. TELL ME, CALDER, HOW DID YOU SPOT THAT THESE YANKS WERE JERRIES IN DISGUISE?

WELL, IT JUST DIDN'T MAKE SENSE, SARGE. I COULD HAVE UNDERSTOOD A FEW BLOKES FROM THE YANKEE FIFTH ARMY BEING WITH FIRST ARMY BLOKES, BECAUSE THEY WERE FIGHTING SIDE BY SIDE. BUT THE YANKEE SEVENTH ARMY IS WAY DOWN FAR SOUTH OF HERE.

THE YANKEE PARATROOPS HAVEN'T BEEN IN THE FRONT-LINE SINCE THEY WERE DROPPED AT NIJMEGEN AND EINDHOVEN LAST SEPTEMBER. SO YOU SEE, SARGE, THEY COULDN'T HAVE HAD A MIXED BUNCH LIKE THAT IN THE FRONT LINE. AND IF THEY'D BEEN REAL YANKS, THEY WOULDN'T HAVE CUT LOOSE AT US THE WAY THEY DID.

Suddenly.

LISTEN!

WHAT IS IT, CALDER?

Sam's acute sense of hearing had detected the first rumbling of the German guns as they launched an attack on a weak spot in the American lines.

"Cut off from our own lines!"

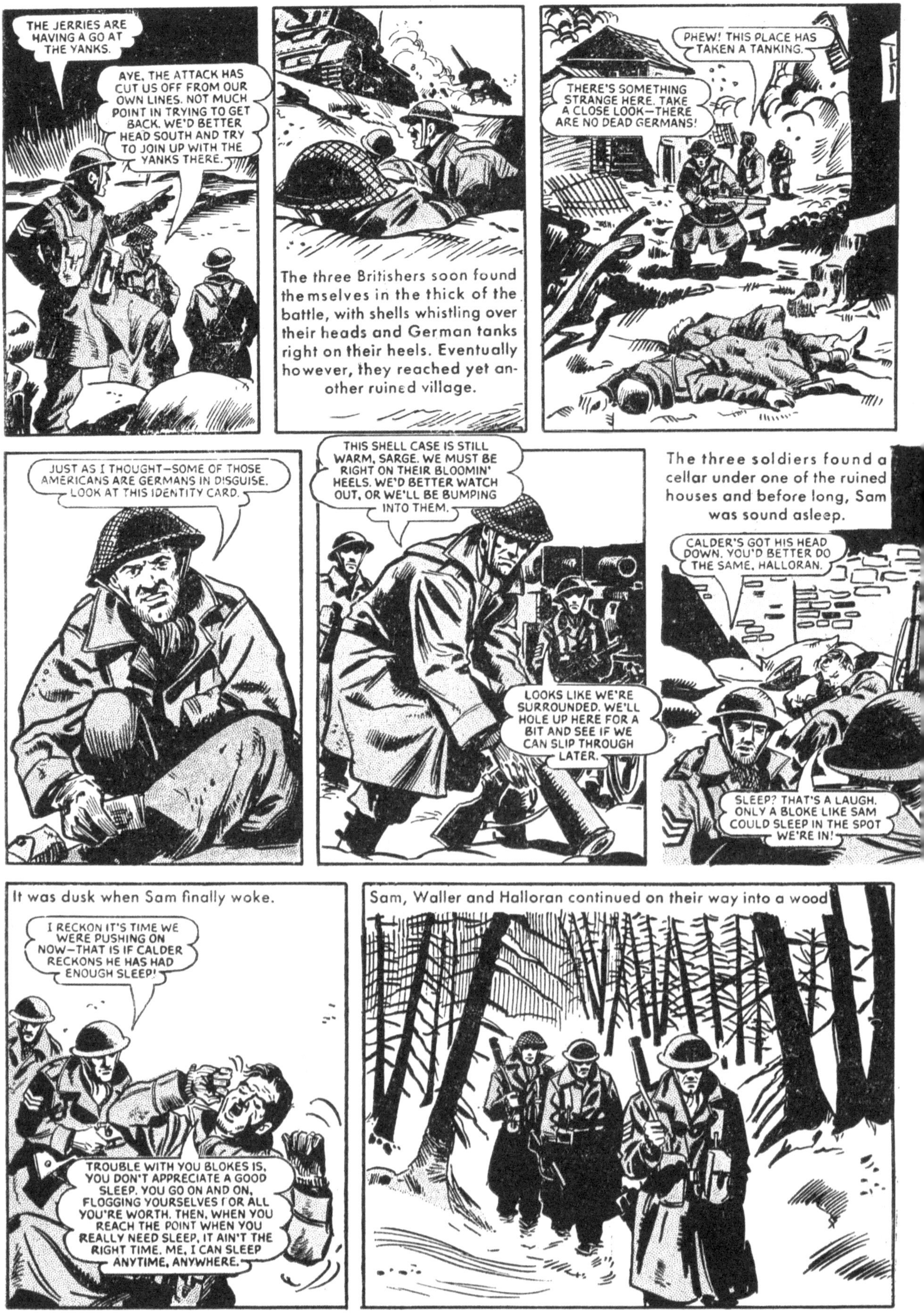
THE JERRIES ARE HAVING A GO AT THE YANKS.
AYE, THE ATTACK HAS CUT US OFF FROM OUR OWN LINES. NOT MUCH POINT IN TRYING TO GET BACK. WE'D BETTER HEAD SOUTH AND TRY TO JOIN UP WITH THE YANKS THERE.
The three Britishers soon found themselves in the thick of the battle, with shells whistling over their heads and German tanks right on their heels. Eventually however, they reached yet another ruined village.
PHEW! THIS PLACE HAS TAKEN A TANKING.
THERE'S SOMETHING STRANGE HERE. TAKE A CLOSE LOOK—THERE ARE NO DEAD GERMANS!
JUST AS I THOUGHT—SOME OF THOSE AMERICANS ARE GERMANS IN DISGUISE. LOOK AT THIS IDENTITY CARD.
THIS SHELL CASE IS STILL WARM, SARGE. WE MUST BE RIGHT ON THEIR BLOOMIN' HEELS. WE'D BETTER WATCH OUT, OR WE'LL BE BUMPING INTO THEM.
LOOKS LIKE WE'RE SURROUNDED. WE'LL HOLE UP HERE FOR A BIT AND SEE IF WE CAN SLIP THROUGH LATER.
The three soldiers found a cellar under one of the ruined houses and before long, Sam was sound asleep.
CALDER'S GOT HIS HEAD DOWN. YOU'D BETTER DO THE SAME, HALLORAN.
SLEEP? THAT'S A LAUGH. ONLY A BLOKE LIKE SAM COULD SLEEP IN THE SPOT WE'RE IN!
It was dusk when Sam finally woke.
I RECKON IT'S TIME WE WERE PUSHING ON NOW—THAT IS IF CALDER RECKONS HE HAS HAD ENOUGH SLEEP!
TROUBLE WITH YOU BLOKES IS, YOU DON'T APPRECIATE A GOOD SLEEP. YOU GO ON AND ON, FLOGGING YOURSELVES FOR ALL YOU'RE WORTH. THEN, WHEN YOU REACH THE POINT WHEN YOU REALLY NEED SLEEP, IT AIN'T THE RIGHT TIME. ME, I CAN SLEEP ANYTIME, ANYWHERE.
Sam, Waller and Halloran continued on their way into a wood

"I'll get even with those Jerries!"

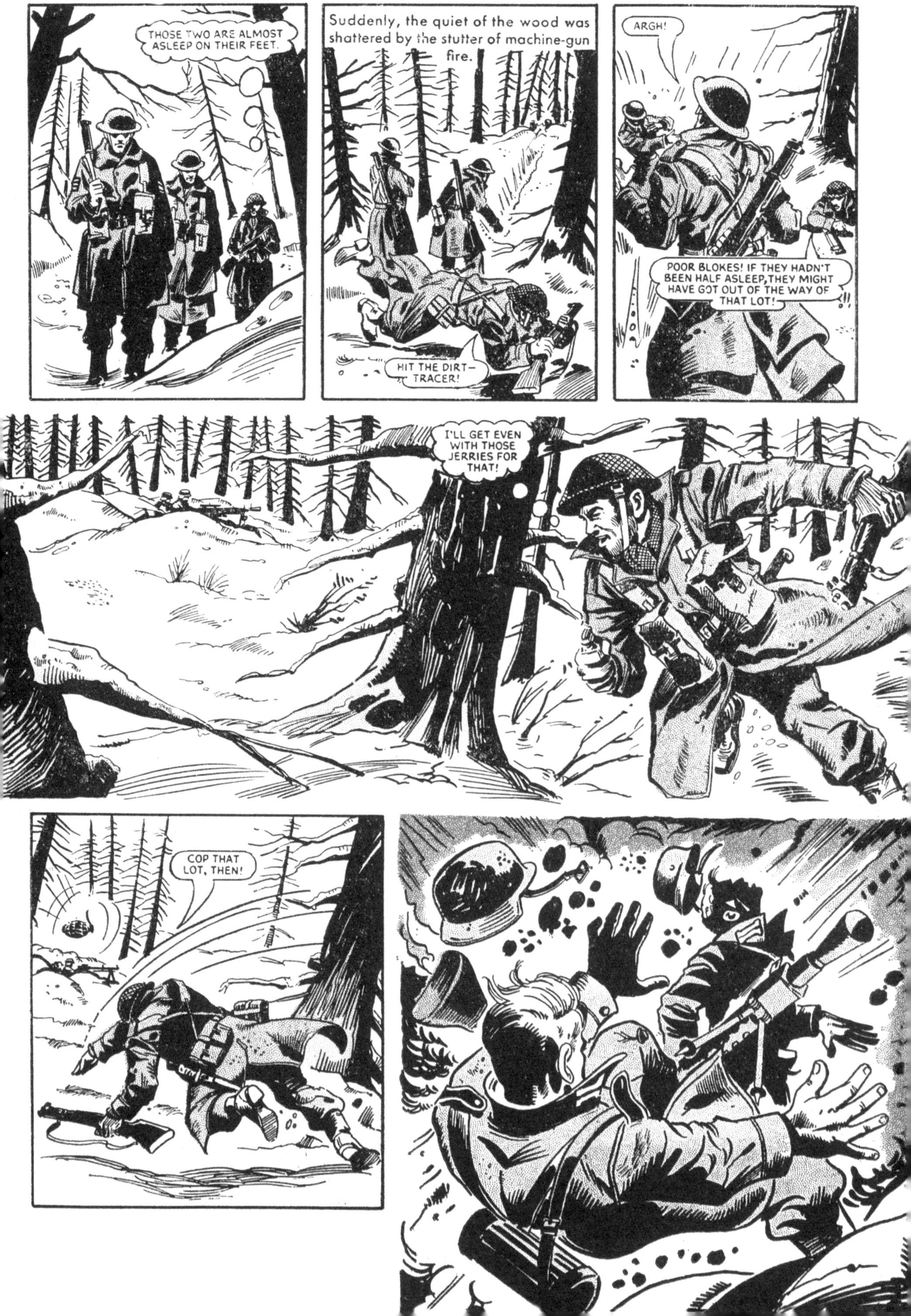
THOSE TWO ARE ALMOST ASLEEP ON THEIR FEET.
Suddenly, the quiet of the wood was shattered by the stutter of machine-gun fire.
HIT THE DIRT—TRACER!
ARGH!
POOR BLOKES! IF THEY HADN'T BEEN HALF ASLEEP, THEY MIGHT HAVE GOT OUT OF THE WAY OF THAT LOT!
I'LL GET EVEN WITH THOSE JERRIES FOR THAT!
COP THAT LOT, THEN!

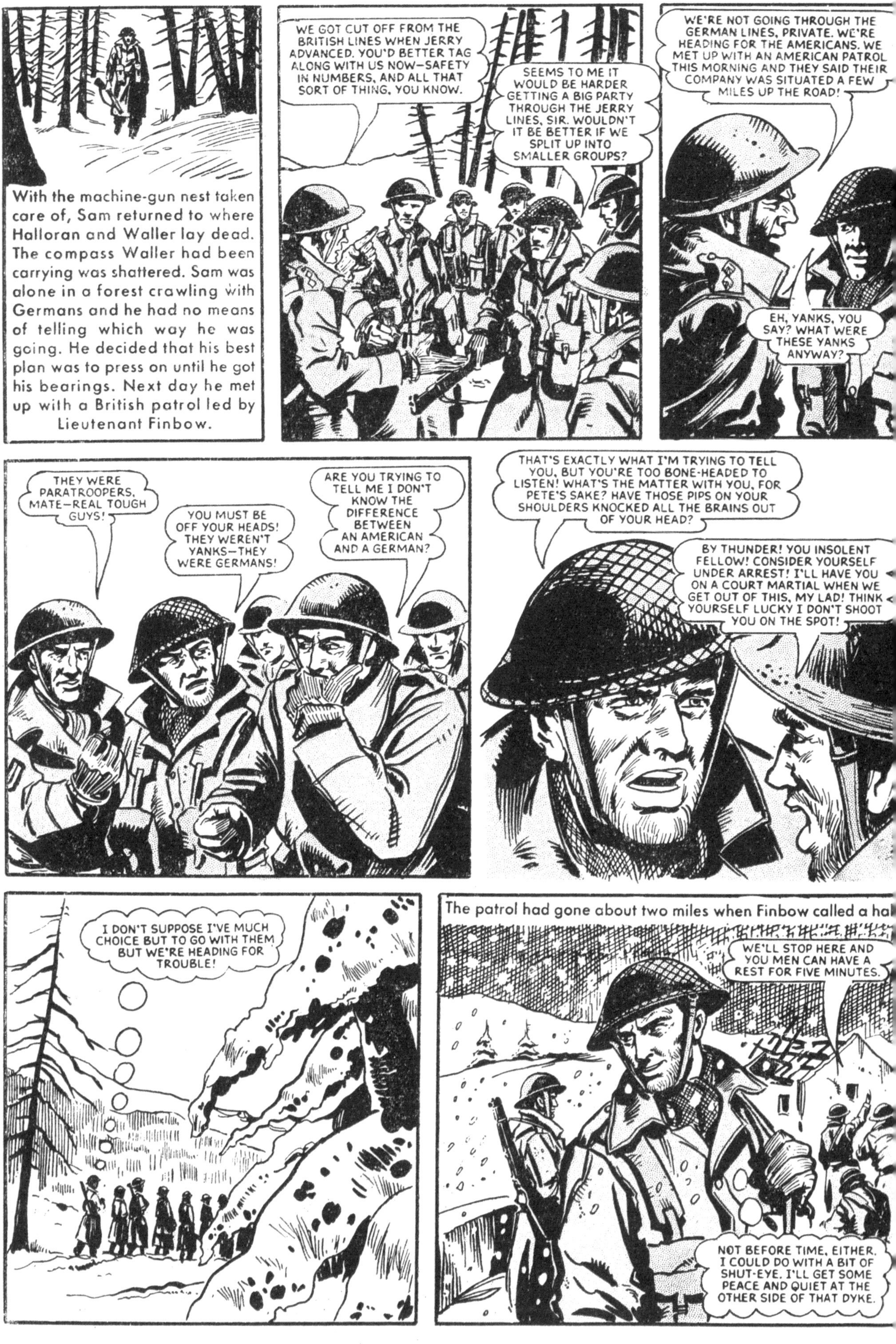

With the machine-gun nest taken care of, Sam returned to where Halloran and Waller lay dead. The compass Waller had been carrying was shattered. Sam was alone in a forest crawling with Germans and he had no means of telling which way he was going. He decided that his best plan was to press on until he got his bearings. Next day he met up with a British patrol led by Lieutenant Finbow.
WE GOT CUT OFF FROM THE BRITISH LINES WHEN JERRY ADVANCED. YOU'D BETTER TAG ALONG WITH US NOW—SAFETY IN NUMBERS, AND ALL THAT SORT OF THING, YOU KNOW.
SEEMS TO ME IT WOULD BE HARDER GETTING A BIG PARTY THROUGH THE JERRY LINES, SIR. WOULDN'T IT BE BETTER IF WE SPLIT UP INTO SMALLER GROUPS?
WE'RE NOT GOING THROUGH THE GERMAN LINES, PRIVATE. WE'RE HEADING FOR THE AMERICANS. WE MET UP WITH AN AMERICAN PATROL THIS MORNING AND THEY SAID THEIR COMPANY WAS SITUATED A FEW MILES UP THE ROAD!
EH, YANKS, YOU SAY? WHAT WERE THESE YANKS ANYWAY?
THEY WERE PARATROOPERS, MATE—REAL TOUGH GUYS!
YOU MUST BE OFF YOUR HEADS! THEY WEREN'T YANKS—THEY WERE GERMANS!
ARE YOU TRYING TO TELL ME I DON'T KNOW THE DIFFERENCE BETWEEN AN AMERICAN AND A GERMAN?
THAT'S EXACTLY WHAT I'M TRYING TO TELL YOU, BUT YOU'RE TOO BONE-HEADED TO LISTEN! WHAT'S THE MATTER WITH YOU, FOR PETE'S SAKE? HAVE THOSE PIPS ON YOUR SHOULDERS KNOCKED ALL THE BRAINS OUT OF YOUR HEAD?
BY THUNDER! YOU INSOLENT FELLOW! CONSIDER YOURSELF UNDER ARREST! I'LL HAVE YOU ON A COURT MARTIAL WHEN WE GET OUT OF THIS, MY LAD! THINK YOURSELF LUCKY I DON'T SHOOT YOU ON THE SPOT!
I DON'T SUPPOSE I'VE MUCH CHOICE BUT TO GO WITH THEM BUT WE'RE HEADING FOR TROUBLE!
The patrol had gone about two miles when Finbow called a ha
WE'LL STOP HERE AND YOU MEN CAN HAVE A REST FOR FIVE MINUTES.
NOT BEFORE TIME, EITHER. I COULD DO WITH A BIT OF SHUT-EYE. I'LL GET SOME PEACE AND QUIET AT THE OTHER SIDE OF THAT DYKE.

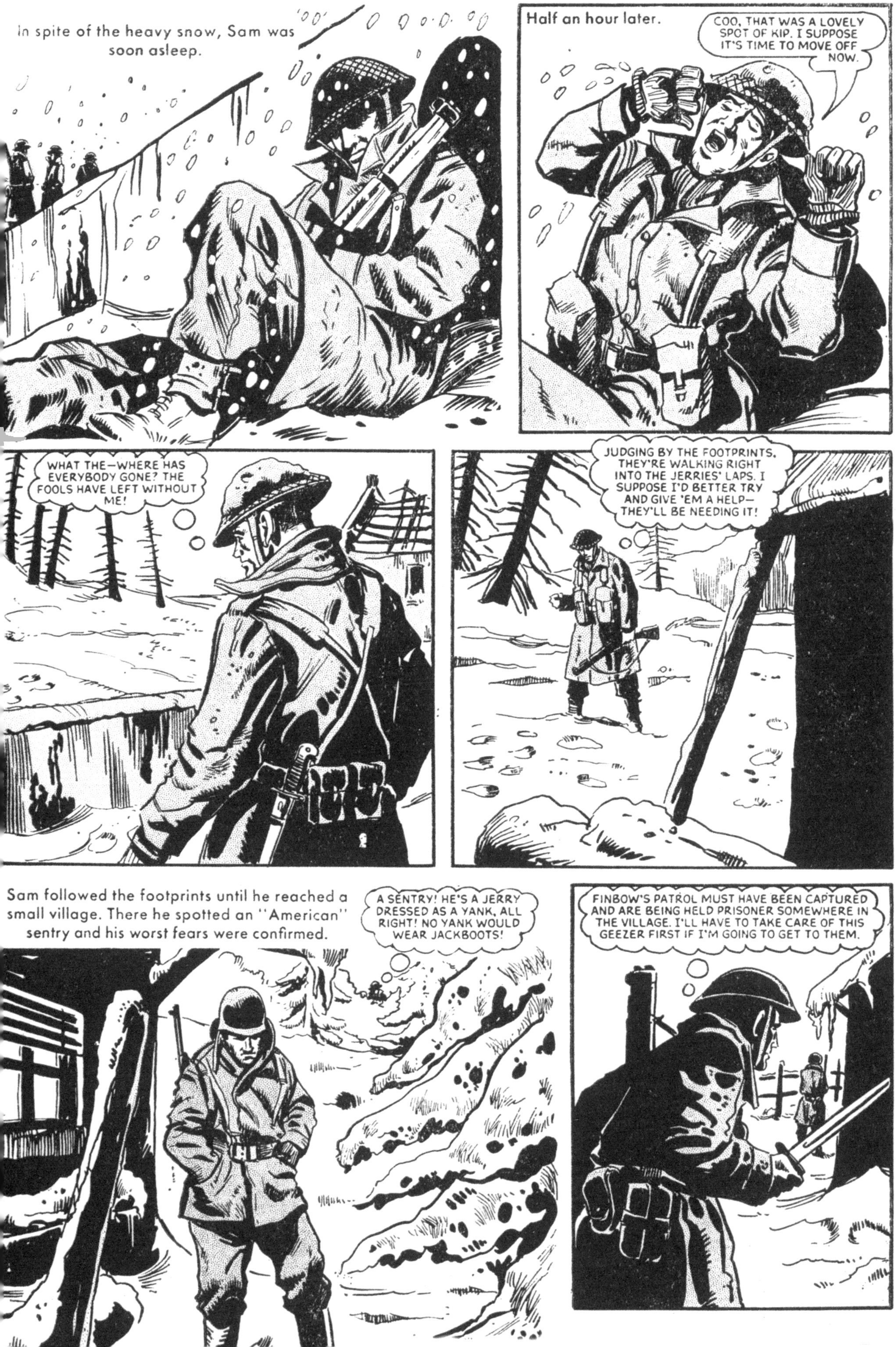
In spite of the heavy snow, Sam was soon asleep.
Half an hour later.
COO, THAT WAS A LOVELY SPOT OF KIP. I SUPPOSE IT'S TIME TO MOVE OFF NOW.
WHAT THE—WHERE HAS EVERYBODY GONE? THE FOOLS HAVE LEFT WITHOUT ME!
JUDGING BY THE FOOTPRINTS, THEY'RE WALKING RIGHT INTO THE JERRIES' LAPS. I SUPPOSE I'D BETTER TRY AND GIVE 'EM A HELP—THEY'LL BE NEEDING IT!
Sam followed the footprints until he reached a small village. There he spotted an "American" sentry and his worst fears were confirmed.
A SENTRY! HE'S A JERRY DRESSED AS A YANK, ALL RIGHT! NO YANK WOULD WEAR JACKBOOTS!
FINBOW'S PATROL MUST HAVE BEEN CAPTURED AND ARE BEING HELD PRISONER SOMEWHERE IN THE VILLAGE. I'LL HAVE TO TAKE CARE OF THIS GEEZER FIRST IF I'M GOING TO GET TO THEM.

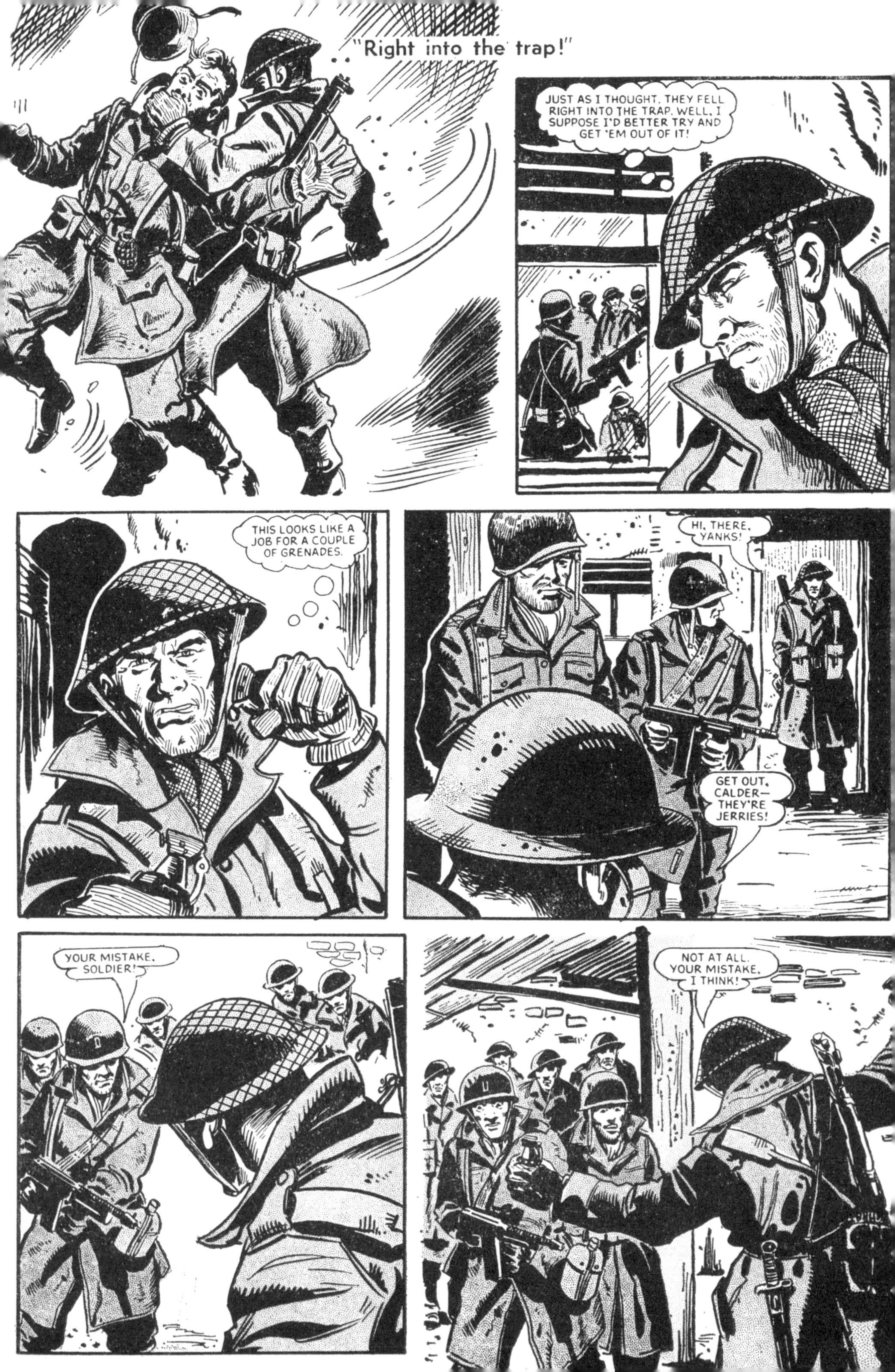
"Right into the trap!"
JUST AS I THOUGHT. THEY FELL RIGHT INTO THE TRAP. WELL, I SUPPOSE I'D BETTER TRY AND GET 'EM OUT OF IT!
THIS LOOKS LIKE A JOB FOR A COUPLE OF GRENADES.
HI, THERE, YANKS!
GET OUT, CALDER— THEY'RE JERRIES!
YOUR MISTAKE, SOLDIER!
NOT AT ALL. YOUR MISTAKE, I THINK!

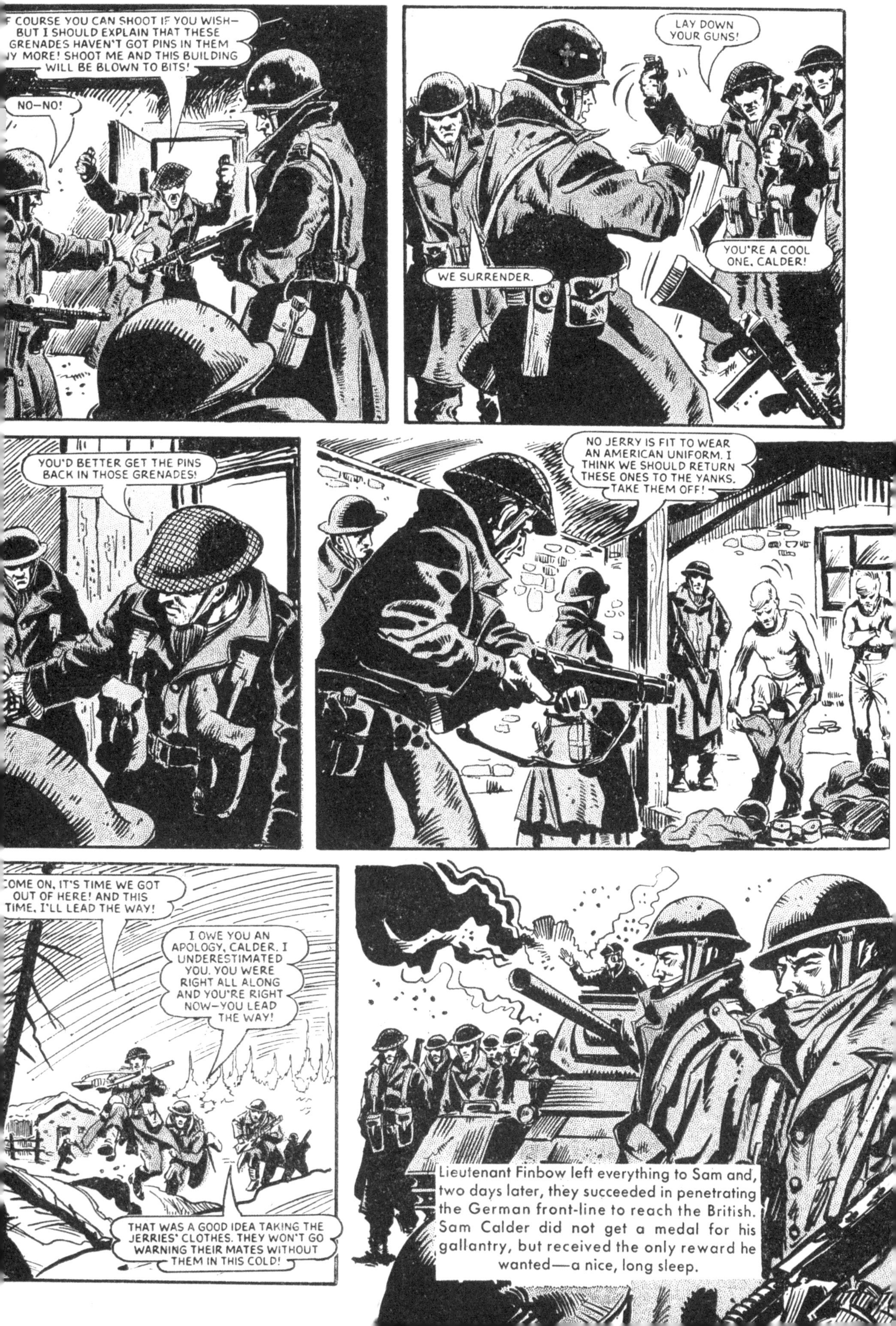
F COURSE YOU CAN SHOOT IF YOU WISH—BUT I SHOULD EXPLAIN THAT THESE GRENADES HAVEN'T GOT PINS IN THEM NY MORE! SHOOT ME AND THIS BUILDING WILL BE BLOWN TO BITS!
NO—NO!
LAY DOWN YOUR GUNS!
WE SURRENDER.
YOU'RE A COOL ONE, CALDER!
YOU'D BETTER GET THE PINS BACK IN THOSE GRENADES!
NO JERRY IS FIT TO WEAR AN AMERICAN UNIFORM. I THINK WE SHOULD RETURN THESE ONES TO THE YANKS. TAKE THEM OFF!
COME ON, IT'S TIME WE GOT OUT OF HERE! AND THIS TIME, I'LL LEAD THE WAY!
I OWE YOU AN APOLOGY, CALDER. I UNDERESTIMATED YOU. YOU WERE RIGHT ALL ALONG AND YOU'RE RIGHT NOW—YOU LEAD THE WAY!
THAT WAS A GOOD IDEA TAKING THE JERRIES' CLOTHES. THEY WON'T GO WARNING THEIR MATES WITHOUT THEM IN THIS COLD!
Lieutenant Finbow left everything to Sam and, two days later, they succeeded in penetrating the German front-line to reach the British. Sam Calder did not get a medal for his gallantry, but received the only reward he wanted—a nice, long sleep.

THE FIGHT OF FORGOTTEN PUNCHES

A GREAT ROAR came from the crowd in the packed stadium as "Steel" Kirby swung into the attack, his great arms swinging like pistons. His opponent, who suddenly seemed to grow smaller, went staggering against the ropes as a left hook exploded against his chest, knocking every ounce of breath out of his body.

My hands were clenched as I saw the thin smile creep over Kirby's face. I had waited what seemed years for this match and now it seemed to be taking only seconds for all my hopes and plans to be smashed to a pulp.

They had said Steel Kirby was unbeatable, and I had set out to prove them wrong. I hated that giant, vicious bully as much as any man could, and I wanted to show him up for the mean coward he was. The only way to do that was in the ring. But how do you take away the crown of the British heavy-weight champion, the man tipped to take the world title?

I thought I had the answer in Mike Chester, the lad I had trained to within a hair's-breadth of perfection. But here was Mike being battered from one end of the ring to the other. Where had things gone wrong?

* * * * *

Barney Roberts is my name, and it was a name that meant something to quite a few people

> No mercy from the fists of 'Steel' Kirby!

in the boxing game a few years back. Then I suffered a leg injury and had to pack in the game. I couldn't leave boxing altogether, though, and I opened a small gym where I coached likely youngsters. When Mike Chester first came along I could tell at a glance that here was the ideal material for a heavy-weight, but he had a long way to go before

he would get a crack at the champ.

Mike was a miner and was built of muscle, without an ounce of spare fat. His reflexes were fantastically quick and even without any real boxing skill he put up such a good show in the ring that I resolved there and then to do all I could to give him a real start in the boxing game.

Mike was a good pupil. He was quick to learn, and soon he was developing his natural ability so much that I really began to think he was championship material. Above all Mike had patience, and he willingly accepted my often tough criticism and tried to build up on his weak points.

Publicity Punches

THROUGH my old contacts in the fight game I heard that Steel Kirby was visiting our town for a day or so. I had never met the man myself, but like everyone else I had read of his rocket-like rise to success.

He'd been taken on by some very shrewd managers, given all the right breaks, and was now very definitely on his way to the top.

Like Mike, he had started in industry, and had worked in a steel foundry. That explained his nickname. But he had far better training facilities than I could provide for Mike in my tiny gym.

He gave up his work altogether and spent his whole time in training, whereas Mike could only come along in between shifts. As I said, this was because Kirby had been taken on by some very smart operators, and I knew they were men who worked in a ruthless way. They were out to make this man a champion, and money was no object.

To give my lads a bit of a boost, I invited Kirby along to the gym and perhaps hand out a word of encouragement here and there. His managers saw publicity possibilities in this and they agreed.

Kirby arrived with a bunch of photographers in tow. His chief manager was a keen-eyed man named Totten who organised everything.

"I want pictures of Steel patting some of these youngsters on the back," he instructed the photographers. He turned to my lads. "I want you to show some admiration for the man who's going to be British heavy-weight champ before long."

My lads tried to do what he said while the flash-bulbs popped. Kirby smirked and I took a dislike to him when I saw the way he switched his smirk off as soon as the photographers had finished. He wasn't a bit interested in what was going on and he looked impatient when I suggested he watch some of my youngsters in action.

"I've got a better idea than that," Totten piped up. "Come on, Steel—get changed into kit and we'll have some pictures of you actually sparring with these boys."

Steel agreed with very bad grace and changed into his kit. I decided to put Mike in the ring with him for the photographs. Dancing round the ring, Steel flicked a few fancy punches in Mike's direction as the photographers popped away.

Mike was very serious and he was carefully weighing up Steel's methods just as I had taught him to do.

"Okay, youngster," Totten called, "let's see you try to take a swing at Steel for just one more picture."

Mike nodded. Suddenly he was

under Steel's guard and hammering away at his body before anyone—including Steel—realised what was happening. A look of astonishment and then anger flashed over Steel's face. Those punches had hurt, but what had hurt most was the speed with which Mike had fooled him.

Steel pushed Mike away and

Steel Kirby was taken completely by surprise by the barrage of blows from the young boxer.

retreated to a corner while he regained his breath. Then he danced across the ring towards Mike again. I felt a cold chill as I saw the look in Steel's eyes. This was the real thing for him, now, and he was out to get Mike.

A straight left headed viciously for Mike's shoulder, but the lad bobbed neatly out of the way. Steel closed in on him and began to crowd him into a corner, both fists working like machine-guns.

Steel's face was black with fury as Mike weaved and dodged and then slid out from under the trap. Mike brought round a right hook

lost his temper he might have been able to take advantage of Mike's inexperience.

Totten realised what was happening, and when one of the photographers snapped Steel staggering against the ropes after a hook from Mike, he decided to step in.

"That's enough, lads," he said, separating the two boxers.

There was cold fury in Steel's eyes as he changed. Totten made the photographers take all the film out of their cameras and expose it, so it couldn't be used.

"Who is that lad?" he asked me thoughtfully.

I told him about Mike and his

One of the photographers had managed to fool Totten by not destroying all his pictures and I could imagine the fury of the manager when he saw this.

Ambush

THAT night Mike was on his way home from the mine when two men suddenly appeared alongside him. Before he knew what was happening, he was pushed down a lonely side street. Two other

Mike Chester had proved that he was good enough to reach the top in boxing — but there were some who didn't want him to make it!

that connected with Steel's ear and brought a howl of fury from the bigger man. Now his temper had really gone.

"We'd better stop this," I said to Totten, but he shrugged.

"Your lad provoked him," the manager said. "I'll let Steel work off his temper now."

But things just weren't working out like that. Mike was on top of his form and he was coolly countering every one of the other man's moves with a greater turn of speed.

It wasn't all one-way traffic, and Mike took quite a hammering, but he was making Steel look foolish. If the other man had not

ambition to become a professional.

"I wouldn't encourage him in that," Totten said casually. "It's a tough game and I don't reckon he's got the staying power to make it."

I was tempted to say that his staying power seemed pretty good compared with Steel's, but I decided it would be more diplomatic to remain silent.

The next morning I picked up my paper and glanced at the sports page. There was a picture of Mike connecting with a left jab with Steel's chest, and the headline read: "Unknown Amateur Rocks Kirby."

men approached from the other end.

He didn't stand a chance against the four of them. Using boots and coshes they beat him to the ground. Mike fought back savagely, but a blow on the head stunned him. My gym was just round the corner and when I heard the noise of the scuffling I opened the door to take a look.

When I saw what was happening, I shouted to the lads in the gym,

"Come on—Mike's in trouble!"

As we all spilled out of the gym the four men saw us, hesitated, and then started to run the other way. We gave chase, but they all piled into a car at the end of the street and roared away.

We helped the unconscious Mike into the gym and called a doctor. He was still not fully conscious when the doctor examined him.

"Plenty of bruises," the doctor said after a while, "and he'll be suffering from concussion. It looks as though they were trying to break his wrists when you disturbed them."

That didn't surprise me. Once his wrists were broken, Mike would never have been a serious boxer again. And it was clear this attack had been made to make sure he wouldn't ever be a challenge to Kirby.

In fact the police were never able to discover the attackers.

But I was more concerned about Mike himself. He spent a couple of days in bed, and when I went to see him he said he felt fit enough.

"Leave it for a few more days before you come back to the gym," I advised him. "Those thugs gave you a good going over and it's best not to rush things."

Mike was puzzled. "I don't understand why they should be so upset because I had a go at Steel."

"It's not that," I explained. "They're looking to the future. Totten saw how good you really were, and how, with training, you could present a real challenge to Steel—even getting that British title. They've got a lot of money invested in him, and they reckon you present a big risk to their investment. So they decided to put you out of the picture."

I was relieved that Mike had not been more badly hurt, and when he came to the gym at the week-end I got him to put on the gloves right away.

"Come on, Mike," I said, squaring up to him. "Let's see you dish out a bit more of that Steel medicine!"

Mike came towards me hesitantly. There was something wrong. He put up his gloves, but his stance was awkward and his arms moved unsteadily. He attempted to swing at me, but over-reached and almost lost his balance. I could have dropped him with one blow.

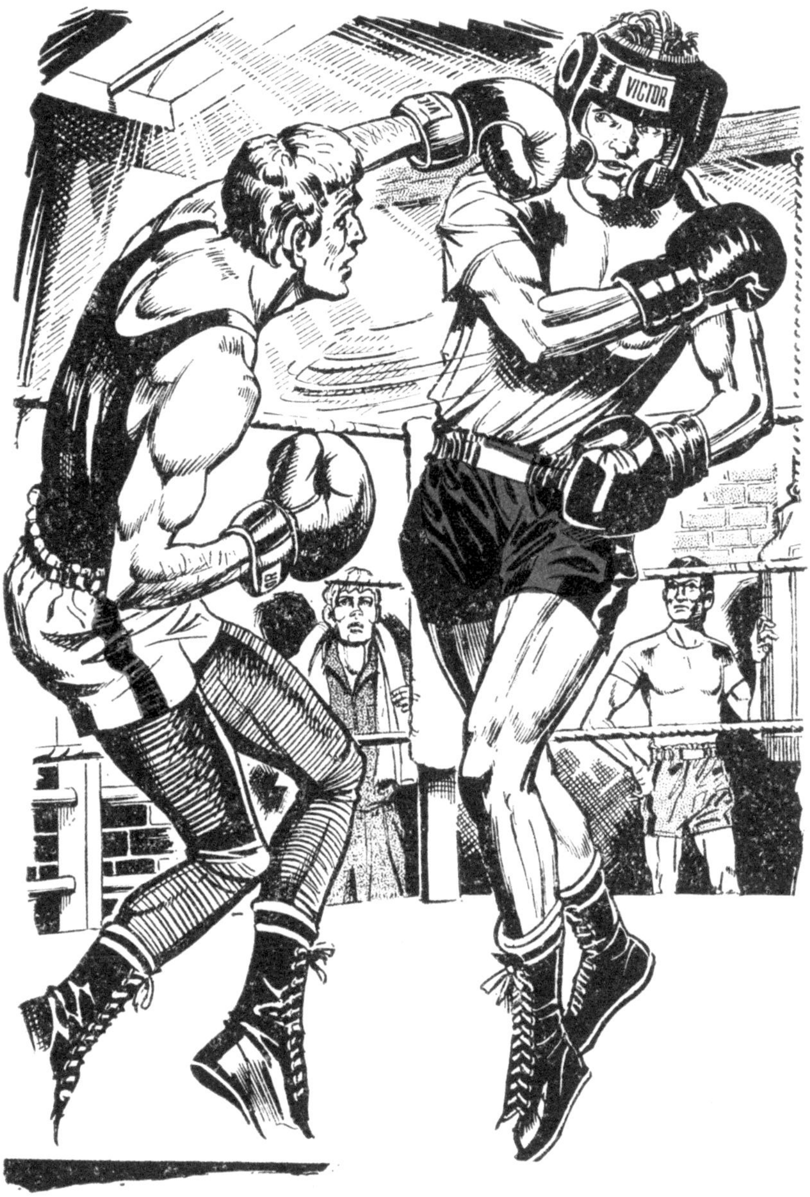
VICTOR

Barney Roberts was horrified — his bright young boxer had forgotten how to box!

He moved in closer and tried to do his famous rat-tat on my ribs with both fists. But he couldn't time the rhythm, and found himself pushing both gloves forward at once.

His face was white and strained as I stopped him, and took him round to see the doctor again.

After a long examination, the doctor gave his verdict.

"The concussion has affected his memory, but not completely. What is blanked out is that part of his mind that controlled his boxing skill. Quite simply, he's forgotten how to box!"

Cave-In

IN a lonely, derelict cottage on the moors, I taught Mike to fight again. It took two solid years of work to teach him how to use his arms and legs like a boxer and to learn a new skill.

It was not the natural skill that he had when I first took him on. This was something learned slowly and laboriously according to the text books.

A crazy scheme from crazy people.

Mike became, in fact, a textbook boxer and it was only his dedication and fierce ambition that lifted him out of the ordinary run of fighters.

It was a task that I would have dismissed as crazy if anyone had suggested it in normal circumstances. But these circumstances were not normal. Both Mike and I vowed to repay Steel Kirby for what he had done, and we agreed to devote all our time and energy to toppling Steel from his throne.

To do this, I decided to give Mike a new identity, so Steel and saw Steel eventually gain the British title. As a boxer he was improving all the time, and I could well understand those commentators who saw in him a world champ. But I was determined to bring out an even better boxer who had the guts and the decency that Steel never had.

Looking back, the whole scheme seems crazy. Sure, we were crazy, but it takes crazy people to clear out thugs like Steel and his crowd.

By the end of two years, Mike was ready for the professional ring. He was a smooth, polished

I'd done a bit about altering his appearance, by cutting his thick black hair very short and trimming down his bushy eyebrows. It's surprising how much difference that can make to a man's appearance.

Ted won every one of his fights in the first six months of his new career, and by now people were taking notice of him. Through my contacts in the game, I was able to fix up the right matches to bring him to the attention of the bigger promoters.

Eventually the sportswriters were

The hooter at the mine went off! There had been an accident and Mike Chester knew he'd be needed.

his men would not get wind of what we were doing. While I kept the gym on, Mike never went there. As far as most people were concerned, he'd given up boxing completely. In fact, every night he went straight to a lonely, empty cottage well outside the town, where I met him.

There I had rigged up a rough-and-ready ring and it was there we spent countless hours, starting right with the basics of boxing and painfully conquering the secret of every move, every punch in the book.

While this was going on, we performer who threw the right punches at the right time, made the right moves and could take his punishment. I was proud of him, of course, but I've been in boxing all my life and what I look for in any fighter is that natural style that really makes a man great. That's just what was missing from Mike's new identity.

Under his new name of Ted Morris he started on the circuit and in a few months was making quite a name for himself. Not many people watching him would recognise Mike Chester in the ring.

beginning to refer to him as a likely contender for the British title. They noted his smooth, text-book style and began to ask when Steel was going to agree to a contest.

Steel was in no hurry to meet an unknown, but eventually, with a bit of behind-the-scenes pressure on my part, the publicity became a bit too much. He finally agreed to a match.

The night before the match, Mike and I had a last training session at the cottage that had been our headquarters for so long. When we had finished, I said,

The human pit-prop!

"That's it, Mike. If anyone can lick that thug, Ted Morris can. And that's just what you're going to do tomorrow."

Just as we were leaving the cottage, the sound of a hooter in a series of short blasts travelled across the moor towards us.

"Strange," I said. "That sounds like the hooter at the mine—but they don't sound it at this time."

Mike snatched up his jacket. "That's the accident signal—it means someone's trapped below ground!"

He was off like the wind, sprinting across the moor towards the mine. Mike was a miner, and those were his mates in trouble.

I had to follow on more slowly. By the time I reached the mine, Mike had already descended.

"It's a fall in No. 3 shaft," one of the crowd at the pit-head told me. "Mike knows that shaft better than any man here, and he's leading the rescue party."

I heard later how Mike crawled through the tangle of broken props and rubble, leading the rescue party to where the injured men were trapped. They had to break through a solid barrier of rock to reach them. There was an ominous groaning from the remaining props as they started to drag the injured men clear. Mike spotted the key prop and, standing beneath it, took the weight of it on his massive shoulders.

Sweat poured from him as the work went on slowly and the roof of the shaft began to settle more and more. Finally the last man was clear. Mike dropped away from the prop and hurled himself back as the roof caved in with a shattering roar. He got clear with about half a second to spare.

On the surface I looked at his black, blood-streaked face and said bluntly, "I'm going to cancel the match for tomorrow. You're not up to it after that."

But he shook his head. "I feel fine, Barney. And we've worked hard to get this match. If we cancel it, we'll never get another chance."

He refused to be budged, and finally I agreed. It was a decision I was to regret as soon as he went into the ring.

Style Swop

AS the bell rang for the start of the first round, I watched Steel closely. But there was no sign of recognition on his face for the man he had met briefly two years previously. He began slowly, trying a few experimental shots to probe Mike's defences.

There was no doubt the champion had improved his technique a lot since that night he had been in my gym. His temper was completely under control and he knew just what he was doing.

But I just couldn't understand Mike. I had trained him in every punch in the book to counter Steel's attacks, but now it was

As the tunnel roof groaned and cracked, threatening to bury both rescuers and rescued, Mike Chester took the strain!

Scuppered by a style switch!

as if he had never heard of them. He was completely unsure of himself and Steel's punches were hitting home hard and often.

As the round went on, Steel became more and more sure of himself. In a clinch, he hissed in Mike's ear,

"You're not getting off lightly, Morris. I'm going to chop you up into little pieces before I finish you off!"

This was a charming habit Steel had, of threatening his opponents in an effort to put them off.

By the end of the first round, people in the crowd were muttering about Mike being out of his class. And I was beginning to agree with them.

At the end of the round, I said to Mike,

"Are you sure that nothing happened to you in the mine last night?"

"I'm fine," he replied. "I managed to get clear before the roof caved in. All that hit me was a piece of flying stone."

During the second round I watched Steel punching Mike from one side of the ring to the other. Where had I gone wrong? Then something clicked in my mind.

At the end of round two Mike wasn't looking too good at all.

I said to him, "Listen, Mike. That stone that hit you on the head must have brought back your memory!"

He looked puzzled, as I went on, "Can't you see what's happening? You're trying to box the way

I taught you during the past two years, but all you're doing is getting in the way of the real Mike Chester, who really wants to have a go!"

Mike nodded slowly. "You mean my original style is getting mixed up with the new one—and that's why I can't do any good? Then what should I do?"

"Just this," I said. "Get out there and forget everything I ever taught you. Just leave it to your fists to do your thinking for you!"

Mike went into the next round like a new man. There was a confidence that had been lacking before as he watched Steel bore into the attack.

Steel aimed a vicious right hook at Mike's head and if it had connected that would have been the end of the match. But Mike slid neatly out of the way and his own right crashed into the champion's chest before he knew what was happening.

Steel was surprised. He swung round and before he could home a punch on Mike's chest, he was staggering under a rain of blows. He forced a clinch, and then, very quietly, Mike whispered in his ear,

"Know what my real name is, Champ? It's Mike Chester—the lad you met in Barney Roberts' gym!"

His words had far more effect than Steel's ever had on his opponents. As the ref separated them, I could see the look of disbelief on the champion's face. This was followed by a look of

fury as he realised how he had been fooled.

Steel lost his temper then, and by doing so he lost his title. He flung himself at Mike, his fists raining a barrage of blows, any one of which could have meant a knockout. But Mike easily danced clear and weighed his opponent up with cool seriousness. As Steel's attack faded away, Mike was in there with three short, sharp jabs that rocked Steel's head from side to side. Steel's anger exploded into another attack.

This time Mike stood his ground, slid under the champion's blows, and brought a right like a rocket up from the floor. It hit Steel's chin and lifted him off his feet. He staggered backwards across the ring and sagged on the ropes.

Mike was waiting for him as he stood up again. With cool calculation he beat Steel to the floor, where the ref started his count. On the count of eight Steel started to get up, but I got the impression he saw Mike's face waiting there for him. That was enough, and he slumped back to the floor utterly defeated.

Now Mike is the champ, of course, and there's no doubt he'll get that world title some day. His natural style still leaves a lot to be desired, and now I'm giving it the same polish that Ted Morris had. We don't train in a derelict cottage any more, but once I get these two styles working together, there'll be only one word to describe this boy—he'll be the greatest!

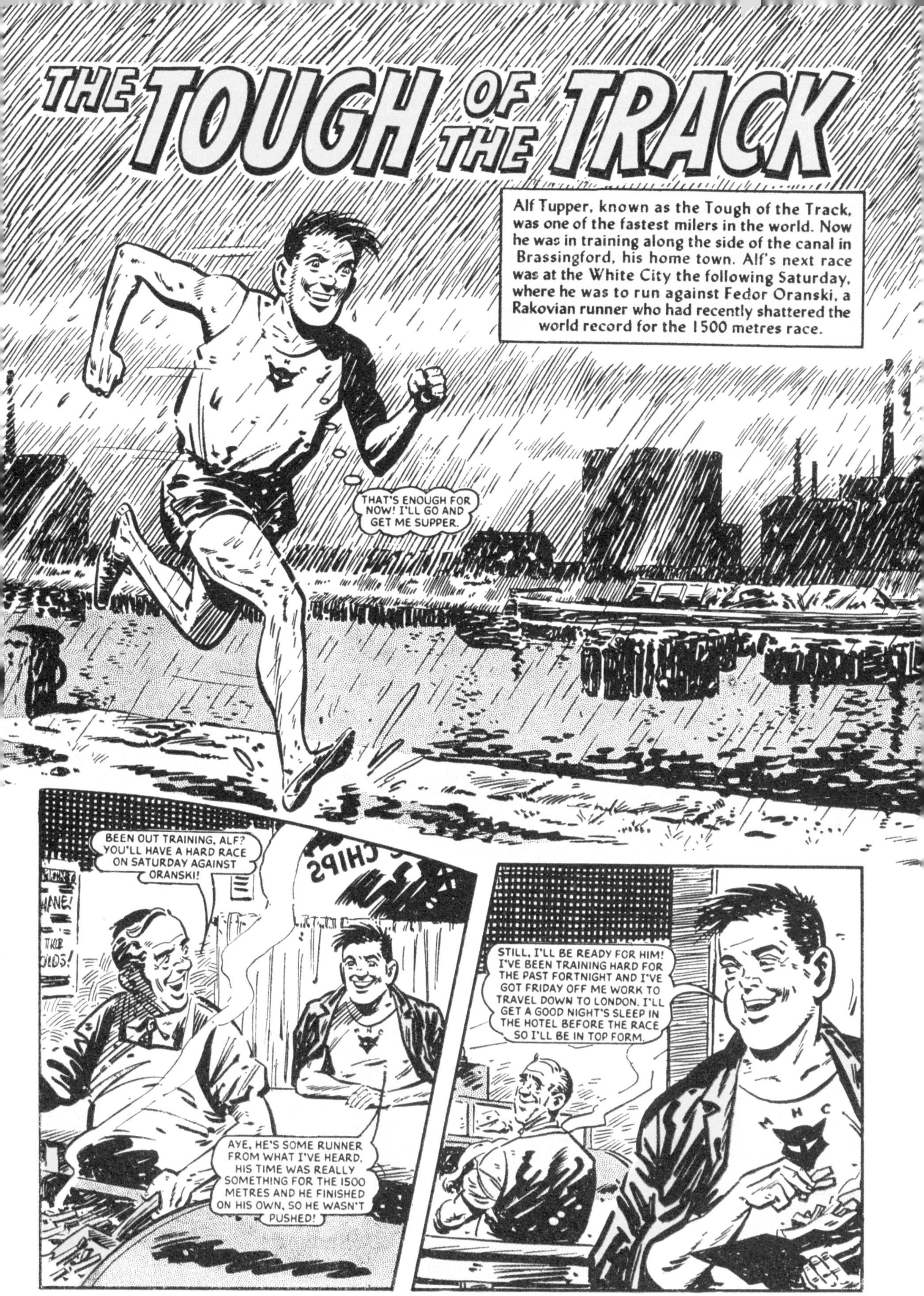
THE TOUGH OF THE TRACK
Alf Tupper, known as the Tough of the Track, was one of the fastest milers in the world. Now he was in training along the side of the canal in Brassingford, his home town. Alf's next race was at the White City the following Saturday, where he was to run against Fedor Oranski, a Rakovian runner who had recently shattered the world record for the 1500 metres race.
THAT'S ENOUGH FOR NOW! I'LL GO AND GET ME SUPPER.
BEEN OUT TRAINING, ALF? YOU'LL HAVE A HARD RACE ON SATURDAY AGAINST ORANSKI!
AYE, HE'S SOME RUNNER FROM WHAT I'VE HEARD. HIS TIME WAS REALLY SOMETHING FOR THE 1500 METRES AND HE FINISHED ON HIS OWN, SO HE WASN'T PUSHED!
STILL, I'LL BE READY FOR HIM! I'VE BEEN TRAINING HARD FOR THE PAST FORTNIGHT AND I'VE GOT FRIDAY OFF ME WORK TO TRAVEL DOWN TO LONDON. I'LL GET A GOOD NIGHT'S SLEEP IN THE HOTEL BEFORE THE RACE SO I'LL BE IN TOP FORM.

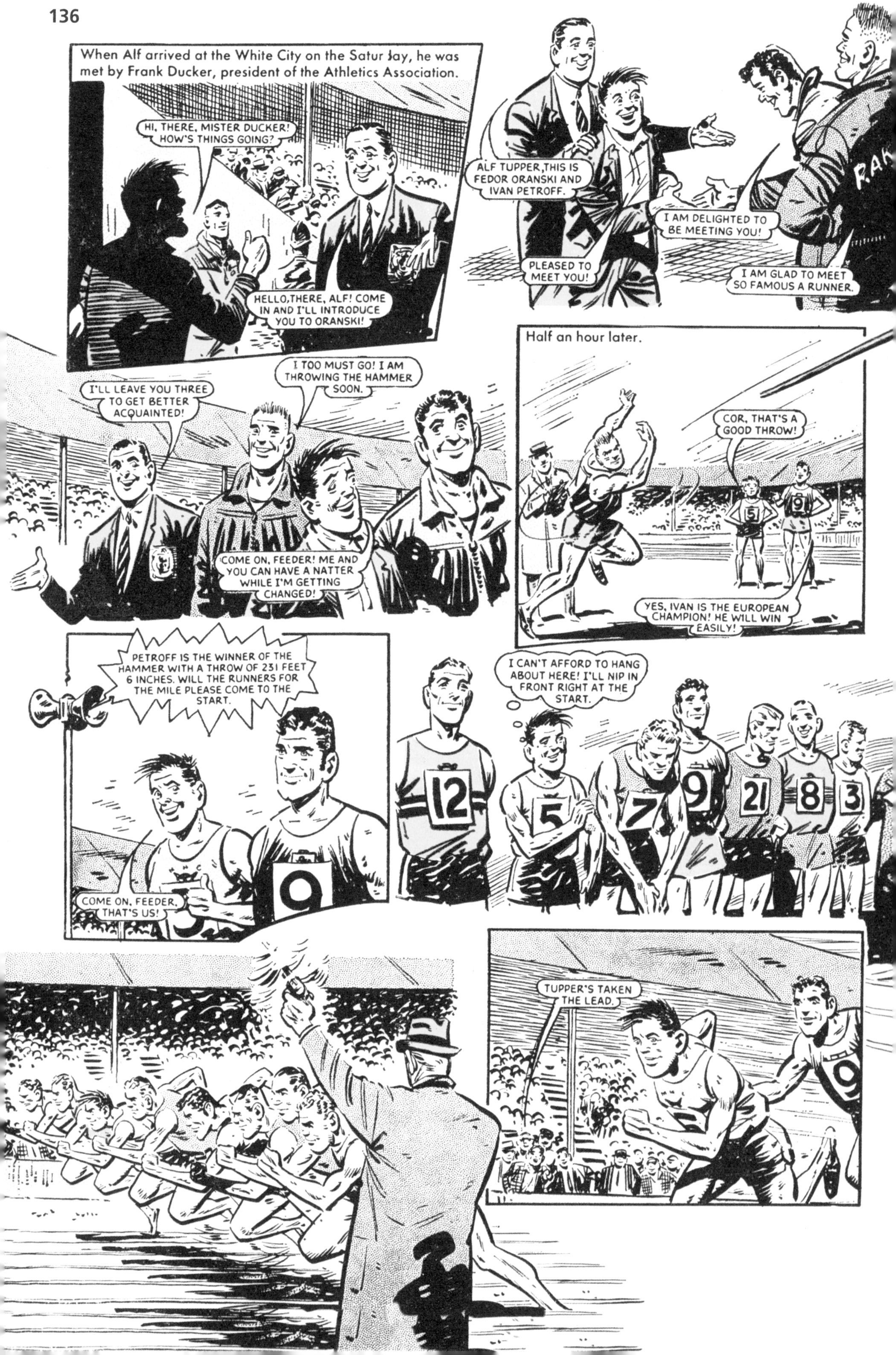
When Alf arrived at the White City on the Satur Jay, he was met by Frank Ducker, president of the Athletics Association.
HI, THERE, MISTER DUCKER! HOW'S THINGS GOING?
HELLO,THERE, ALF! COME IN AND I'LL INTRODUCE YOU TO ORANSKI!
ALF TUPPER,THIS IS FEDOR ORANSKI AND IVAN PETROFF.
PLEASED TO MEET YOU!
I AM DELIGHTED TO BE MEETING YOU!
I AM GLAD TO MEET SO FAMOUS A RUNNER.
I'LL LEAVE YOU THREE TO GET BETTER ACQUAINTED!
I TOO MUST GO! I AM THROWING THE HAMMER SOON.
COME ON, FEEDER! ME AND YOU CAN HAVE A NATTER WHILE I'M GETTING CHANGED!
Half an hour later.
COR, THAT'S A GOOD THROW!
YES, IVAN IS THE EUROPEAN CHAMPION! HE WILL WIN EASILY!
PETROFF IS THE WINNER OF THE HAMMER WITH A THROW OF 231 FEET 6 INCHES. WILL THE RUNNERS FOR THE MILE PLEASE COME TO THE START.
COME ON, FEEDER, THAT'S US!
I CAN'T AFFORD TO HANG ABOUT HERE! I'LL NIP IN FRONT RIGHT AT THE START.
TUPPER'S TAKEN THE LEAD.

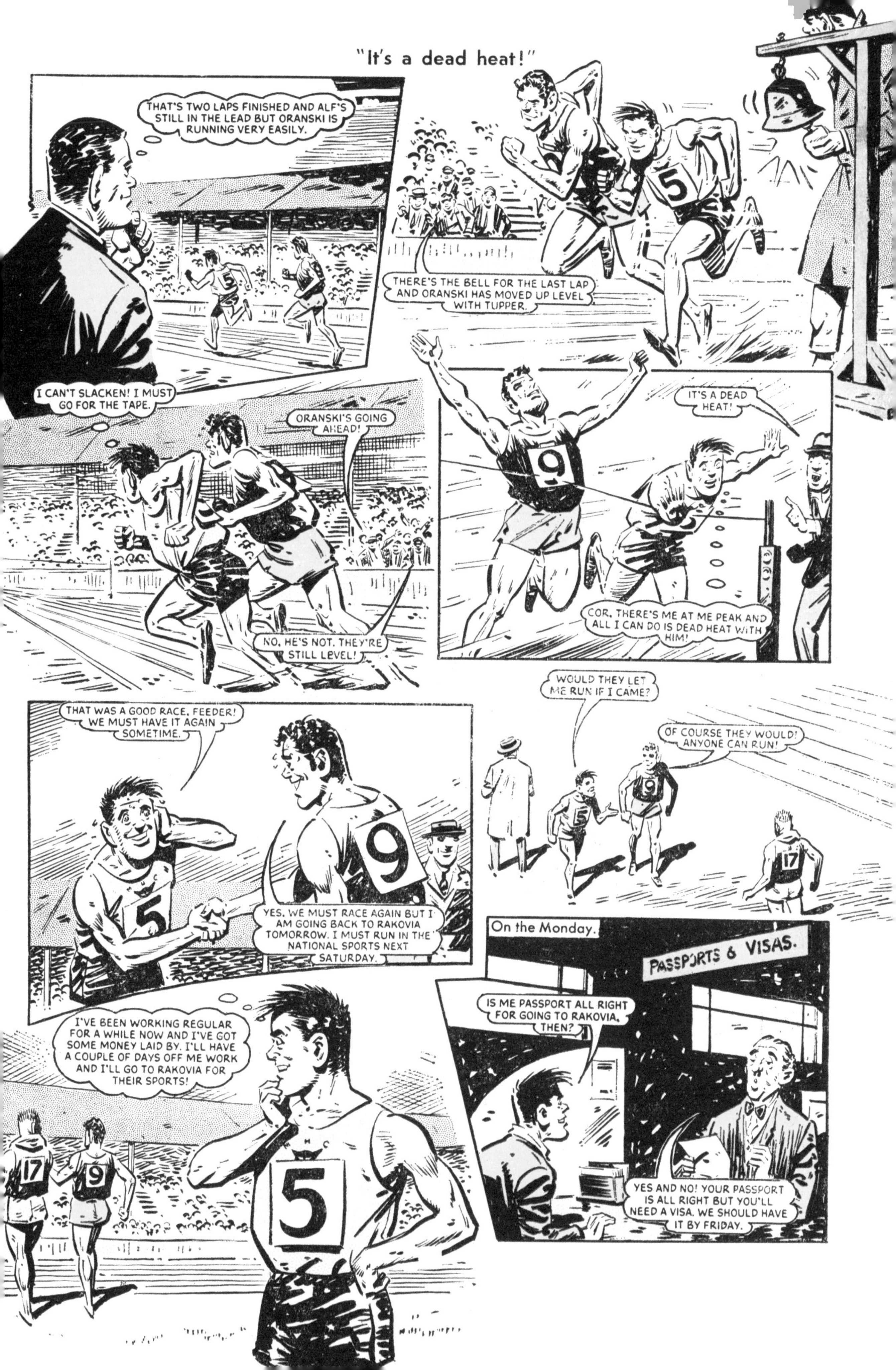
"It's a dead heat!"
THAT'S TWO LAPS FINISHED AND ALF'S STILL IN THE LEAD BUT ORANSKI IS RUNNING VERY EASILY.
THERE'S THE BELL FOR THE LAST LAP AND ORANSKI HAS MOVED UP LEVEL WITH TUPPER.
I CAN'T SLACKEN! I MUST GO FOR THE TAPE.
ORANSKI'S GOING AHEAD!
NO, HE'S NOT. THEY'RE STILL LEVEL!
IT'S A DEAD HEAT!
COR, THERE'S ME AT ME PEAK AND ALL I CAN DO IS DEAD HEAT WITH HIM!
THAT WAS A GOOD RACE, FEEDER! WE MUST HAVE IT AGAIN SOMETIME.
YES, WE MUST RACE AGAIN BUT I AM GOING BACK TO RAKOVIA TOMORROW. I MUST RUN IN THE NATIONAL SPORTS NEXT SATURDAY.
WOULD THEY LET ME RUN IF I CAME?
OF COURSE THEY WOULD! ANYONE CAN RUN!
I'VE BEEN WORKING REGULAR FOR A WHILE NOW AND I'VE GOT SOME MONEY LAID BY. I'LL HAVE A COUPLE OF DAYS OFF ME WORK AND I'LL GO TO RAKOVIA FOR THEIR SPORTS!
On the Monday.
PASSPORTS & VISAS.
IS ME PASSPORT ALL RIGHT FOR GOING TO RAKOVIA, THEN?
YES AND NO! YOUR PASSPORT IS ALL RIGHT BUT YOU'LL NEED A VISA. WE SHOULD HAVE IT BY FRIDAY.

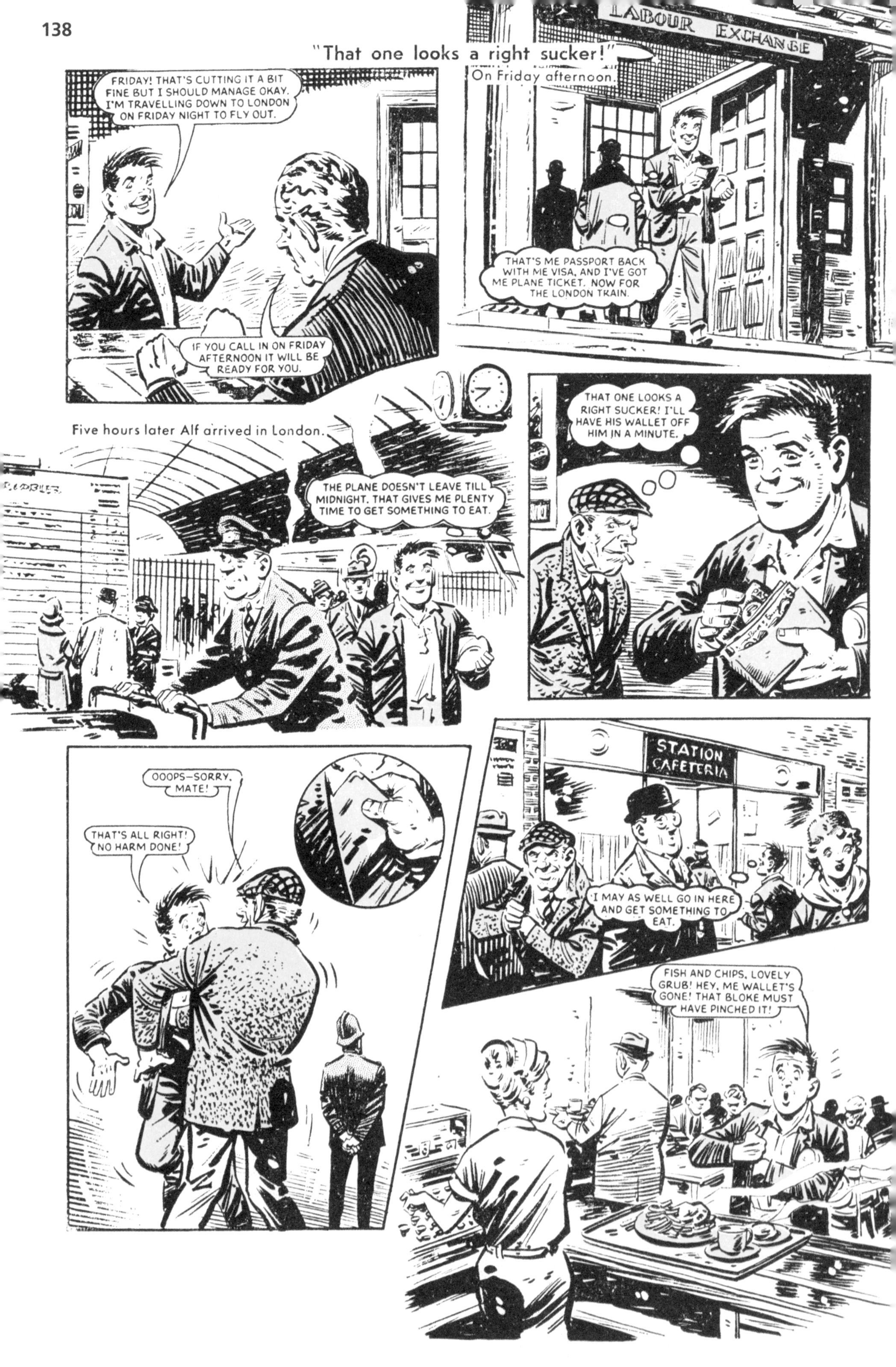
"That one looks a right sucker!"
FRIDAY! THAT'S CUTTING IT A BIT FINE BUT I SHOULD MANAGE OKAY. I'M TRAVELLING DOWN TO LONDON ON FRIDAY NIGHT TO FLY OUT.
IF YOU CALL IN ON FRIDAY AFTERNOON IT WILL BE READY FOR YOU.
On Friday afternoon.
LABOUR EXCHANGE
THAT'S ME PASSPORT BACK WITH ME VISA, AND I'VE GOT ME PLANE TICKET. NOW FOR THE LONDON TRAIN.
Five hours later Alf arrived in London.
THE PLANE DOESN'T LEAVE TILL MIDNIGHT. THAT GIVES ME PLENTY TIME TO GET SOMETHING TO EAT.
THAT ONE LOOKS A RIGHT SUCKER! I'LL HAVE HIS WALLET OFF HIM IN A MINUTE.
OOOPS—SORRY, MATE!
THAT'S ALL RIGHT! NO HARM DONE!
STATION CAFETERIA
I MAY AS WELL GO IN HERE AND GET SOMETHING TO EAT.
FISH AND CHIPS, LOVELY GRUB! HEY, ME WALLET'S GONE! THAT BLOKE MUST HAVE PINCHED IT!

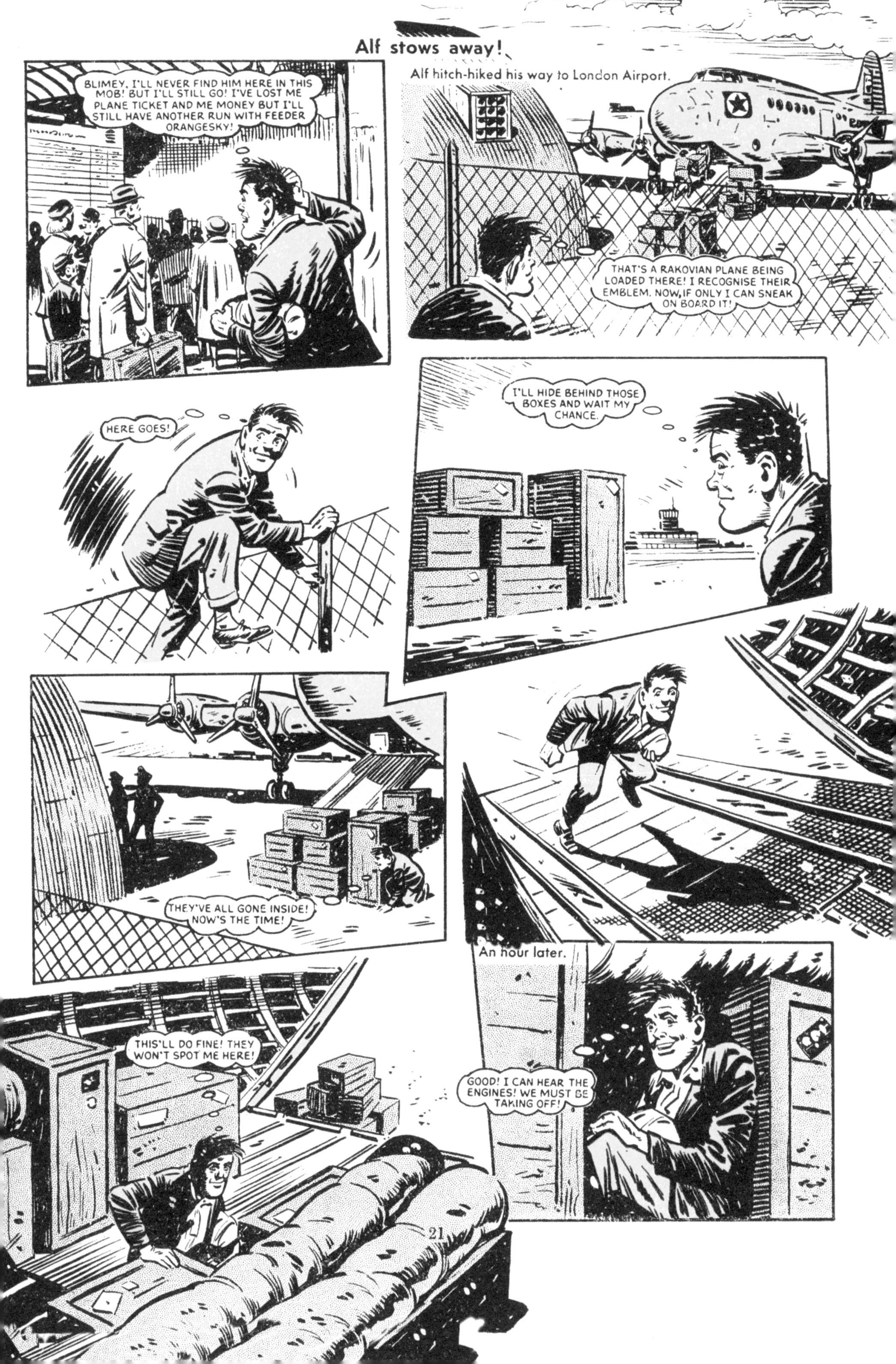
Alf stows away!
BLIMEY, I'LL NEVER FIND HIM HERE IN THIS MOB! BUT I'LL STILL GO! I'VE LOST ME PLANE TICKET AND ME MONEY BUT I'LL STILL HAVE ANOTHER RUN WITH FEEDER ORANGESKY!
Alf hitch-hiked his way to London Airport.
THAT'S A RAKOVIAN PLANE BEING LOADED THERE! I RECOGNISE THEIR EMBLEM. NOW, IF ONLY I CAN SNEAK ON BOARD IT!
HERE GOES!
I'LL HIDE BEHIND THOSE BOXES AND WAIT MY CHANCE.
THEY'VE ALL GONE INSIDE! NOW'S THE TIME!
THIS'LL DO FINE! THEY WON'T SPOT ME HERE!
An hour later.
GOOD! I CAN HEAR THE ENGINES! WE MUST BE TAKING OFF!

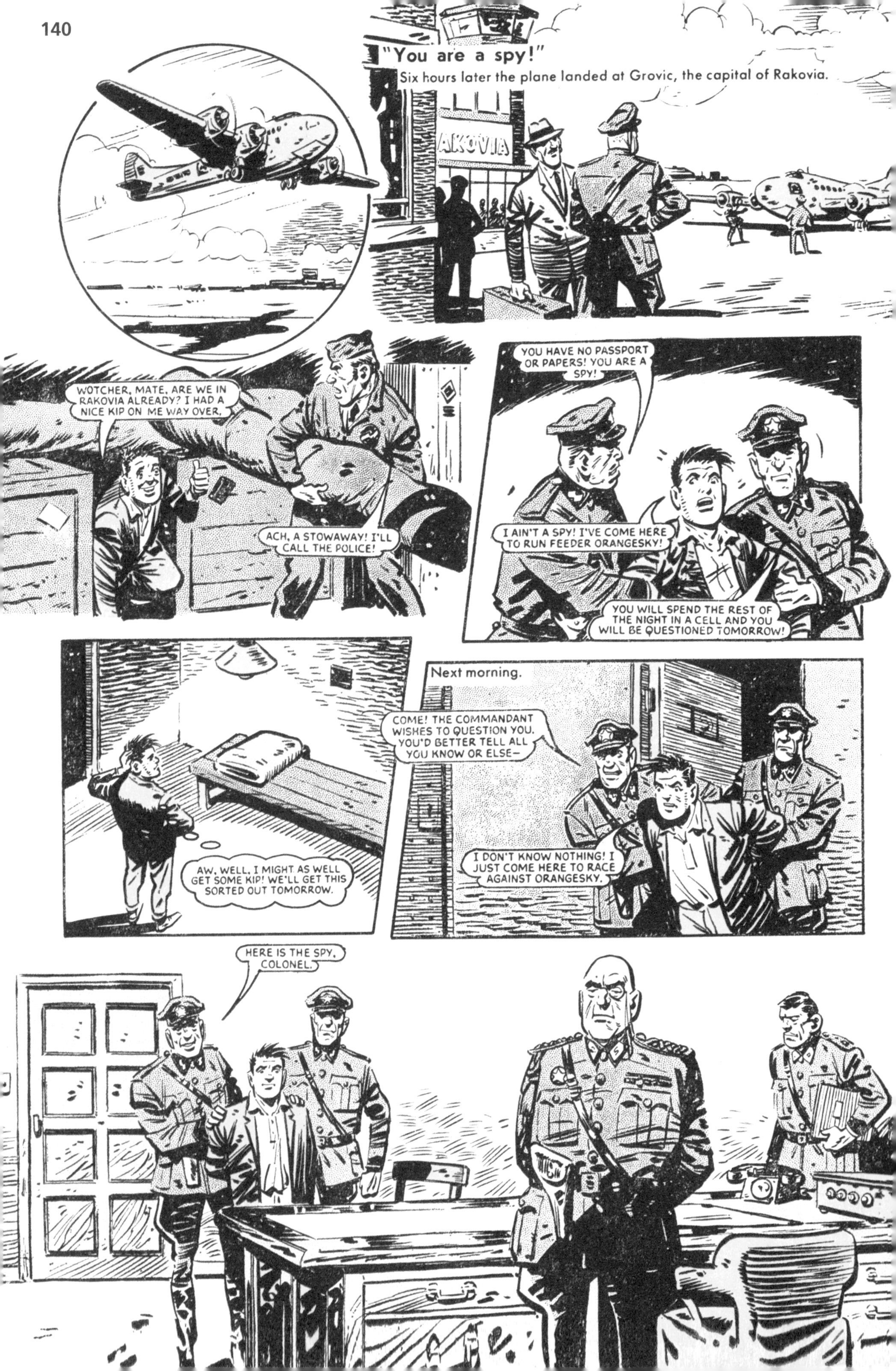
"You are a spy!"
Six hours later the plane landed at Grovic, the capital of Rakovia.
AKOVIA
WOTCHER, MATE, ARE WE IN RAKOVIA ALREADY? I HAD A NICE KIP ON ME WAY OVER.
ACH, A STOWAWAY! I'LL CALL THE POLICE!
YOU HAVE NO PASSPORT OR PAPERS! YOU ARE A SPY!
I AIN'T A SPY! I'VE COME HERE TO RUN FEEDER ORANGESKY!
YOU WILL SPEND THE REST OF THE NIGHT IN A CELL AND YOU WILL BE QUESTIONED TOMORROW!
AW, WELL, I MIGHT AS WELL GET SOME KIP! WE'LL GET THIS SORTED OUT TOMORROW.
Next morning.
COME! THE COMMANDANT WISHES TO QUESTION YOU. YOU'D BETTER TELL ALL YOU KNOW OR ELSE–
I DON'T KNOW NOTHING! I JUST COME HERE TO RACE AGAINST ORANGESKY.
HERE IS THE SPY, COLONEL.

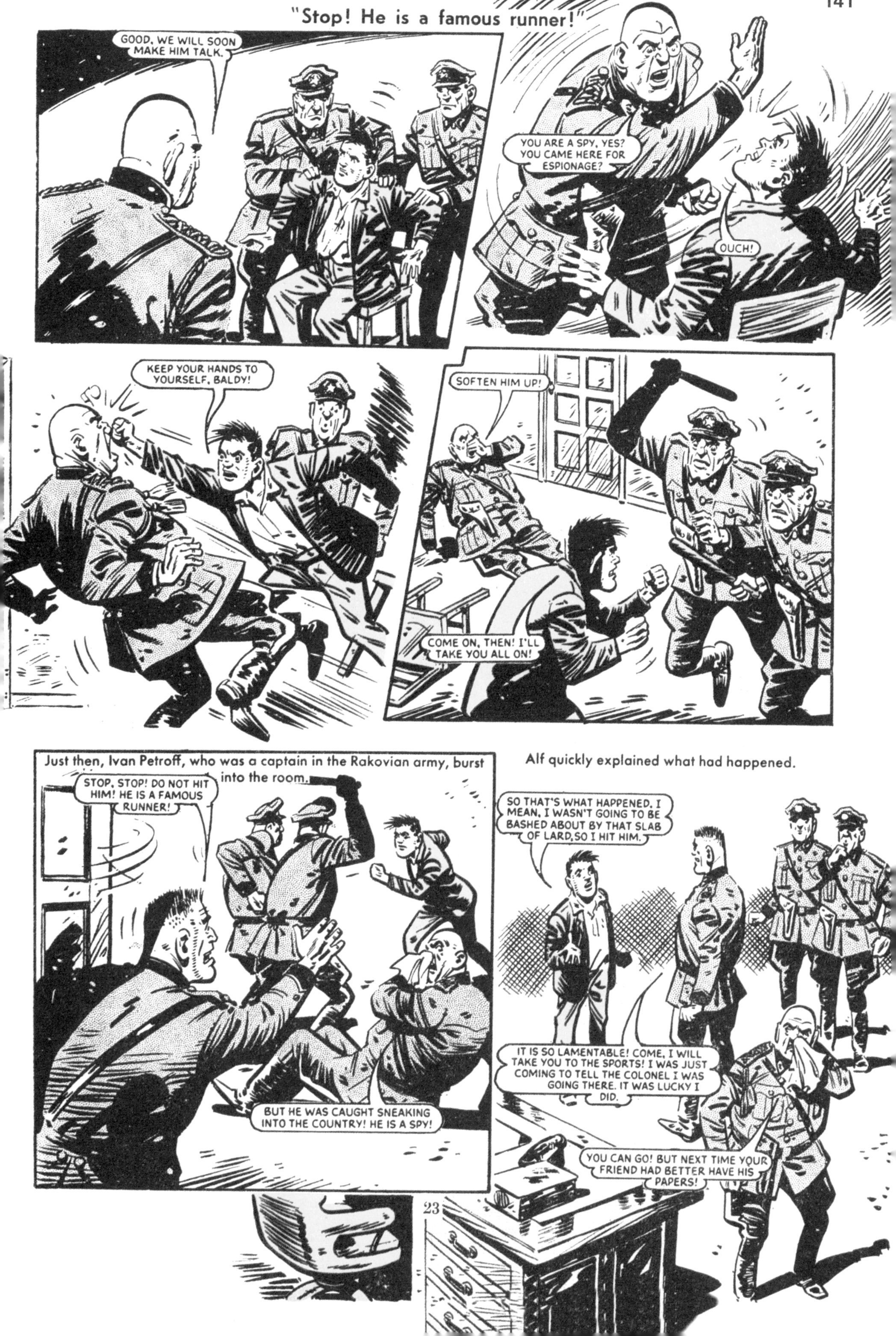
"Stop! He is a famous runner!"
GOOD, WE WILL SOON MAKE HIM TALK.
YOU ARE A SPY, YES? YOU CAME HERE FOR ESPIONAGE?
OUCH!
KEEP YOUR HANDS TO YOURSELF, BALDY!
SOFTEN HIM UP!
COME ON, THEN! I'LL TAKE YOU ALL ON!
Just then, Ivan Petroff, who was a captain in the Rakovian army, burst into the room.
STOP, STOP! DO NOT HIT HIM! HE IS A FAMOUS RUNNER!
BUT HE WAS CAUGHT SNEAKING INTO THE COUNTRY! HE IS A SPY!
Alf quickly explained what had happened.
SO THAT'S WHAT HAPPENED. I MEAN, I WASN'T GOING TO BE BASHED ABOUT BY THAT SLAB OF LARD, SO I HIT HIM.
IT IS SO LAMENTABLE! COME, I WILL TAKE YOU TO THE SPORTS! I WAS JUST COMING TO TELL THE COLONEL I WAS GOING THERE. IT WAS LUCKY I DID.
YOU CAN GO! BUT NEXT TIME YOUR FRIEND HAD BETTER HAVE HIS PAPERS!
23

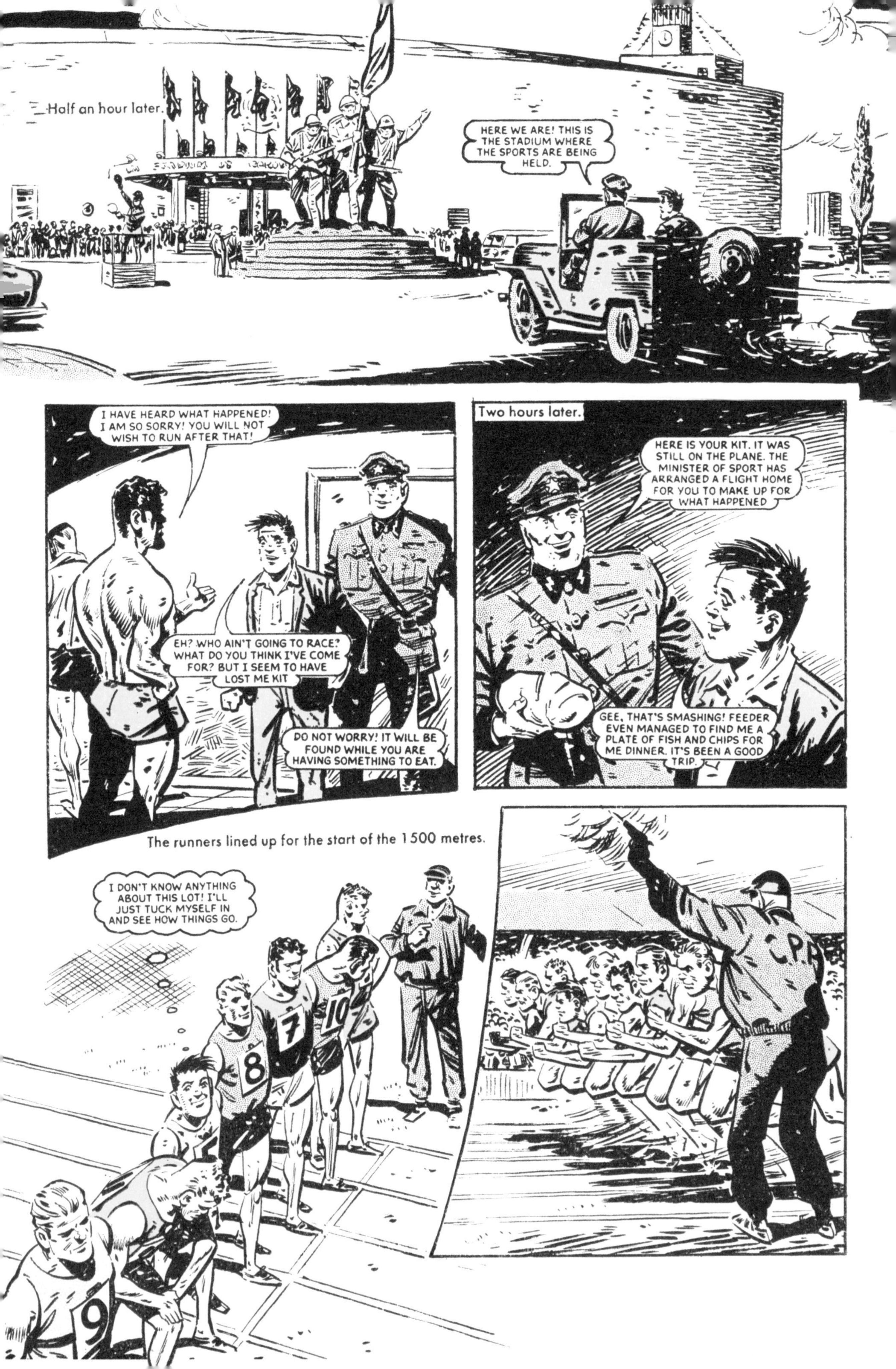
Half an hour later.
HERE WE ARE! THIS IS THE STADIUM WHERE THE SPORTS ARE BEING HELD.
I HAVE HEARD WHAT HAPPENED! I AM SO SORRY! YOU WILL NOT WISH TO RUN AFTER THAT!
EH? WHO AIN'T GOING TO RACE? WHAT DO YOU THINK I'VE COME FOR? BUT I SEEM TO HAVE LOST ME KIT
DO NOT WORRY! IT WILL BE FOUND WHILE YOU ARE HAVING SOMETHING TO EAT.
Two hours later.
HERE IS YOUR KIT. IT WAS STILL ON THE PLANE. THE MINISTER OF SPORT HAS ARRANGED A FLIGHT HOME FOR YOU TO MAKE UP FOR WHAT HAPPENED
GEE, THAT'S SMASHING! FEEDER EVEN MANAGED TO FIND ME A PLATE OF FISH AND CHIPS FOR ME DINNER. IT'S BEEN A GOOD TRIP.
The runners lined up for the start of the 1500 metres.
I DON'T KNOW ANYTHING ABOUT THIS LOT! I'LL JUST TUCK MYSELF IN AND SEE HOW THINGS GO.
7
10
8
9
C.P.R

"This British runner is not so good!"

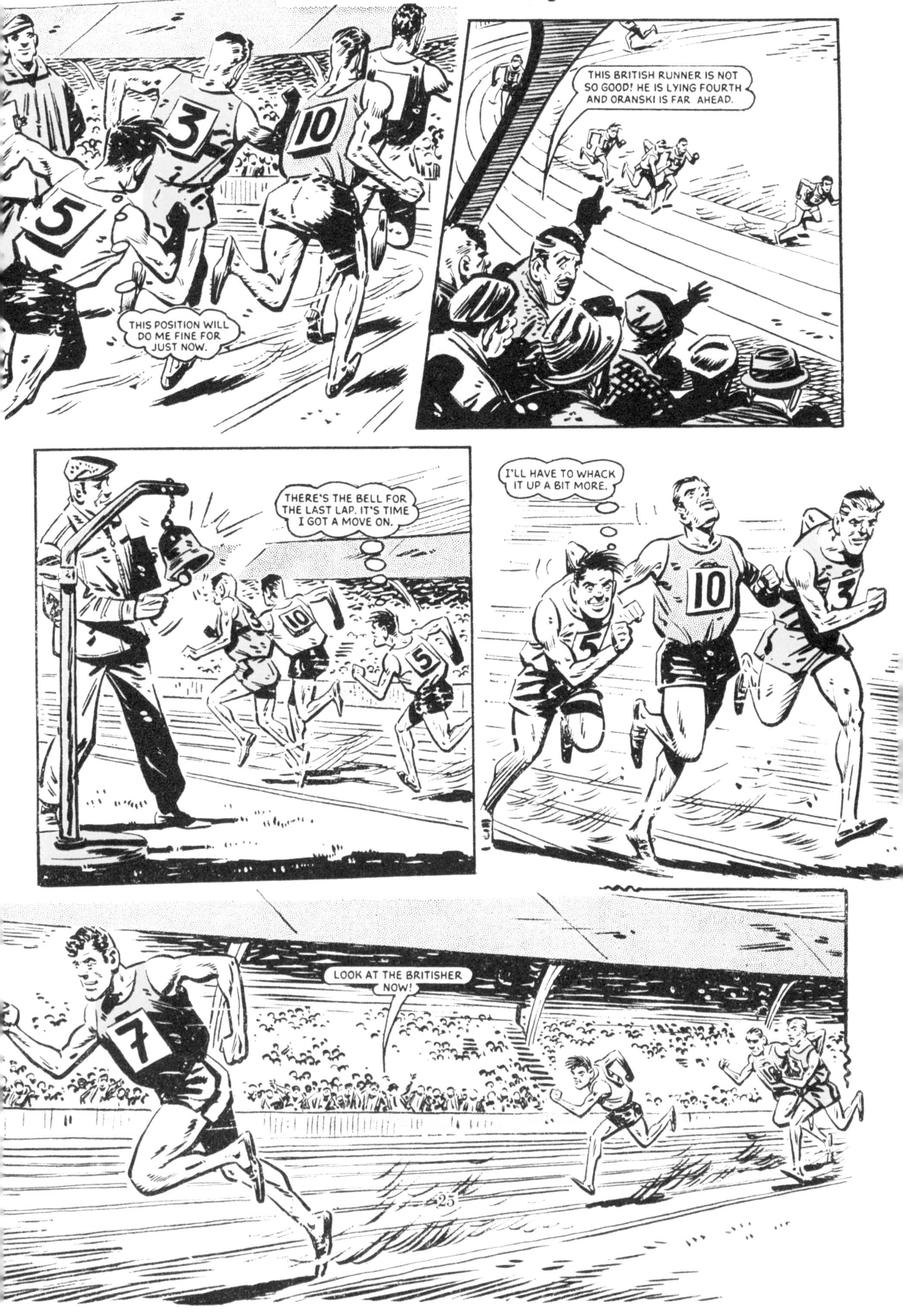
THIS POSITION WILL DO ME FINE FOR JUST NOW.
THIS BRITISH RUNNER IS NOT SO GOOD! HE IS LYING FOURTH AND ORANSKI IS FAR AHEAD.
THERE'S THE BELL FOR THE LAST LAP. IT'S TIME I GOT A MOVE ON.
I'LL HAVE TO WHACK IT UP A BIT MORE.
LOOK AT THE BRITISHER NOW!

"I just don't like getting beat."

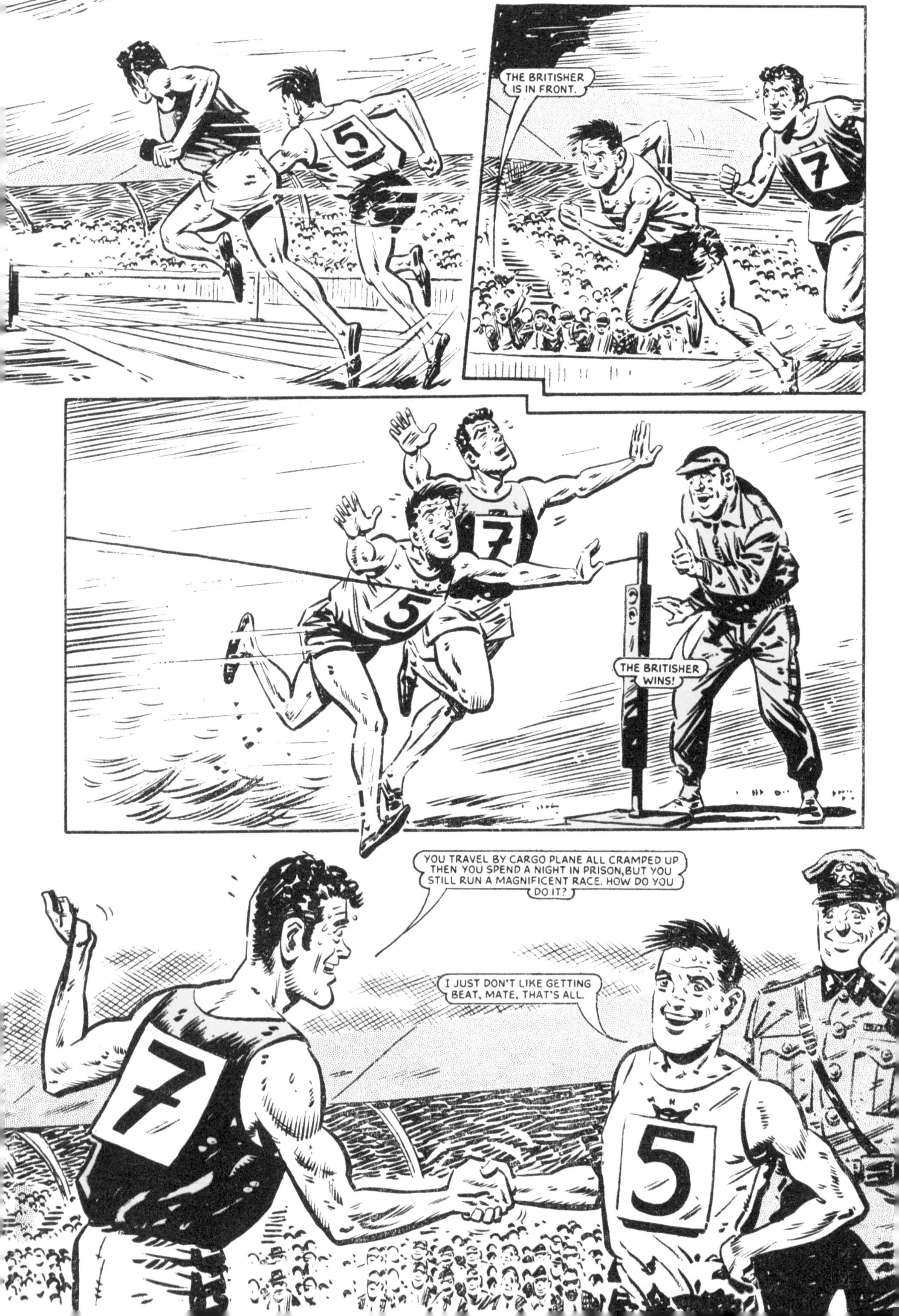
THE BRITISHER IS IN FRONT.
THE BRITISHER WINS!
YOU TRAVEL BY CARGO PLANE ALL CRAMPED UP THEN YOU SPEND A NIGHT IN PRISON, BUT YOU STILL RUN A MAGNIFICENT RACE. HOW DO YOU DO IT?
I JUST DON'T LIKE GETTING BEAT, MATE, THAT'S ALL.

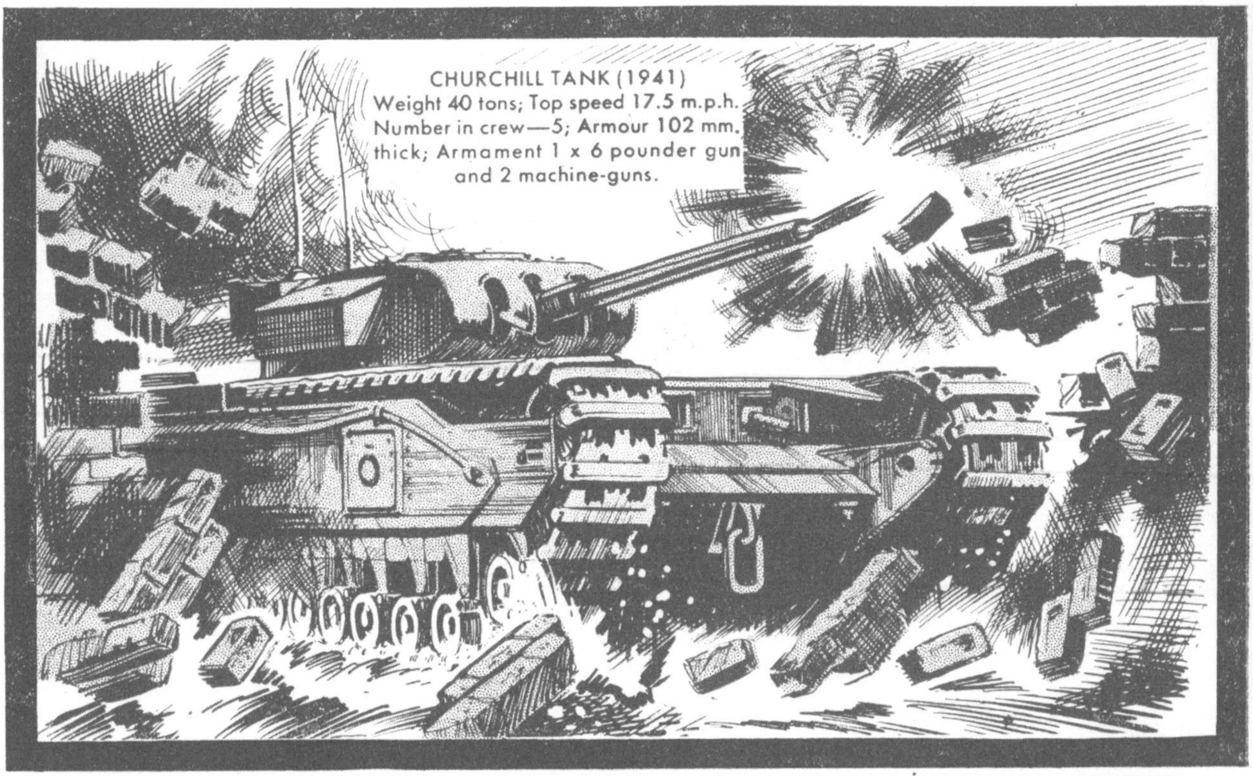
CHURCHILL TANK (1941)
Weight 40 tons; Top speed 17.5 m.p.h. Number in crew—5; Armour 102 mm. thick; Armament 1 x 6 pounder gun and 2 machine-guns.

THE TANKS

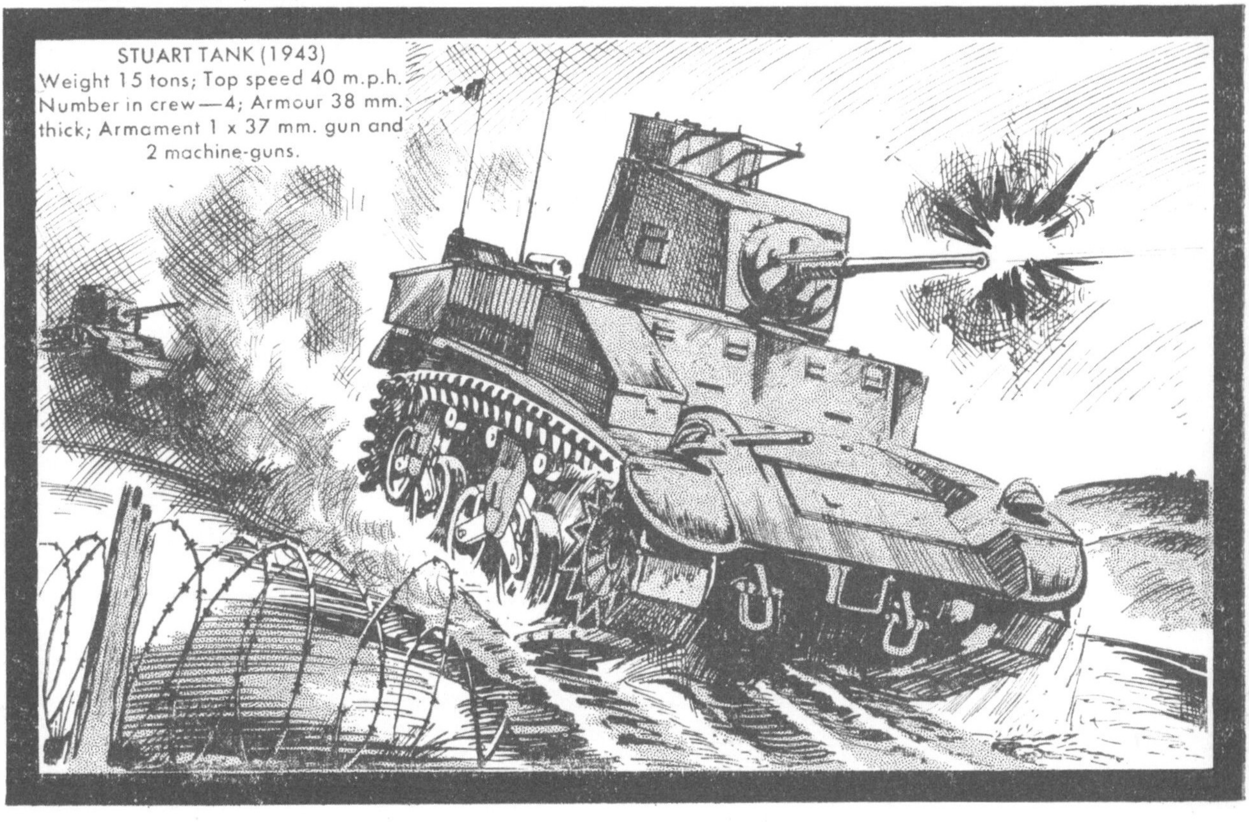
STUART TANK (1943)
Weight 15 tons; Top speed 40 m.p.h. Number in crew—4; Armour 38 mm. thick; Armament 1 x 37 mm. gun and 2 machine-guns.